Champion Horses

Maurizio Bongianni

Champion Horses

Illustrations by Piero Cozzaglio

Bonanza Books
New York

Produced by ERVIN s.r.l., Rome, under the supervision of Adriano Zannino
Editorial assistant Serenella Genoese Zerbi

The publisher wishes to thank:

The Italian Jockey Club and the Senior Steward Avv. Sergio Arnaldi, and his assistant Sig. Franco Mercuri
The Ente Nazionale Corse al Trotto (ENCAT), as represented by Sig. Gennarino D'Alicandro
The Associazione Nazionale Allevatori Cavallo Trottatore (ANACT), and Sig. Berto Celletti
The United States Trotting Association
The Société d'Encouragement à l'Elevage du Cheval Français
The Japan Riding Association
The Società Gestione Ippodromi di Maia S.p.A.
The Hipodromo de Las Américas
The Società degli Steeple-Chases d'Italia, especially the President Sig.ra Anna Grisi
The Società Gestione Ippodromo delle Capannelle

Translated by Jennifer Clay
Copyright © 1983 Arnoldo Mondadori Editore S.p.A., Milan
English translation copyright © 1984 Arnoldo Mondadori
Editore S.p.A., Milan

This 1984 edition published by Bonanza Books, distributed by
Crown Publishers, Inc.

Printed and bound in Italy by Arnoldo Mondadori Officine Grafiche, Verona

Library of Congress Cataloging in Publication Data

Bongianni, Maurizio.
  Champion horses.

  Translation of: I grandi cavalli.
  Includes index.
  1. Horse-racing—History. 2. Race horses—History.
3. Steeplechasing—History. 4. Harness racing—History.
5. Harness racehorses—History. I. Cozzaglio, Piero.
II. Title.
SF335.A1B6613   1984   798.4'009   84-11012
ISBN 0-517-43933-6

h g f e d c

PREFACE

This beautifully illustrated book is a fascinating guide to horse racing. The wealth of factual information it contains will enable the reader, whether a newcomer to the sport or a confirmed enthusiast, to learn about every aspect of the world of racing, from discovering the pedigree of a particular horse to studying the layout of a famous racecourse.

The author is an official trainer and as such is able to draw on firsthand experience, particularly in the field of flat racing, to provide an interesting account both of the history of horse racing and of the careers of the greatest international champions. Writing with warmth and charm, he brings to life some of the most exciting moments in the history of this sport, taking us through its development from the equestrian competitions of ancient Greece and Rome to the major races of the present day.

This is a comprehensive study which is both informative and enjoyable to read. Piero Cozzaglio's magnificent illustrations of each horse lift the book out of the ordinary, making it a work of artistic value which will delight anyone who shares the author's enthusiasm for this subject.

A. GIUBILO

INTRODUCTION

My intention in writing this book has been to provide a guide to the world of horse racing that will appeal to both enthusiasts and to those approaching the subject for the first time.

The book is divided into three main sections covering flat racing, steeplechasing and trotting. Each section opens with a brief history outlining the development of each type of horse racing, and the lines of descent which have produced the champion horses in each field. This is followed by a selection of representative horses, chosen either by virtue of their outstanding achievements on the track or for their contribution to the improvement of the breed, with a description of their physical attributes and details of their career. This information is complemented by tables showing the horses' ancestry and track record. Completing each section are championship records and layouts of some of the major international racecourses.

Flat racing champions are ordered chronologically, illustrating the development of the English thoroughbred. This section also devotes a few pages to some of the best-known racing colours. The section on steeplechasing covers five of the most important international races, from their origins to the present day, whilst that on trotting is subdivided into examples of American and French trotters, pacers and German-bred stock.

It should be noted that the placings given for trotting refer to second and third places in the case of American races, whereas in Europe they include fourth place. Since trotting races tend to be made up of several heats, the number of wins quoted in this section refer to individual heats contested, with the exception of Peter the Great for whom only the final overall result has been taken into consideration, as in his day races consisted of as many as seven heats.

I have tried to cover the entire racing world and to be as informative as possible. It has not been an easy task, especially since contradictions and gaps in the sources of information have created a great many problems. Sometimes the research carried out on the subject has led to conclusions which differ substantially from those dictated by scientific argument. An example of this is the case of Tartar who, in the Bobinski Tables (which is a standard work), is said to be a bay; in actual fact, since he was the product of two chestnuts, he could only have been a chestnut himself and so he has been described as such here.

The choice of individual horses covered in detail is inevitably a subjective one, and constraints of space have obliged me to leave out equally noteworthy representatives.

THE AUTHOR

CONTENTS

In the pedigree and championship records the following symbols and abbreviations have been used:

♀   mare – m.   ◆   black – bl.
♂   horse – h.   □   grey – gr.
◇   chestnut – ch.
○   bay – b.
●   dark bay – dk.b.

USA – United States   FR – France   ITY – Italy   IRE – Ireland

The Flat

FLAT RACING

The roots of flat racing, the ultimate aim of which, besides any competitive spirit, should be to advance the English thoroughbred, can be traced back to distant times long before the creation of this breed. In the civilizations of Greece or Rome, equestrian competitions were of special importance, but they differed from modern races in that the ability of the horse was always secondary to that of the rider. The first record of racing in England dates back to 1074, whereas in France races were held from 1370 in Saumur and also in Brittany.

In 1465 in Rome, Pope Paul II was the patron of the Corse dei Berberi (Berber races) which took place along the Via del Corso and ended at the present-day Piazza Venezia. Here the pontiff built the Palazzo di Venezia, and took pleasure in watching these wild competitions from its windows.

In England, the first races on the Epsom Downs using Oriental horses took place thanks to Richard the Lion-Hearted (1157–99) who was passionately fond of horses and was also the first person to offer money as a prize for the winners. In 1511, during the reign of Henry VIII, the town of Chester became the home of England's first racecourse. The following year the organizers of the Chester Fair offered a decorative wooden ball as a prize for the race being run on that occasion, which was later replaced by a silver cup. In 1609 the Sheriff of Chester, Sir Ambrye, dissatisfied with the way the cup had been cast, had a duplicate made and then yet another, thus ending up with three silver cups which he decided to award to the first three horses, a tradition which has continued ever since. As early as 1603 the so-called "sweepstake" races were held in Chester, in which the stakes comprised the amount collected from the entrants in addition to a winner's prize. Races also took place at Newmarket as early as the beginning of the seventeenth century and by 1625 provision was made to regulate entries and withdrawals. Silver cups were provided for the owner of the winning horse and its rider but penalties as severe as prison sentences were imposed on jockeys guilty of improper riding during the race.

When Charles I was condemned to death in 1649, Oliver Cromwell came to power. He was so opposed to horse racing that in 1654 he issued a decree banning it. On his death in 1658, he was succeeded by his son Richard who was replaced a year later by King Charles II. The restored king was such an enthusiastic supporter of racing that he himself rode in races, and during his reign (1660–85) he gave considerable impetus to English horse racing. Meanwhile "betting races" took place in France in 1651, the most famous being the one between the Prince d'Harcourt and the Duke de Joyeuse (1,000 écus) held on 15 May that year. In America, the first so-called official races date from 1666 and took place on Long Island, on ground handed over for the purpose by the Governor of New York which today is the site of the Aqueduct Racetrack. Two years earlier America's first racetrack was built – the Newmarket course at Hempstead, but before we can speak of races in the sense in which we use the term today, we must move on to 1750 when the Jockey Club was founded in England. At first this association had jurisdiction only over races run at Newmarket, but its influence later spread to Epsom (1844), Ascot (1857) and Goodwood (1858) and gradually throughout the United Kingdom. The first two-year-old races in England date from around 1770, while in 1776 the St. Leger was first run, though not until two years later did it take its name from the colonel who suggested the race. It was won in the first year (over the original distance of two miles) by a filly belonging to Lord Rockingham, Alabaculia, sired by Sampson. The Oaks was first run in 1779. This is a race for three-year-old fillies and takes its name from Lord Derby's house near Epsom, where it was held. The following year, 1780 the Derby was instituted, taking its name from the same Earl who helped to start it. This race, still of fundamental importance today, was first run over a mile, but after four years the distance was increased to a mile and a half, like the Oaks, and was run on the same track. In 1790, the English Stud Book was first published. Its aim was to register the births of all thoroughbred horses. In 1809 the 2,000

Guineas was run for the first time over a mile at Newmarket.

An important promoter of racing in France was the Count d'Artois, Louis XVI's brother, who built the Champ-de-Mars racecourse, and it was during the reign of Louis XVI that spring and autumn meetings began to be held regularly at the Sablons, on the plain which is now the site of Longchamp racecourse. A year later (1777) racing began at Fontainebleau and in 1781, at Vincennes. At that time races were already regulated as regards entry requirements, the weights and handicaps for horses coming from abroad. In 1805 a decree issued by Napoleon instituted races, starting in 1808, in the regions most involved in breeding horses. These races provided a form of selection in that the winners had the right to take part in a Grand Prix in Paris. In 1833 the Société d'Encouragement pour l'Amélioration des Races de Chevaux en France was founded and the Duke d'Orléans began compiling the Stud Book. The Jockey Club was founded in 1834 and two years later the Jockey Club Cup was contested for the first time; this came to be of equivalent significance to the Derby. Longchamp racecourse was built in Paris in 1856 and in 1863, 20 years after the Prix de Diane, the Grand Prix de Paris was run for the first time. The other great French race, the Prix de l'Arc de Triomphe, is a comparatively recent addition, as it was first run in 1920.

Racing in America developed alongside its English counterpart, drawing on England for ideas and inspiration as well as for high-quality horses; as early as 1798 they imported Diomed, the first Epsom Derby winner.

In Germany the Deutsches Gestütbuch (German Stud Book) was introduced in 1811, whereas racing in Italy did not become established until somewhat later due to the political turmoil of the era. The first official Italian races were run in Turin in the early 1800s although the first recorded race took place in 1739 in Livorno. Racing clubs began to emerge in 1835; the first was set up in Turin and was followed by clubs in many of the major cities, but it was not until 1880, when the Italian Jockey Club was founded (a year after the introduction of the Stud Book) that Italian racing assumed its definitive form. In 1884 the Capannelle racecourse was built in Rome and in the same year the first Italian Derby was run there. The San Siro racecourse in Milan was inaugurated in 1888, races having previously been held at Castellazzo di Rho outside Porta Sempione. The oldest existing Italian race is the Premio dell'Arno which dates back to 1827 when, under the title of Sottoscrizione dell'Arno (Arno Subscription, where each subscription was ten *zecchini*) it was run in Florence and won by Riber, a four-year-old grey.

Following this description of events relating to the history of horse racing in those countries which from the very beginning have been most closely involved with this sport, we should turn to Japan, perhaps the most recent of the newcomers. The Japan Racing Association, which became recognized internationally in 1955, is making commendable progress which is enabling Japanese racing to develop rapidly. In Japan too, the origins of racing can be traced back to ancient times. Races took place as early as 701 in the form of ceremonies at the Imperial Court, and in 1093 races are known to have been held at Kyoto in the Kamo Sanctuary where they assumed the significance of a sacred rite. The history of modern Western-style horse racing, however, began in Japan in 1861 with the organization of the first meetings at Yokohama. The following year the Yokohama Race Club was established and inaugurated official races on an oval track.

TYPES OF RACES

Races can be divided into weight for age races, conditions races, handicaps, claiming races, selling races, maidens' and newcomers' races. In weight for age races, allotted weight is fixed from a special table, whereas in conditions races it depends on the total number and type of races won over a fixed period of time and so is calculated by a process where weight is added or allowed for accordingly. In handicaps, the weight is set by the person responsible (handicapper), taking into account the horse's most recent form without neglecting his career as a whole.

Handicaps can be divided into descending and ascending groups. In descending handicaps, the weight scale begins with the highest weights (with a maximum of 10 st 3 lb (65kg) rising, in exceptional circumstances, to 11 st 11 lb (70 kg) and then dropping to the lowest ones; in ascending handicaps the opposite is the case and the handicapper bases his assessment on the horses that will have to carry the least weight (minimum weight 7 st 1 lb (45 kg) rising up the scale with no limit imposed. The purpose of handicaps is to make each horse's chance equal as far as possible, so that all are in a position to win. It should be said, however, that ascending handicaps in which the more humbly bred horses take part are run mostly in Italy, whereas in most other countries the word handicap signifies a descending handicap.

In claiming races all the runners are for sale and can be bought by making a higher bid than the price fixed for each individual horse; the bid must be handed in in a sealed envelope no later than five minutes after the end of the race. The price the buyer has to pay to the horse owner is based on the whole fixed price made up by the entire prize due to the winner or by its complement (the difference between the prize won and the prize due to the winner) depending on whether the horse is placed or not. In selling races, which attract the lowest category horses, the winner is put up for auction immediately after the race, starting at a price previously fixed at the time of entering the race. All the other horses can be claimed by a procedure similar to the one described. Maiden races are open to horses that have not yet won a race, while newcomers' races, as the name implies, are for horses running in a race for the first time. Apart from professional races, there are also amateur and ladies' races in which the competititive spirit sometimes triumphs over financial interest.

The most important of all races are the Pattern races which are divided, according to their value, into Group I, Group II and Group III races. Included among these are the Classics, most of which are reserved for three-year-olds. These races serve to draw attention to the best horses of the current generation. Clearly, the ultimate purpose of Group races is to select the horses that will be tomorrow's best sires. Apart from Group races, there are also the "Listed" races which are less important but considered good indicators for the purposes of evaluation.

Horses which race on the flat appear for the first time as two-year-olds after April (in Italy) but this date varies from country to country. The distance of two-year-old races is initially 5 furlongs (1,000 m) (or 4 furlongs (800 m) for the very first races of the year) but is gradually increased as the year goes on. As regards distance, races can be divided into sprints, 5 – 7 furlongs (1,000–1,400 m), middle distance races, 1 mile 2 furlongs (1,600–2,000 m), long distance races, 12 – 15 furlongs (2,400–3,000 m), very long distance races, up to 2½ miles (4,000 m) and extremely long distance races, over 2½ miles (4,000 m). There are also races which fall between these distances, but they still come within these five categories.

The current planning tendency seems to be to reduce the distance of some races more than in the past but the major Classic races usually are not altered and the Derby, which is the Classic race par excellence, is run in most countries over 12 furlongs (2,400m), with a few exceptions such as in the United States where the most important of all, the Kentucky Derby, is run over 10 furlongs (2,000 m), (and similarly the Hollywood Derby), whereas in other countries the distance is even less.

THE ENGLISH THOROUGHBRED

Thoroughbred means "purely bred" and this has been the ambition which, in the course of almost three centuries, has led to the creation of this breed of horse for which speed is all important. The origins of the English thoroughbred date back to the early 18th century, a time which saw the importation into England of the three horses which must undoubtedly be considered the foundation sires of the breed and the ancestors in the direct male line of all existing horses belonging to this line. These were the dark bay Byerley Turk (of Turkish origin), the bay Darley Arabian (of Arab origin) and another dark bay, the Godolphin Arabian (of Berber origin).

These three stallions came to England somewhere between the late 17th century and the first quarter of the 18th century. They were not the only three stallions originally to contribute towards the foundation of the breed, however, and according to calculations made in 1881 by Joseph Osborne at least another 475 horses (all of oriental origin) made an initial contribution although they failed to secure a descendancy in the direct male line which was capable of continuing up until the present day. Similarly only about 40 of the 100 brood mares originally entered in the Stud Book managed to keep their direct female line alive through their descendants. This initial

nucleus of brood mares was made up of the "Royal Mares," especially selected by the Royal family for breeding. These horses represented the results of painstaking work carried out by cross-breeding with the constant determining strain of oriental blood.

Various families exist in the breed of the English thoroughbred, distinguished by a number which refers back to the original foundation brood mare. This acts as a sort of surname which is transferred from the mother (dam) to her offspring. This distinguishing number is found in the pedigree alongside the names of the furthest removed ancestors under consideration. Horses descending from brood mares not entered from the very beginning in the first volume of the English Stud Book are marked with an asterisk, a dash or an O. Using this system, devised in the mid 19th century by an Australian named Bruce Lowe, it is possible to establish which female lines successfully combine to pass on those qualities necessary to a racehorse to be firstly a good runner and secondly a successful stud. Many of the original families are now extinct but, as mentioned previously, about 40 of them still exist, continuing to produce champions and ensuring the perpetuation of the breed.

Three progenitors descend directly from

the three foundation sires of the English thoroughbred. From Byerley Turk, in the fourth generation, comes Herod (b. 1758); from Darley Arabian, also in the fourth generation, comes Eclipse (ch. 1764); and from the Godolphin Arabian, this time in the second generation comes Matchem (b. 1748). All the representatives of the breed which at present exist in the world derive from these three lines. From the point of view of conformation the English thoroughbred does not have very well-blended features since selection was made on the basis of the competitive qualities of the studs and not on their physical characteristics. Thus there are horses of heights varying from a minimum of 14.3 hands (1.50 m) to a maximum of 16.3 hands (1.70 m).

Other features also vary considerably, to the extent that the thoroughbred can be divided into three physical types, differing from each other as regards aptitude too. The "sprinter" is taller, has an elongated back and loins, a deeper chest, slanting croup and a fairly straight shoulder. The "stayer" is smaller, has a roomier chest, shorter back, flat croup and sloping shoulder. Lastly comes the "middle-distancer" with its slanting croup but sloping shoulder and rather short back, which shows particular aptitude for steeplechases.

14

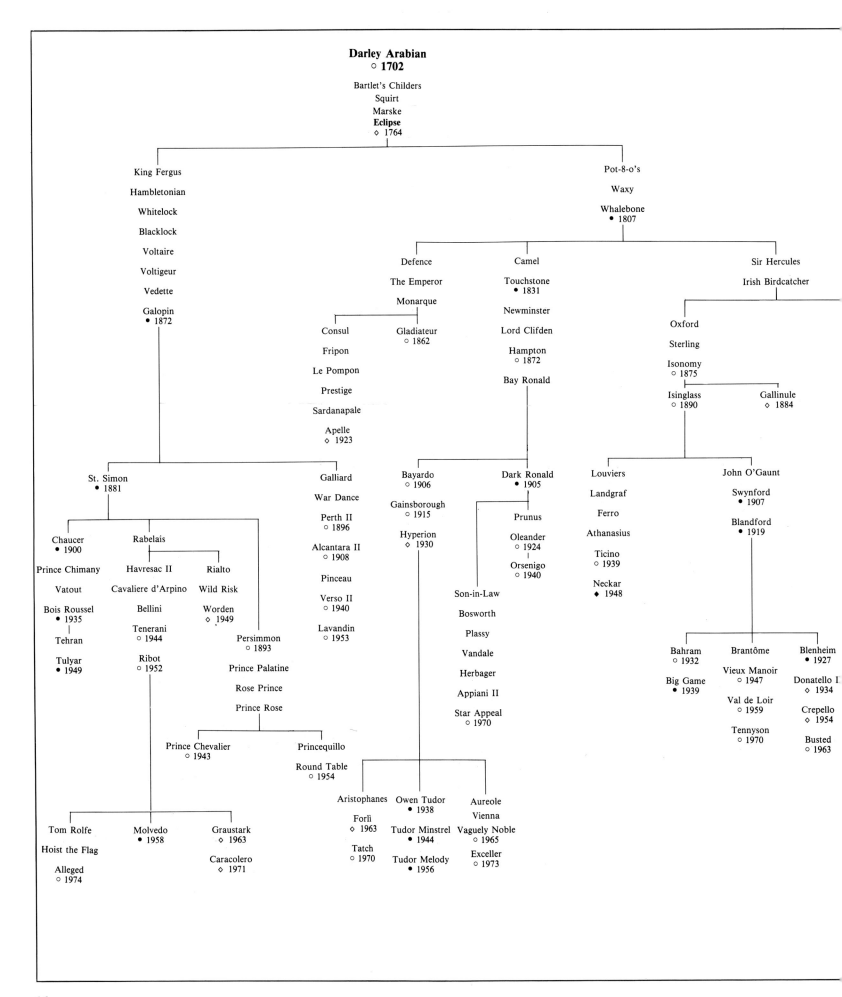

Darley Arabian
○ **1702**

Bartlet's Childers

Squirt

Marske

Eclipse
◇ 1764

King Fergus

Hambletonian

Whitelock

Blacklock

Voltaire

Voltigeur

Vedette

Galopin
● 1872

Pot-8-o's

Waxy

Whalebone
● 1807

Defence

The Emperor

Monarque

Consul

Fripon

Le Pompon

Prestige

Sardanapale

Apelle
◇ 1923

Gladiateur
○ 1862

Camel

Touchstone
● 1831

Newminster

Lord Clifden

Hampton
○ 1872

Bay Ronald

Sir Hercules

Irish Birdcatcher

Oxford

Sterling

Isonomy
○ 1875

Isinglass
○ 1890

Gallinule
◇ 1884

St. Simon
● 1881

Galliard

War Dance

Perth II
○ 1896

Alcantara II
○ 1908

Pinceau

Verso II
○ 1940

Lavandin
○ 1953

Bayardo
○ 1906

Gainsborough
○ 1915

Hyperion
◇ 1930

Dark Ronald
● 1905

Prunus

Oleander
○ 1924

Orsenigo
○ 1940

Louviers

Landgraf

Ferro

Athanasius

Ticino
○ 1939

Neckar
◆ 1948

John O'Gaunt

Swynford
● 1907

Blandford
● 1919

Chaucer
● 1900

Prince Chimany

Vatout

Bois Roussel
● 1935

Tehran

Tulyar
● 1949

Rabelais

Havresac II

Cavaliere d'Arpino

Bellini

Tenerani
○ 1944

Ribot
○ 1952

Rialto

Wild Risk

Worden
◇ 1949

Persimmon
○ 1893

Prince Palatine

Rose Prince

Prince Rose

Prince Chevalier
○ 1943

Princequillo

Round Table
○ 1954

Son-in-Law

Bosworth

Plassy

Vandale

Herbager

Appiani II

Star Appeal
○ 1970

Bahram
○ 1932

Big Game
● 1939

Brantôme

Vieux Manoir
○ 1947

Val de Loir
○ 1959

Tennyson
○ 1970

Blenheim
● 1927

Donatello I
◇ 1934

Crepello
◇ 1954

Busted
○ 1963

Tom Rolfe

Hoist the Flag

Alleged
○ 1974

Molvedo
● 1958

Graustark
◇ 1963

Caracolero
◇ 1971

Aristophanes

Forlì
◇ 1963

Tatch
○ 1970

Owen Tudor
● 1938

Tudor Minstrel
● 1944

Tudor Melody
● 1956

Aureole

Vienna

Vaguely Noble
○ 1965

Exceller
○ 1973

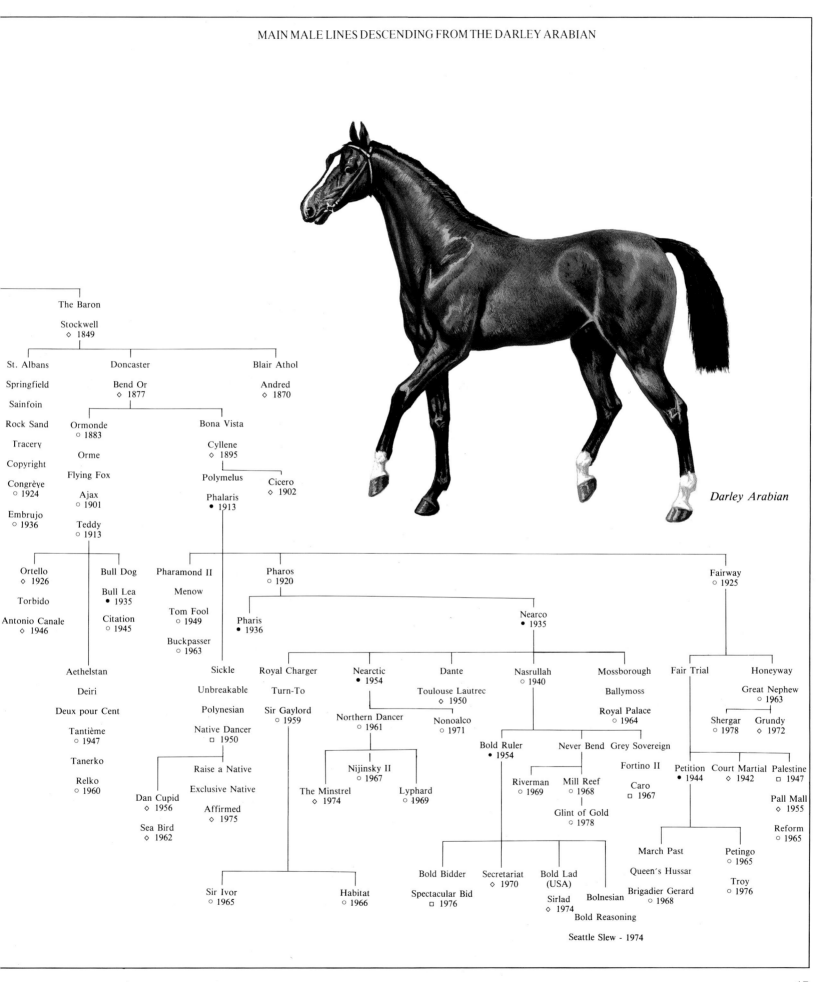

The Baron

Stockwell
◇ 1849

St. Albans   Doncaster   Blair Athol

Springfield   Bend Or   Andred
                 ◇ 1877   ◇ 1870

Sainfoin

Rock Sand   Ormonde   Bona Vista
             ○ 1883

Tracery   Orme   Cyllene
                     ◇ 1895

Copyright

Congrève   Flying Fox   Polymelus   Cicero
○ 1924   ◇ 1902

           Ajax   Phalaris
Embrujo   ○ 1901   ● 1913
○ 1936

            Teddy
            ○ 1913

Darley Arabian

Ortello   Bull Dog   Pharamond II   Pharos   Fairway
◇ 1926   ○ 1920   ○ 1925

       Bull Lea   Menow
Torbido   ● 1935

                  Tom Fool   Nearco
Antonio Canale   Citation   ○ 1949   Pharis   ● 1935
◇ 1946   ○ 1945   ● 1936

                  Buckpasser
                  ○ 1963

Aethelstan   Sickle   Royal Charger   Nearctic   Dante   Nasrullah   Mossborough   Fair Trial   Honeyway
                                 ● 1954   ○ 1940

Deiri   Unbreakable   Turn-To   Toulouse Lautrec   Ballymoss   Great Nephew
                                               ◇ 1950   ○ 1963

Deux pour Cent   Polynesian   Sir Gaylord   Nonoalco   Royal Palace
                          ○ 1959   ○ 1971   ○ 1964   Shergar   Grundy
Tantième   Native Dancer   Northern Dancer   ○ 1978   ◇ 1972
○ 1947   □ 1950   ○ 1961   Bold Ruler   Never Bend   Grey Sovereign

                                             ● 1954   Fortino II
Tanerko   Raise a Native   Petition   Court Martial   Palestine
                                   Nijinsky II   Riverman   Mill Reef   Caro   ● 1944   ◇ 1942   □ 1947
Relko   Exclusive Native   ○ 1967   Lyphard   ○ 1969   ○ 1968   □ 1967
○ 1960   Dan Cupid   The Minstrel   ○ 1969
          ◇ 1956   Affirmed   ◇ 1974   Glint of Gold   Pall Mall
                     ◇ 1975   ○ 1978   ◇ 1955
          Sea Bird
          ◇ 1962   March Past   Petingo   Reform
                                                                       ○ 1965   ○ 1965

                                                 Queen's Hussar
                  Sir Ivor   Habitat   Bold Bidder   Secretariat   Bold Lad   Troy
                  ○ 1965   ○ 1966   Spectacular Bid   ○ 1970   (USA)   Brigadier Gerard   ○ 1976
                                                  □ 1976   Sirlad   Bolnesian   ○ 1968
                                                              ◇ 1974
                                                                 Bold Reasoning

                                               Seattle Slew - 1974

17

Byerley Turk

MALE LINES DESCENDING FROM BYERLEY TURK

Byerley Turk
• 1689

Jigg

Partner

Tartar

Herod
○ 1758

Woodpecker

Buzzard

Selim — Castrel

Sultan — Pantaloon

Bay Middleton — Windhound

Flying Dutchman — Thormanby
• 1846

Dollar — Atlantic
○ 1860

Androclès — Le Sancy

Cambyse — Le Samaritain

Gardefeu — Roi Hérode

Chouberski — The Tetrarch
□ 1911

Brûleur

Ksar — Tetratema — Salmon Trout
◇ 1918 — □ 1917 — ○ 1921

Tourbillon — Bactériophage — King Salmon
○ 1928 — ○ 1930

Téléférique

Alizier — Cobalt
○ 1947 — ◇ 1950

Djebel — Timor
○ 1937

Pronto
○ 1958

Practicante
○ 1966

Clarion — Hugh Lupus — Le Levandou

Klairon — Hethersett — Le Levanstell

Luthier — Blakeney — Le Moss
• 1965 — ○ 1966 — ◇ 1975

MALE LINES DESCENDING FROM THE GODOLPHIN ARABIAN

Godolphin Arabian
• 1724

Cade

Matchem
○ 1748

Conductor

Trumpator

Sorcerer

Comus

Humphrey Clinker

Melbourne
• 1834

West Australian
○ 1850

Solon — Australian

Barcaldine — Spendthrift

Marco — Hastings

Marcovil — Fair Play

Hurry On — Man o' War
◇ 1913 — ◇ 1917

Coronach — Precipitation — War Admiral — War Relic
◇ 1923 — • 1934

Niccolò — Sheshoon — Relic
dell'Arca — ♦ 1945
○ 1938 — Sassafras
○ 1967

Polic — Pieces of Eight
• 1953 — • 1963

Polyfoto — Stateff
• 1962 — ◇ 1974

18

BYERLEY TURK

dk.b.h. c.1680

Of the three foundation sires of the breed this horse, also called The Byerley Turk, is the one whose origins can be traced farthest back in time and about which we have received the least comprehensive information. He is thought to have been foaled in 1685 in Turkey and imported to England to be used as a charger by Captain Byerley, whose name he took according to the custom of the time. He was a dark bay horse, easy to handle and extremely fast, so much so that he was considered to be an exceptional racehorse in his day, even though he never took part in official track races. The only certain piece of information is that in breeding he proved to be an excellent stud, producing six winners. It was his great-great-grandson Herod, son of Tartar (ch.h.1743) who continued the line, ensuring that it descended directly into the present day with The Tetrarch lines.

Owner: Captain Byerley
Did not take part in track races

DARLEY ARABIAN

b.h. 1700

Among the foundation sires of the breed the Darley Arabian is the one who through his descendants has, without doubt, contributed most to the evolution of the thoroughbred.

He was an Arab of the Kochiani breed and his original name was Mannika (or Manak according to some authors). He was imported at the age of three from the Orient by Thomas Darley, the British Consul in Aleppo, who, having exchanged him for a rifle, sent him to his father Sir Richard in Yorkshire. The Darley Arabian was quite a tall horse for an Arab of that period, measuring almost 15 hands (1.5 m) at the withers, and immediately striking owing to his handsome appearance and exceedingly elegant carriage. As a stud, he made a name for himself by having sired two horses, Bartlet's Childers (b.h. 1716)(from whom Eclipse was to descend in the third generation) and his brother Flying Childers (b.h. 1714 out of Betty Leedes), both of which were bred, as the name suggests, by a man named Childers.

Flying Childers lived up to his name and is remembered in history for his speed. The Duke of Devonshire bought him to use as a hunter but was so impressed by his exceptional qualities that he decided to race him. The horse certainly lived up to his expectations: he won all his races with ridiculous ease and in the last one, over a distance of 4 miles, he led his rivals by 2 furlongs (400m). He was withdrawn from racing as a result of repeated threats to his owner and only many years later was his reputation overshadowed by Eclipse. At stud he was unable to sire good quality stallions so as to assure the continuation of his line, despite the fact that many of his progeny were winners. His influence has been keenly felt, however, in the making of the American Trotter, especially through his son Blaze (1733).

Owner: Thomas and Richard Darley
Did not take part in races

GODOLPHIN ARABIAN

dk.b.h. 1724

His Berber origin should have meant that he was called the Godolphin Barb, but the fashion at that time dictated that he should be called the Godolphin Arabian. He was foaled in Morocco and in 1731 was given together with four other eastern stallions as a gift from the Bey of Tunis to King Louis XVI. The French sovereign showed no appreciation for the eastern horses and

so arrangements were made to sell them. After some time an Englishman, Mr Coke, noticed a horse on the Pont Neuf in Paris whose appearance was reasonably impressive and even though the horse had been reduced to a pitiful condition and harnessed to a water-cart, Mr Coke was so struck by the fate which had befallen such a handsome animal that he bought him for 75 francs. The purchaser brought Curven's Bay Barb (such was the horse's name at that time) to England with him and later sold him to a friend, a Mr Williams, the owner of a tavern in St. James's. Williams was unsuccessful in racing him (because of the horse's difficult temperament) and therefore decided to sell him to Lord Godolphin who used him on his Gogmagog stud farm, near Cambridge, as a teaser to bring the mares into heat. From that moment the horse acquired his new name.

At stud the Godolphin Arabian covered a very valuable Arab brood mare named Roxana, producing one of the most valuable racehorses of that period, Lath, who was foaled in 1732. Lath earned his sire fame as a stallion. In 1738 at Newmarket, where three races were being contested respectively by the Godolphin Arabian's sons, Regulus, Cade and Lath, it is said that Lord Godolphin, who was so convinced that they would all win, led the Godolphin Arabian on to the racecorse so as to let him share in the victory of his three "sons" who promply won, living up to the expectations of their eccentric owner. Cade sired Matchem who ensured the continuation of his illustrious progenitor's line.

Owner: Lord Godolphin
Did not run

Godolphin Arabian

MATCHEM

b.h. 1748 – No. 4 Fam. – foaled in England

This grandson of the Godolphin Barb is one of the three foundation sires of the breed. He was a small horse (14.3 hands (1.51m), but very tough, a quality which he inherited from his sire Cade and later passed on to his progeny. His background was excellent and he had no problem in winning the races he entered in two or three heats, managing to run over a distance of almost 4 miles (6,400m) three times in one day. He died at the age of 33 and in his career as a stallion sired 354 winners.

Matchem's line became established in the mid nineteenth century through West Australian, the first winner of the English Triple Crown (Derby, 2,000 Guineas, St. Leger), and through his offspring: Australian (b.h. 1858) and Solon (b.h. 1861). The former was exported ot the USA where he began a line of which Man o'War was the most outstanding descendant, while the latter originated a line in Europe of which Hurry On is the main exponent.

Breeder: Mr Fenwick
Owner: John Holmes
Racing Career: 13 starts; 11 wins

Matchem	Cade ○ 1734	Godolphin Arabian ● 1724	— —	— —
			— —	—
		Roxana ○ 1718	Bald Galloway	St. Victor's Barb 0 Grey Whynot 15
			Akaster Turk Mare	Akaster Turk 0 Cream Cheeks 6
	Partner Mare ○ 1735	Partner ◇ 1718	Jigg	Byerley Turk 0 Spanker Mare 6
			Curwen Bay Barb Mare	Curwen Bay Barb 0 Old Spot Mare 9
		Brown Farewell ● 1710	Makeless	Oglethorpe Arabian 0 —
			Brimmer Mare	Brimmer 0 Place's White Turk Mare 4

HEROD

b.h. 1758 – No. 26 Fam. – foaled in Great Britain

This horse, who was also known as King Herod (a name which was later abbreviated for practical reasons), was a well-built and muscular animal. Throughout his racing career from the age of five to nine he achieved many wins and was defeated only twice, displaying extraordinary tenacity and speed at all times. Herod also excelled at stud, siring 497 winners, one of which has ensured the continuation of the line down to the present day. He was Woodpecker (ch. 1773) who, through his son Buzzard (ch. 1787), was the originator of two distinguished lines in France, one of which leads to Tourbillon and the other to The Tetrarch, both of whom are recognized in history as great horses. Other sons of Herod who deserve a mention are Florizel (b.b. 1768), who sired Diomed (ch.h. 1777), winner of the first Epsom Derby and exported to the United States at the age of 21 after having served as a stallion in England, and Highflyer (b.h. 1774). High-flyer was unbeaten in 12 races and sired 470 winners including three Derby winners, four Doncaster St. Leger winners and a filly who won the Oaks.

Breeder: Duke of Cumberland
Owners: Duke of Cumberland – Sir John Moore
Racing career: Winner of numerous matches

Herod	Tartar ◇ 1743	Partner ◇ 1718	Jigg	Byerley Turk / 0 Spanker Mare / 6
			Curwen Bay Barb Mare	Curwen Bay Barb / 0 Old Spot Mare / 9
		Meliora ◇ 1729	Fox	Clumsy / 11 Bay Peg / 6
			Milkmaid	Sir E. Blackett's Snail / 43 Shields Galloway / 48
	Cypron ○ 1750	Blaze ○ 1733	Flying Childers	Darley Arabian / 0 Betty Leedes / 6
			Confederate Filly	Grey Grantham / 0 Duke of Rutland's Black Barb Mare / 61
		Selima ◆ 1733	Bethell's Arabian	— —
			Graham's Champion Mare	Graham's Champion / 53 Darley Arabian Mare / 26

ECLIPSE

ch.h. 1764 – No. 12 Fam. – foaled in Great Britain

This horse was named Eclipse because he was foaled on 5 April 1764, a day when England witnessed a total eclipse of the sun. This coincidence was in a certain sense a premonition of what were to be the fortunes of his line in the future. Not only did this horse "eclipse" all his rivals on the racecourse but he was just as successful at stud. He relegated the progeny of Herod and Matchem to a position of merely marginal importance, at least as regards numbers, since nowadays 90 per cent of existing thoroughbreds descend in their direct male line from this exceptional horse. The history of the thoroughbred abounds with fortuitous events due to chance or fate and Eclipse was one of those. Eclipse's great grandsire, Bartlet's Childers (sired by the Darley Arabian) could not be trained, but when he was sent to stud he sired a colt named Squirt. One day, because of Squirt's unsoundness, his owner decided to have him shot. The stable lad in charge of him did all he could to try and prevent the horse from meeting such a dismal end and managed to convince the owner to change his mind and hand over the horse to him. It is said that in exchange for Squirt the stable boy sang the owner a song.

At the age of 17 Squirt produced Marske, Eclipse's sire. As a yearling Eclipse was nothing special and rather low at the front in addition to having a fairly difficult temperament. After the death of the Duke of Cumberland the effects of his stud farm were sold at auction and Eclipse was bought by a Mr Wildman who took him to the countryside. As time passed the horse began to change in his physical appearance and demonstrated unusual strength and speed but at the same time he became increasingly difficult. The new owner was concerned and discussed him with Captain O'Kelly, who suggested to him a solution which could suit them both: Eclipse would be placed in the hands of an Irishman named Sullivan, the head lad at O'Kelly's stables, who was able to handle any horse, and after the horse had begun racing his price would be fixed and the Captain would be able to buy half of him. Sullivan shut himself in the box with the horse and a short time later he had Eclipse as docile as a lamb. At this point training began. Work was carried out at unusual times, in an attempt to remove the horse from the gaze of inquisitive eyes, with the hope of doing well as regards the bets that would be placed when the horse began racing. At the age of five, on 3 May 1769, Eclipse took part in his first race over a distance of almost 4 miles (6.40 km). It was a double event consisting of two heats: he won the first effortlessly and in the second left his rivals more than a furlong (200 m) behind, just as Captain O'Kelly had bet (1,000 guineas to 500). After the race he bought half the horse, as agreed, for 650 guineas. That year, Eclipse went from win to win; on 29 May at Epsom, 13 and 15 June at Winchester, 23 and 26 June at Salisbury, 25 July at Canterbury, 27 July at Lewes and 19 September at Lichfield. He reappeared in public in the spring of the following year, winning effortlessly over Bucephalus, a horse who until then had been unbeaten.

After such a success, the threats which had been made previously became stronger and so Wildman, intimidated, sold his half for 1,100 guineas to his partner who continued to race the horse with constant success until September. Later O'Kelly too, under threat, decided to declare publicly that on 3 and 4 October Eclipse would run his last two races. So on 4 October, in a walk-over, cheered by a mass of people, Eclipse bade farewell to the trace. In 1771 the horse began his career as a stallion at a fee of 25 guineas and there were always a great many requests from the breeders, even when the fee was raised to 50 guineas. In 1789, at the age of 25, Eclipse died of colic, having sired 344 winners in his lifetime. The most significant fact revealed by the post mortem, apart from the strength and hardness of his bones, was the weight of his heart: 14.3 lb (6.5 kg).

Two great lines with numerous and important ramifications descend from Eclipse, particularly from King Fergus (ch.h. 1775) and Pot-8-o's (ch.h. 1773). The spelling of the latter's name should have been Potatoes, but when the breeder instructed a stableman to write down the horse's name the man, in his ignorance, misspelt it.

Breeder: Duke of Cumberland
Owner: Wildman and O'Kelly

Racing Career		
Age	Starts	Wins
5	9	9
6	12	12
Total	21	21

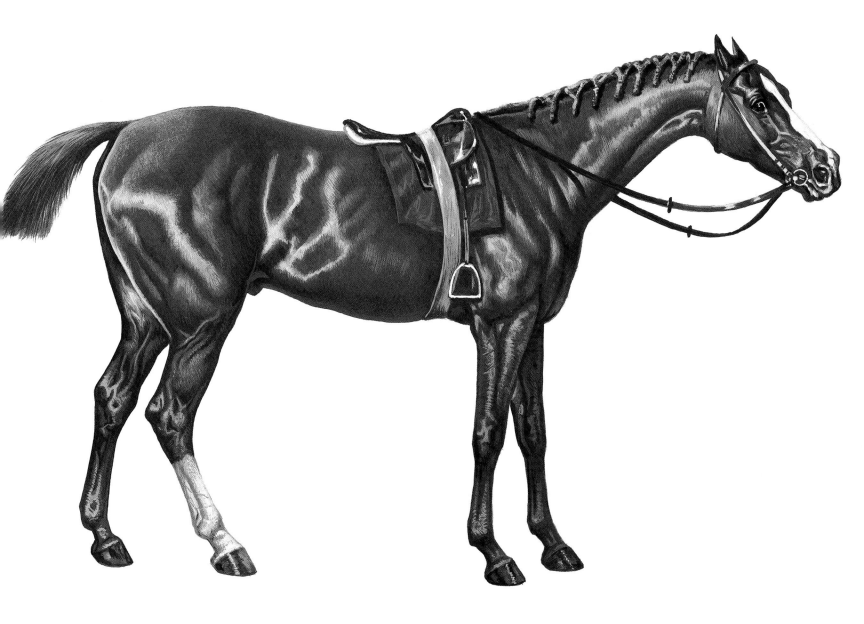

			Bartlet's Childers	Darley Arabian	0
	Squirt			Betty Leeds	6
	◇ 1732		Snake Mare	Snake	0
Marske				Clumsey	11
● 1750	Blacklegs Mare		Hutton's Blacklegs	Hutton's Bay Barb	0
				Coneyskins Mare	34
			Bay Bolton Mare	Bay Bolton	0
Eclipse				Fox Cub Mare	8
	Regulus		Godolphin Arabian	—	
	○ 1739			—	
			Grey Robinson	Bald Galloway	15
Spilletta				Snake Mare	11
○ 1749	Mother Western		Easby Snake	Lister's Snake	11
	1731			Akaster Turk Mare	70
			Old Montagu Mare	Old Montagu	0
				Hautboy Mare	12

TOUCHSTONE

dk.b.h. 1831 – No. 14 Fam. – foaled in Great Britain

He was a rather small horse, standing 15 hands, (1.51m), with a decidedly elongated form (he had one extra dorsal vertebra and two extra ribs like Eclipse) and was without doubt a high-caliber racehorse. He had considerable stamina but was slow to get going, apparently because of problems with the joints of his forelegs. He had, however, a final sprint which was very effective and ran from the age of two to six before proving a successful sire. He died at the age of 30 having sired three Derby winners, two Doncaster St. Leger winners, four 2,000 Guineas winners, a filly that won the 1,000 Guineas and another that won the Oaks.

His line has come down to us through his son Newminster, winner of the St. Leger in 1851, through two branches which originate from the latter's grandson, Bay Ronald (b. 1893) by Hampton, out of Black Duchess. One of the lines stems from Bayardo (b. 1906) who is most famous as paternal grandsire of Hyperion and the other from Dark Ronald (dk. b. 1905) who had a great reputation in Germany above all as grandsire of Oleander. It is, however, important to mention that Dark Ronald is the sire of Son-in-Law (dk. b. 1911) whose presence in the pedigree is a guarantee of stamina. Despite his excellent racing career, however, Touchstone's long-lasting reputation owes at least as much to his achievements at stud and those of his progeny.

Breeder: Lord Westminster
Owner: Lord Westminster
Most important wins: St. Leger, Ascot Gold Cup (twice) Doncaster Cup (twice)

Touchstone	Camel • 1822	Whalebone • 1807	Waxy	Pot-8-o's	Eclipse 12 / Sportsmistress 38
				Maria	Herod 26 / Lisette 18
			Penelope	Trumpator	Conductor 12 / Brunette 14
				Prunella	**Highflyer** 13 / Promise 1
		Selim Mare ○ 1812	Selim	**Buzzard**	Woodpecker 1 / Misfortune 3
				Alexander Mare	Alexander 13 / Highflyer Mare 2
			Maiden	**Sir Peter**	**Highflyer** 13 / Papillon 3
				Phoenomenon Mare	Phoenomenon 2 / Matron 24
	Banter • 1826	Master Henry ○1815	Orville	Beningbrough	King Fergus 6 / Herod Mare 7
				Evelina	**Highflyer** 13 / Termagant 8
			Miss Sophia	Stamford	**Sir Peter** 3 / Horatia 30
				Sophia	**Buzzard** 3 / Huncamunca 3
		Boadicea ○ 1807	Alexander	**Eclipse**	Marske 8 / Spilletta 12
				Grecian Princess	William's Forester 2 / Coalition Colt Mare 13
			Brunette	Amaranthus	Old England 15 / Second Mare 4
				Mayfly	Matchem 4 / Starling Mare 14

Racing Career		
Age	**Starts**	**Wins**
2	2	1
3	6	5
4	4	2
5	2	2
6	1	1
Total	15	11

MELBOURNE

dk.b.h. 1834 – No. 1 Fam. – foaled in Great Britain

Melbourne was a moderately good race-horse of reasonably sturdy build but his racing career, which lasted from the age of four to seven, certainly gave no indication of the enormous success he was to have as a sire. He was in fact one of the most extraordinary stallions ever to be bred in England and of his many offspring it is West Australian (b. 1850) who stands out most of all. West Australian was the first winner of the Triple Crown, and was beaten only once.

After losing his first race West Australian went on to win ten consecutive starts and the last two in which he took part as a three-year-old, one at Doncaster and the other at Newmarket, were walk-overs. At four, having been sold to Lord Londesborough, West Australian won the Ascot Gold Cup. He was sent to stud in 1855 and stood in Yorkshire but in 1860 was exported to France. As a stallion his best products were Solon from whom Hurry On and Australian descend in the fourth generation, the latter being Man o'War's third grandsire. In addition to this exceptional horse, Melbourne also got a series of top-class mares who later showed themselves to be high caliber brood mares. After having headed the Stallion List in England from 1853 to 1857, Melbourne died in 1859 at the age of 25.

Breeder: Mr Robinson
Owner: Mr Robinson

Racing Career

Age	Starts	Wins
4	7	3
5	8	6
6	1	0
7	1	0
Total	17	9

					Conductor	12
Melbourne	Humphrey Clinker ○ 1822	Comus ◇ 1809	Sorcerer	**Trumpator**	Conductor	12
					Brunette	14
				Y. Giantess	Diomed	6
					Giantess	6
			Houghton Lass	**Sir Peter**	**Highflyer**	13
					Papillon	3
				Alexina	King Fergus	6
					Lardella	25
		Clinkerina ● 1812	Clinker	**Sir Peter**	**Highflyer**	13
					Papillon	3
				Hyale	Phoenomenon	2
					Rally	6
			Pewett	Tandem	Syphon	9
					Regulus Mare	17
				Termagant	Tantrum	21
					Cantatrice	8
	Cervantes Mare ○ 1825	Cervantes ○ 1806	Don Quixote	Eclipse	Marske	8
					Spilletta	12
				Grecian Princess	William's Forester	2
					Coalition Colt Mare	13
			Evelina	**Highflyer**	Herod	26
					Rachel	13
				Termagant	Tantrum	21
					Cantatrice	8
		Golumpus Mare ● 1818	Golumpus	Gohanna	Mercury	9
					Herod Mare	24
				Catherina	Woodpecker	1
					Camilla	11
			Paynator Mare	Paynator	**Trumpator**	14
					Mark A. Mare	18
				St. George Mare	St. George	9
					Abigail	1

STOCKWELL

ch.h. 1849 – No. 3 Fam. – foaled in Great Britain

If a prize for perseverance were to be awarded to breeders of racehorses there would be no doubt as to the person who should receive it – William Theobald. He was the owner of Pocahontas, the brood mare who, after being sent to the stallion The Baron for eight consecutive years, came in foal, later foaling a chestnut colt who fortunately did not inherit her tendency to roar. The colt was named Stockwell after the village of the same name, then on the outskirts of London, where he was foaled. He was bought by the eccentric Lord Exeter and was second and fourth in his two races as a two-year-old. The next season Stockwell won the 2,000 Guineas and the St. Leger, but was decisively beaten in the Derby in which he was unplaced. As a four-year-old his best performance was second place in the Gold Cup at Ascot, but it was at stud where he won his real fame.

In his new role, Stockwell earned himself the name of "Emperor of Stallions" and produced three Derby winners, four 2,000 Guineas winners and six St. Leger winners, and headed the stallions list in England seven times between 1860 and 1867. His line was continued down to the present day by St. Albans and Doncaster.

St. Albans began a line in which the name of Congreve (b. 1924) is the most outstanding, while Doncaster sired Bend Or (ch. 1877) from whom one of today's dominant stallion lines descends. Bend Or's sons Ormonde and Bona Vista started off two dynasties, one which was headed by Teddy and the other by Phalaris. At this point, however, it should be said that there is a certain amount of doubt as to the validity of Bend Or's pedigree due to a suspicion (which continued to exist even after an inquiry had been held) of there having been a change of identity involving him and Tadcaster, also sired by Doncaster but by a different dam, which could have occurred in the transfer from the stud farm to the Russley training center.

Breeder: W. Theobald
Owner: Lord Exeter
Most important wins: 2,000 Guineas, St. Leger

Stockwell					
The Baron ◇ 1842	Irish Birdcatcher ◇ 1833	Sir Hercules	Whalebone	**Waxy** **Penelope**	18 / 1
			Peri	Wanderer Thalestris	11 / 2
		Guiccioli	Bob Booty	Chanticleer Ierne	3 / 23
			Flight	Escape Y. Heroine	57 / 11
	Echidna ○ 1838	Economist	**Whisker**	**Waxy** **Penelope**	18 / 1
			Floranthe	Octavian Caprice	8 / 36
		Miss Pratt	Blacklock	Whitelock Coriander Mare	2 / 2
			Gadabout	**Orville** Minstrell	8 / 24
Pocahontas ○ 1837	Glencoe ◇ 1831	Sultan	Selim	Buzzard Alexander Mare	3 / 2
			Bacchante	Williamson's Ditto Mercury Mare	7 / 8
		Trampoline	Tramp	Dick Andrews Gohanna Mare	9 / 3
			Web	**Waxy** **Penelope**	18 / 1
	Marpessa ○ 1830	Muley	**Orville**	Beningbrough Evelina	7 / 8
			Eleanor	Whiskey Y. Giantess	2 / 6
		Clare	Marmion	**Whisker** Y. Noisette	1 / 28
			Harpalice	Gohanna Amazon	24 / 3

Racing Career

Age	Starts	Wins
2	2	0
3	14	11
4	4	0
Total	20	11

GLADIATEUR

b.h. 1862 – No. 5 Fam. – foaled in France

When Gladiateur, who was bred in France, was taken to Chantilly to be broken in, the trainer Charles Pratt advised against attempting to race him since an injury to a joint which he had sustained as a foal gave him a tendency to lameness. The owner therefore chose to consult the British trainer Tom Jennings, who was favourably impressed with the horse and began training him in England. Gladiateur's racing career, which was of a high standard, took place mostly in England. As a two-year-old he met with mixed fortune, winning only one race from three, but as a three-year-old he was beaten only once. Despite the fact that at birth his front legs appeared rather fragile, Gladiateur grew into quite a large horse. He won the 2,000 Guineas, beating Archimedes by a neck in an exciting finish in which five horses, including the favourite, Liddington, who came third, arrived at the post in a tight bunch, the distances separating the first five being neck – neck – head – head.

Although he was frequently lame, Gladiateur was trained for the Derby and started favourite. He triumphed at Epsom, winning in a field of 30 runners after having held back until the finishing straight. At Tattenham Corner he was tenth, but in the home stretch Gladiateur really let himself go with very little coaxing from his jockey Grimshaw, and won with the greatest of ease. For the first time, the Derby had been won by a horse foaled outside Great Britain. After having carried off the Grand Prix de Paris at Longchamp, Gladiateur triumphed in the Doncaster St. Leger and then again in Paris in the Prix Royal Oak, as well as winning the Newmarket Derby by 40 lengths. As a four-year-old he won all four of his races, including the Ascot Gold Cup. Sadly, after his excellent racing career, Gladiateur left no notable descendants when he died in 1876.

Breeder: Count F. de Lagrange
Owner: Count F. de Lagrange
Most important wins: 2,000 Guineas, Derby Stakes, St. Leger Stakes, Grand Prix de Paris, Prix Royal Oak, Ascot Gold Cup

Racing Career

Age	Starts	Wins
2	3	1
3	10	9
4	6	6
Total	19	16

Gladiateur	Monarque ○ 1852	The Emperor ◇ 1841	Defence	**Whalebone**	**Waxy** 18 / **Penelope** 1
				Defiance	Rubens 2 / Little Folly 5
			Reveller Mare	Reveller	Comus 25 / Rosette 19
				Design	**Tramp** 3 / **Defiance** 5
		Poetess ○ 1838	Royal Oak	Catton	Golumpus 11 / Lucy Gray 2
				Smolensko Mare	Smolensko 18 / Lady Mary 13
			Ada	Whisker	**Waxy** 18 / **Penelope** 1
				Anna Bella	Shuttle 21 / Drone Mare 19
	Miss Gladiator ○ 1854	Gladiator ◇ 1833	Partisan	Walton	Sir Peter 3 / Arethusa 7
				Parasol	Pot-8-o's 38 / Prunella 1
			Pauline	Moses	**Whalebone** 1 / Gohanna Mare 5
				Quadrille	Selim 2 / Canary Bird 22
		Taffrail ● 1845	Sheet Anchor	Lottery	**Tramp** 3 / Mandane 11
				Morgiana	Muley 6 / Miss Stephenson 12
			The Warwich Mare	Merman	**Whalebone** 1 / Mermaid 9
				Ardrossan Mare	Ardrossan 2 / Shepherdess 5

HAMPTON

b.h. 1872 – No. 10 Fam. – foaled in Great Britain

This horse was smaller than average, at 15 hands (1.55m) or a little more, and proved to be a late developer. Hampton made his debut as a two-year-old in a selling race and his career continued with little success (it is said that he even ran in steeplechases) until he was four years old, when having shown great staying power, he was trained in secret for the Goodwood Cup for which he ended up favourite at six to four. Before this, however, he could have been backed at 40 to 1 and so when he won, albeit by only three-quarters of a length from Admiral Byng, he guaranteed huge winnings for his backers.

At five Hampton improved further, winning the Doncaster Cup and the Goodwood Cup, which he took for the second year running. At six he reappeared at Epsom, just beating Verneuil to win the Gold Cup. Verneuil, however, took his revenge by winning the Ascot Gold Cup, in which Hampton could finish only fourth. That year he was second in the Goodwood Stakes and the Doncaster Cup. He was fourth to Isonomy in the Cambridgeshire in a field of 38 when giving the winner 27 lb.

Hampton's racing career had its high moments but it could certainly not have been described as awe-inspiring, and was in no way indicative of the enormous success he was to have as a stallion. Hampton sired many fine horses, including two Epsom Derby winners, but his name is best known in connection with that of his son Bay Ronald who, although one of the less brilliant of his offspring on the track, had the distinction of siring Bayardo and Dark Ronald, grandsires of Hyperion and Oleander respectively. Hampton died in 1897 at the age of 25.

Breeder: Lord Norreys
Owners: J. Nightingall, B.B.C. Herwey, Fred Hobson, Lord Ellesmere
Most important wins: Goodwood Cup (twice), Epsom Gold Cup, Doncaster Cup

Hampton					
Lord Clifden ○ 1860	Newminster ○ 1848	Touchstone	Camel	Whalebone	1
				Selim Mare	24
			Banter	Master Henry	3
				Boadicea	14
		Beeswing	Dr. Syntax	Paynator	18
				Beningbrough Mare	37
			Ardrossan Mare	Ardrossan	2
				Lady Eliza	8
	The Slave ○ 1852	Melbourne	Humphrey Clinker	Comus	25
				Clinkerina	8
			Cervantes Mare	Cervantes	8
				Golumpus Mare	1
		Volley	Voltaire	Blacklock	2
				Phantom Mare	12
			Martha Lynn	Mulatto	5
				Leda	2
Lady Langden ● 1868	Kettledrum ◇ 1858	Rataplan	The Baron	Irish Birdcatcher	11
				Echidna	24
			Pocahontas	Glencoe	1
				Marpessa	3
		Hybla	The Provost	The Saddler	3
				Rebecca	4
			Otisina	**Liverpool**	11
				Otis	3
	Haricot ● 1847	Lanercost	**Liverpool**	Tramp	3
				Whisker Mare	11
			Otis	Bustard	10
				Election Mare	3
		Queen Mary	Gladiator	Partisan	1
				Pauline	22
			Plenipotentiary Mare	Plenipotentiary	6
				Myrrha	10

Racing Career		
Age	**Starts**	**Wins**
2	5	3
3	5	2
4	3	1
5	10	8
6	10	5
Total	33	19

ORMONDE

b.h. 1883 – No. 16 Fam. – foaled in Great Britain

Ormonde was a good-looking animal, standing 16.2 hands (1.65m) with a sturdy frame complemented by elegant lines, even though his head was rather ordinary. His racing career lasted from two to four and he was unbeaten in 16 races. He was fourth winner of the Triple Crown and although he was a roarer (caused by paralysis of the larynx accompanied by a characteristic whistling noise), he was without doubt an exceptional racehorse. He won the Epsom Derby beating The Bard by a length and a half, while the next horse was referred to as a "bad third" owing to the enormous gap between him and the second. Ormonde was such an extremely docile horse that the Duke of Westminster himself rode him to a reception at Grosvenor House in celebration of Queen Victoria's Jubilee. Ormonde received an extremely warm welcome, especially from the ladies, but when he began to feed on the flowers that decorated their hats and dresses the Queen herself intervened and remarked to Ormonde: "Your horse is too greedy," at which the Duke was mortified.

Ormonde was sired by Bend Or who was also a fine racehorse (10 wins out of 14 starts). Bend Or won the Epsom Derby, and was also an exceptional sire having produced Bona Vista from whom the Phalaris dynasty descends. In his role as a stallion, through his son Orme (b. 1889) and his grandson Flying Fox (b. 1896), Ormonde headed a very important line of which Teddy is the most outstanding representative.

Ormonde was exported to Argentina for £12,000 in 1889 but was sold four years later to a Californian, William O'Brien, since he was not proving very productive. He died in the United States in 1904 and his remains were transported to London where they are now preserved in the Natural History Museum in South Kensington.

Breeder: Duke of Westminster
Owner: Duke of Westminster
Most important wins: 2,000 Guineas, Derby Stakes, St. Leger Stakes, Champion Stakes, Dewhurst Stakes, July Cup, Rous Memorial Stakes, Hardwicke States, St. James's Palace Stakes

Racing Career

Age	Starts	Wins
2	3	3
3	10	10
4	3	3
Total	16	16

Ormonde	Bend Or ◇ 1877	Doncaster ◇ 1870	Stockwell	The Baron	**Irish Birdcatcher** 11 / Echidna 24
				Pocahontas	Glencoe 1 / Marpessa 3
			Marigold	Teddington	Orlando 13 / Miss Twickenham 2
				Ratan Mare	Ratan 9 / Melbourne Mare 5
		Rouge Rose ◇ 1865	Thormanby	Windhound *	**Pantaloon** 17 / Phryne 3
				Alice Hawthorn	Muley Moloch 9 / Rebecca 4
			Ellen Horne	Redshank	Sandbeck 8 / Johanna 15
				Delhi	Plenipotentiary 6 / Pawn Junior 1
	Lily Agnes ○ 1871	Macaroni ○ 1860	Sweetmeat	Gladiator	Partisan 1 / Pauline 22
				Lollypop	Starch of Voltaire 12 / Belinda 21
			Jocose	**Pantaloon**	Castrel 2 / Idalia 17
				Banter	Master Henry 3 / Boadicea 14
		Polly Agnes ○ 1865	The Cure	Physician	Brutandorf 11 / Primette 21
				Morsel	Mulatto 5 / Linda 6
			Miss Agnes	**Irish Birdcatcher**	Sir Hercules 2 / Guiccioli 11
				Agnes	Clarion 6 / Annette 16

* or Melbourne (No. 1 Fam.)

29

ISONOMY

b.h. 1875 – No. 19 Fam. – foaled in Great Britain

This horse was a bit smaller than average (15.3 hands)(1.58m) but had a deep chest and extremely muscular hindquarters. He had a few defects, however, which fortunately he did not pass on to his progeny, like flat thighs, light bone structure and high heels. Isonomy's racing career lasted from two to five. As a two-year-old he won only one of his starts, coming second in the other two, while as a three-year-old he appeared on the track only once, easily winning the Cambridgeshire in a field of 38 runners, but carrying only 7 st 1 lb (45 kg) and starting at 50/1. Hampton finished third, carrying 9 st 2 lb (58 kg).

As a four-year-old, after finishing second in a handicap race at Newmarket with 9 st (57.5 kg), Isonomy had a series of six consecutive wins including the Gold Vase, the Ascot Gold Cup, the Goodwood Cup and the Doncaster Cup. The year ended, however, with defeat in the Cambridgeshire in which he was given the huge weight of 9 st 9 lb (61.5 kg). As a five-year-old, Isonomy won both his starts, the Manchester Cup, in which he conceded 3 st 2 lb (20 kg) to The Abbot, and The Ascot Gold cup for the second year running.

Even though Isonomy was a good racehorse, it was at stud that he really showed his greatness, siring numerous champions, the best known being Gallinule, sire of Pretty Polly and Isinglass, sixth winner of the Triple Crown who lost only one out of his 12 starts. It was Isinglass who ensured the continuation of his paternal line through two of his sons – Louviers, who started off a branch which numbers, among others, the German horse Ticino and John O'Gaunt, the sire of Swynford whose son Blandford was a stallion of the highest quality.

Breeder: Mr Graham
Owner: F. Gretton
Most important wins: Ascot Gold Cup (twice), Goodwood Cup, Doncaster Cup, Gold Vase, Cambridgeshire Handicap, Manchester Cup

Racing Career		
Age	Starts	Wins
2	3	1
3	1	1
4	8	6
5	2	2
Total	14	10

Pedigree

Isonomy					
Sterling ○ 1868	Oxford ◇ 1857	Irish Birdcatcher	Sir Hercules	Whalebone / Peri	1 / 2
			Guiccioli	Bob Booty / Flight	23 / 11
		Honey Dear	Plenipotentiary	Emilius / Harriet	28 / 6
			My Dear	Bay Middleton / Miss Letty	1 / 12
	Whisper ○ 1857	Flatcatcher	Touchstone	Camel / Banter	24 / 14
			Decoy	Filho de Puta / Finesse	12 / 3
		Silence	Melbourne	Humphrey Clinker / Cervantes Mare	8 / 1
			Secret	Hornsea / Solace	15 / 12
Isola Bella ○ 1868	Stockwell ◇ 1849	The Baron	Irish Birdcatcher	Sir Hercules / Guiccioli	2 / 11
			Echidna	Economist / Miss Pratt	36 / 24
		Pocahontas	Glencoe	Sultan / Trampoline	8 / 1
			Marpessa	Muley / Clare	6 / 3
	Isoline ◇ 1860	Ethelbert	Faugh-a-Ballagh	Sir Hercules / Guiccioli	2 / 11
			Espoir	Liverpool / Esperance	11 / 12
		Bassishaw	The Prime Warden	Cadland / Zarina	12 / 17
			Miss Whinney	Sir Hercules / Euphrosyne	2 / 19

ANDREINA

ch.m. 1881 – No. 6 Fam. – foaled in Italy

Andreina was a mare with elegant lines and a particularly gently temperament. She raced from two to five and, had she been used more wisely, would almost certainly have ended her racing career unbeaten. Unfortunately she merely wandered round Italy from one racecourse to the other running a total of 39 races, 29 of which she won. As a two-year-old Andreina appeared on the track just once, finishing unplaced in the Varese Criterium. As a three-year-old she won 17 of her 18 starts and was only beaten in Rome by Parthenope, and on that same day she had her 17th race.

Andreina was the winner of the first Italian Derby and for this reason her name, more than any other, is linked to this classic. That same year she won other important races including the Omnium in Rome, the Premio Firenze, the Gran Premio Lombardia at Catellazzo, and the Premio Principe Amedeo, the City of Turin Cup in Turin and the Premio Varese.

As a four-year-old she ran in 14 races winning 12 of them, including the Jockey Club Cup in Rome and the Premio di Firenze for the second time; she walked over for the City of Milan Cup and came second in her remaining starts. As a five-year-old Andreina took part in six races, managing to win only one, however, since the burden of an exhausting career was by now taking its toll. As a brood mare she did not yield the results hoped of her although in 1896 she gave birth to Marcantonio, a handsome golden horse with a sturdy frame and well-proportioned conformation, who proved to be a of classic caliber.

Breeder: Thomas Rook
Owner: Thomas Rook
Most important wins: Italian Derby, Premio Omnium (twice), Premio Principe Amedeo, City of Turin Cup

Racing Career

Age	Starts	Wins
2	1	0
3	18	17
4	14	12
5	6	1
Total	39	30

Andreina	Andred ◇ 1870	Blair Athol ◇ 1861	Stockwell	The Baron	Irish Birdcatcher	11
					Echidna	24
				Pocahontas	Glencoe	1
					Marpessa	3
			Blink Bonny	**Melbourne**	Humphrey Clinker	8
					Cervantes Mare	1
				Queen Mary	Gladiator	22
					Plenipotentiary M.	10
		Woodcraft ○ 1861	**Voltigeur**	Voltaire	Blacklock	2
					Phantom Mare	12
				Martha Lynn	Mulatto	5
					Leda	2
			Venison Mare	Venison	Partisan	1
					Fawn	11
				Wedding-Day	Camel	24
					Margellina	11
	Orpheline ○ 1865	Norton ○ 1854	**Voltigeur**	Voltaire	Blacklock	2
					Phantom Mare	12
				Martha Lynn	Mulatto	5
					Leda	2
			Lucy Dashwood	Sheet Anchor	Lottery	11
					Morgiana	12
				Patty	Whisker	1
					Miss Patrick	4
		Britannia ○ 1857	Brocket	**Melbourne**	Humphrey Clinker	8
					Cervantes Mare	1
				Miss Slick	Muley Moloch	9
					Whisker Mare	1
			Protection	Defence	Whalebone	1
					Defiance	5
				Testatrix	Touchstone	14
					Y. Worry	6

ST. SIMON

dk.b.h. 1881 – No. 11 Fam. – foaled in Great Britain

St. Simon was bred by the Hungarian Prince Batthyany and when the latter died while he was waiting to watch the victory of Galliard in the 2,000 Guineas, the horse was bought by the Duke of Portland.

Due to a Jockey Club rule which was in force at that time, all the entries made by his deceased owner became void and so the horse had to be content with running in relatively modest races. St. Simon ran at two and three, always winning with extreme ease, never needing to be taxed to his limit and ended his career unbeaten. The distance of the races he contested varied between 6 furlongs (1,200 m) and 2½ miles (4,000 m) and never caused him the slightest problem. As a two-year-old he won the Halnaker Stakes, a maiden race, the Devonshire Nursery (in a field of 19 runners), the Prince of Wales's Nursery, carrying top-weight of 9 st (57 kg), and a match at Newmarket.

At three, after having walked over for the Epsom Gold Cup he won the Ascot Gold Cup, 20 lengths ahead of Tristan, he won the Newcastle Gold Cup with the greatest of ease and in the Goodwood Cup he beat the St. Leger winner Ossian by 20 lengths. St. Simon was a formidable galloper with an extremely nervous temperament which was revealed not only on the racetrack but also in training. One day his jockey, Fred Archer, on the instructions of St. Simon's trainer Mat Dawson, touched him with his spurs so as to coax him out of his laziness. St. Simon put on such a sprint that he soon disappeared from the view of his owner and trainer who later saw him being led back by the jockey, who swore he would never dare repeat the experiment again.

However outstanding St. Simon was as a racehorse he was even more remarkable at stud and can rightly be considered one of the greatest thoroughbred horses of all time. The influence of his stock was felt through the stallion lines of Persimmon (b. 1893), Chaucer (dk.b. 1900) and Rabelais (b. 1900) all of which are still very important today; the great Ribot descends in the fifth remove from Rabelais. In addition to these horses which have guaranteed a continuation through the direct male line, St. Simon also sired other high-class horses like St. Frusquin (dk.b. 1893), Desmond (dk.b. 1896) and Diamond Jubilee (b. 1897).

Diamond Jubilee, a full brother of Florizel II and Persimmon, had a terrible temperament and a pronounced aversion to jockeys, who had the greatest difficulty getting into the saddle. His trainer noticed that the horse behaved in a completely different manner with Herbert Jones, the stable boy, who was promoted to jockey and rode Diamond Jubilee in the 2,000 Guineas which he won by four lengths. From that day Jones rode him for the rest of the horse's career, winning the Triple Crown. St Simon died in 1908 at the age of 27.

St. Simon	Galopin • 1872	Vedette • 1854	Voltigeur	**Voltaire**	Blacklock / Phantom Mare	2 / 12
				Martha Lynn	Mulatto / Leda	5 / 2
			Mrs. Ridgway	Irish Birdcatcher	Sir Hercules / Guiccioli	2 / 11
				Nan Darrell	Inheritor / Nell	4 / 19
		Flying Duchess ○ 1853	Flying Dutchman	Bay Middleton	**Sultan** / Cobweb	8 / 1
				Barbelle	Sandbeck / Darioletta	8 / 3
			Merope	**Voltaire**	Blacklock / Phantom Mare	2 / 12
				Velocipede's Dam	Juniper / Sorcerer Mare	9 / 3
	St. Angela ○ 1865	King Tom ○ 1851	Harkaway	Economist	Whisker / Floranthe	1 / 36
				Fanny Dawson	Nabocklish / Miss Tooley	4 / 2
			Pocahontas	Glencoe	**Sultan** / Trampoline	8 / 1
				Marpessa	Muley / Clare	6 / 3
		Adeline ○ 1851	Jon	Cain	Paulowitz / Paynator Mare	8 / 8
				Margaret	Edmund / Medora	12 / 4
			Little Fairy	Hornsea	Velocipede / Cerberus Mare	3 / 15
				Lacerta	Zodiac / Jerboa	1 / 11

ST. SIMON

Breeder: Prince Batthyany
Owner: Duke of Portland
Most important wins: Ascot Gold Cup, Goodwood Cup

Racing Career		
Age	Starts	Wins
2	5	5
3	4	4
Total	9	9

PERSIMMON

b.h. 1893 – No. 7 Fam. – foaled in Great Britain

Persimmon, full brother to Florizel II (dk.b.h. 1891) and Diamond Jubilee (b.h. 1897), was a big, powerful horse with a long dorsolumbar line. He made his racing debut by winning the Coventry Stakes at Ascot and later that summer he took the Richmond Stakes at Goodwood. Persimmon was beaten only twice in his three seasons' racing, the first time as a two-year-old when he came third behind St. Frusquin and Omladina in the Middle Park Plate.

The other occasion on which Persimmon was beaten was as a three-year-old in the Prince of Wales's Stakes· when he was second when giving 3 lb to St. Frusquin, another son of St. Simon. But in the Derby at Epsom, Persimmon had crossed swords with St. Frusquin for the second time finally getting the better of him by only a neck after a struggle which lasted for the whole of the finishing straight. St. Frusquin had previously won the 2,000 Guineas in which Persimmon did not take part, missing the chance of winning the Triple Crown, which, all things considered, he really deserved. He won the Doncaster St. Leger at 11 to 2 on and ended his three-year-old days by winning the Jockey Club Stakes from the older horses Sir Visto and Ladas.

As a four-year-old Persimmon ran only twice, but they were very important races – the Eclipse Stakes and the Ascot Gold Cup, both of which he won. At stud, apart from the great Sceptre, he sired Prince Palatine (b.h. 1908) who ensured the continuation of the line which was to produce Prince Rose from whom Prince Chevalier, Prince Bio and Princequillo descend, all of whom, in turn, headed very important branches. Persimmon died in 1908 at the age of 15.

Breeder: H.R.H. the Prince of Wales
Owner: H.R.H. the Prince of Wales
Most important wins: Derby, St. Leger, Eclipse Stakes, Ascot Gold Cup, Coventry Stakes, Jockey Club Stakes

				Voltaire	12

			Voltigeur	Voltaire	12
		Vedette		Martha Lynn	2
			Mrs. Ridgway	Irish Birdcatcher	11
	Galopin			Nan Darrell	19
	• 1872		Flying Dutchman	Bay Middleton	1
		Flying Duchess		Barbelle	3
			Merope	Voltaire	12
St. Simon				Velocipede's Dam	3
• 1881			Harkaway	Economist	36
		King Tom		Fanny Dawson	2
			Pocahontas	Glencoe	1
	St. Angela			Marpessa	3
	○ 1865		Jon	Cain	8
		Adeline		Margaret	4
			Little Fairy	Hornsea	15
				Lacerta	11
			Newminster	Touchstone	14
		Lord Clifden		Beeswing	8
			The Slave	Melbourne	1
	Hampton			Volley	2
	○ 1872		Kettledrum	Rataplan	3
		Lady Langden		Hybla	3
			Haricot	Lanercost	3
				Queen Mary	10
Perdita II			Melbourne	Humphrey Clinker	8
○ 1881		Young Melbourne		Cervantes Mare	1
			Clarissa	Pantaloon	17
	Hermione			Glencoe Mare	25
	• 1875		St. Albans	Stockwell	3
		La Belle Hélène		Bribery	2
			Teterrima	Voltigeur	2
				Ellen Middleton	7

(Persimmon)

Racing Career

Age	Starts	Wins
2	3	2
3	4	3
4	2	2
Total	9	7

CYLLENE

s.h. 1895 – No. 9 Fam. – foaled in Great Britain

He was an extremely small horse and so late a foal that he was not entered for the classics. There is no doubt, however, that he was the outstanding horse of his generation in a career which lasted from two to four years old, and in which he proved his excellent qualities as a stayer.

He was beaten only twice, as a two-year-old in the Imperial Produce Stakes and once the following year in the Column Produce Stakes, winning all his other races including the Ascot Gold Cup and the Jockey Club Stakes. Cyllene went in 1900 to stud and proved himself an exceptional stallion siring four Epsom Derby winners, one of whom was Cicero (ch.h. 1902), but he was never greatly favoured by breeders. The greatest achievement to be attributed to Cyllene was that he sired Polymelus who on the track was no more than a good handicapper, but at stud, showed unexpected qualities by siring Phalaris who headed the stallion lines which today, particularly through Nearco, dominate the world's bloodstock breeding circles. In 1905 he was bought by the important brewer, Sir William Bass, who made no attempt to conceal his ambition to secure the chance of closely inbreeding Cyllene (3 × 3) with Bend Or's line by means of a union with his famous brood mare Sceptre. The best product of this mating was Maid of the Mist who gave good results as a brood mare, after a somewhat inconclusive racing career. In 1908 Cyllene was exported to Argentina where he died in 1925 at the age of 30.

Breeder: C.D. Rose
Owner: C.D. Rose
Most important wins: Jockey Club Stakes, Ascot Gold Cup, National Breeders' Produce Stakes, Newmarket Stakes

Racing Career

Age	Starts	Wins
2	5	4
3	4	3
4	2	2
Total	11	9

Cyllene	Bona Vista ◇ 1889	Bend Or ◇ 1877	Doncaster	**Stockwell**	The Baron / **Pocahontas** / 24 / 3
				Marigold	Teddington / Ratan Mare / 2 / 5
			Rouge Rose	Thormanby	Windhound * / Alice Hawthorn / 3 / 4
				Ellen Horne	Redshank / Delhi / 15 / 1
		Vista ◇ 1879	Macaroni	Sweetmeat	Gladiator / Lollypop / 22 / 21
				Jocose	Pantaloon / Banter / 17 / 14
			Verdure	King Tom	Harkaway / **Pocahontas** / 2 / 3
				May-Bloom	**Newminster** / Lady Hawthorn / 8 / 4
	Arcadia ◇ 1887	Isonomy ○ 1875	Sterling	Oxford	Irish Birdcatcher / Honey Dear / 11 / 12
				Whisper	Flatcatcher / Silence / 3 / 12
			Isola Bella	**Stockwell**	The Baron / **Pocahontas** / 24 / 3
				Isoline	Ethelbert / Bassishaw / 12 / 19
		Distant Shore ◇ 1880	Hermit	**Newminster**	Touchstone / Beeswing / 14 / 8
				Seclusion	Tadmor / Miss Sellon / 12 / 5
			Land's End	Trumpeter	Orlando / Cavatina / 13 / 1
				Faraway	Young Melbourne / Maid of Masham / 25 / 9

* or Melbourne (No. 1 Fam.)

SCEPTRE

b.m. 1899 – No. 16 Fam. – foaled in Great Britain

Sceptre was bought by Mr Robert S. Sievier at an auction following the death of the Duke of Westminster, for the sale of all the contents of his stud farm. Her career in racing lasted from two to five and in her first year she won two of her three races. As a three-year-old she won the 1,000 and 2,000 Guineas, and though she was unlucky in the Derby, failing to do better than fourth place after a bad start, she made up for it two days later by winning the Oaks.

She then went to France and ran unplaced in the Grand Prix de Paris but on her return to England won three races including the St. James's Palace Stakes and the Doncaster St. Leger. At the end of her three-year-old season she had had a busy career and some of her defeats could have been avoided. Her owner had been conceited enough to train her himself in her classic season and although Sceptre won four of the five classics, Sievier had to sell her for financial reasons.

After one last run for Sievier as a four-year-old Sceptre was sold to William Bass and carried off five wins, as well as being just beaten by Ard Patrick after an epic battle for the Eclipse. As a five-year-old the mare ran in three more races but failed to win.

Sceptre was sent to stud with great hopes but did not succeed in producing the great champion expected of her. Her best colt was Grosvenor, who gave a good performance as a stallion, while her best filly was Maid of the Mist who was a successful brood mare. During her career at stud Sceptre was bought by Lord Glanely and it was he who owned her when she died in 1926.

				Voltigeur	2
			Vedette	Mrs. Ridgway	19
		Galopin			
			Flying Duchess	Flying Dutchman	3
	St. Simon			Merope	3
	• 1881		King Tom	Harkaway	2
				Pocahontas	3
		St. Angela			
Persimmon			Adeline	Jon	4
○ 1893				Little Fairy	11
			Lord Clifden	Newminster	8
				The Slave	2
		Hampton			
	Perdita II		Lady Langden	Kettledrum	3
	○ 1881			Haricot	10
			Young Melbourne	Melbourne	1
				Clarissa	25
		Hermione			
			La Belle Hélène	St. Albans	2
Sceptre					Teterrima	7
			Stockwell	The Baron	24
				Pocahontas	3
		Doncaster			
			Marigold	Teddington	2
	Bend Or			Ratan Mare	5
	◇ 1877		Thormanby	Windhound *	3
				Alice Hawthorn	4
		Rouge Rose			
			Ellen Horne	Redshank	15
				Delhi	1
			Sweetmeat	Gladiator	22
				Lollypop	21
		Macaroni			
Ornament			Jocose	Pantaloon	17
○ 1887				Banter	14
	Lily Agnes		The Cure	Physician	21
	○ 1871			Morsel	6
		Polly Agnes			
			Miss Agnes	Irish Birdcatcher	11
				Agnes	16

* or Melbourne (No. 1 Fam.)

Breeder: Duke of Westminster
Owners: R.S. Sievier – Sir W. Bass
Most important wins: 1,000 Guineas, 2,000 Guineas, Oaks, St. Leger, Champion Stakes, Jockey Club Stakes, Hardwicke Stakes

Racing Career

Age	Starts	Wins
2	3	2
3	12	6
4	7	5
5	3	0
Total	25	13

CHAUCER

dk.b.h. 1900 – No. 1 Fam. – foaled in Great Britain

Chaucer was smaller than average, measuring no more than 15.3 hands (1.58 m) and having a dark bay coat with no white markings whatsoever. He ran from two to six, never really excelling, but proving to be a good handicapper, with an exceptionally competitive spirit, which drove him to struggle on bravely right up to the last yard.

As a stallion Chaucer sired a series of fillies who proved to be excellent brood mares. Among these were Canyon (dam of Colorado), Scapa Flow (dam of Pharos and Fairway) and Selene (dam of Sickle, Pharamond II and Hyperion), dams of stallions who head some of the dynasties which nowadays are among the most successful in the world. In addition to siring brood mares, Chaucer also sired two colts of considerable merit – Stedfast (ch. 1908), winner of the Coronation Cup, the Prince of Wales's Stakes, the St. James's Palace Stakes, the Hardwicke Stakes and the Jockey Club Stakes; and Prince Chimay (ch. 1915) who in the Jockey Club Stakes had the distinction of beating no less a horse than Gainsborough.

It was Prince Chimay who was left to continue the paternal line since the other horse, Stedfast, was unable to equal his track performance as a stallion. Prince Chimay sired Vatout (dk.b.h. 1926) who, following his union with the great Plucky Liège produced Bois Roussel (dk.b.h. 1935), winner of the Epsom Derby. At stud Bois Roussel proved to be a reasonably successful stallion and perpetuated Chaucer's line by originating two branches headed by Tehran, sire of Tulyar, and by Migoli who sired Gallant Man in the United States.

Breeder: Lord Derby
Owner: Lord Derby
Most important wins: Gimcrack Stakes

Racing Career

Age	Starts	Wins
2	5	2
3	4	0
4	10	3
5	11	2
6	5	1
Total	35	8

Chaucer	St. Simon • 1881	Galopin • 1872	Vedette	Voltigeur	**Voltaire** 12 / Martha Lynn 2
				Mrs. Ridgway	Irish Birdcatcher 11 / Nan Darrell 19
			Flying Duchess	Flying Dutchman	Bay Middleton 1 / Barbelle 3
				Merope	**Voltaire** 12 / Velocipede's Dam 3
		St. Angela ○ 1865	King Tom	Harkaway	Economist 36 / Fanny Dawson 2
				Pocahontas	Glencoe 1 / Marpessa 3
			Adeline	Jon	Cain 8 / Margaret 4
				Little Fairy	Hornsea 15 / Lacerta 11
	Canterbury Pilgrim ◊ 1893	Tristan ◊ 1878	Hermit	Newminster	Touchstone 14 / Beeswing 8
				Seclusion	Tadmor 12 / Miss Sellon 5
			Thrift	Stockwell	The Baron 24 / **Pocahontas** 3
				Braxey	Moss Trooper 18 / Queen Mary 10
		Pilgrimage ◊ 1875	The Palmer *	Beadsman	Weatherbit 12 / Mendicant 13
				Madame Eglantine	Cowl 2 / Diversion 5
			Lady Audley	Macaroni	Sweetmeat 21 / Jocose 14
				Secret	Melbourne 1 / Mystery 1

* or The Earl (No. 12 Fam.)

PRETTY POLLY

ch.m. 1901 – No. 14 Fam. – foaled in Ireland

Pretty Polly had a white sock on her left forefoot and a star on her forehead. When she was handed over to Peter Purcell Gilpin for training she had a dull coat and was lazy and apathetic. One morning on an important work-out she was used by Gilpin along with two other horses to accompany a fast two-year-old called Delaunay, who was highly thought of in the stables. To the great amazement of her trainer, who on that occasion had brought her on to the track with no great confidence, she won by ten lengths. This did not stop the public laughing at her coat which was certainly not worthy of a thoroughbred. Her trainer therefore made her make the return journey crowded into a box with four other horses and wrapped in three woollen blankets with the aim of making her really sweat. When she arrived at Newmarket this result had been achieved, and when the groom began to brush her the dullness gradually disappeared leaving a wonderful chestnut coat in its place. Thus, for the first time in her life, Pretty Polly actually looked like a racehorse.

Her career continued until she was five, with her most important victories coming in the 1,000 Guineas, the Oaks, the Doncaster St. Leger, the Coronation Stakes, the Jockey Club Cup and the Coronation Cup, which she won twice, while as a two-year-old Pretty Polly won races like the National Breeders' Produce, the Champagne, Criterion and Cheveley Park Stakes.

She was not entered for the Epsom Derby. That year she won the Free Handicap, carrying 9 st 7 lb (60.5 kg), but in the autumn she also suffered her first defeat in France in the Prix du Conseil Municipal, finishing second behind Preston II who was however carrying 7 lb (3.5 kg) less. The other defeat in Pretty Polly's career came when she was five in the Ascot Gold Cup when she was beaten a length by Bachelor's Button. Pretty Polly was without doubt an extraordinary race mare, perhaps the greatest of all time. She loved the crowd, the public, the applause and the cheers, just like Carbine, the champion of Australia who, when he won, demanded the warm approval of the spectators and would not leave the enclosure until he had received it, whereas if he lost he stayed in a corner, dejected and sad.

Pretty Polly was the leading character in another tale which was both curious and pathetic at the same time. It concerned her deep affection for Joey, a small cob whose box was next to hers. After every race she sought out her friend and would not let her saddle be removed until she had shared the joy of her victory with him. When they were in their boxes the two horses spent many hours communicating with each other and exchanging neighs. When the trainer was informed of this friendship he had a blanket made for the cob which was identical to Pretty Polly's and let him travel behind the mare on every one of her trips. For the big races, Gilpin obtained authorization from the stewards for Pretty Polly to be accompanied by her friend during the parade and in the canter up to the starting post. Joey died in 1906 and a few days later, strangely enough, Pretty Polly lost the Ascot Gold Cup, the only defeat she suffered in England.

At stud she foaled good horses such as King John, winner of the Irish Derby, but above all she produced four fillies who have continued the direct female line down to the present day, producing among others, the Derby winners St. Paddy and Psidium.

Breeder: Major E. Loder
Owner: Major E. Loder
Most important wins: 1,000 Guineas, Oaks, St. Leger, Coronation Cup (twice)

Racing Career		
Age	**Starts**	**Wins**
2	9	9
3	8	7
4	5	5
5	2	1
Total	24	22

				Oxford	Irish Birdcatcher	11
					Honey Dear	12
		Isonomy ○ 1875	Sterling	Whisper	Flatcatcher	3
					Silence	12
	Gallinule ◇ 1884		Isola Bella	Stockwell	The Baron	24
					Pocahontas	3
				Isoline	Ethelbert	12
					Bassishaw	19
		Moorhen ●/◆ 1873	Hermit	Newminster	Touchstone	14
					Beeswing	8
				Seclusion	Tadmor	12
					Miss Sellon	5
			Skirmisher Mare	Skirmisher	Voltigeur	2
					Gardham Mare	2
Pretty Polly				Vertumna	Stockwell	3
					Garland	19
		Saraband ◇ 1883	Muncaster	Doncaster	Stockwell	3
					Marigold	5
				Windermere	Macaroni	14
					Miss Agnes	16
			Highland Fling	Scottish Chief	Lord of the Isles	4
					Miss Ann	12
	Admiration ◇ 1892			Masquerade	Lambourne	14
					Burlesque	4
		Gaze ○ 1886	Thuringian Prince	Thormanby	Windhound *	3
					Alice Hawthorn	4
				Eastern Princess	Surplice	2
					Tomyris	12
			Eye Pleaser	Brown Bread	Weatherbit	12
					Brown Agnes	16
				Wallflower	Rataplan	3
					Chaperon	14

* or Melbourne (No. 1 Fam.)

AJAX

b.h. 1901 – No. 2 Fam. – foaled in France

At the auction following the death of the Duke of Westminster, M. Edmond Blanc acquired Flying Fox, winner of the Triple Crown in 1899, after he had been left with the Derby at his mercy when the French horse, Holocauste, fell only 2½ furlongs (500 m) from the post and fractured a leg. Flying Fox did not race as a four-year-old and in his first year at stud he sired Ajax, repaying Monsieur Blanc for the financial sacrifice he had made when he bought the horse for 37.500 guineas, after having met with strong opposition in the form of higher bids by the Prince of Wales and a group of American breeders.

Ajax began his racing in the Prix Saint–Firmin at Chantilly over 6 furlongs (1,200 m) which he won. As a three-year-old he won the Prix Noailles over 1 mile 2 furlongs (2,000 m), the Prix Lupin over 10½ furlongs (2,100 m) the Prix du Jockey Club over 1½ miles (2,400 m) and the Grand Prix de Paris over 1 mile 7 furlongs (3,000 m). In the Grand Prix Ajax got to the front close home to beat Turenne who had led from the start even though he had had to contend with fierce competition from one of the winner's stablemates, Gouvernant, for the entire race.

After this very short but brilliant career, Ajax was sent to stud and proved to be a great stallion too, especially as sire of Teddy from whom two famous horses descend, Bull Dog (dk.b.h. 1927), sire of Bull Lea, and Tantième (b.h. 1944), grand-sire of Relko. Like his sire, Ajax died prematurely, at the early age of 14.

Ajax					
	Flying Fox ○ 1896	Orme ○ 1889	Ormonde	Bend Or	Doncaster 5 / Rouge Rose 1
				Lily Agnes	**Macaroni** 14 / Polly Agnes 16
			Angelica	**Galopin**	Vedette 19 / Flying Duchess 3
				St. Angela	King Tom 3 / Adeline 11
		Vampire ● 1889	**Galopin**	Vedette	Voltigeur 2 / Mrs. Ridgway 19
				Flying Duchess	**Flying Dutchman** 3 / Merope 3
			Irony	Rosebery	Speculum 1 / Ladylike 22
				Sarcasm	Breadalbane 10 / Jeu d'Esprit 7
	Amie ◇ 1893	Clamart ◇ 1888	Saumur	Dollar	**Flying Dutchman** 3 / Payment 1
				Finlande	Ion 4 / Fraudulent 5
			Princess Catherine	Prince Charlie	Blair Athol 10 / Eastern Princess 12
				Catherine	**Macaroni** 14 / Selina 3
		Alice ● 1887	Wellingtonia	Chattanooga	Orlando 13 / Ayacanora 3
				Araucaria	Ambrose 16 / Pocahontas 3
			Asta	Cambuslang	Cambuscan 19 / Hepatica 19
				Lady Superior	Caterer 7 / Penance 2

Breeder: Edmond Blanc
Owner: Edmond Blanc
Most important wins: Prix du Jockey Club, Prix Lupin, Grand Prix de Paris, Prix Noailles

Racing Career		
Age	Starts	Wins
2	1	1
3	4	4
Total	5	5

SIGNORINETTA

b.m. 1905 – No. 23 Fam. – foaled in Great
Britain

In 1880, the Chevalier Odoardo Ginistrelli,
dissatisfied with the way things were going
in Italy, moved his whole stud farm from
Portici, near Naples, to England. He was,
according to all reports, somewhat eccentric and had taken it into his head to beat
the English on their own ground. His
successes began with a filly named Signor-
ina who, after a healthy racing career went
to stud in 1892 at the age of five.

In the meantime Ginistrelli had had a
small house built in Newmarket. After a
great many disappointments he decided in
1904 to send his mare to Isinglass, a very
popular stallion at that time. One day,
while she was being led to the appoint-
ment, she met and was attracted by the call
of a rather ordinary stallion named
Chaleureux. The two horses stopped and
turned to look at each other, drawing the
attention of Ginistrelli who immediately
came to his own conclusions: he would
encourage their affection even if he still had
to pay the 300 guineas stud fee for Isinglass
just the same. Thus it was that Signorinetta
was foaled.

She raced only in England at two and
three, appearing on the track 13 times to
win on only three occasions. As a two-year-
old Signorinetta won only one of her six
starts but as a three-year-old she had two
exceptional wins – the Epsom Derby and
the Oaks in the space of just two days. Her
owner's dream had therefore come true
and his filly had beaten the English horses
in their two most prestigious classics.

At stud Signorinetta did not produce any
great offspring, but of her progeny The
Winter King is worth remembering. He
went to stud in Italy as did Signorinetta's
half-brother Signorino.

Breeder: Odoardo Ginistrelli
Owner: Odoardo Ginistrelli
Most important wins: Derby, Oaks

Racing Career		
Age	Starts	Wins
2	6	1
3	7	2
Total	13	3

Signorinetta	Chalereux ○ 1894	Goodfellow ○/● 1887	Barcaldine	Solon	West Australian / Darling's Dam / 7 / 23
				Ballyroe	Belladrum / Bon Accord / 22 / 23
			Ravissante	Clanronald	Blair Athol / Isilia / 10 / 12
				Makeshift	**Voltigeur** / Makeless / 2 / 2
		L'Eté ◇ 1880	John Devis	**Voltigeur**	Voltaire / Martha Lynn / 12 / 2
				Jamaica	Liverpool / Preserve / 11 / 1
			Fandango Mare	Fandango	Barnton / Castanette / 2 / 5
				Sleight of Hand Mare	Sleight of Hand / Hampton Mare / 3 / 15
	Signorina ● 1887	St. Simon ● 1881	Galopin	Vedette	**Voltigeur** / Mrs. Ridgway / 2 / 19
				Flying Duchess	Flying Dutchman / Merope / 3 / 3
			St. Angela	King Tom	Harkaway / Pocahontas / 2 / 3
				Adeline	Jon / Little Fairy / 4 / 4
		Star of Portici ○ 1871	Heir at Law	Newminster	Touchstone / Beeswing / 14 / 8
				The Heiress	Irish Birdcatcher / Inheritress / 11 / 4
			Verbena	De Ruyter	Lanercost / Barbelle / 3 / 3
				Singleton Lass	St. Lawrence / Gaberlunzie Mare / 21 / 23

ALCANTARA II

b.h. 1908 – No. 4 Fam. – foaled in France

Alcantara II was a son of Perth II, winner of the four major French races (Poule d'Essai des Poulains, Prix du Jockey-Club, Grand Prix de Paris and Prix Royal Oak), as well as the Prix du Cadran over 2½ miles (4,000 m). He was a horse whose overall appearance could certainly not be described as attractive, the line of his body denoting a lack of distinction. He had a rather hollow back in addition to badly formed forelegs, and yet he proved to be physically quite powerful and mentally extremely well-balanced.

Alcantara's most important win in a two season racing career came in the Prix du Jockey-Club (the French Derby) and his most notable sons when he went to stud were Kantar, who was exported to the United States in 1936, and Pinceau, winner of the Prix Royal Oak, the Grand Prix de Saint Cloud, the Prix Ganay and the Grand International d'Ostende. Both proved to be excellent stallions by siring Victrix (b.h. 1934) and Verso II (b.h. 1940) respectively.

It was Pinceau who took on the role of continuing the paternal line through Verso II (Prix du Jockey-Club, Prix Royal Oak and Prix de l'Arc de Triomphe), sire of Osborne (b.h. 1947), winner of the Doncaster Cup at the age of seven and of Lavandi (b.h. 1953) winner of the Epsom Derby. Alcantara II also showed that he was an excellent sire of brood mares, and his daughters produced such valuable horses as Brumeux, Pantaloon and Festnet.

Alcantara II	Perth II ○ 1896	War Dance ○ 1887	Galliard	Galopin	Vedette 19 / Flying Duchess 3
				Mavis	Macaroni 14 / Merlette 13
			War Paint	Uncas	Stockwell 3 / Nightingale 1
				Piracy	Buccaneer 14 / Newminster Mare 1
		Primrose Dame ○ 1885	Barcaldıne	Solon	West Australian 7 / Darling's Dam 23
				Ballyroe	Belladrum 22 / Bon Accord 23
			Lady Rosebery	Lord Clifden	**Newminster** 8 / The Slave 2
				Violet	**Thormanby** 4 / Woodbine 8
	Toison d'Or ▢ 1901	Le Sancy ▢ 1884	Atlantic	**Thormanby**	Windhound * 3 / Alice Hawthorn 4
				Hurricane	Wild Dayrell 7 / Midia 3
			Gem of Gems	Strathconan	**Newminster** 8 / Souvenir 11
				Poinsettia	Young Melbourne 25 / Lady Hawthorn 4
		Harfleur II ◇ 1890	Archiduc	Consul	Monarque 19 / Lady Lift 35
				The Abbess	Atherstone 11 / Convent 1
			Hauteur	Rosicrucian	Beadsman 13 / Mad.me Eglantine 5
				Hawthorndale	Kettledrum 3 / Lady A. Hawthorn 4

* or Melbourne (No. 1 Fam.)

Breeder: Baron M. de Rothschild
Owner: Baron M. de Rothschild
Most important wins: Prix du Jockey Club, Prix Lupin, Prix de la Rochette

Racing Career		
Age	Starts	Wins
2	6	3
3	14	4
Total	20	7

THE TETRARCH

gr.h. 1911 – No. 2 Fam. – foaled in Ireland

The Tetrarch's racing career lasted only one year, when he was two, since he was prevented by an accident which occurred while training for the Derby from appearing on the track again. He made his debut by winning a maiden race at Newmarket making a handy sum for his entourage who had seen him in a trial where he beat the seven-year-old General Symons carrying the same weight (8 st 7 lb)(55 kg), and had as much as 5 to 1 to their money. When he appeared on the track before the race he was a source of public amusement due above all to his curious spotted coat. After the finish, however, the judgement was very different and instead of being called "rocking-horse" he was given the name "the Spotted Wonder."

The horse went on to win the Woodcote Stakes at Epsom, the Coventry Stakes at Ascot and the National Breeders' Produce Stakes at Sandown Park. In this last race he won by a neck, although he had been left 20 lengths at the start. His wins continued with the Rous Memorial Stakes at Goodwood, the Champion Breeders' Foal Stakes at Derby and the Champagne Stakes at Doncaster. He ended his career unbeaten, proving himself to be a horse of exceptional caliber.

The Tetrarch was a powerful horse with extraordinarily strong hindquarters. He also had a very expressive head denoting his strong personality. He had been reluctant to appear on the track and behaved similarly as a stallion, where he sired only 130 horses although these were of an unquestionably high quality. One of his best colts was Tetratema, while his most illustrious filly was Mumtaz Mahal, but in addition to these two excellent horses, The Tetrarch also sired three St. Leger winners (Caligula, Polemarch and Salmon Trout). He headed the stallions' list in 1919, but as the years passed by The Tetrarch became sterile, and he retired in 1925, eight years before he died.

Breeder: Mr E. Kennedy
Owner: Major Dermot McCalmont
Most important wins: National Breeders' Produce Stakes, Woodcote Stakes, Champagne Stakes

Racing Career		
Age	Starts	Wins
2	7	7

				Atlantic	**Thormanby**	4
			Le Sancy		Hurricane	3
		Le Samaritain □ 1895		Gem of Gems	Strathconan	11
					Poinsettia	4
			Clementina	**Doncaster**	Stockwell	3
	Roi Hérode □ 1904				Marigold	5
				Clemence	Newminster	8
					Eulogy	2
			War Dance	Galliard	Galopin	3
					Mavis	13
		Roxelane ◊ 1894		War Paint	Uncas	1
					Piracy	1
			Rose of York	**Speculum**	Vedette	19
					Doralice	1
				Rouge Rose	**Thormanby**	4
The Tetrarch					Ellen Horne	1
			Bend Or	**Doncaster**	Stockwell	3
					Marigold	5
		Bona Vista ◊ 1889		**Rouge Rose**	**Thormanby**	4
					Ellen Horne	1
			Vista	**Macaroni**	Sweetmeat	21
					Jocose	14
	Vahren ◊ 1897			Verdure	**King Tom**	3
					May-Bloom	4
			Hagioscope	**Speculum**	Vedette	19
					Doralice	1
		Castania ◊ 1889		Sophia	**Macaroni**	14
					Zelle	23
			Rose Garden	Kingcraft	**King Tom**	3
					Woodcraft	11
				Eglantine	Hermit	5
					Mabille	2

PHALARIS

dk.b.h. 1913 – No. 1 Fam. – foaled in Great Britain

Phalaris was the son of an ordinary brood mare named Bromus and of Polymelus. He had statuesque lines although a rather hollow back, a defect which was accentuated by muscular hindquarters and high withers. His racing career covered the years of the First World War, and he raced from two to five years old, proving an excellent handicapper at his best over a mile (1,600 m).

He served as a stallion at Lord Derby's stud farm with a group of brood mares of the highest caliber at his disposal, but this was certainly not the only reason for his great success as a stallion. Phalaris in fact proved to be an excellent transmitter, capable of passing on to his sons above all the qualities of early maturity and speed without, however, putting his own stamp on them which is why they were so different from each other both in their appearance and character. The most famous of Phalaris's offspring were Pharos (1920) sire of Nearco; Manna (1922) winner of the Epsom Derby and the 2,000 Guineas; Colorado (1923), sire of Felicitation and Colorado Kid; Fairway (1925), full brother of Pharos; Sickle (1924) sire of Unbreakable, and Pharamond II (1925), sire of Menow.

Through these talented and varied sons, Phalaris's blood was dispersed throughout all the continents and his name appears in many present-day pedigrees establishing him as one of the greatest stallion of this century and one of the most important in history.

Phalaris	Polymelus ○ 1902	Cyllene ◇ 1895	Bona Vista	Bend Or	Doncaster 5 / Rouge Rose 1
				Vista	Macaroni 14 / Verdure 4
			Arcadia	Isonomy	Sterling 12 / Isola Bella 19
				Distant Shore	Hermit 5 / Land's End 9
		Maid Marian ● 1886	Hampton	**Lord Clifden**	Newminster 8 / The Slave 2
				Lady Langden	Kettledrum 3 / Haricot 10
			Quiver	Toxophilite	Longbow 21 / Legerdemain 3
				Young Melbourne Mare	Young Melbourne 25 / Brown Bess 3
	Bromus ○ 1905	Sainfoin ◇ 1887	**Springfield**	St. Albans	**Stockwell** 3 / Bribery 2
				Viridis	Marsyas 12 / Maid of Palmyra 12
			Sanda	Wenlock	**Lord Clifden** 2 / Mineral 4
				Sandal	**Stockwell** 3 / Lady Evelyn 2
		Cheery ● 1892	St. Simon	Galopin	Vedette 19 / Flying Duchess 3
				St. Angela	King Tom 3 / Adeline 11
			Sunrise	**Springfield**	St. Albans 2 / Viridis 12
				Sunray	King of the Forest 31 / Sunshine 1

Breeder: Lord Derby
Owner: Lord Derby

Racing Career

Age	Starts	Wins
2	3	2
3	7	3
4	9	7
5	5	3
Total	24	15

HURRY ON

ch.h. 1913 – No. 2 Fam. – foaled in Great Britain

Hurry On was an attractive horse with well proportioned features. He was tall, considerably above the average height (17 hands)(1.73 m) with a girth of 81 in (206 cm) and circumference of cannon bone of 9.4 in (24 cm). A son of Marcovil, a stallion of little value, and Toute Suite, a small brood mare, he remained unbeaten throughout his short racing career, winning all six of his races as a three-year-old. He was a horse with great stamina winning over distances up to 2 miles 2 furlongs (3,600 m). Among the races won by Hurry On was the St. Leger which that year, due to the First World War, was run at Newmarket as the September Stakes instead of Doncaster.

Once he was sent to stud he proved to be one of the best stallions of his day, appearing high on the stallions' list in England for several years. In addition to the Derby winner Captain Cuttle (ch.h. 1919), Hurry On sired Coronach (Derby and St. Leger Stakes) who was, however, rumoured to be a roarer, and Precipitation, who became the sire of Chamossaire and Airborne.

He was also the sire of a number of first class fillies and brood mares, like Toboggan (dam of Citàtion), Nuvolona (dam of Navarro), Instantaneous (dam of Court Martial) and Jiffy, dam of Ocean Swell (winner of the Epsom Derby and the Ascot Gold Cup). One of Hurry On's peculiarities at stud was that while some of his offspring were tenacious and competitive, others were seen to be extremely poor fighters, having just one speed and capable only of front-running. It is, however, interesting to note that the name of St. Simon does not appear anywhere in his pedigree, a factor which has proved favourable when his offspring have been crossed with strains which were, at that time, very popular but nevertheless saturated with the blood of this horse.

				West Australian	7
			Solon	Darling's Dam	23
		Barcaldine		Belladrum	22
	Marco ◇ 1892		Ballyroe	Bon Accord	23
			Hermit	Newminster	8
		Novitiate		Seclusion	5
Marcovil ◇ 1903			Retty	Lambton	9
				Fern	3
			Speculum	Vedette	19
		Hagioscope		Doralice	1
			Sophia	Macaroni	14
	Lady Willikins ◇ 1885			Zelle	23
			Hermit	Newminster	8
		Dinah		Seclusion	5
			The Ratcatcher's Daughter	Rataplan	3
				Lady Alicia	12
Hurry On			St. Albans	**Stockwell**	3
		Springfield		Bribery	2
			Viridis	Marsyas	12
	Sainfoin ◇ 1887			Maid of Palmyra	12
			Wenlock	Lord Clifden	2
		Sanda		Mineral	4
			Sandal	**Stockwell**	3
				Lady Evelyn	2
Tout Suite ◇ 1904			Cremorne *	Parmesan	7
		Thurio		Rigolboche	2
			Verona	Orlando	13
	Star ◇ 1887			Iodine	2
			Thunderbolt	**Stockwell**	3
		Meteor		Cordelia	11
			Duty	Rifleman	8
				D. of Sleight of H.	2

* or Tibthorpe (No. 16 Fam.)

Breeder: V. Murland
Owner: J. Buchanan
Most important wins: St. Leger, Jockey Club Cup

Racing Career

Age	Starts	Wins
3	6	6

TEDDY

b.h. 1913 – No. 2 Fam. – foaled in France

Teddy was a son of Ajax and a mediocre brood mare named Rondeau, and was sold by his breeder at the age of two for a ridiculously small sum. In 1916 the great French races were not run because of the war and so Teddy began his career in Spain in the San Sebastian Grand Prix (1½ miles (2,400m)) which he won. At the same racecourse he also won the San Sebastian St. Leger (1 mile 4½ furlongs (2,500 m)), but seven days later he suffered his first defeat when he came third in the Coppa d'Oro del Re. In France, in October of that year, he won the Prix de Darnay (1 mile 3 furlongs (2,200 m)) and the Prix des Trois Ans (1½ miles (2,400 m)), which was, in a way, supposed to be a substitute for the Prix du Jockey-Club, not run from 1915 to 1918. However, he achieved only third place at Mont-de-Marsan, where he was beaten in the Prix d'Elevage (1½ miles (2,400 m)).

The following year he won only one race, at Chantilly, the Prix des Sablonnières over 1 mile 2 furlongs (2,000 m). Teddy went to stud and assumed such an important rôle that he became known as "The Sire of Sires." Besides being proven as a fine stallion capable of imprinting his unmistakable stamp on all his progeny, Teddy sired a series of brood mares which have spread his reputation worldwide.

The most important of his offspring are Sir Gallahad III (b.h. 1920), exported to the United States in 1925, and Bull Don (1927) who followed him five years later. In addition to these two good stallions, Teddy sired an excellent horse in Italy named Ortello and another called Salpiglossis (b.h. 1928) while in France his offspring included Aethelstan (b.h. 1922) sire of Deiri (also later exported to America), Astérus (b.h. 1923) bred by Marcel Boussac, and Brumeux (b.h. 1925), exported to England. Teddy died in 1937 in the United States where he had been exported from France at the age of 18.

Breeder: Edmond Blanc
Owner: J. Davis Cohn
Most important wins: San Sebastian Grand Prix, Prix des Trois Ans

Racing Career

Age	Starts	Wins
3	7	5
4	1	1
Total	8	6

Teddy						
	Ajax ○ 1901	Flying Fox ○ 1896	Orme	Ormonde	**Bend Or**	1
					Lily Agnes	16
				Angelica	**Galopin**	3
					St. Angela	11
				Vampire	**Galopin**	Vedette	19
					Flying Duchess	3
				Irony	Rosebery	22
					Sarcasm	7
		Amie ◇ 1893	Clamart	Saumur	Dollar	1
					Finlande	5
				Princess Catherine	Prince Charlie	12
					Catherine	3
			Alice	Wellingtonia	Chattanooga	3
					Araucaria	3
				Asta	Cambuslang	19
					Lady Superior	2
	Rondeau ○ 1900	Bay Ronald ○ 1893	Hampton	Lord Clifden	Newminster	8
					The Slave	2
				Lady Langden	Kettledrum	3
					Haricot	10
			Black Duchess	Galliard	**Galopin**	3
					Mavis	13
				Black Corrie	Sterling	12
					Wild Dayrell Mare	3
		Doremi ◇ 1894	**Bend Or**	Doncaster	Stockwell	3
					Marigold	5
				Rouge Rose	Thormanby	4
					Ellen Horne	1
			Lady Emily	Macaroni	Sweetmeat	21
					Jocose	14
				May Queen	Claret	24
					Lady Blanche	2

MAN O'WAR

ch.h. 1917 – No. 4 Fam. – foaled in the United States

Nicknamed "Big Red," Man o'War raced in the United States at two and three, carrying the colours of Samuel D. Riddle, who bought him at auction for 5,000 dollars. In his first year he won all his races except one, the Sanford Memorial Stakes, in which he was beaten by Upset to whom he had, however, given 15 lb (6½ kg). It should also be said that Upset won by only half a length after Man o'War had been the victim of a bad start.

However, "Big Red" took his revenge on Upset just ten days later, beating him in the Grand Union Hotel Stakes by an early length. Man o'War's most important wins as a two-year-old were the Hopeful Stakes and the Belmont Futurity. At three he won all his starts with great ease, becoming something of a legend. Only once did a rival succeed in troubling him, when John P. Grier was beaten a length and a half in the Dwyer Stakes at Aqueduct after being narrowly in front a furlong from home. Man o'War could have been the first winner of the American Triple Crown, as he won the Preakness Stakes and the Belmont Stakes, but he was never entered for the Kentucky Derby.

When he was retired from racing in 1921 his owner turned down the fabulous amount of one million dollars offered to him for the horse, saying that anyone could have owned such a lot of money but only one person could own "Big Red." At stud Man o'War failed to live up to expectations but was still able to sire 220 winners, 64 of whom won stakes races. The best horses he produced were War Admiral (dk.b.h. 1934), sire of several excellent brood mares, and War Relic (ch.h. 1938) who continued the paternal line. Man o'War's fillies were also outstanding and proved to be excellent brood mares who foaled 124 stakes winners. In 1943 Man o'War was retired from stud and four years later, at the age of 30, he died.

			Australian	West Australian	7
		Spendthrift		Emilia	11
	Hastings		Aerolite	Lexington	12
	● 1893			Florine	13
			Tomahawk *	King Tom	3
Fair Play		Cinderella		Mincemeat	3
◇ 1905			Manna	Brown Bread	16
				Tartlet	21
			Doncaster	Stockwell	3
		Bend Or		Marigold	5
	Fairy Gold		Rouge Rose	Thormanby	4
	◇ 1896			Ellen Horne	1
			Galliard	**Galopin**	3
		Dame Masham		Mavis	13
			Pauline	**Hermit**	5
Man o'War				Lady Masham	9
			Springfield	St. Albans	2
		Sainfoin		Viridis	12
	Rock Sand		Sanda	Wenlock	4
	● 1900			Sandal	2
			St. Simon	**Galopin**	3
		Roquebrune		St. Angela	11
			St. Marguerite	**Hermit**	5
				Devotion	4
Mahubah			Hampton	Lord Clifden	2
○ 1910		Merry Hampton		Lady Langden	10
			Doll Tearsheet	Broomielaw	10
	Merry Token			Mrs. Quickly	22
	○ 1891		Macgregor	Macaroni	14
		Mizpah		Necklace	4
			Underhand Mare	Underhand	43
				Slayer Mare	4

* or Blue Ruin (No. 2 Fam.)

Breeder: Major August Belmont II
Owner: Samuel D. Riddle
Most important wins: Hopeful Stakes, Belmont Futurity, Preakness Stakes, Belmont Stakes, Travers Stakes, Lawrence Realization Stakes, Jockey Club Stakes

Racing Career		
Age	**Starts**	**Wins**
2	10	9
3	11	11
Total	21	20

BLANDFORD

dk.b.h. 1919 – No. 3 Fam. – foaled in Great Britain

Blandford suffered from an attack of pneumonia when still a foal and later, as a yearling, he met with an accident in the paddock. His body was poor in appearance, with unharmonious lines, ugly forelimbs, short forearms and a slightly hollow back. His weak constitution meant that his racing career was limited to only four appearances, which were spread over his second and third year and include no Classic wins.

At stud his activity was also rather limited and he only covered a small number of mares. Some of his offspring, however, inherited such talent that Blandford became fundamentally important in pedigrees as a carrier of the classic qualities which make up the required balance between stamina and speed.

Those of his progeny who ensured the continuation of his line were Blenheim (dk.b. 1927), Umidwar (b. 1931), Brantôme (b. 1931) and Bahram (b. 1932). Few would have thought that such a fragile horse could play such an important part in the development of the breed over these last 50 years. On the other hand, even Blandford's sire, Synford, broke a fetlock after winning the Doncaster St. Leger and the Eclipse Stakes, and it was a miracle that he was ever sent to stud. Blandford died relatively young in 1935 at the age of only 16.

			Isonomy	**Sterling**	12
		Isinglass		Isola Bella	19
	John O' Gaunt		Dead-Lock	Wenlock	4
	○ 1901			Malpractice	3
			St. Simon	**Galopin**	3
Swynford		La Flêche		St. Angela	11
● 1907			Quiver	Toxophilite	3
				Young Melb. Mare	3
			Hermit	Newminster	8
		Tristan		Seclusion	5
	Canterbury Pilgrim		Thrift	Stockwell	3
	◇ 1893			Braxey	10
			The Palmer *	Beadsman	13
		Pilgrimage		Madame Eglantine	5
			Lady Audley	Macaroni	14
				Secret	1
Blandford			**Isonomy**	**Sterling**	12
		Gallinule		Isola Bella	19
			Moorhen	**Hermit**	5
	White Eagle			Skirmisher Mare	19
	◇ 1905		**Galopin**	Vedette	19
		Merry Gal		Flying Duchess	3
			Mary Seaton	**Isonomy**	19
				Marie Stuart	5
Blanche			Ben Battle	Rataplan	3
○ 1912		Bendigo		Young Alice	4
			Hasty Girl	Lord Gough	12
	Black Cherry			Irritation	9
	● 1892		Galliard	**Galopin**	3
		Black Duchess		Mavis	13
			Black Corrie	**Sterling**	12
* or The Earl (No. 12 Fam.)				Wild Dayrell Mare	3

Breeder: The National Stud
Owner: R.C. and S.C. Dawson
Most important wins: Princess of Wales's Stakes

Racing Career		
Age	**Starts**	**Wins**
2	2	1
3	2	2
Total	4	3

APELLE

ch.h. 1923 – No. 5 Fam. – foaled in Italy

Apelle was the first horse to be bred in Italy who could truly be considered of international caliber. His racing career lasted from two to five and includes important wins both in Italy and outside that country.

As a two-year-old he won the Critérium de Maisons-Laffitte and in Italy he ran in four races being beaten only once in the Gran Criterium Internazionale by Scopello with the excuse of being tired as a result of the return journey from France. As a three-year-old Apelle won the Italian Derby and the Gran Premio di Milano with the greatest of ease but in the Premio Parioli, due to a tactical error, he was beaten by Toce and in the Gran Premio d'Italia by his stable mate, Cranach (sired by Cannobie).

Apelle was also unplaced in the Grand Prix de Paris but in finishing fifth only two lengths behind the winner Take My Tip, his effort was so admired that it encouraged a group of foreign owners to purchase him.

He ran again in France with the new colours of M. Caillault, where he won the Coupe d'Or de Maisons-Laffitte but was unplaced in the Prix de l'Arc de Triomphe, won by Biribi. He was then transferred to England where this time he raced for Mr. R. McCreery, winning the Sandown Anniversary Cup and the Durham Stakes. At five Apelle won all three of his races – the Coronation Cup, the Bottisham Stakes and, for the second year running, the Sandown Anniversary Cup. In 1929 he was sent to stud and sired good colts such as Cappiello (Prix Lupin and Grand Prix de Paris) and excellent fillies like Tofanella (dam Tenerani). In 1937 Apelle returned to Italy where three years later he died.

Breeder: Federico Tesio
Owner: Federico Tesio – M Caillault – R. McCreery
Most important wins: Critérium de Maisons-Laffitte, Italian Derby, Gran Premio di Milano, Coupe d'Or de Maisons-Laffitte, Coronation Cup, Sandown Anniversary Cup (twice)

Racing Career

Age	Starts	Wins
2	6	4
3	9	5
4	5	2
5	3	3
Total	23	14

Apelle	Sardanapale ○ 1911	Prestige ○ 1903	Le Pompon	Fripon	Consul 35 / Folle Avoine 22
				La Foudre	The Scottish Chief 12 / La Noue 18
			Orgueilleuse	Révérend	Energy 27 / Rêveuse 17
				Oroya	**Bend Or** 1 / Freia 17
		Gemma ○ 1903	Florizel II	**St. Simon**	Galopin 3 / St. Angela 11
				Perdita II	**Hampton** 10 / Hermione 7
			Agnostic	Rosicrucian	Beadsman 13 / Mad.me Eglantine 5
				Bonnie Agnes	Blair Athol 10 / Little Agnes 16
	Angelina ●1913	St. Frusquin ● 1893	**St. Simon**	Galopin	Vedette 19 / Flying Duchess 3
				St. Angela	King Tom 3 / Adeline 11
			Isabel	Plebeian	Joskin 5 / Queen Elizabeth 11
				Parma	Parmesan 7 / Archeress 22
		Seraphine ◇ 1907	Cyllene	Bona Vista	**Bend Or** 1 / Vista 4
				Arcadia	Isonomy 19 / Distant Shore 9
			Virginal	Ladas	**Hampton** 10 / Illuminata 1
				Wise Virgin	Wisdom 7 / Elizabeth 5

OLEANDER

b.h. 1924 – No. 6 Fam. – foaled in Germany

Oleander can be considered as the most typical example of German breeding. Despite the fact that at two he met with a serious accident which even placed his future activity on the track in doubt, he continued his racing career until he was five years old. He never ran in a classic but to make up for it tried twice to win the Prix de l'Arc de Triomphe. The best result he obtained in this race was third place in the year when Ortello won. Although outside Germany he failed to achieve the results expected of him in his own country he performed very well indeed by winning the Grosser Preis von Baden over a distance of 1½ miles (2,400 m) three years in a row.

At stud Oleander continued the line of Dark Ronald and made a name for himself principally through his son Orsenigo (b.h. 1940) an excellent sire of brood mares and of horses with great stamina and considerable sprinting ability. It was Orsenigo, small but well-proportioned, who ensured a valuable line first in Italy but, more importantly, in South America after his export to Brazil, siring among others Escorial, the winner in Argentina of the Gran Premio Carlos Pellegrini.

As well as Orsenigo, Oleander sired horses like Randford whose son Garnier won the Moscow Derby in 1958. Perhaps his native Germany has least benefitted from this bloodline, which descends from the winner of the German Derby, Sturmvogel, who did not produce any great results at stud, from the more positive Asterios, winer of the German St. Leger, and from Nuvolari, a stallion of ordinary caliber although he sired several excellent brood mares.

Oleander	Prunus ○ 1915	Dark Ronald ● 1905	Bay Ronald	**Hampton**	Lord Clifden 2 / Lady Langden 10
				Black Duchess	Galliard 13 / Black Corrie 3
			Darkie	Thurio	Cremorne* 2 / Verona 2
				Insignia	Blair Athol 10 / Decoration 9
		Pomegranate ○ 1901	Persimmon	**St. Simon**	Galopin 3 / St. Angela 11
				Perdita II	**Hampton** 10 / Hermione 7
			Briar Root	**Springfield**	St. Albans 2 / Viridis 12
				Eglentyne	Hermit 5 / Mabille 2
	Orchidee II ◇ 1910	Galtee More ○ 1894	Kendal	**Bend Or**	Doncaster 5 / Rouge Rose 1
				Windermere	Macaroni 14 / Miss Agnes 16
			Morganette	**Springfield**	St. Albans 2 / Viridis 12
				Lady Morgan	**Thormanby** 4 / Morgan la Faye 5
		Orseis ○ 1897	Saint Serf	**St. Simon**	Galopin 3 / St. Angela 11
				Feronia	**Thormanby** 4 / Woodbine 8
			Orsova	**Bend Or**	Doncaster 5 / Rouge Rose 1
				Fenella	Cambuscan 19 / La Favorite 6

* or Tibthorpe (No. 16 Fam.)

Breeder: Gestüt Schlenderhan
Owner: Alfred von Oppenheim
Most important wins: Grosser Preis von Baden (3 times), Grosser Preis von Berlin (twice)

Racing Career		
Age	**Starts**	**Wins**
2	2	2
3	7	6
4	7	5
5	5	4
Total	21	17

FAIRWAY

b.h. 1925 – No. 13 Fam. – foaled in Great Britain

Fairway was a horse with rather elongated lines, a slightly hollow back, and imperfect knees and hocks. He was an exceptional racehorse but his extremely excitable and nervous temperament cost him a victory in the Epsom Derby. His track activity took place from two to four as when he was five he was withdrawn from racing as a result of an injury to a tendon received during training for the Gold Cup. During his career he won over distances of between 5 furlongs (1,000 m) and 2¼ miles (3,620 m) and was beaten only three times: the first as a two-year-old in his maiden race, the Eglinton Stakes, when he was second to Grandmaster, the second in the Epsom Derby when he was unplaced, and the third as a four-year-old in the Eclipse Stakes when he was beaten by Royal Minstrel.

At stud Fairway's varied progeny included fast horses and stayers, although most of the latter category were of poor quality. His line was perpetuated by the offspring of his son Fair Trial (ch. 1932), the sire of Court Martial (ch. 1942), Petition (d.b. 1944) and Palestine (gr. 1947). Fair Trial generally sired horses best suited to speed, but his fillies, if crossed properly, have also foaled horses well able to stay more demanding distances. Some of the best of Fair Trial's offspring were three winners of the 2,000 Guineas in Lambert Simnel, Palestine and Court Martial and the Eclipse winner Petition. The best of them was Court Martial who was third to Dante in the Derby. Another high class horse sired by Fairway was Blue Peter (ch. 1936) winner of the 2,000 Guineas, the Derby and the Eclipse Stakes. At stud he sired an excellent stayer in Botticelli (dk.b. 1951) whose name is remembered in connection with the Italian Derby and the Ascot Gold Cup.

Breeder: Lord Derby
Owner: Lord Derby
Most important wins: St. Leger, Coventry Stakes, Champion Stakes (twice), Eclipse Stakes, Champagne Stakes, July Cup, Jockey Club Cup, Newmarket Stakes, Rous Memorial Stakes, Princess of Wales's Stakes

Racing Career

Age	Starts	Wins
2	4	3
3	5	4
4	6	5
Total	15	12

				Bona Vista	Bend Or	1
Fairway	Phalaris • 1913	Polymelus ○ 1902	Cyllene		Vista	4
				Arcadia	Isonomy	19
					Distant Shore	9
			Maid Marian	Hampton	Lord Clifden	2
					Lady Langden	10
				Quiver	Toxophilite	3
					Y. Melbourne Mare	3
		Bromus ○ 1905	Sainfoin	Springfield	St. Albans	2
					Viridis	12
				Sanda	Wenlock	4
					Sandal	2
			Cheery	**St. Simon**	Galopin	3
					St. Angela	11
				Sunrise	Springfield	12
					Sunray	1
	Scapa Flow ◊ 1914	Chaucer • 1900	**St. Simon**	Galopin	Vedette	19
					Flying Duchess	3
				St. Angela	King Tom	3
					Adeline	11
			Canterbury Pilgrim	Tristan	**Hermit**	5
					Thrift	10
				Pilgrimage	The Palmer*	5
					Lady Audley	1
		Anchora ◊ 1905	Love Wisely	Wisdom	Blinkhoolie	10
					Aline	7
				Lovelorn	Philammon	4
					Gone	11
			Eryholme	Hazlehatch	**Hermit**	5
					Hazledean	11
				Ayrsmoss	Ayrshire	8
					Rattlewings	13

* or The Earl (No. 12 Fam.)

53

ORTELLO

ch.h. 1926 – No. 16 Fam. – foaled in Italy

Ortello, a son of Teddy, was a great stayer, and like many of that exceptional stallion's offspring he was well built but less consistent than his sire. Ortello won all his races except three: the Grand Critérium in which he was second behind Aruntius, the Premio Chiusura as a three-year-old, and the Prix de l'Arc de Triomphe the next season in which he came fourth. As a two-year-old Ortello won the Premio Chiusura from Erba and from that day until the same race the following year he was unbeaten.

In Italy as a three-year-old he won the Derby, the Gran Premio di Milano (in which he beat the French horse Pinceau) and the St. Leger, while in France he carried off the Prix de l'Arc de Triomphe, beating the French horse, Kantar, and the German horse Oleander. After gaining only second place in the Premio Chiusura, in 1929 Ortello began winning again, but only less important races. His training for the Gold Cup for which he had been transferred to England was interrupted after a fall during a work-out and he was consequently unable to take part in the great Ascot race. In the autumn, having recovered from his accident, he returned to France to run in the Prix de l'Arc de Triomphe in an attempt to repeat his success of the previous year but, as has already been mentioned, he managed no better than fourth place.

Ortello's career both on the track and at stud, was excellent. He sired a great number of winners and first-class horses like Moroni, Golfo, Torbido and Macherio. He was exported to the United States in 1947 and unfortunately, following a heart attack, died as soon as he arrived in California.

Breeder: Giuseppe de Montel
Owner: Giuseppe de Montel
Most important wins: Italian Derby, Gran Premio di Milano, Prix de l'Arc de Triomphe, Italian St. Leger

				Ormonde	16
			Orme	Angelica	11
		Flying Fox	Vampire	**Galopin**	3
	Ajax			Irony	7
	○ 1901		Clamart	Saumur	5
		Amie		Princess Catherine	3
			Alice	Wellingtonia	3
Teddy				Asta	2
○ 1913			**Hampton**	Lord Clifden	2
		Bay Ronald		Lady Langden	10
			Black Duchess	Galliard	13
	Rondeau			Black Corrie	3
	○ 1900		**Bend Or**	Doncaster	5
		Doremi		Rouge Rose	1
			Lady Emily	Macaroni	14
Ortello				May Queen	2
			Hampton	Lord Clifden	2
		Ladas		Lady Langden	10
			Illuminata	Rosicrucian	5
	Gorgos			Paraffin	1
	● 1903		**St. Simon**	**Galopin**	3
		The Gorgon		St. Angela	11
			Andromeda	Minting	1
				Stella	19
Hollebeck			**St. Simon**	**Galopin**	3
○ 1914		Rabelais		St. Angela	11
			Satirical	Satiety	2
	Hilda II			Chaff	14
	○ 1907		Kendal	**Bend Or**	1
		Helen Kendal		Windermere	16
			Helen Hampton	**Hampton**	10
				Helen Agnes	16

Racing Career

Age	Starts	Wins
2	5	4
3	9	8
4	5	4
Total	19	16

TOURBILLON

b.h. 1928 – No. 13 Fam. – foaled in France

Tourbillon could certainly not be described as a model horse as far as his conformation was concerned as he had very badly bowed hocks. He was never a gentle-natured horse and his character became progressively worse as the years went by. His racing career lasted 2 seasons during which time he won six races including the Prix du Jockey Club and the Prix Lupin in France and the Zukunfts Rennen over 6 furlongs (1,200 m) which he won as a two-year-old at Baden in Germany. His final race was in the Prix de l'Arc de Triomphe in which he was not placed.

At stud he achieved better results proving to be the best perpetuator of Dollar's line, and sired Djebel who ensured its continuation in Europe. In South America, apart from Coaraze in Brazil, another of his colts Timor started off a very interesting branch in Argentina through Pronto (b.h. 1958) who sired Practicante (b.h. 1966). The best racehorse sired by Tourbillon was Caracalla who, unbeaten throughout his career, failed to live up to expectations as a stallion. The current representatives of Tourbillon's line in Europe belong to three branches which descend from Djebel and are traced down to Le Lavandou (sire of Le Levanstell), Clarion and Hugh Lupus (grandsires of Luthier and Blakeney respectively). Tourbillon died in 1954 at the age of 26, having become so difficult towards the end of his life that it was almost impossible to go near him.

Breeder: Marcel Boussac
Owner: Marcel Boussac
Most important wins: Prix du Jockey-Club, Prix Lupin, Prix Greffulhe, Prix Rocquart, Zukunfts Rennen

Racing Career

Age	Starts	Wins
2	4	2
3	7	4
Total	11	6

				Gardefeu	Cambyse	2
			Chouberski		Bougie	6
		Brûleur ◦ 1910		Campanule	The Bard	1
					Saint Lucia	28
			Basse Terre	**Omnium II**	Upas	19
					Bluette	22
	Ksar ◊ 1918			Bijou	**St. Gatien**	16
					Thora	4
			Omnium II	Upas	Dollar	1
					Rosemary	19
		Kizil Kourgan ◊ 1899		Bluette	Wellingtonia	3
					Blue Serge	22
			Kasbah	Vigilant	Vermouth	3
					Virgule	11
				Katia	Guy Dayrell	1
Tourbillon					Keepsake	3
			Rabelais	**St. Simon**	Galopin	3
					St. Angela	11
		Durbar ◦ 1911		Satirical	Satiety	2
					Chaff	14
			Armenia	Meddler	**St. Gatien**	16
					Busybody	1
	Durban ◦ 1918			Urania	Hanover	15
					Wanda	0
			Irish Lad	Candlemas	Hermit	5
					Fusee	22
		Banshee ◦ 1910		Arrowgrass	Enquirer *	A18
					Sparrowgrass	0
			Frizette	Hamburg	Hanover	15
					Lady Reel	23
* or Bramble (No. 9 Fam.)				Ondulee	**St. Simon**	11
					Ornis	13

55

HYPERION

ch.h. 1930 – No. 6 Fam. – foaled in Great Britain

Hyperion was a gentle-natured, sociable horse who always seemed in an excellent mood and showed great interest in everything that surrounded him. In stature, he was well below the average height measuring less than 15.2 hands (1.55 m) when he won the Derby, with a girth of 67 in (170 cm) and cannon bone of 7½ in (19 cm). He was sired by Gainsborough (winner of the Triple Crown) and his racing career lasted three years, from two to four. In his first race, a maiden race at Doncaster, he finished fourth in a field of 19 runners, and he later won dead-heated at Goodwood and before being defeated again at Newmarket he then won the Dewhurst Stakes, so his two-year-old career was clearly erratic.

As a three-year-old Hyperion matured and despite his small size clearly showed his classic ability by winning all four of his starts, including the Derby from King Salmon and 22 others, and the St. Leger beating Felicitation. As a four-year-old Hyperion was decisively beaten in the Ascot Gold Cup, won by Felicitation, emphasizing his limitations over long distances.

Once he was sent to stud he became outstanding and, through many of his offspring, from Owen Tudor to Aureole, Khaled and Aristophanes, his blood was diffused throughout the whole world. Owen Tudor proved to be the sire of excellent sprinters while among his fillies Hydroplane foaled the great Citation.

Hyperion was without doubt one of the greatest and most important stallions of this century. The successful crossing known as the "nicking" of his fillies with Nearco was an interesting experiment that was repeated on countless occasions and almost invariably produced good results. Hyperion lived to the ripe old age of 30, and kept his vitality and spirit right to the very end.

Breeder: Lord Derby
Owner: Lord Derby
Most important wins: Derby, St. Leger, Dewhurst Stakes, Prince of Wales's Stakes, Chester Vase

Hyperion						
	Gainsborough ○ 1915	Bayardo ○ 1906	Bay Ronald	Hampton	Lord Clifden	2
					Lady Langden	10
				Black Duchess	Galliard	13
					Black Corrie	3
			Galicia	**Galopin**	Vedette	19
					Flying Duchess	3
				Isoletta	Isonomy	19
					Lady Muncaster	10
		Rosedrop ◇ 1907	St. Frusquin	**St. Simon**	**Galopin**	3
					St. Angela	11
				Isabel	Plebeian	11
					Parma	22
			Rosaline	Trenton	Musket	3
					Frailty	18
				Rosalys	Bend Or	1
					Rosa May	2
	Selene ○ 1919	Chaucer ● 1900	**St. Simon**	**Galopin**	Vedette	19
					Flying Duchess	3
				St. Angela	King Tom	3
					Adeline	11
			Canterbury Pilgrim	Tristan	Hermit	5
					Thrift	10
				Pilgrimage	The Palmer *	5
					Lady Audley	1
		Serenissima ○ 1913	Minoru	Cyllene	Bona Vista	4
					Arcadia	9
				Mother Siegel	Friar's Balsam	2
					Galopin Mare	5
			Gondolette	Loved One	See Saw	6
					Pilgrimage	1
				Dongola	Doncaster	5
					Douranee	6

* or The Earl (No. 12 Fam.)

Racing Career		
Age	**Starts**	**Wins**
2	5	3
3	4	4
4	4	2
Total	13	9

BAHRAM

b.h. 1932 – No. 16 Fam. – foaled in Great Britain

A horse with a perfect conformation, Bahram in addition to aesthetic qualities also possessed considerable stamina and sprinting ability. His racing career lasted two years and he won all nine of the races he contested. At two Bahram won five races including the Gimcrack Stakes and the Middle Par Stakes, while the next season he won the Triple Crown and the St. James's Palace Stakes. A brief but brilliant career in which, according to his trainer Frank Butters, due to his laziness he never revealed his possibilities to the full.

At stud his best offspring were Big Game and Persian Gulf. He was exported to the United States in 1940 and six years later was moved to Argentina, but as fate would have it, the horse which was really to continue the paternal line was not Bahram but Blenheim (dk.b. 1927) who met with an accident soon after winning the Epsom Derby. Blenheim was inferior to Bahram as a racehorse but at stud won a place of absolute supremacy. The most illustrious of Blenheim's offspring was Mahmoud (gr.h. 1933) who proved to be an excellent sire of brood mares, whilst in Italy another of his progeny, Donatello II (ch.h. 1934) also showed himself to be of international class even though he met the only defeat of his career outside his home country.

Donatello II was beaten in the Grand Prix de Paris by Clairvoyant but in that race he performed so well that he was bought by a syndicate of English breeders to be taken to Great Britain where he served as a stallion and sired excellent horses like Alycidon and Crepello. Bahram did not sire great champions in America but he did get many winners the best being Jet Pilot (Kentucky Derby). Bahram died in Argentina in 1956 at the age of 24.

Breeder: Aga Khan
Owner: Aga Khan
Most important wins: 2,000 Guineas, Derby, St. Leger, Middle Park Stakes, Gimcrack Stakes, St. James's Palace Stakes

Racing Career

Age	Starts	Wins
2	5	5
3	4	4
Total	9	9

				Isinglass	**Isonomy** Dead-Lock	19 3
Bahram	Blandford • 1919	Swynford • 1907	John O'Gaunt	La Flêche	**St. Simon** Quiver	11 3
			Canterbury Pilgrim	Tristan	Hermit Thrift	5 10
				Pilgrimage	The Palmer* Lady Audley	5 1
		Blanche ○ 1912	White Eagle	Gallinule	**Isonomy** Moorhen	19 19
				Merry Gal	**Galopin** Mary Seaton	3 5
			Black Cherry	Bendigo	Ben Battle Hasty Girl	4 9
				Black Duchess	Galliard Black Corrie	13 3
	Friar's Daughter • 1921	Friar Marcus • 1912	Cicero	Cyllene	Bona Vista Arcadia	4 9
				Gas	Ayrshire Illuminata	8 1
			Prim Nun	Persimmon	**St. Simon** Perdita II	11 7
				Nunsuch	Nunthorpe La Morlaye	11 20
		Garron Lass ○ 1917	Roseland	William the Third	**St. Simon** Gravity	11 2
				Electric Rose	Lesterlin Arc Light	9 26
			Concertina	**St. Simon**	**Galopin** St. Angela	3 11
				Comic Song	Petrarch Frivolity	10 16

* or The Earl (No. 12 Fam.)

NEARCO

dk.b.h. 1935 – No. 4 Fam. – foaled in Italy

He was a horse with such a well proportioned conformation that he appeared smaller than he actually was. At a mature age he measured 16 hands (1.67 m), just slightly above average. His sire, Pharos, was certainly not the most outstanding racehorse among Phalaris's progeny having won only 14 of his 30 races, but Nearco was the greatest Italian horse of all time, not only as regards track performance but also and more especially for his contribution through his descendants to world bloodstock breeding, and in 1959 about 100 of his sons were serving as stallions throughout the world.

Nearco remained unbeaten throughout his racing career, winning all the Italian Classics and triumphing in France in the Grand Prix de Paris in spite of the fact that he was not really a stayer. In this race, which established him as a champion of international standard, the Epsom Derby winner, Bois Roussel, was beaten into third place, 2½ lengths behind the winner. After this success, which confirmed that he was a first class racehorse, he was bought by a syndicate of English breeders and went to stud.

During the Second World War a bunker was built for him at Newmarket to protect him from air raids. Only now, 40 years later, is it possible to make an overall assessment of his performance as a stallion. His performance at stud was extraordinary and in this century came second only to that of his grandsire, Phalaris. The most outstanding of his progeny on the track were Dante (Derby, Coventry Stakes, Middle Park Stakes), Syajirao (St. Leger, Irish Sweeps Derby) and Nimbus (2,000 Guineas, Derby). At stud it has mainly been the winners of the smallest number of races, Nasrullah, Royal Charger, Mossborough and Nearctic, who have been chiefly responsible for heading a series of bloodlines which have been of great importance both in Europe and America in the second half of this century.

The names speak for themselves – Sir Ivor and Habitat (who descends from Royal Charger), Northern Dancer and Nijinsky (son and grandson respectively of Nearctic), Bold Ruler, Never Bend, Bold Lad (USA), Bold Lad (IRE), Caro, Mill Reef, Secretariat and Spectacular Bid, all of which are descendants of Nasrullah. In 1982 a yearling son of Nijinsky, and great-grandson of the marvellous Nearco, was bought in the United States by Robert Sangster for the amazing sum of 4,250,000 dollars.

Nearco	Pharos ○ 1920	Phalaris • 1913	Polymelus	Cyllene	Bona Vista 4 / Arcadia 9
				Maid Marian	Hampton 10 / Quiver 3
			Bromus	Sainfoin	Springfield 12 / Sanda 2
				Cheery	**St. Simon** 11 / Sunrise 1
		Scapa Flow ◊ 1914	Chaucer	**St. Simon**	**Galopin** 3 / St. Angela 11
				Canterbury Pilgrim	Tristan 10 / Pilgrimage 1
			Anchora	Love Wisely	Wisdom 7 / Lovelorn 11
				Eryholme	Hazlehatch 11 / Ayrsmoss 13
	Nogara ○ 1928	Havresac II • 1915	Rabelais	**St. Simon**	**Galopin** 3 / St. Angela 11
				Satirical	Satiety 2 / Chaff 14
			Hors Concours	Ajax	Flying Fox 7 / Amie 2
				Simona	**St. Simon** 11 / Flying Footstep 8
		Catnip ○ 1910	Spearmint	Carbine	Musket 3 / Mersey 2
				Maid of the Mint	Minting 1 / Warble 1
			Sibola	The Sailor Prince	Albert Victor 13 / Hermita 19
				Saluda	Mortemer 1 / Perfection 4

Breeder: F. Tesio
Owner: F. Tesio
Most important wins: Gran Criterium, Italian Derby, Gran Premio d'Italia, Gran Premio di Milano, Grand Prix de Paris

Racing Career		
Age	Starts	Wins
2	7	7
3	7	7
Total	14	14

BULL LEA

dk.b.h 1935 – No. 9 Fam. – foaled in the United States

Bull Lea's sire, Bull Dog (full brother of Sir Gallahad III) was primarily responsible for diffusing Teddy's blood in America. He was a strong, muscular, average-sized horse with four white socks, with only one on the off hind leg clearly visible, a powerful neck and a deep chest. His racing career lasted from two to four but includes no wins of any great importance. Generally speaking he was a good but not excellent racehorse and although a reasonable winner, every time he was faced with a demanding challenge, as occurred in the Kentucky Derby and the Preakness, he finished unplaced. Bull Lea did, however, win ten races including the Blue Grass Stakes, and he was second seven times.

In contrast to his style as a racehorse, Bull Lea acquired great fame at stud. He headed the stallions' list in the United States five times and was celebrated as a sire of brood mares. The most famous of his offspring were Hill Gail and Iron Liège, winners of the Kentucky Derby, and the gelding, Armed. But the individuality of Citation (b.h. 1945) stands out most among the 276 winners he produced from 1943 to 1963. In five years of activity on the racecourse Citation collected 32 wins out of 45 starts, wins which included those races that make up the American Triple Crown: the Kentucky Derby, the Preakness Stakes and the Belmont Stakes. This exceptional son of Bull Lea was also able to cover the mile, carrying 9 st 1 lb (58 kg) in 1 minute 33 ⅗ seconds.

Citation should have been the natural choice to continue the line but at stud he was disappointing. So Bull Lea, who had an ability to sire excellent gallopers and brood mares (he headed the Sire of Brood Mares List from 1958 to 1961) was unfortunately unable to produce a horse worthy of a great sire to ensure his descent in the direct male line.

Breeder: Coldstream Stud
Owner: Calumet Farm
Most important wins: Blue Grass Stakes, Widener Handicap

Bull Lea					
Bull Dog ○/● 1927	Teddy ○ 1913	Ajax	Flying Fox	Orme / Vampire	11 / 7
			Amie	Clamart / Alice	3 / 2
		Rondeau	Bay Ronald	Hampton / Black Duchess	10 / 3
			Doremi	Bend Or / Lady Emily	1 / 2
	Plucky Liège ○ 1912	Spearmint	Carbine	Musket / Mersey	3 / 2
			Maid of the Mint	Minting / Warble	1 / 1
		Concertina	St. Simon	Galopin / St. Angela	3 / 11
			Comic Song	Petrarch / Frivolity	10 / 16
Rose Leaves ● 1916	Ballot ◇ 1904	Voter	Friar's Balsam	**Hermit** / The Flower of Dorset	5 / 2
			Mavourneen	Barcaldine / Gaydene	23 / 1
		Cerito	Lowland Chief	Lowlander / Bathilde	19 / 23
			Merry Dance	Doncaster / Highland Fling	5 / 14
	Colonial ○ 1897	Trenton	Musket	Toxophilite / W. Australian Mare	3 / 3
			Frailty	Goldsbrough / Flora McIvor	13 / 18
		Thankful Blossom	Paradox	Sterling / Casuistry	12 / 1
			The Apple	**Hermit** / Black Star	5 / 9

Racing Career

Age	Starts	Wins
2	9	2
3	16	7
4	2	1
Total	27	10

DJEBEL

b.h. 1937 – No. 5 Fam. – foaled in France

Djebel was rather a small horse but had a slender figure. His racing career lasted from the age of two to five in which time he won 15 of his 25 races and never finished lower than third. He had an excellent track career which was crowned when he was five years old with seven wins out of the same number of starts. The most outstanding of his important wins were the Middle Park Stakes as a two-year-old; the 2,000 Guineas and the Poule d'Essai des Poulains the next year; as a four-year-old the Prix Boiard and d'Harcourt and as a five-year-old the Prix de l'Arc de Triomphe, the Grand Prix de Saint-Cloud and, for the second year running, the Prix Boiard and d'Harcourt.

Among his most honourable defeats were the Prix de Chantilly, which that year replaced the Prix du Jockey-Club and was won by Quicko, and third place in the 1941 Prix de l'Arc de Triomphe won by Le Pacha.

Djebel was sired by Tourbillon and continued the line decisively, although his offspring did tend to inherit a certain amount of fragility along with the qualities of their sire. As regards his offspring some of the most remarkable colts he produced were Clarion, grandsire of Luthier (dk.b.h 1965), My Babu, winner of the 2,000 Guineas and an excellent sire of brood mares, Le Lavandou, sire of Le Levanstell (b.h. 1957) and Hugh Lupus, grandsire of the Epsom Derby winner, Blakeney.

The best filly sired by Djebel was Coronation (b.m. 1946), very closely inbred to Tourbillon (2 × 2), winner of the Prix Robert Papin and of the Poule d'Essai des Pouliches and Prix de l'Arc de Triomphe. Djebel died in 1957 at the age of 20.

Breeder: Marcel Boussac
Owner: Marcel Boussac
Most important wins: 2,000 Guineas, Poule d'Essai des Poulains, Middle Park Stakes, Grand Prix de Saint-Cloud, Prix de l'Arc de Triomphe, Prix Ganay, Prix d'Harcourt (twice)

Racing Career

Age	Starts	Wins
2	5	2
3	4	3
4	6	3
5	7	7
Total	22	15

Djebel						
	Tourbillon ◦ 1928	Ksar ◇ 1918	Brûleur	Chouberski	Gardefeu	6
					Campanule	28
				Basse Terre	Omnium II	22
					Bijou	4
			Kizil Kourgan	Omnium II	Upas	19
					Bluette	22
				Kasbah	Vigilant	11
					Katia	3
		Durban ◦ 1918	Durbar	Rabelais	St. Simon	11
					Satirical	14
				Armenia	Meddler	1
					Urania	0
			Banshee	Irish Lad	Candlemas	22
					Arrowgrass	0
				Frizette	Hamburg	23
					Ondulee	13
	Loïka ◇ 1926	Gay Crusader ◦ 1914	Bayardo	Bay Ronald	Hampton	10
					Black Duchess	3
				Galicia	Galopin	3
					Isoletta	10
			Gay Laura	Beppo	Marco	3
					Pitti	2
				Galeottia	Galopin	3
					Agave	1
		Coeur à Coeur ◇ 1921	Teddy	Ajax	Flying Fox	7
					Amie	2
				Rondeau	Bay Ronald	3
					Doremi	2
			Ballantree	Ayrshire	Hampton	10
					Atalanta	8
				Abeyance	Touchet	14
					Minnie Hauk	5

TICINO

b.h. 1939 – No. 3 Fam. – foaled in Germany

This horse can be considered the most important and interesting product of German breeding and certainly the first to make his influence felt outside his country of origin.

Ticino's racing career lasted four years from the age of two and as it took place during the Second World War his racing activities were limited to within the confines of Germany and Austria.

He was without doubt a horse of above average ability which he proved by frequently winning races with the greatest of ease and by completing the final year of his racing career unbeaten. The most important of his wins came in the German Derby the Grosser Preis von Berlin, which he won three times, and the Grosser Preis von Baden. At stud he headed the stallions' list in Germany for nine years with a number of high class winners until unfortunately, he became infertile at the age of 16.

Niederlander (b.h. 1947) was probably the best all-round, powerful horse sired by Ticino, but he was sent to stud in East Germany. Neckar (bl.h. 1948) was another and the most elegant and refined of Ticino's progeny. He was the first to begin the task of continuing his paternal line which he did by siring Hogarth (b.h. 1965), an Italian Derby winner and reasonably successful at stud, when based at Dormello. In addition to Neckar, Orsini (dk.b.h. 1954) also upheld Ticino's reputation at stud, repeating his sire's performance by siring four German winners, one fewer than Neckar.

Apart from these unquestionably valuable colts, all of whom won the German Derby, Ticino also sired some good fillies, especially the top class Bella Paola (dk.b. 1955). She was bred in France by M. François Dupré, and won the Grand Critérium, the 1,000 Guineas, the Oaks, the Prix Vermeille and the Champion Stakes, and was the dam of Pola Bella (dk.b. 1965), of the Poule d'Essai des Pouliches. Neckar and Orsini were outstanding sires of fillies and brood mares.

Ticino					
Athanasius • 1931	Ferro • 1923	Landgraf	Louviers	Isinglass	3
				St. Louvaine	1
			Ladora	Ladas	1
				Dorothea	27
		Frauenlob	Caius	Reverend	17
				Choise	19
			Farandole	Saphir	16
				Franche Comte	5
	Athanasie ○ 1924	Laland	Fels	**Hannibal**	1
				Festa	16
			Ladyland	Kendal	16
				Glare	1
		Athene	Ariel	**Ard Patrick**	5
				Ibidem	9
			Salamis	**Hannibal**	1
				Semiramis	16
Terra • 1929	Aditi • 1922	Dark Ronald	Bay Ronald	**Hampton**	10
				Black Duchess	3
			Darkie	Thurio	2
				Insignia	9
		Aversion	Nuage	Simonian	5
				Nepthe	5
			Antwort	**Ard Patrick**	5
				Alveole	9
	Teufelrose • 1918	Robert le Diable	Ayrshire	**Hampton**	10
				Atalanta	8
			Rose Bay	Melton	8
				Rose of Lancaster	1
		Rosanna	St. Maclou	St. Simon	11
				Mimi	12
			Rose of Jeddah	Gallinule *	19
				Rose d'Amour	20

* or Kendal Royal (No. 22 Fam.)

Breeder: Gestüt Erlenhof
Owner: Gestüt Erlenhof
Most important wins: German Derby, Grosser Preis von Berlin (three times), Grosser Preis von Baden (three times)

Racing Career

Age	Starts	Wins
2	2	1
3	7	4
4	5	2
5	7	7
Total	21	14

NASRULLAH

dk.b.h. 1940 – No. 9 Fam. – foaled in Great Britain

Nasrullah was certainly not one of the best track performers of Nearco's sons, proving to have a very difficult temperament which he handed down to some of his offspring. Nasrullah raced for two years. He was third in his first race, the Wilburton Stakes won by Nearly, and then won the Great Bradley Stakes and the Coventry Stakes, both over 6 furlongs (1,200 m), but was beaten in the Middle Park Stakes by Ribbon. As a three-year-old he won the Chatteris Stakes over a mile, the Caversham Stakes over 10 furlongs (2,000 m) and the Champion Stakes over the same distance. In the New Derby, however, he finished behind Straight Deal and Umiddad, and was un-placed in the 2,000 Guineas and New St. Leger.

At stud Nasrullah had exceptionally good results siring a series of high-class horses. One of his most well-known sons was Bold Ruler who, at Belmont Park, set the truly phenomenal time of 1:09 over 6 furlongs (1,200 m), carrying 9 st 7 lb (60½ kg). Besides this extraordinary racehorse, Nasrullah also sired other top class horses including Never Say Die, winner of the Epsom Derby and the Doncaster St. Leger, Nashua (Preakness Stakes and Belmont Stakes) and Grey Sovereign, who were also outstanding stallions. Nevertheless, out of more than 70 stallions, all sons of Nasrullah in service at studs throughout the world, Bold Ruler still has the most outstanding record with top class winners like Bold Lad (USA), Bold Lad (IRE), Successor, Bold Bidder, King Emperor and, last in chronological order, Secretariat. Bold Ruler headed the stallions' list in the United States from 1963 and 1969 and died in 1971 from widespread cancer. His notable progeny have without doubt guaranteed him a position of supremacy as a stallion, but above all have produced descendants which form solid foundations for the perpetuation of a blood line. Nasrullah was exported to the United States in 1949, and died there ten years later.

Nasrullah	Nearco ● 1935	Pharos ○ 1920	Phalaris	Polymelus	Cyllene 9 / Maid Marian 3
				Bromus	Sainfoin 2 / Cheery 1
			Scapa Flow	Chaucer	**St. Simon** 11 / **Canterbury Pilgrim** 1
				Anchora	Love Wisely 11 / Eryholme 13
		Nogara ○ 1928	Havresac II	Rabelais	**St. Simon** 11 / Satirical 14
				Hors Concours	Ajax 2 / Simona 8
			Catnip	Spearmint	Carbine 2 / Maid of the Mint 1
				Sibola	The Sailor Prince 19 / Saluda 4
	Mumtaz Begum ○ 1932	Blenheim ● 1927	Blandford	Swynford	John O'Gaunt 3 / **Canterbury Pilgrim** 1
				Blanche	White Eagle 5 / Black Cherry 3
			Malva	Charles O'Malley	Desmond 16 / Goody Two Shoes 5
				Wild Arum	Robert le Diable 1 / Marliacea 1
		Mumtaz Mahal □ 1921	The Tetrarch	Roi Hérode	Le Samaritain 2 / Roxelane 1
				Vahren	Bona Vista 4 / Castania 2
			Lady Josephine	Sundridge	Amphion 12 / Sierra 2
				Americus Girl	Americus 0 / Palotta 9

Breeder: Aga Khan
Owner: Aga Khan
Most important wins: Champion Stakes, Coventry Stakes

Racing Career

Age	Starts	Wins
2	4	2
3	6	3
Total	10	5

NASRULLAH

TENERANI

b.h. 1944 – No. 6 Fam. – foaled in Italy

The racing career of this horse was greatly influenced by the dislike which Federico Tesio had for him. Tenerani was in fact a rather lazy horse in training and that, added to the fact that he had a bad habit of climbing up the walls of his box was more than enough to make him go down in the estimation of his trainer. As a two-year-old he ran in seven races, winning only three, none of which was particularly important: the Premio Settimo over 5 furlongs (1,000 m), the Premio Luino over 6 furlongs (1,200 m) and the Premio Valate over 7 furlongs (1,400 m), but at three the horse showed definite signs of improvement by winning the Premio Merano at the beginning of the season. After this Tenerani had to comply with the wishes of his trainer by allowing himself to be beaten in the Premio Emanuele Filiberto by his stable companion, Duccio, who was more in favour with the "Wizard of Dormello." This excellent performance opened the doors of the Italian Derby which he won narrowly beating Scanno by a neck.

After his success in the Derby Tenerani won the Gran Premio d'Italia and the Gran Premio di Milano, but was defeated in the City of Milan Cup by the filly Zambra to whom he was giving 6 lb (3 kg). After this unexpected reverse Tenerani won the Italian St. Leger, the Jockey Club Cup (beating Duccio by 10 lengths), and the Premio Duca d'Aosta, and the following year he won all his races except the Gran Premio di Milano in which he was pipped at the post by Astolfina who carried the same colours. One of the most important races he won in Italy was the Premio Omnium while in England that year he gained his two best victories, the first at Ascot in the Queen Elizabeth Stakes, beating Black Tarquin, and the second in the Goodwood Cup when, admittedly, the odds on Arbar broke down.

He went to stud in 1949 and after having stood in Italy was moved in 1952 to England where he sired several quality horse including Tenterhooks (Goodwood Cup), Fighting Charlie, twice winner of the Ascot Gold Cup, and Bonnard (Doncaster Cup), while in Italy in his first year he sired the great Ribot and in 1953 Tissot, winner of the Premio Emanuele Filiberto, the Italian Grand Prix, the Jockey Club Cup, the Rome Cup, the Milan Gold Cup and the Premio Presidente della Repubblica. Like his sire Tenerani, Ribot too was out of favour with Federico Tesio who incidentally also showed similar feelings towards his dam, Romanella, to such an extent that when Tesio referred to him he said "the son of those two" showing, with this phrase, the low regard he had for the three. Tenerani returned to Italy in 1960 and ended his days at the Fonte di Papa stud farm on the outskirts of Rome in 1965.

Tenerani					
	Bellini ○ 1937	Cavaliere d'Arpino ○ 1926	Havresac II	Rabelais	**St. Simon** 11 Satirical 14
				Hors Concours	Ajax 2 Simona 8
			Chuette	Cicero	**Cyllene** 9 Gas 1
				Chute	Carbine 2 Weir 4
		Bella Minna ◇ 1923	Bachelor's Double	Tredennis	Kendal 16 St. Marguerite 4
				Lady Bawn	Le Noir 29 Milady 21
			Santa Minna	Santoi	Queen's Birthday 11 Merry Wife 1
				Minnow	William the Third 2 Mino 2
	Tofanella ◇ 1931	Apelle ◇ 1923	Sardanapale	Prestige	Le Pompon 18 Orgueilleuse 4
				Gemma	Florizel II 7 Agnostic 16
			Angelina	St. Frusquin	**St. Simon** 11 Isabel 22
				Seraphine	**Cyllene** 9 Virginal 5
		Try Try Again ○ 1922	Cylgad	**Cyllene**	Bona Vista 4 Arcadia 9
				Gadfly	Hampton 10 Merry Duchess 22
			Perseverance II	Persimmon	**St. Simon** 11 Perdita II 7
				Reminiscence	Carlton 10 Recollection 6

Breeder: Dormello-Ogliata stud farm
Owner: Dormello-Ogliata stud farm
Most important wins: Italian Derby, Gran Premio d'Italia, Gran Premio di Milano, Italian St. Leger, Jockey Club Cup, Queen Elizabeth Stakes, Goodwood Cup

Racing Career		
Age	Starts	Wins
2	7	3
3	9	7
4	8	7
Total	24	17

TULYAR

dk.b.h. 1949 – No. 22 Fam. – foaled in Ireland

Tulyar was a horse with an extremely promising pedigree. His racing career was unremarkable to begin with, but as he grew older it improved. In fact, as a two-year-old Tulyar won only two races, the Buggins Farm Nursery Stakes (1 mile) at Haydock Park and Kineton Nursery at Birmingham, over the same distance, finishing second once and third once and unplaced in two other races.

As a three-year-old things were different, and after having won the Henry VIII Stakes at Hurst Park over 7 furlongs (1,400 m) he took the Ormonde Stakes over 1 mile 6 furlongs (2,800 m) at Chester. Tulyar then won the Derby Trial at Lingfield before he triumphed at Epsom, beating Gay Time by three quarters of a length. After the Derby he swept on to victory in the Eclipse Stakes, the King George VI and Queen Elizabeth Stakes and the Doncaster St. Leger, but though it seemed likely at one time that he would stay in training as a four-year-old his owner decided to sell him to the Irish National Stud.

In 1955 he was sold to an American syndicate, but in Kentucky he suffered a serious illness which threatened his life. In 1958 he resumed his activities at stud, but unfortunately his achievements as a stallion were disappointing apart from Ginetta (Poule d'Essai des Pouliches, Prix du Moulin de Longchamp) and Fiorentina (Irish 1,000 Guineas). His best son was perhaps Empire (b.h. 1957), who won several races in France and later was exported to Italy as a stallion where he failed to win favour with the breeders, although he did sire several good products including Brioche (Premio Regina Elena). In the United States Tulyar sired a number of good mares including Castle Forbes (Gardenia Stakes), Paris Pike (Hollywood Oakes), Dringle Bay (Hollywood Oaks) and Tularia (International Handicap). Tulyar died in 1960.

Tulyar	Tehran ○ 1941	Bois Roussel ● 1935	Vatout	Prince Chimany	**Chaucer** 1 / Gallorette 8
				Vasthi	Sans Souci II 3 / Vaya 3
			Plucky Liège	**Spearmint**	Carbine 2 / Maid of the Mint 1
				Concertina	St. Simon 11 / Comic Song 16
		Stafaralla ○ 1935	Solario	Gainsborough	Bayardo 10 / Rosedrop 2
				Sun Worship	Sundridge 2 / Doctrine 26
			Mirawala	**Phalaris**	Polymelus 3 / Bromus 1
				Miranda	Gallinule 19 / Admiration 14
	Neocracy ● 1944	Nearco ● 1935	Pharos	**Phalaris**	Polymelus 3 / Bromus 1
				Scapa Flow	**Chaucer** 1 / Anchora 13
			Nogara	Havresac II	Rabelais 14 / Hors Concours 8
				Catnip	**Spearmint** 1 / Sibola 4
		Harina ○ 1933	Blandford	Swynford	John O'Gaunt 3 / Canterbury Pilgrim 1
				Blanche	White Eagle 5 / Black Cherry 3
			Athasi	Farasi	Desmond 16 / Molly Morgan 3
				Athgreany	Galloping Simon* 8 / Fairyland 22

* or His Majesty (No. 13 Fam.)

Breeder: Aga Khan
Owner: Aga Khan
Most important wins: Derby, Eclipse Stakes, King George VI and Queen Elizabeth Stakes, St. Leger Stakes

Racing Career		
Age	Starts	Wins
2	6	2
3	7	7
Total	13	9

TULYAR

NATIVE DANCER

gr.h. 1950 – No. 5 Fam. – foaled in the United States

Sired by Polynesian, a stallion who was renowned for his ability to produce extremely healthy offspring, Native Dancer was taller than average with a powerful muscular neck, extremely well-developed hindquarters, very high withers and sturdy shoulders, and in action he achieved a great length of stride. He was one of the greatest champions produced by American bloodstock breeding and his racing career lasted three years from the age of two, during which time he made 22 appearances.

He was beaten on only one occasion, in the Kentucky Derby, when he was hampered on the first bend and Dark Star beat him by a head. This defeat not only broke his unbeaten record but also denied him the American Triple Crown, a prize which he had given ample proof of deserving. Native Dancer made his two-year-old debut at the Jamaican racetrack on 19 April, when he won without difficulty and just four days later, on the same course, he took the Youthful Stakes. He reappeared in early August and in the course of a month won four races at Saratoga, including the Saratoga Special Stakes and the Hopeful Stakes. Less than a month later he made two appearances, with just six days in-between, at Belmont Park, firstly winning a routine race and then taking the Futurity Stakes. The year ended for Native Dancer at Jamaica with victory in the East View Stakes over a distance of 8½ furlongs (1,700 m).

At the start of his three-year-old season he reappeared on the same course, to win the important Gotham and Wood Memorial Stakes with only seven days rest in-between. A week later Native Dancer was unexpectedly beaten in the Derby at Churchill Downs, a real stroke of bad luck, considering that the horse that won had always lost to him on previous occasions. In May he had two more prestigious wins: the Withers Stakes at Pimlico only seven days later, where he beat Jamie K by a neck. Native Dancer continued the year with a series of wins, taking the Belmont Stakes (beating Jamie K by the same distance as in the Preakness), the Dwyer Stakes at Aqueduct, the Arlington Classic, the Travers Stakes at Saratoga and the American Derby at Washington Park.

As a four-year-old he appeared on the track three times, his most important win being in the Metropolitan Handicap at Belmont Park, carrying 9st 4 lb (59 kg), catching Straight Face near the line to win by a neck. Native Dancer won over distances ranging from 5 furlongs (1,000 m) to a mile and a half (2,400 m) proving that he had all the requirements of a classic racehorse.

The name "Flying Grey" was highly appropriate for him and, though the colour of his coat was not very popular in America, Native Dancer was loved and appreciated both as a racehorse and a stallion. At stud he sired a series of first class horses including Dan Cupid (ch. 1956) sire of Sea Bird II; Raise a Native (ch. 1961) sire of Majestic Prince, winner of the Kentucky Derby and the Preakness Stakes; Dancer's Image (gr. 1965) sire of Godswalk, and the filly Natalma (b. 1957) dam of the famous Northern Dancer.

				Polymelus	3
			Phalaris	Bromus	1
		Sickle			
			Selene	Chaucer	1
	Unbreakable ♦ 1935			Serenissima	6
			Prince Palatine	Persimmon	7
				Lady Lightfoot	1
		Blue Glass			
			Hour Glass II	Rock Sand	4
Polynesian ○ 1942				Hautesse	4
			Polymelus	Cyllene	9
		Polymelian		Maid Marian	3
			Pasquita	Sundridge	2
	Black Polly ○ 1936			Pasquil	7
			Pompey	Sun Briar	8
		Black Queen		Cleopatra	3
			Black Maria	Black Toney	10
				Bird Loose	14
Native Dancer			Fair Play	Hastings	21
		Display		Fairy Gold	9
			Cicuta	Nassoviav	14
	Discovery ◇ 1931			Hemlock	2
			Light Brigade	Picton	7
		Ariadne		Bridge of Sighs	8
			Adrienne	His Majesty	23
				Adriana	23
Geisha □ 1943			Whisk Broom II	Broomstick	16
		John P. Grier		Audience	4
			Wonder	Disguise II	10
	Miyako □ 1935			Curiosity	8
			Sweep	Ben Brush	A1
		La Chica		Pink Domino	8
			La Grisette	Roi Hérode	1
				Miss Fiora	5

Breeder: A.G. Vanderbilt
Owner: A.G. Vanderbilt
Most important wins: Saratoga Special Stakes, Hopeful Stakes, Futurity Stakes, Wood Memorial Stakes, Withers Stakes, Preakness Stakes, Belmont Stakes, Arlington Classic Stakes, Travers Stakes, American Derby, Metropolitan Handicap

Racing Career

Age	Starts	Wins
2	9	9
3	10	9
4	3	3
Total	22	21

RIBOT

b.h. 1952 – No. 4 Fam. – foaled in Italy

Ribot was one of the greatest champions of this century if not, as is the opinion of many people, the greatest of all. Throughout his racing career, he raced from two to four, and was unbeaten in 16 of his starts, always winning in a clear convincing manner, with the exception of his last race as a two-year-old, the Gran Criterium in which he was held up to get the trip and won by only a head from Gail. He was not engaged in the Italian classics, but his international wins were so significant that he has been placed on a level above all others.

As a two-year-old Ribot won three races, including the Criterium Nazionale and the Gran Criterium, while as a three-year-old his six successes included the Premio Emanuele Filiberto and the Premio del Jockey Club in Italy and the Prix de l'Arc de Triomphe in France. In this great French race, the cream of flat races, he had no difficulty in beating his 22 opponents. As a four-year-old he won seven times. After he had taken the Gran Premio di Milano he won the King George VI and Queen Elizabeth Stakes at Ascot, and in October at Longchamp he won the Prix de l'Arc de Triomphe for the second year running, beating Talago by 6 lengths with Tanerko third.

Ribot went to stud in 1957 and began his new career at Lord Derby's Woodland Stud at Newmarket, returning to Italy at the end of the season. Leased out to America in 1960, he continued his activities as a stallion at the Darby Dan Farm at Lexington in Kentucky. At stud too, Ribot was outstanding. In his first year he sired Latin Lover, exported as a stallion to Australia, and Molvedo, winner of the Prix de l'Arc de Triomphe in which his illustrious sire had twice triumphed.

In the generations that followed Ribot's most successful offspring have been Romulus (1959), Europe's Millers' champion miler in 1962 and then exported to Japan; Ragusa (1960), winner of the Irish Sweeps Derby, the Doncaster St. Leger and the King George VI and Queen Elizabeth Stakes, who turned out to be an excellent stallion but unfortunately died prematurely; Prince Royal (1961) winner of the Prix de l'Arc de Triomphe; Tom Rolfe (1962) winner of the Preakness Stakes; Graustark (1963) an outstanding stallion; Ribocco (1964) winner of the Observer Gold Cup, the Irish Sweeps Derby and the St. Leger; Ribero (1965) another winner of the Irish Sweeps Derby and the Doncaster St. Leger, Arts and Letters (1966) winner of the Jockey Club Gold Cup and the Belmont Stakes; His Majesty (1968) head of the stallions' list in the USA in 1982; Regal Exception (1969) winner of the Irish Guinness Oaks; and Filiberto (1970) winner of the Prix Morny.

With so many top class sons to follow him, Ribot's line has been built on solid foundations. Nowadays it is unnecessary and irrelevant to discuss his success or to make predictions about the quality of his offspring, since his grandchildren and great-grandchildren have already proved to be fine animals, excelling first on the race-track and later at stud. Hoist the Flag, sire of Alleged, is just one of the many possible examples. Ribot died in 1972 at the age of 22.

Ribot	Tenerani ○ 1944	Bellini ○ 1937	Cavaliere d'Arpino	Havresac II	Rabelais 14 / Hors Concours 8
				Chuette	Cicero 1 / Chute 4
			Bella Minna	Bachelor's Double	Tredennis 4 / Lady Bawn 21
				Santa Minna	Santoi 1 / Minnow 2
		Tofanella ◇ 1931	Apelle	Sardanapale	Prestige 4 / Gemma 16
				Angelina	St. Frusquin 22 / Seraphine 5
			Try Try Again	Cylgad	Cyllene 9 / Gadfly 22
				Perseverance II	Persimmon 7 / Reminiscence 6
	Romanella ◇ 1943	El Greco ◇ 1934	Pharos	Phalaris	Polymelus 3 / Bromus 1
				Scapa Flow	Chaucer 1 / Anchora 13
			Gay Gamp	Gay Crusader	Bayardo 10 / Gay Laura 1
				Parasol	Sunstar 5 / Cyclamen 14
		Barbara Burrini • 1937	Papyrus	Tracery	Rock Sand 4 / Topiary 19
				Miss Matty	Marcovil 12 / Simonath 16
			Bucolic	Buchan	Sunstar 5 / Hamoaze 16
				Volcanic	Corcyra 6 / La Soufrière 4

Breeder: Dormello-Ogliata stud farm
Owner: Dormello-Ogliata stud farm
Most important wins: Gran Criterium, Gran Premio del Jockey Club, Prix de l'Arc de Triomphe (twice), Gran Premio di Milano, King George VI and Queen Elizabeth Stakes

Racing Career		
Age	**Starts**	**Wins**
2	3	3
3	6	6
4	7	7
Total	16	16

NEARCTIC

dk.b.h. 1954 – No. 14 Fam. – foaled in Canada

Nearctic's dam was imported into Canada by E.P. Taylor when she was in foal and it was here that she gave birth to Nearctic, sired by Nearco, who raced for four years from two to five and won 21 of his 47 races. As a two-year-old he won the Clarendon Stakes at Woodbine over 5 furlongs (1,000 m) and, on the same track, the Victoria Stakes over 5½ furlongs (1,100 m). Later that year Nearctic won the Saratoga Special Stakes (6 furlongs (1,200 m) and, again at Saratoga, was only fourth in the Hopeful Stakes before winning the Carleton Stakes over 6 furlongs (1,200 m) at Woodbine.

At three Nearctic won the International Handicap at Fort Eric carrying 8 st 11 lb (56 kg), recording a time of 1'43"⅖ over 8½ furlongs (1,000 m). There were more wins the following year. In Canada he took the Bold Venture Handicap (58"⅕ over 5 furlongs (1,000 m)) and the Vigil Handicap at Fort Erie, the Swynford Stakes, the Jacques Cartier Stakes (1'09"⅘ over 6 furlongs (1,200 m) and the Canadian Maturity Stakes (1 mile 1 furlong (1,800 m)) at Woodbine. After travelling to Detroit Nearctic won in the Michigan Mile and, on his return to Canada, won the Sandown Stakes, the Greenwood Handicap and the Seaway Handicap at Woodbine. As a five-year-old he raced just three times, and repeated his success of the previous year in the Vigil Handicap.

Nearctic's racing career was average, and certainly gave no hint of the enormous success he was to enjoy as a stallion. At stud Nearctic sired 335 foals and proved himself a sire of brood mares, but his main achievement was to have sired Northern Dancer (b.h. 1961) who, after a brilliant racing career, proved to be an exceptional stallion by siring a series of top class animals. Nearctic died in 1973 at the age of 19.

Nearctic	Nearco • 1935	Pharos ○ 1920	Phalaris	Polymelus	Cyllene 9 / Maid Marian 3
				Bromus	Sainfoin 2 / Cheery 1
			Scapa Flow	**Chaucer**	**St. Simon** 11 / **Canterbury Pilgrim** 1
				Anchora	Love Wisely 11 / Eryholme 13
		Nogara • 1928	Havresac II	Rabelais	**St. Simon** 11 / Satirical 14
				Hors Concours	Ajax 2 / Simona 8
			Catnip	Spearmint	Carbine 2 / Maid of the Mint 1
				Sibola	The Sailor Prince 19 / Saluda 4
	Lady Angela ◊ 1944	Hyperion ◊ 1930	Gainsborough	Bayardo	Bay Ronald 3 / Galicia 10
				Rosedrop	St. Frusquin 22 / Rosaline 2
			Selene	**Chaucer**	**St. Simon** 11 / **Canterbury Pilgrim** 1
				Serenissima	Minoru 5 / Gondolette 6
		Sister Sarah • 1930	Abbots Trace	Tracery	Rock Sand 4 / Topiary 19
				Abbots Anne	Right-Away 11 / Sister Lumley 4
			Sarita	Swynford	John O'Gaunt 3 / **Canterbury Pilgrim** 1
				Molly Desmond	Desmond 16 / Pretty Polly 14

Breeder: E.P. Taylor
Owner: E.P. Taylor – Windfields Farm
Most important wins: Clarendon Stakes, Saratoga Special Stakes, Michigan Mile, Canadian Maturity Stakes

Racing Career

Age	Starts	Wins
2	13	7
3	13	4
4	18	9
5	3	1
Total	47	21

ROUND TABLE

b.h. 1954 – No. 2 Fam. – foaled in the United States

Round Table was smaller than average (15.3 hands) (1.56 m) but well-proportioned and had perfectly sound limbs. He had an amazingly competitive spirit and was unplaced only ten times from 66 starts in four years. Holder in the United States of the mile and a quarter (2,000 m) record with a time of 1 minute 59.4 seconds, which is a truly exceptional performance, he was one of the most extraordinary gallopers ever to appear on the American tracks.

At stud he was no less outstanding and sired an uninterrupted sequence of excellent offspring many of which have risen to the challenge of diffusing his blood throughout the world. These include horses like Baldric II (b. 1961) winner of the 2,000 Guineas and the Champion Stakes, and later exported to Japan; Advocator (b.h. 1962); Upper Case (b.h. 1969) winner of the Florida Derby and the Wood Memorial Stakes; Targowice (b.h. 1970); Apalachee (b.h. 1971) winner of the Observer Gold Cup; Cellini (b.h. 1971) winner of the William Hill Dewhurst Stakes, and Artaius (b.h. 1974) winner of the Eclipse Stakes and the Sussex Stakes. In addition to these Round Table produced other excellent winners such as Drumtop, He's a Smoothie, Knightly Manner and Duel who have won big prizes in America.

Round Table descends from Persimmon's line and was sired by Princequillo whose influence on American breeding can be detected in the pedigrees of many of the great champions foaled in America over the last 30 years.

Round Table	Princequillo ○ 1940	Prince Rose ○ 1928	Rose Prince	Prince Palatine	**Persimmon** 7 / Lady Lightfoot 1
				Eglantine	Perth 8 / Rose de Mai 11
			Indolence	Gay Crusader	Bayardo 10 / Gay Laura 1
				Barrier	Grey Leg 6 / Bar the Way 10
		Cosquilla ○ 1933	Papyrus	Tracery	Rock Sand 4 / Topiary 19
				Miss Matty	Marcovil 12 / Simonath 16
			Quick Thought	White Eagle	**Gallinule** 19 / Merry Gal 5
				Mindful	Minoru 5 / Noble Martha 1
	Knight's Daughter ○ 1941	Sir Cosmo ● 1926	The Boss	Orby	Orme 11 / Rhoda B. 26
				Southern Cross II	Meteor 3 / Resplendent 24
			Ayn Hali	Desmond	St. Simon 11 / L'abbesse de Jouarre 16
				Lalla Rookh	Hackler 7 / Lady Gough 6
		Feola ● 1933	Friar Marcus	Cicero	Cyllene 9 / Gas 1
				Prim Nun	**Persimmon** 7 / Nunsuch 20
			Aloe	Son-in-Law	Dark Ronald 9 / Mother-in-Law 5
				Alope	**Gallinule** 19 / Altoviscar 2

Breeder: Claiborne Farm
Owner: Kerr Stable
Most important wins: Hollywood Gold Cup, Hawthorne Gold Cup (twice), American Derby, Bay Meadows Derby, Blue Grass Stakes, United Nations Handicap (twice), San Antonio Stakes, Santa Anita Handicap, Gulfstream Park Handicap

Racing Career		
Age	Starts	Wins
2	10	5
3	22	15
4	20	14
5	14	9
Total	66	43

MARGUERITE VERNAUT

ch.m. 1957 – No. 14 Fam. – foaled in Italy

She was by Toulouse Lautrec, and had an unusually athletic build which she took from her sire who had inherited it from his dam Tokamura. The male side of Marguerite Vernaut's pedigree is very interesting in that Toulouse Lautrec was by Dante who was perhaps the best of Nearco's offspring on the racecourse, winning the Epsom Derby and being defeated on only one occasion in the 2,000 Guineas by Court Martial.

Marguerite Vernaut raced for two years and she won over distances of between 5 furlongs (1,000 m) and 1½ miles (2,400 m).

As a two-year-old she won the Premio Primi Passi, the Criterium Nazionale and the Gran Criterium while as a three-year-old, after having lost the Italian Derby (probably due to the wrong racing tactics), she won the Premio Emanuele Filiberto and the Premio d'Italia. Her best win was at Newmarket where she triumphed in the Champion Stakes beating Never Too Late, winner of the 1,000 Guineas and the Oaks. As often occurs, however, this fine mare's performance at stud was disappointing and did not earn her the renown she had acquired on the racecourse.

Marguerite Vernaut	Toulouse Lautrec ◇ 1950	Dante ○ 1942	Nearco	Pharos	Phalaris 1 / Scapa Flow 13
				Nogara	Havresac II 8 / Catnip 4
			Rosy Legend	Dark Legend	Dark Ronald 9 / Golden Legend 9
				Rosy Cheeks	St. Just 12 / Purity 3
		Tokamura ○ 1940	Navarro	Michelangelo	Signorino 23 / Fausta 2
				Nuvolona	Hurry On 2 / Nera di Bicci 4
			Tofanella	Apelle	Sardanapale 16 / Angelina 5
				Try Try Again	Cylgad 22 / Perseverance II 6
	Mariebelle ◇ 1948	Mieuxcé ○ 1933	Massine	Consols	Doricles 20 / Console 3
				Mauri	Ajax 2 / La Camargo 12
			L'Olivète	Opott	Maximum II 13 / Oussouri 4
				Jonicole	St. Just 12 / S.te Fiole 7
		Myrtle Green ◇ 1937	Trigo	Blandford	Swynford 1 / Blanche 3
				Athasi	Farasi 3 / Athgreany 22
			Simone Vergnes	Diadumenos	Orby 26 / Donnetta 2
				Incense	Roi Hérode 1 / Sacred Ibis 14

Breeder: Dormello-Olgiata stud farm
Owner: Dormello-Olgiata stud farm
Most important wins: Gran Griterium, Gran Premio d'Italia, Champion Stakes

Racing Career

Age	Starts	Wins
2	5	5
3	5	4
Total	11	9

MOLVEDO

dk.b.h 1958 – No. 16 Fam. – foaled in Italy

A good-sized horse, 16.2 hands (1.68 m), Molvedo closely resembled his sire Ribot in his overall appearance. His two-season racing career saw him win seven of his eight races over distances of between 5 furlongs (1,000 m) and 1 mile 5 furlongs (2,600 m). As a two-year-old he ran four races and won three, including the Gran Criterium (Group II), suffering the only defeat of his career in the Criterium Nazionale, won by Adrasto.

As a three-year-old, a strained muscle prevented him from racing until July, but he reappeared in the Premio d'Estate which he won without any difficulty. After this triumphant return, Molvedo went to France and won the Grand Prix du Centenaire de Deauville over 1 mile 5 furlongs (2,600 m), beating Misti in a field of 15. But by far the most important prize he won was the Prix de l'Arc de Triomphe in which he beat Right Royal, Misti and 16 others. Molvedo's career ended in Italy with his win in the Gran Premio del Jockey in which he beat Rio Marin by 4 lengths.

Molvedo began his career as a stallion in Italy at Gornate, and after the compulsory three years his owners refused a very attractive offer. Twenty years later there is still a great deal of interest in him, as he sired some fine quality offspring even though he did not have the advantages of the same brood mares at his disposal as did the other sons of Ribot. His best sons and daughters include Maestrale (Premio Presidente della Repubblica), Red Arrow (Italian Derby, Gran Premio d'Italia), Salado (John Porter Stakes), La Milanaise (Grand Prix de Vichy), Barado (Prix Gladiateur) and Scherzo (Prix Daru). Molvedo headed the stallions, list in Italy in 1976 and topped that for the sire of brood mares in 1975 and 1979.

Molvedo	Ribot ○ 1952	Tenerani ○ 1944	Bellini	Cavaliere d'Arpino	**Havresac II** 8 / Chuette 4
				Bella Minna	Bachelor's Double 21 / Santa Minna 2
			Tofanella	Apelle	Sardanapale 16 / Angelina 5
				Try Try Again	Cylgad 22 / Perseverance II 6
		Romanella ◇ 1943	El Greco	**Pharos**	Phalaris 1 / Scapa Flow 13
				Gay Gamp	Gay Crusader 1 / Parasol 14
			Barbara Burrini	Papyrus	Tracery 19 / Miss Matty 16
				Bucolic	Buchan 16 / Volcanic 4
	Maggiolina • 1946	Nakamuro ○ 1940	Cameronian	**Pharos**	Phalaris 1 / Scapa Flow 13
				Una Cameron	Gainsborough 2 / Cherimoya 1
			Nogara	**Havresac II**	Rabelais 14 / Hors Concours 8
				Catnip	Spearmint 1 / Sibola 4
		Murcia ◇ 1940	Pilade	Captain Cuttle	Hurry On 2 / Bellavista 22
				Piera	Wool Winder 4 / Partridge 1
			Muci	Tetrameter	The Tetrarch 2 / Mandola 5
				Pearl Maiden	Phaleron 8 / Seashell 16

Breeder: Ticino Stud
Owner: Ticino Stud
Most important wins: Gran Criterium, Gran Premio del Jockey Club, Prix de l'Arc de Triomphe, Grand Prix de Deauville

Racing Career

Age	Starts	Wins
2	4	3
3	4	4
Total	8	7

RELKO

b.h. 1960 – No. 16 Fam. – foaled in France

Relko was a very nervous horse and slightly above average height, 16.1 hands (1.63 m). He raced from two to four winning nine out of 13 starts. In the first year he won twice over 5 furlongs (1,000 m), in the Prix Isard II and the Prix Gladiateur, before finishing second in the Critérium de Maisons-Laffitte and the Prix Thomas Bryon, and fourth in the Grand Critérium. As a three-year-old Relko achieved important victories in both France and England winning the Poule d'Essai des Poulains (French 2,000 Guineas), the Epsom Derby, the Prix Royal Oak (French St. Leger) and the Prix de Guiche. Relko's career as a three-year-old is however marred by his withdrawal from the Irish Derby at the start where he was very lame, maybe due to a sudden feverish attack which had side effects on his kidneys, and by his performance in the Prix de l'Arc de Triomphe in which he failed to gain a place.

As a four-year-old this son of Tanerko was unbeaten in three races – the Prix Ganay, the Coronation Cup and the Grand Prix de Saint-Cloud. The most impressive victory in his career was, however, his triumph in the Epsom Derby, when he beat Merchant Venturer and Ragusa. Later that year Ragusa won the Irish Derby, the King George VI and Queen Elizabeth Stakes and the Doncaster St. Leger.

Relko went to stud in 1965 and sired numerous winners of Group races including Breton (Grand Critérium and Prix de la Salamandre), Relay Race (Jockey Club Stakes and Hardwicke Stakes), Relkino (Benson and Hedges Gold Cup and Lockinge Stakes), Tierceron (Gran Premio d'Italia, Gran Premio del Jockey Club and Italian St. Leger) and Irish Star (Grosser Preis der Stadt Gelsenkirchen).

				Deiri	Aethelstan	23
			Deux pour Cent		Desra	14
		Tantième ○ 1947		Dix pour Cent	Feridoon	11
					La Chansonnerie	11
				Indus	**Alcantara II**	4
			Terka		Himalaya	16
	Tanerko ● 1953			La Furka	**Blandford**	3
					Brenta	20
				Fairway	Phalaris	1
			Fair Copy		Scapa Flow	13
		La Divine ● 1943		Composure	Buchan	16
					Serenissima	6
				Blue Skies	**Blandford**	3
			La Diva		Blue Pill	5
Relko				La Traviata	**Alcantara II**	4
					Tregaron	12
				Man o'War	Fair Play	9
			War Relic		Mahubah	4
		Relic ◆ 1945		Friar's Carse	Friar Rock	9
					Problem	1
				Black Toney	Peter Pan	2
			Bridal Colors		Belgravia	10
	Relance III ◇ 1952			Vaila	Fariman	9
					Padilla	8
				Tourbillon	Ksar	3
			Le Volcan		Durban	13
		Polaire II ● 1947		Eroica	Banstar	13
					Macedonienne	5
				Papyrus	Tracery	19
			Stella Polaris		Miss Matty	16
				Crépuscule	Galloper Light	3
					Terra d'Ombra	16

Breeder: François Dupré
Owner: François Dupré
Most important wins: Poule d'Essai des Poulains, Derby, Prix Royal Oak, Prix Ganay, Coronation Cup, Grand Prix de Saint-Cloud

Racing Career		
Age	**Starts**	**Wins**
2	5	2
3	5	4
4	3	3
Total	13	9

NORTHERN DANCER

b.h. 1961 – No. 2 Fam. – foaled in Canada

This horse was quite small in stature and when fully grown was just under 15.3 hands (1.60 m). Although he was not a precocious horse he was the best two-year-old of 1963 in Canada, winning seven out of nine starts and twice finishing second. His major successes as a two-year-old included the Summer Stakes (one mile (1,600 m)) at Port Erie, the Coronation Futurity (1 mile 1 furlong (1,800 m)) at Woodbine, the Carleton Stakes (7 furlongs (1,400 m)) at Greenwood and the Remsen Stakes (one mile (1,600 m)) at Aqueduct in the United States.

In his first race as a three-year-old he was bumped and finished only third, but after a seven lengths win in an exhibition race with no prize and no betting, Northern Dancer took the Flamingo Stakes, the Florida Derby ahead of The Scoundrel, the Blue Grass Stakes, the Kentucky Derby and the Preakness Stakes, again beating The Scoundrel.

He failed to complete the Triple Crown in the Belmont Stakes at Aqueduct, however, as he could only manage coming in third behind Quadrangle and Roman Brother. Northern Dancer ended his career by winning the Queen's Plate over 1 mile 2 furlongs (2,000 m) at Woodbine in Canada, to produce a tally of 14 wins out of 8 starts with two seconds and two thirds in two seasons.

He started at stud in Canada and served as a stallion from 1965 to 1968 at the Oshawa Stud, before being transferred to Maryland, and he has proved to be one of the greatest successes. He headed the stallions' list in the United States in 1971 and 1977 and in Britain in 1970 and 1977. His exceptional offspring include the great Nijinsky (1967), Viceregal (1966), North-fields (1968), Lyphard (1969), The Minstrel (1974) and Be My Guest (1974), all of whom have been most successful stallions. In 1982 two of his sons, Be My Guest and Nijinsky, filled the first two places in the stallions' list in England. Few may have expected such good results both on the track and at stud from Northern Dancer, who failed to reach his reserve of $25,000 as a yearling but at the end of his career was syndicated for $2,400,000 (£1,600,000) and later a share in him (one fortieth of the horse) was valued at $190,000 (£125,000).

				Polymelus	3
			Phalaris	Bromus	1
		Pharos		Chaucer	1
	Nearco • 1935		Scapa Flow	Anchora	13
			Havresac II	Rabelais	14
		Nogara		Hors Concours	8
			Catnip	Spearmint	1
Nearctic • 1954				Sibola	4
			Gainsborough	Bayardo	10
		Hyperion		Rosedrop	2
	Lady Angela ◇ 1944		Selene	Chaucer	1
				Serenissima	6
		Sister Sarah	Abbots Trace	Tracery	19
				Abbots Anne	4
			Sarita	Swynford	1
Northern Dancer				Molly Desmond	14
			Unbreakable	Sickle	6
		Polynesian		Blue Glass	4
	Native Dancer □ 1950		Black Polly	Polymelian	7
				Black Queen	14
		Geisha	Discovery	Display	2
				Ariadne	23
			Miyako	John P. Grier	8
				La Chica	5
	Natalma ○ 1957		Blenheim	Blandford	3
		Mahmoud		Malva	1
			Mah Mahal	Gainsborough	2
	Almahmoud ◇ 1947			Mumtaz Mahal	9
		Arbitrator	Peace Chance	Chance Shot	3
				Peace	10
			Mother Goose	Chicle	31
				Flying Witch	2

Breeder: E.P. Taylor
Owner: E.P. Taylor
Most important wins: Flamingo Stakes, Florida Derby, Blue Grass Stakes, Kentucky Derby, Preakness Stakes

Racing Career		
Age	Starts	Wins
2	9	7
3	9	7
Total	18	14

SEA BIRD

ch.h. 1962 – No. 2 Fam. – foaled in France

Sired by the American stallion Dan Cupid, Sea Bird was an average sized horse, 16.1 hands (1.67 m), well-built with a nicely sloping shoulder which enabled wide sweeping movements, and well-developed hindquarters. He raced at two to three and was beaten only once – in the Grand Critérium when he was beaten by Grey Dawn after being slowly away. As a two-year-old he took the Prix de Blaison over 7 furlongs (1,400 m) and the Critérium de Maisons Laffitte over the same distance.

At three, after winning the Prix Greffulhe and the Prix Lupin (Group I) both over 1 mile 2½ furlongs (2,100 m), he triumphed in the Epsom Derby beating Meadow Court in a mere canter. This brilliant success was followed by easy victories in the Grand Prix de Saint-Cloud and in the Prix de l'Arc de Triomphe where he swept home six lengths ahead of Reliance with Diatôme five lengths behind. Sea Bird's career was comparatively brief but he was so obviously champion material that Timeform allotted him 10 st 5 lb (67 kg), a weight they had never before given to any horse.

In his first season at stud he sired Gyr who won the Prix Daru, Prix Hocquart and Grand Prix de Saint-Cloud and was second in the Derby, to Nijinsky. Sea Bird's other great claim to fame as a stallion was Allez France, one of the most notable fillies ever to appear on the world's racetracks. The horse was exported to the United States in 1966 but, except for this great racemare, he failed to perform as had been hoped. In 1973 he returned to Europe where he died shortly afterwards due to an illness, before he could cover any mares.

Sea Bird	Dan Cupid ◇ 1956	Native Dancer ◻ 1950	Polynesian	Unbreakable	**Sickle** 6 / Blue Glass 4
				Black Polly	Polymelian 7 / Black Queen 14
			Geisha	Discovery	Display 2 / Ariadne 23
				Miyako	John P. Grier 8 / La Chica 5
		Vixenette ◇ 1944	**Sickle**	Phalaris	Polymelus 3 / Bromus 1
				Selene	Chaucer 1 / Serenissima 6
			Lady Reynard	Gallant Fox	Sir Gallahad III 16 / Marguerite 4
				Nerva	Fair Play 9 / Zephyretta 4
	Sicalade ○ 1956	Sicambre • 1948	Prince Bio	Prince Rose	Rose Prince 11 / Indolence 10
				Biologie	Bactériophage 25 / Eponge 1
			Sif	Rialto	**Rabelais** 14 / La Grêlée 12
				Suavita	Alcantara II 4 / Shocking 7
		Marmelade ○ 1949	Maurepas	Aethelstan	Teddy 2 / Dédicace 23
				Brocéliande	La Farina 4 / Reine Mab 12
			Couleur	Biribi	**Rabelais** 14 / La Bidouze 27
				Colour Bar	Colorado 3 / Lady Disdain 2

Breeder: Jean Ternynck
Owner: Jean Ternynck
Most important wins: Derby, Prix Lupin, Grand Prix de Saint-Cloud, Prix de l'Arc de Triomphe, Prix Greffulhe

Racing Career		
Age	Starts	Wins
2	3	2
3	5	5
Total	8	7

BUCKPASSER

b.h. 1963 – No. 1 Fam. – foaled in the United States

Buckpasser was without doubt one of the greatest champions to have appeared on American tracks. At 16.3 hands (1.65 m), his elegant lines gave him perfect conformation in all respects. In his three-season racing career he won many major stakes and he was unplaced only once in 31 appearances over distances from 5½ furlongs (1,100 m) to 2 miles (3,200 m). As a two-year-old he won the Arlington-Washington Futurity, the National Stallion Stakes (dead-heating with Hospitality), the Tremont Stakes, the Champagne Stakes at Aqueduct, the Sapling Stakes at Monmouth Park and the Hopeful Stakes at Saratoga as well as being second in the Futurity Stakes at Aqueduct.

As a three-year-old Buckpasser took the Flamingo Stakes at Hialeah just beating Abe's Hope, but after this performance,

which had not totally convinced his trainer Eddie Neloy, he was sidelined due to a crack on the inside of his right fore-hoof. He therefore had to miss the classics and reappeared on the track winning a handicap at Belmont Park on the same day that the last race of the Triple Crown was run there. After this victorious return Buckpasser began winning races of major importance again starting off with the Leonard Richard Stakes at Delaware. He then took the Arlington Classic, setting a world mile record – on a level track – with a time of 1'32"⅗, and the Chicagoan Stakes. Through the rest of the year Buckpasser went from success to success, the Brooklyn Handicap, the American Derby at Arlington beating Jolly Jet and Stupendous, the Everglades Stakes, the Lawrence Realization Stakes over 1 mile 5 furlongs (2,600 m)

at Aqueduct, the Woodward Stakes on the same course beating Royal Gunner, Baffle and Tom Rolfe, the Travers Stakes at Saratoga, the Malibu Stakes at Santa Anita, and the Jockey Club Gold Cup at Aqueduct over 2 miles (3,200 m). He was elected Horse of the Year.

As a four-year-old Buckpasser carried off other important wins in the Suburban Handicap at Aqueduct, the San Fernando Stakes at Santa Anita, beating Fleet Host and Pretense, and the Metropolitan Handicap at Aqueduct, carrying 9 st 4 lb (59 kg). He was second in the Woodward Stakes, the Brooklyn Handicap and the Bowling Green Handicap. As well as being Horse of the Year as a three-year-old, Buckpasser was also champion two-year-old in 1965, 1966 and handicap champion in 1967.

He went to stud in 1968 and confirmed his qualities by siring two first class fillies, Numbered Account (14 wins) and La Prévoyante (25 wins), as well as L'Enjôleur (Manitoba Derby, Quebec Derby, Laurel Futurity, Coronation Futurity and Horse of the Year in Canada at two and three), Pass The Glass, and Quick as Lightning (1,000 Guineas).

Buckpasser	Tom Fool ○ 1949	Menow ● 1935	Pharamond II	Phalaris	Polymelus 3 / Bromus 1
				Selene	Chaucer 1 / Serenissima 6
			Alcibiades	Supremus	Ultimus 14 / Mandy Hamilton 32
				Regal Roman	Roi Hérode 1 / Lady Cicero 8
		Gaga ○ 1942	Bull Dog	**Teddy**	Ajax 2 / Rondeau 2
				Plucky Liège	Spearmint 1 / Concertina 16
			Alpoise	Equipoise	Pennant 8 / Swinging 5
				Laughing Queen	Sun Briar 8 / Cleopatra 3
	Busanda ♦ 1947	War Admiral ● 1934	Man o'War	Fair Play	Hastings 21 / Fairy Gold 9
				Mahubah	Rock Sand 4 / Merry Token 4
			Brushup	Sweep	Ben Brush A1 / Pink Domino 8
				Annette K.	Harry of Hereford 1 / Bathing Girl 11
		Businesslike ○ 1939	Blue Larkspur	Black Servant	Black Toney 10 / Padula 8
				Blossom Time	North Star III 4 / Vaila 8
			La Troienne	**Teddy**	Ajax 2 / Rondeau 2
				Hélène de Troie	Helicon 22 / Lady of Pedigree 1

Breeder: Ogden Phipps
Owner: Ogden Phipps
Most important wins: Arlington-Washington Futurity, Champagne Stakes (USA), Sapling Stakes, Hopeful Stakes, Flamingo Stakes, Jockey Club Gold Cup, Woodward Stakes, Travers Stakes, Suburban Handicap, Metropolitan Handicap, Brooklyn Handicap

Racing Career

Age	Starts	Wins	
2	11	9	
3	14	13	
4	6	3	x
Total	31	25	

GREAT NEPHEW

b.h. 1963 – No. 14 Fam. – foaled in Great Britain

Great Nephew is of average height at 16 hands (1.625 m) and won five races from two to four in all-over distances varying from 6 furlongs (1,200 m) to 1 mile 2 furlongs (2,000 m). As a two-year-old he had only one win, in the Norfolk Stakes at Newmarket but in his other six starts he was second once and third twice.

At three he won the Prix Michael Houyvet at Deauville after being beaten by a short head by Kashmir II in the 2,000 Guineas. He was beaten by only a head by Silver Shark in the Prix du Moulin and in the Lockinge Stakes by Silly Season as well as being third in the St. James's Stakes and the Queen Anne Stakes.

As a four-year-old, after having won the Prix de Pâques, Great Nephew achieved his most significant wins in the Prix Dollar and the Prix du Moulin de Longchamp, as well as being second in the Eclipse Stakes to Busted and in the Prix Ganay to Behistoun. He completed his career by coming fourth in the Prix de la Forêt.

Great Nephew went to stud in 1968 and is best known by far for Grundy (ch.h. 1972) and Shergar (b.h. 1978), both winners of the Epsom Derby, the Irish Sweeps Derby and the King George and Queen Elizabeth Diamond Stakes. He was leading sire in Britain in 1975 and 1981. Mrs Penny (ch. 1977) is one of his best fillies with wins in the William Hill Chevely Park Stakes, the Prix de Diane de Revlon and the Prix Vermeille. Great Nephew stands at the Dalham Hall Stud at Newmarket.

Great Nephew	Honeyway ● 1941	Fairway ○ 1925	**Phalaris**	Polymelus	Cyllene	9
					Maid Marian	3
				Bromus	Sainfoin	2
					Cheery	1
			Scapa Flow	**Chaucer**	St. Simon	11
					Canterbury Pilgrim	1
				Anchora	Love Wisely	11
					Eryholme	13
		Honey Buzzard ◇ 1931	Papyrus	**Tracery**	Rock Sand	4
					Topiary	19
				Miss Matty	Marcovil	12
					Simonath	16
			Lady Peregrine	White Eagle	Gallinule	19
					Merry Gal	5
				Lisma	Persimmon	7
					Luscious	9
	Sybil's Niece ◇ 1951	Admiral's Walk ◇ 1936	Hyperion	Gainsborough	Bayardo	10
					Rosedrop	2
				Selene	**Chaucer**	1
					Serenissima	6
			Tabaris	Roi Hérode	Le Samaritain	2
					Roxelane	1
				Tip-toe	Royal Realm	7
					Lady Lightfoot	1
		Sybil's Sister ○ 1943	Nearco	Pharos	**Phalaris**	1
					Scapa Flow	13
				Nogara	Havresac II	8
					Catnip	4
			Sister Sarah	Abbots Trace	**Tracery**	19
					Abbots Anne	4
				Sarita	Swynford	1
					Molly Desmond	14

Breeder: J.P. Philipps
Owner: J.P. Philipps
Most important wins: Prix Moulin de Longchamp, Prix Dollar

Racing Career

Age	Starts	Wins
2	7	1
3	9	1
4	6	3
Total	22	5

ROYAL PALACE

b.h. 1964 – No. 1 Fam. – foaled in Great Britain

Royal Palace is a very muscular horse of average height (15.3 hands), and raced from two to four winning over distances of between 6 furlongs (1,200 m) and 1½ miles (2,400 m). At two he won the Acomb Stakes (6 furlongs (1,200 m)) and the Royal Lodge Stakes over a mile. At three, after beating Taj Dewan in the 2,000 Guineas and winning the Epsom Derby he unfortunately had to be withdrawn from the Doncaster St. Leger due to injury and though he reappeared in the Champion Stakes he was beaten by Reform and Taj Dewan.

As a four-year-old Royal Palace proved that he had fully regained all his strength and won all his five races – the Coronation Stakes over 1 mile 2 furlongs (2,000 m) at Sandown Park, the Coronation Cup at Epsom over 1½ miles (2,400 m), the Prince of Wales's Stakes at Ascot over 1 mile 2 furlongs (2,000 m), the Eclipse Stakes over 1 mile 2 furlongs (2,000 m) at Sandown Park beating Taj Dewan and Sir Ivor, and the King George VI and Queen Elizabeth Stakes over 1½ miles (2,400 m) at Ascot.

Royal Palace has been at stud since 1969 and has unfortunately not come up to the standard expected of him. His best product in racing has been the filly Dunfermline, owned by Her Majesty Queen Elizabeth II and winner of the Epsom Oaks and Doncaster St. Leger.

Royal Palace	Ballymoss ◊ 1954	Mossborough ◊ 1947	Nearco	Pharos	**Phalaris** 1 / Scapa Flow 13
				Nogara	Havresac II 8 / Catnip 4
			All Moonshine	Bobsleigh	**Gainsborough** 2 / Toboggan 3
				Selene	Chaucer 1 / Serenissima 6
		Indian Call ◊ 1936	Singapore	**Gainsborough**	Bayardo 10 / Rosedrop 2
				Tetrabbazia	The Tetrarch 2 / Abbazia 8
			Flittemere	Buchan	Sunstar 5 / Hamoaze 16
				Keysoe	Swynford 1 / Keystone II 2
	Crystal Palace ◊ 1956	Solar Slipper ◊ 1945	Windsor Slipper	Windsor Lad	Blandford 3 / Resplendent 19
				Carpet Slipper	**Phalaris** 1 / Simon's Shoes 5
			Solar Flower	Solario	**Gainsborough** 2 / Sun Worship 26
				Serena	Winalot 3 / Charmione 10
		Queen of Light ◊ 1949	Borealis	Brumeux	Teddy 2 / La Brume 27
				Aurora	Hyperion 6 / Rose Red 1
			Picture Play	Donatello II	Blenheim 1 / Delleana 14
				Amuse	**Phalaris** 1 / Gesture 1

Breeder: H.J. Joel
Owner: H.J. Joel
Most important wins: 2,000 Guineas, Derby, Eclipse Stakes, King George VI and Queen Elizabeth Stakes

Racing Career		
Age	**Starts**	**Wins**
2	3	2
3	3	2
4	5	5
Total	11	9

VAGUELY NOBLE

b.h. 1965 – No. 1 Fam. – foaled in Great Britain

Vaguely Noble, a horse with elegant conformation, raced for two years at two and three. In his first year he won twice and was second twice out of four starts. The first win was in the Sandwich Stakes over 7 furlongs (1,400 m) which he won by 12 lengths and in a field of 18, and the other was in the Observer Gold Cup, when he came home seven lengths ahead of Doon with Riboccare third and Connaught fifth. In December that year the horse appeared at the Newmarket December sales and was bought by Mrs Robert Franklyn for 136,000 guineas. He was sent to France where he won the Prix de Guiche and the Prix du Lys, but in the Grand Prix de Saint-Cloud he was beaten by Hopeful Venture and Minamoto, perhaps partly because Vaguely Noble was not suited to a left-handed course.

He then won the Prix de Chantilly before his greatest win in the Prix de l'Arc de Triomphe when he beat Sir Ivor by three lengths in a field which included classic winners such as Roselière (Prix de Diane), La Lagune (Oaks) and Dhaudevi (Grand Prix de Paris and Prix Royal Oak). Vaguely Noble was almost immediately syndicated for five million dollars and went to stud in the United States. He proved an excellent sire with winners like Dahlia (winner of 11 Group I races in Europe and America), Ace of Aces (Sussex Stakes), Noble Decree (Observer Gold Cup), Royal and Regal (Florida Derby), Mississipian (Grand Critérium), Nobiliary (Washington D.C. International, Prix Saint-Alary), Exceller (Grand Prix de Paris) and Empery (Derby).

Vaguely Noble	Vienna ◊ 1957	Aureole ◊ 1950	**Hyperion**	Gainsborough	Bayardo 10 / Rosedrop 2
				Selene	**Chaucer** 1 / Serenissima 6
			Angelola	Donatello II	Blenheim 1 / Delleana 14
				Feola	Friar Marcus 20 / Aloe 2
		Turkish Blood ○ 1944	Turkhan	**Bahram**	Blandford 3 / Friar's Daughter 16
				Theresina	Diophon 2 / Teresina 6
			Rusk	Manna	**Phalaris** 1 / Waffles 22
				Baby Polly	**Spearmint** 1 / Pretty Polly 14
	Noble Lassie ○ 1956	Nearco • 1935	Pharos	**Phalaris**	Polymelus 3 / Bromus 1
				Scapa Flow	**Chaucer** 1 / Anchora 13
			Nogara	Havresac II	Rabelais 14 / Hors Concours 8
				Catnip	**Spearmint** 1 / Sibola 4
		Belle Sauvage ◊ 1949	Big Game	**Bahram**	Blandford 3 / Friar's Daughter 16
				Myrobella	Tetratema 14 / Dolabella 6
			Tropical Sun	**Hyperion**	Gainsborough 2 / Selene 6
				Brulette	Brûleur 4 / Seaweed 1

Breeder: Major L.B. Holliday
Owners: Mrs L.B. Holliday, Mrs R.A. Franklyn and Mr N.B. Hunt
Most important wins: Prix de l'Arc de Triomphe, Observer Gold Cup, Prix du Lys

Racing Career		
Age	Starts	Wins
2	4	2
3	5	4
Total	9	6

SIR IVOR

b.h. 1965 – No. 8 Fam. – foaled in the United States

Of average height at 16 hands (1.63 m), this horse is of a build which is the exact American version of the Nearco type, more muscular and rounded, but still graceful and elegant. Sir Ivor proved to have a lively, sociable character, and to be very easy to handle.

He raced almost exclusively in Europe, having run only one race in his country of origin. He was unplaced in his first race as a two-year-old, the Tyros Stakes at The Curragh on 1 July, but was unbeaten for the rest of the year, winning the National Stakes over 7 furlongs (1,400 m) and the Probationer Stakes over the same distance, both at The Curragh, while in Paris he broke the tradition of the Grand Critérium always being won by French-trained horses.

As a three-year-old, after having spent the winter in Pisa, he won the 2,000 Guineas Trial over 7 furlongs (1,400 m) at Ascot before landing that classic by beating Petingo and Jimmy Reppin. Sir Ivor went on to triumph in the Epsom Derby, in which he beat Connaught, but in the Irish Derby he was beaten by Ribero and in the Eclipse Stakes he finished a close third behind Royal Palace and Taj Dewan. Sir Ivor was then twice beaten in France, by Prince Sao in the Prix Henry Delamarre and then by Vaguely Noble in the Prix de l'Arc de Triomphe, before he came back to winning form with his defeat of Locris and Candy Cane in the Champion Stakes and his career ended on the best possible note when he won the Washington D.C. International at Laurel Park, the only race he ever ran in America and the last one of his career.

According to Lester Piggott, who almost always rode him, of all the good horses that he has ever ridden Sir Ivor, the European two-year-old champion and Horse of the Year in England in 1968, was the best of all and this judgement must be much respected. Sir Ivor entered stud in 1969 and produced a large number of Group race winners including Optimistic Gal, Cave Doro (Ballymoss Stakes), Sir Penfro (Gallinule Stakes, Desmond Stakes), Ivanjica (Prix de l'Arc de Triomphe, Poule d'Essai des Pouliches, Prix Vermeille), Ercolano (Prix du Lys), Malinowski (Craven Stakes) and Godetia (Goffs Irish 1,000 Guineas, Irish Guinness Oaks). So far, Sir Ivor's performance at stud is most notable for the high-quality fillies he has sired since the great colt on which hopes for continuing the line can be based has still not arrived.

Sir Ivor	Sir Gaylord ○ 1959	Turn-to ○ 1951	Royal Charger	Nearco	**Pharos** 13
					Nogara 4
				Sun Princess	Solario 26
					Mumtaz Begum 9
			Source Sucrée	Admiral Drake	Craig an Eran 16
					Plucky Liège 16
				Lavendula II	**Pharos** 13
					Sweet Lavender 1
		Somethingroyal ○ 1952	Princequillo	Prince Rose	Rose Prince 11
					Indolence 10
				Cosquilla	Papyrus 16
					Quick Thought 1
			Imperatrice	Caruso	Polymelian 7
					Sweet Music 2
				Cinquepace	Brown Bud 2
					Assignation 2
	Attica ◇ 1953	Mr. Trouble ◇ 1947	Mahmoud	Blenheim	Blandford 3
					Malva 1
				Mah Mahal	Gainsborough 2
					Mumtaz Mahal 9
			Motto	Sir Gallahad III	Teddy 2
					Plucky Liège 16
				Maxima	Sir Martin 9
					Minima 13
		Athenia ● 1943	Pharamond II	Phalaris	Polymelus 3
					Bromus 1
				Selene	Chaucer 1
					Serenissima 6
			Salaminia	Man o'War	Fair Play 9
					Mahubah 4
				Alcibiades	Supremus 32
					Regal Roman 8

Breeder: Mill Ridge Farm
Owner: R.R. Guest
Most important wins: Grand Critérium, 2,000 Guineas, Derby Champion Stakes, Washington D.C. International

Racing Career

Age	Starts	Wins
2	4	3
3	9	5
Total	13	8

PRACTICANTE

b.h. 1966 – No. 8 Fam. – foaled in Argentina

Practicante was not an attractive horse and had a rather ordinary appearance, but he was very powerful. He raced from two to six, and his first wins included the Clasico Miguel Cane (7½ furlongs (1,500 m)) at Palermo, but was beaten in the Polla de Potrillos (the Argentine 2,000 Guineas) by Martinet. He got his revenge on that rival, however, in the Gran Premio Jockey Club, beating him by 1½ lengths, and then won the most important three-year-old classic, the Gran Premio Nacional which is, in practice, the Argentine Derby, by 4 lengths from Bluff Albertinto, while Martinet was only fourth. Practicante beat Martinet once again by 2½ lengths over a distance of 1 mile 7 furlongs (3,000 m) by a decisive sprint in the final stretch of the Gran Premio Carlos Pellegrini at San Isidro, proving that he was the best three-year-old horse in the whole of South America.

He was taken to Ireland as a four-year-old and was second in the Desmond Stakes while that same year in France he finished unplaced in the Prix Foy. His racing career continued in the USA when he was five and six years old, and he recorded important successes such as the Seneca Handicap, the San Luis Obispo Handicap and San Juan Capistrano Invitational Handicap, as well as being third in the Man o' War Stakes.

Practicante went to stud in 1973 and headed the stallions' list in Argentina in 1979, siring good winners like Vituperante and Auxiliante. Practicante is the most successful perpetuator of Tourbillon's line which still continues in America. His sire, Pronto, had the conformation typical of horses belonging to this line, even though his loins were shorter than those of his grandsire, Tourbillon.

Practicante	Pronto ○ 1958	Timor ◇ 1944	Tourbillon	Ksar	Brûleur 4 / Kizil Kourgan 3
				Durban	Durbar 0 / Banshee 13
			Samya	Nimbus	Elf II 4 / Nepenthe 5
				Sapience	Gorgoss 19 / Sapientia 19
		Prosperina ○ 1949	Gusty	Bois Roussel	Vatout 3 / Plucky Liège 16
				Heavenly Wind	Tai Yang 3 / Godetia 1
			Beoka	Badruddin	Blandford 3 / Mumtaz Mahal 9
				Deyanira	Mineral 9 / Divertida 20
	Extraneza ○ 1956	Penny Post ◇ 1945	Embrujo	Congreve	Copyright 2 / Per Noi 1
				Encore	Your Majesty 22 / Efilet 1
			Encomienda	Parwiz	Phalaris 1 / Waffles 22
				Estampilla	Saint Wolf 5 / Espatula 9
		Epatante ○ 1947	British Empire	Colombo	Manna 22 / Lady Nairne 11
				Rose of England	Teddy 2 / Perce Neige 3
			Spit Fire	Silurian	Swynford 1 / Glacier 3
				Partenope	Perrier 2 / Mystify 8

Breeder: Haras el Turf
Owner: Stud el Turf
Most important wins: Gran Premio Nacional, Gran Premio Carlos Pellegrini

Racing Career

Age	Starts	Wins
2	2	1
3	5	4
4	2	0
5	8	1
6	11	2
Total	28	8

PRACTICANTE

HABITAT

b.h. 1966 – No. 4 Fam. – foaled in the United States

This son of Sir Gaylord, with his elegant conformation and slightly above-average stature (16.1 hands (1.65 m)) was bought as a yearling at Keeneland for $105,000. He raced only as a three-year-old and proved a high-class miler. All his races were over that distance except the first two which were over 1 mile 2 furlongs (2,000 m) and in which he finished unplaced and second respectively. That first race was the only poor result in the whole of his racing career.

In England Habitat won the Lockinge Stakes at Newbury, beating Jimmy Reppin and Tower Walk, and then the Wills Mile at Goodwood from Lucyrowe and, once again, Jimmy Reppin; but in the St. James's Palace Stakes at Ascot he was beaten by Right Tack. In France Habitat had two successes: the first in the Prix Quincey ahead of Mige and Furibondo, and the second, which was more important, in the Prix du Moulin de Longchamp where he beat Boysie Boy and Montevideo II.

Habitat went to stud in 1970 and immediately proved to be an exceptional stallion, with numerous Group race winners: Habat (William Hill Middle Park Stakes), Rose Bowl (Champion Stakes), Hot Spark (Flying Childers Stakes), Steel Heart (William Hill Middle Park Stakes), Flying Water (1,000 Guineas, Prix Jacques le Marois, Champion Stakes), Hittite Glory (William Hill Middle Park Stakes and Flying Childers Stakes), Habitony (Santa Anita Derby), Double Form (King's Stand Stakes), Marwell (William Hill July Cup, William Hill Cheveley Park Stakes) and Sigy (Prix de l'Abbaye de Longchamp). Habitat headed the stallions' list in England in 1983 and stands at the Grangewilliam Stud in Ireland.

Habitat	Sir Gaylord ○ 1959	Turn-to ○ 1951	Royal Charger	Nearco	**Pharos** 13 / Nogara 4
				Sun Princess	Solario 26 / Mumtaz Begum 9
			Source Sucrée	Admiral Drake	Craig an Eran 16 / **Plucky Liège** 16
				Lavendula II	**Pharos** 13 / Sweet Lavender 1
		Somethingroyal ○ 1952	Princequillo	Prince Rose	Rose Prince 11 / Indolence 10
				Cosquilla	Papyrus 16 / Quick Thought 1
			Imperatrice	Caruso	Polymelian 7 / Sweet Music 2
				Cinquepace	Brown Bud 2 / Assignation 2
	Little Hut ○ 1952	Occupy ○ 1941	Bull Dog	Teddy	Ajax 2 / Rondeau 2
				Plucky Liège	Spearmint 1 / Concertina 16
			Miss Bunting	Bunting	Pennant 8 / Frillery 0
				Mirthful	North Star 4 / Dismiss 23
		Savage Beauty ○ 1934	Challenger II	Swynford	John O'Gaunt 3 / Canterbury Pilgrim 1
				Sword Play	Great Sport 6 / Flash of Steel 2
			Khara	Kai-Sang	The Finn 4 / Kiluna 9
				Decree	Wrack 4 / Royal Message 4

Breeder: Nuckols Bros
Owner: C.W. Engelhard
Most important wins: Prix du Moulin de Longchamp, Lockinge Stakes, Prix Quincey, Wills Mile

Racing Career		
Age	**Starts**	**Wins**
3	8	5

SASSAFRAS

b.h. 1967 – No. 8 Fam. – foaled in France

Sassafras was very close to average height, 16 hands (1.63 m), and during his two season career he ran over distances varying between 7 furlongs (1,400 m) and 1 mile 7½ furlongs (3,100 m). As a two-year-old he only won one race at Vichy but as he grew older he showed considerable progress which, with an impressive crescendo, led him to victory in the Prix de l'Arc de Triomphe. In this race, after an exciting struggle, he beat the great Nijinsky by a head. Sassafras had previously won the Prix du Jockey Club and the Prix Royal Oak but he won this last race only after the first horse to finish, Hallez, was relegated from first place following a stewards' enquiry.

In the same year Sassafras also won two less important races, one at Maisons Laffitte and the other at Longchamp, in addition to an honourable third place behind Stintino and Dragoon in the Prix Lupin. He went to stud in 1971 and in ten years Sassafras has produced numerous Group race winners, both European and non-European, like Henri le Balafre (Prix Royal Oak), Glenaris (Hollywood Oaks), Dom Alaric (Grand Prix de Deauville), Naasiri (Prix Greffulhe), Galway Bay (Coventry Stakes and, in Australia, V.R.C. Craven "A" Stakes), Marmolada (Oaks d'Italia and Premio Lydia Tesio) and Lotar (Premio Emanuele Filiberto and Premio Principe Amedeo).

These excellent results should, however, come as no surprise since Sassafras's pedigree was full of promise. His sire, Sheshoon, half-brother of Charlottesville, was an excellent stayer (winner of the Ascot Gold Cup, the Grand Prix de Saint-Cloud and the Grosser Preis von Baden) and was outstanding as a sire of brood mares, while his dam, Ruta, was half-sister to Roi Dagobert. Moreover, Sassafras's second dam, Dame d'Atour, was related to the successful stallion Shantung, which presents us with direct or collateral lines of descent which are extremely interesting for the purpose of reproduction. Sassafras was exported in 1980 to the United States where he is now standing.

Sassafras	Sheshoon ◇ 1956	Precipitation ◇ 1933	**Hurry On**	Marcovil	Marco 3 / Lady Willikins 12
				Tout Suite	Sainfoin 2 / Star 2
			Double Life	Bachelor's Double	Tredennis 4 / Lady Bawn 21
				Saint Joan	Willbrook 5 / Flo Desmond 2
		Noorani ◇ 1950	Nearco	Pharos	Phalaris 1 / Scapa Flow 13
				Nogara	Havresac II 8 / Catnip 4
			Empire Glory	Singapore	**Gainsborough** 2 / Tetrabbazia 8
				Skyglory	Sky-rocket 16 / Simone 14
	Ruta ◦ 1960	Ratification ◦ 1953	Court Martial	Fair Trial	Fairway 13 / Lady Juror 9
				Instantaneous	**Hurry On** 2 / Picture 1
			Solesa	Solario	**Gainsborough** 2 / Sun Worship 26
				Mesa	Kircubbin 9 / Mackwiller 1
		Dame d'Atour ◦ 1955	Cranach (FR)	Coronach	**Hurry On** 2 / Wet Kiss 4
				Reine Isaure	Blandford 3 / Oriane 12
			Barley Corn	Hyperion	**Gainsborough** 2 / Selene 6
				Schiaparelli	Schiavoni 6 / Aileen 8

Breeder: Dollarstown Stud Establishment
Owner: A. Plesh
Most important wins: Prix de l'Arc de Triomphe, Prix du Jockey Club, Prix Royal Oak

Racing Career		
Age	**Starts**	**Wins**
2	4	1
3	7	5
Total	11	6

SASSAFRAS

NIJINSKY

NIJINSKY

b.h. 1967 – No. 8 Fam. – foaled in Canada

Breeder: E.P. Taylor
Owner: C.W. Engelhard
Most important wins: Dewhurst Stakes, 2,000 Guineas, Derby Stakes, St. Leger Stakes, Irish Sweeps Derby, King George VI and Queen Elizabeth Stakes

Racing Career

Age	Starts	Wins
2	5	5
3	8	6
Total	13	11

Nijinsky was sired by the great Canadian stallion Northern Dancer, and raced at two and three exclusively in Europe. He had a pleasant temperament, extremely powerful hindquarters and light but strong forelimbs. According to his trainer, Vincent O'Brien, Nijinsky was easy to train and a born racer. As a two-year-old he was unbeaten in his five races, one of which was the Dewhurst Stakes at Newmarket over a distance of 7 furlongs (1,400 m), and as a three-year-old he took the Triple Crown, a feat which had last been achieved 35 years before by Bahram. As a three-year-old Nijinsky also had two more important successes in the Irish Sweeps Derby and the King George VI and Queen Elizabeth Stakes where he beat Blakeney, the previous year's winner, but in the autumn Nijinsky suffered two unexpected defeats: the first in France in the Prix de l'Arc de Triomphe when he was beaten by Sassafras, though by only a head and the other in England, in the Champion Stakes, by Lorenzaccio.

He went to stud in 1971 and has sired Group race winners including Green Dancer (Observer Gold Cup, Poule d'Essai des Poulains), Ile de Bourbon (Coronation Cup, King George VI and Queen Elizabeth Diamond Stakes), Princesse Lida (Prix de la Salamandre), Caucasus (Irish St. Leger, Sunset Handicap), Czaravich (Metropolitan Handicap), Niniski (Irish St. Leger, Prix Royal Oak), Upper Nile (Suburban Handicap) and King's Lake (Sussex Stakes).

				Pharos	**Phalaris**	1
Nijinsky	Northern Dancer ○ 1961	Nearctic ● 1954	Nearco		Scapa Flow	13
				Nogara	Havresac II	8
					Catnip	4
			Lady Angela	Hyperion	Gainsborough	2
					Selene	6
				Sister Sarah	Abbots Trace	4
					Sarita	14
		Natalma ○ 1957	Native Dancer	Polynesian	Unbreakable	4
					Black Polly	14
				Geisha	Discovery	23
					Miyako	5
			Almahmoud	Mahmoud	Blenheim	1
					Mah Mahal	9
				Arbitrator	Peace Chance	10
					Mother Goose	2
	Flaming Page ○ 1959	Bull Page ○ 1947	Bull Lea	Bull Dog	Teddy	2
					Plucky Liège	16
				Rose Leaves	Ballot	14
					Colonial	9
			Our Page	Blue Larkspur	Black Servant	8
					Blossom Time	8
				Occult	Dis Donc	31
					Bonnie Witch	4
		Flaring Top ◇ 1947	Menow	Pharamond II	**Phalaris**	1
					Selene	6
				Alcibiades	Supremus	32
					Regal Roman	8
			Flaming Top	Omaha	Gallant Fox	4
					Flambino	17
				Firetop	Man o' War	4
					Summit	8

BRIGADIER GERARD

BRIGADIER GERARD

b.h. 1968 – No. 14 Fam. – foaled in England

Brigadier Gerard was a good-sized horse (16.2 hands (1.68 m)), well-built with a deep chest and a perfect natural stance. His breeder, a well-known racing journalist, managed to obtain this very valuable horse from a brood mare who was only just reasonable, and a stallion with a limited reputation. Brigadier Gerard was out of La Paiva, a mare whose direct female line has to be traced as far back as her great-granddam before a winner can be found.

However, in spite of the fact that La Paiva's dam never ran and her granddam never won, both produced first class offspring. If Brigadier Gerard's pedigree is more closely analyzed it becomes clear that his great-great-granddam, Molly Desmond, daughter of the fantastic Pretty Polly and winner of the Cheveley Park Stakes, produced two excellent horses: Zodiac (Irish St. Leger, Irish Derby) and Spike Island (Irish 2,000 Guineas, Irish Derby).

Although Brigadier Gerard's sire, Queen's Hussar, had not been a great favourite in breeding circles, he was nevertheless the winner of the Lockinge Stakes and the Sussex Stakes. Brigadier Gerard raced for three seasons from the ages of two to four, winning over distances of between 5 furlongs (1,000 m) and 1½ miles (2,400 m). He lost only one race, when he was three, when he was beaten by the Derby winner Roberto in the Benson and Hedges Gold Cup at York. As a two-year-old he won the Berkshire Stakes over 5 furlongs (1,000 m) at Newbury, the Champagne Stakes over 6 furlongs (1,200 m) at Salisbury, the Washington Singer Stakes over 6 furlongs (1,200 m), again at Newbury, and the Middle Park Stakes (Group I) over 6 furlongs (1,200 m) at Newmarket.

As a three-year-old he won the 2,000 Guineas (Group I), the St. James's Palace Stakes (Group II), the Sussex Stakes (Group I), the Goodwood Mile (Group III) and the Queen Elizabeth II Stakes (Group II), all over a mile, and the Champion Stakes (Group I) over 1 mile 2 furlongs (2,000 m). As a four-year-old Brigadier Gerard had seven more wins, taking the Lockinge Stakes (Group II) over 1 mile (1,600 m), the Westbury Stakes (Group III), the Prince of Wales's Stakes (Group II), the Eclispe Stakes (Group I), all over 1 mile 2 furlongs (2,000 m), the King George VI and Queen Elizabeth Stakes (Group I) over 1½ miles (2,400 m) and, for the second time running, the Champion Stakes and the Queen Elizabeth II Stakes.

He has been at stud since 1973 and serves for a syndicate to which the breeder has ceded only 24 shares, with binding clauses concerning the sale and export of both the stallion and his offspring. Each year, those of Brigadier Gerard's sons owned by his breeder which are surplus to his needs have been placed at the disposal of breeders with brood mares, with whom a union could be considered interesting from the point of view of exploiting the bloodline of the stallion as much as possible. Brigadier Gerard has met with only limited success at stud, though he has sired good winners such as Light Cavalry (St. Leger, King Edward Stakes, Princess of Wales's Stakes), R.B. Chesne (Laurent Perrier Champagne Stakes) and Vayrann (Champion Stakes).

Breeder: J. Hislop
Owner: J. Hislop
Most important wins: William Hill Middle Park Stakes, 2,000 Guineas, Sussex Stakes, Eclipse Stakes, King George VI and Queen Elizabeth Stakes, Champion Stakes (twice), Queen Elizabeth II Stakes (twice), St. James's Palace Stakes, Prince of Wales's Stakes

Racing Career

Age	Starts	Wins
2	4	4
3	6	6
4	8	7
Total	18	17

				Fair Trial	Fairway	13
			Petition		Lady Juror	9
		March Past		Art Paper	Artist's Proof	14
		• 1950			Quire	16
				William of Valence	Vatout	3
	Queen's Hussar		Marcelette		Queen Iseult	21
	○ 1960			Permavon	Stratford	1
					Curl Paper	8
				Gold Bridge	Golden Boss*	19
			Vilmorin		Flying Diadem	22
		Jojo		Queen of the Meadows	Fairway	13
		○/□ 1950			Queen of the Blues	7
				Fair Trial	Fairway	13
			Fairy Jane		Lady Juror	9
				Light Tackle	Salmon-Trout	19
					True Joy	19
Brigadier Gerard				Rose Prince	Prince Palatine	1
			Prince Rose		Eglantine	11
		Prince Chevalier		Indolence	Gay Crusader	1
		○ 1943			Barrier	10
				Abbot's Speed	Abbots Trace	4
			Chevalerie		Mary Gaunt	22
	La Paiva			Kassala	Cylgad	22
	◇ 1956				Farizade	9
				Papyrus	Tracery	19
			Horus		Miss Matty	16
		Brazen Molly		Lady Peregrine	White Eagle	5
		○ 1940			Lisma	9
				Phalaris	Polymelus	3
			Molly Adare		Bromus	1
*or Swynford (No. 1 Fam.)				Molly Desmond	Desmond	16
					Pretty Polly	14

MILL REEF

b.h. 1968 – 22 Fam. – foaled in the United States

Mill Reef was a small horse (15.3 hands (1.58 m)) but proved to be a formidable galloper able to give an impressive final sprint. He was trained in England by Ian Balding and raced from two to four. Mill Reef made his racing debut at Salisbury by winning the Salisbury Stakes and after an easy success in the Coventry Stakes he was sent to France where he was beaten by My Swallow in the Prix Robert Papin. Later that year, however, he recorded three more successes by winning the Gimcrack Stakes, the Imperial Stakes and the Dewhurst Stakes.

As a three-year-old, having won the Greenham Stakes, Mill Reef encountered the second and last defeat of his career in the 2,000 Guineas, in which he came second behind Brigadier Gerard but this time beating My Swallow. After this race, the son of Never Bend went from strength to strength, taking the Epsom Derby, the Eclipse Stakes (beating Caro by 4 lengths), the King George VI and Queen Elizabeth Stakes and the Prix de l'Arc de Triomphe. In his four-year season, Mill Reef continued with his series of wins, taking the Prix Ganay in France and the Coronation Cup in England.

On 30 August that year, during training for the Prix de l'Arc de Triomphe, he fractured his near foreleg and this accident put an end to his track career. His sociable, calm temperament helped the course of treatment in which his whole leg was put in a plaster cast, and after he had recovered he was syndicated as a stallion, at the National Stud in England. Mill Reef has already sired the Epsom Derby winner, Shirley Heights (b.h. 1975) and Acamas (b.h. 1975), winner of the Prix du Jockey Club. Two of the best horses to be sired by Mill Reef in subsequent seasons are Glint of Gold, winner of the Italian Derby the first year that race was opened to horses foaled in any country, and Fairy Footsteps, winner of the 1,000 Guineas.

Mill Reef	Never Bend ○ 1960	Nasrullah ○ 1940	Nearco	Pharos	Phalaris 1 / Scapa Flow 13
				Nogara	Havresac II 8 / Catnip 4
			Mumtaz Begum	Blenheim	Blandford 3 / Malva 1
				Mumtaz Mahal	The Tetrarch 2 / Lady Josephine 9
		Lalun ○ 1952	Djeddah	Djebel	Tourbillon 13 / Loïka 5
				Djezima	Astérus 9 / Heldifann 13
			Be Faithful	Bimelech	Black Toney 10 / La Troienne 1
				Blood Root	Blue Larkspur 8 / Knockaney Bridge 19
	Milan Mill ○ 1962	Princequillo ○ 1940	Prince Rose	Rose Prince	Prince Palatine 1 / Eglantine 11
				Indolence	Gay Crusader 1 / Barrier 10
			Cosquilla	Papyrus	Tracery 19 / Miss Matty 16
				Quick Thought	White Eagle 5 / Mindful 1
		Virginia Water □ 1953	Count Fleet	Reigh Count	Sunreigh 8 / Contessina 2
				Quickly	Haste 23 / Stephanie 6
			Red Ray	Hyperion	Gainsborough 2 / Selene 6
				Infra Red	Ethnarch 1 / Black Ray 22

Breeder: Paul Mellon
Owner: Paul Mellon
Most important wins: Derby Stakes, King George VI and Queen Elizabeth Stakes, Eclipse Stakes, Prix de l'Arc de Triomphe, Prix Ganay, Coronation Cup

Racing Career

Age	Starts	Wins
2	6	5
3	6	5
4	2	2
Total	14	12

STAR APPEAL

b.h. 1970 – No. 5 Fam. – foaled in Ireland

A solidly-built average-sized horse (16 hands (1.63 m)), Star Appeal was the son of a stallion from the Dormello Stud, the Italian Derby winner Appiani II and the brood mare Sterna, who was by the German horse Neckar, dam of seven more winners. He was active on the racetracks from the ages of two to five and achieved his victories over distances ranging from 6 furlongs (1,200 m) to 1½ miles (2,400 m). As a two- and three-year-old he won several unimportant races and handicaps but came third in the Irish St. Leger and second in the Gallinule Stakes (Group II).

As a four-year-old in Germany, Star Appeal won the Grosser Preis der Badischen Wirtschaft (Group II) over 1 mile 1 furlong (1,800 m) and the Concentra Pokal des Deutschen Investment Trust (Group II) over 1 mile 2 furlongs (2,000 m) while he was second in the Grosser Preis der Stadt Gelsenkirchen (Group II) and fourth in the Champion Stakes in England. As a five-year-old, Star Appeal proved to be a horse of international caliber, winning the Gran Premio di Milano, the Eclipse Stakes and, most importantly, the Prix de l'Arc de Triomphe. In the Arc, which brought Star Appeal to the forefront in world racing, the horses he beat included Allez France, Ivanjica, Dahlia, Nobiliary, Duke of Marmalade, Bruni and Green Dancer. The totalizator's odds (119 to 1) gives an exact idea of Star Appeal's apparent chance on the eve of this great French race.

In Germany that year he repeated his success in the Grosser Preis der Badischen Wirtschaft, but failed to get better than fourth place in the Grosser Preis von Baden, while, in England, he came third in the Benson and Hedges Cup and fourth in the Champion Stakes and in America he finished fifth in the Washington D.C. International at Laurel Park. In 1976 Star Appeal was sent to stud, where he attracted a great deal of interest from the breeders. One of his fillies, Madam Gay, won the Prix de Diane de Revlon in 1981.

Star Appeal	Appiani II ○ 1963	Herbager ○ 1956	Vandale	Plassy	Bosworth 6 / Pladda 13
				Vanille	La Farina 4 / Vaya 3
			Flagette	Escamillo	**Firdaussi** 1 / Estoril 14
				Fidgette	**Firdaussi** 1 / Boxeuse 16
		Angela Rucellai ○ 1954	Rockefella	Hyperion	Gainsborough 2 / Selene 6
				Rockfel	Felstead 3 / Rockliffe 7
			Aristareta	Niccolò Dell'Arca	Coronach 4 / Nogara 4
				Acquaforte	Blenheim 1 / Althea 4
	Sterna ● 1960	Neckar ◆ 1948	Ticino	Athanasius	Ferro 5 / Athanasie 16
				Terra	Aditi 9 / Teufelsrose 20
			Nixe	Arjaman	**Herold** 4 / Aditja 9
				Nanon	Graf Isolani 1 / Nella da Gubbio 4
		Stammesart ○ 1944	Alchimist	**Herold**	Dark Ronald 9 / Hornisse 4
				Aversion	**Nuage** 5 / Antwort 9
			Stammesfahne	Flamboyant	Tracery 19 / Simonath 16
				Selika	**Nuage** 5 / Safety 5

Breeder: Gestüt Rottgen
Owner: W. Zeitelhack
Most important wins: Gran Premio di Milano, Eclipse Stakes, Prix de l'Arc de Triomphe, Grosser Preis der Badischen Wirtschaft (twice)

Racing Career

Age	Starts	Wins
2	5	2
3	9	3
4	14	2
5	11	4
Total	39	11

SECRETARIAT

SECRETARIAT

ch.b. 1970 – No. 2 Fam. – foaled in the United States

This half-brother of Sir Gaylord was a horse with a short back and very attractive loins. He was 16.2 hands (1.67 m) with a girth of 6 ft 4 ins (1.93 m), a weight of 1,130 lb (513 kg), powerful limbs and straight, lean hocks which enabled him to achieve a long stride. Secretariat raced at two- and three-years old, over almost all distances from 6 furlongs (1,200 m) to 1 mile 5 furlongs (2,600 m).

He made his debut as a two-year-old at Aqueduct, finishing fourth in a maiden race before winning a similar race there only ten days later. After a win at Saratoga, he carried off two important races on that course, the Sanford Stakes over 6 furlongs (1,200 m), the second the Hopeful Stakes over 6½ furlongs (1,300 m). Secretariat then went to Belmont Park where he triumphed in the Futurity Stakes, beating Stop the Music over 6½ furlongs (1,300 m) but in his next race, the 1-mile Champagne Stakes, he finished first, only to be relegated to second in favour of Stop the Music. In the Laurel Futurity Stakes over 8½ furlongs

(1,700 m), Secretariat took immediate revenge on Stop the Music with an 8 lengths victory, and his year ended with a win in the Garden State Stakes over the same distance.

At three, Secretariat started by winning two races in succession at Aqueduct: the Bay Shore Stakes (Group III) over 7 furlongs (1,400 m) and the Gotham Stakes (Group II) over 1 mile (1,600 m), but two weeks later he was only third in the Wood Memorial Stakes on the same track, beaten by Angle Light and Sham. After this disappointing result Secretariat more than restored his reputation by winning the American Triple Crown, the Kentucky Derby over 1 mile 2 furlongs (2,000 m) at Churchill Downs, the Preakness Stakes over 1 mile 1½ furlongs (1,900 m) at Pimlico, beating Sham by 2½ lengths in both races, while in the Belmont Stakes (1½ miles (2,400 m)) he stormed home by 31 lengths.

After winning an invitation race at Arlington by 9 lengths from My Gallant, Secretariat suffered his second defeat of

that year, losing to Onion in the Whitney Stakes at Saratoga, but he immediately redeemed himself, however, by winning the Marlboro Cup Invitational Handicap (Group I) over 1 mile 1 furlong (1,800 m) at Belmont Park. After this win he was beaten again, this time by Prove Out, in the Woodward Stakes at Belmont, over 1½ miles (2,400 m), but he ended his career with two important successes: the first in the Man o' War Stakes (Group I) and the second at Woodbine, in the Canadian International Championship Stakes over 1 mile 5 furlongs (2,600 m), beating Big Spruce by 6½ lengths.

Secretariat went to stud in 1974 and in his first few years has sired some excellent winners both in Europe and America, including General Assembly (Travers Stakes, Hopeful Stakes), Medaille d'Or (Coronation Futurity) and Dactylographer (William Hill Futurity), but from a horse who in 1973 was even given the title "Sportsman of the Year" in the United States, it would perhaps have been reasonable to expect something more.

Breeder: Meadow Stud
Owner: Meadow Stable
Most important wins: Hopeful Stakes, Futurity Stakes, Laurel Futurity, Kentucky Derby, Preakness Stakes, Belmont Stakes, Marlboro Cup Invitational Handicap, Man o' War Stakes, Canadian International Championship Stakes

Racing Career

Age	Starts	Wins
2	9	7
3	12	9
Total	21	16

Secretariat						
	Bold Ruler ● 1954	Nasrullah ○ 1940	Nearco	Pharos	Phalaris Scapa Flow	1 13
				Nogara	Havresac II Catnip	8 4
			Mumtaz Begum	Blenheim	Blandford Malva	3 1
				Mumtaz Mahal	The Tetrarch Lady Josephine	2 9
		Miss Disco ○ 1944	Discovery	Display	Fair Play Cicuta	9 2
				Ariadne	Light Brigade Adrienne	8 23
			Outdone	Pompey	Sun Briar Cleopatra	8 3
				Sweep Out	Sweep On Dugout	A3 8
	Somethingroyal ○ 1952	Princequillo ○ 1940	Prince Rose	Rose Prince	Prince Palatine Eglantine	1 11
				Indolence	Gay Crusader Barrier	1 10
			Cosquilla	Papyrus	Tracery Miss Matty	19 16
				Quick Thought	White Eagle Mindful	5 1
		Imperatrice ○ 1938	Caruso	Polymelian	Polymelus Pasquita	3 7
				Sweet Music	Harmonicon Isette	2 2
			Cinquepace	Brown Bud	Brown Prince June Rose	3 2
				Assignation	Teddy Cinq à Sept	2 2

DAHLIA

ch. m. 1970 – No. 13 Fam. – foaled in the United States

Dahlia was a daughter of Vaguely Noble and in appearance revealed several rather masculine traits. She was a solid, strong mare, of average size but erratic in her performance. In her racing career, which lasted for five seasons, she proved to be a racemare of outstanding qualities. Her wins range from 5 furlongs (1,000 m) to 1 mile 5 furlongs (2,600 m) and include important victories both in Europe and in America. Dahlia achieved her first win in France as a two-year-old in the Prix Yacowlef at Deauville over 5 furlongs (1,000 m). After this she was twice unplaced and she ended her first year with a second in the Prix des Reservoirs at Longchamp.

At three she began by winning the Prix de la Grotte (Group III) over 1 mile (1,600 m), but was only third to Allez France in the Poule d'Essai des Pouliches. After this she won the Prix Saint-Alary (Group I) over 1 mile 2 furlongs (2,000 m), again at Longchamp, but this victory too was followed by another defeat, again by Allez France, in the Prix de Diane. Dahlia then won the Irish Guinness Oaks and only a week later she won the King George VI and Queen Elizabeth Stakes at Ascot in most impressive style. On her return to France she won the Prix Niel (Group III) over 1 mile 3 furlongs (2,200 m), but in the space of less than a month she was to suffer two more defeats, in the Prix Vermeille, won by Allez France, and in the Prix de l'Arc de Triomphe, won by Rheingold. She finished unplaced in both races, but both failures can be attributed at least in part to the injury she sustained in the Vermeille. As usual, however, Dahlia quickly redeemed herself by winning the Washington D.C. International at Laurel in the United States.

As a four-year-old she achieved more important wins, but as had occurred the previous year, every meeting with Allez France ended in defeat. In Europe she won the Grand Prix de Saint-Cloud, triumphed for the second year running in the King George VI and Queen Elizabeth Stakes and took the Benson and Hedges Gold Cup, while in America she achieved two brilliant successes, in the Man o' War Stakes at Belmont Park and in the Canadian International Championship Stakes, Canada's most important race, at Woodbine. In the Washington D.C. International, however, she failed in her attempt to repeat the success of the previous year, not having by any means the best of runs and managing only third place behind Admetus. As a five-year-old, Dahlia won only one race, the Benson and Hedges Gold Cup, repeating the success of the previous year, but she kept going in America as a six-year-old, managing to take one more important win, the Hollywood Invitational Handicap, and, all in all, despite the last two rather disappointing years, she had a brilliant racing career, putting her on a par with the greatest racemares of all time.

Breeder: N.B. Hunt
Owner: N.B. Hunt
Most important wins: Irish Guinness Oaks, King George VI and Queen Elizabeth Stakes (twice), Washington D.C. International, Grand Prix de Saint-Cloud, Benson and Hedges Gold Cup (twice), Man o' War Stakes, Canadian International Championship Stakes, Hollywood Invitational Handicap

Dahlia	Vaguely Noble ○ 1965	Vienna ◇ 1957	Aureole	Hyperion	Gainsborough 2 / Selene 6
				Angelola	Donatello II 14 / Feola 2
			Turkish Blood	Turkhan	Bahram 16 / Theresina 6
				Rusk	Manna 22 / Baby Polly 14
		Noble Lassie ○ 1956	Nearco	Pharos	Phalaris 1 / Scapa Flow 13
				Nogara	Havresac II 8 / Catnip 4
			Belle Sauvage	Big Game	Bahram 16 / Myrobella 6
				Tropical Sun	Hyperion 6 / Brulette 1
	Charming Alibi ◇ 1963	Honeys Alibi ○ 1952	Alibhai	Hyperion	Gainsborough 2 / Selene 6
				Teresina	Tracery 19 / Blue Tit 6
			Honeymoon	Beau Père	Son-in-Law 5 / Cinna 3
				Panoramic	Chance Shot 3 / Dustwhirl 8
		Adorada II ◇ 1947	Hierocles	Abjer	Astérus 9 / Zariba 9
				Loïka	Gay Crusader 1 / Coeur à Coeur 5
			Gilded Wave	Gallant Fox	Sir Gallahad III 16 / Marguerite 4
				Ondulation	Sweeper 8 / Frizette 13

Racing Career

Age	Starts	Wins
2	4	1
3	10	6
4	10	5
5	11	1
6	13	2
Total	48	15

DAHLIA

ALLEZ FRANCE

b.m. 1970 – No. 1 Fam. – foaled in the United States

Allez France is a horse of elegant appearance and rather elongated lines. Her racing career took place mostly in France, and lasted from two to five with her wins confined to distances of between 1 mile (1,600 m) and 1½ miles (2,400 m). She made her racing debut as a two-year-old at Longchamp in September, winning the Prix Toutevoie over 1 mile (1,600 m), after which she went on to win the Critérium des Pouliches over the same course and distance.

As a three-year-old she won the Poule d'Essai des Pouliches on her first appearance, but was unplaced in the Prix Lupin, won by Kalamoun. She nevertheless redeemed herself just under a month later at Chantilly by winning the Prix de Diane over 1 mile 2½ furlongs (2,100 m) but in early September she managed no more than fourth place in the Prix de la Nonette at Longchamp. Allez France came back to her best three weeks later in the Prix Vermeille over 1½ miles (2,400 m) beating Hurry Harriet, after which she was second to Rheingold in the Prix de l'Arc de Triomphe, and in the Champion Stakes, to Hurry Harriet.

Allex France was unbeaten as a four-year-old, carrying off five brilliant victories in the Prix d'Harcourt, the Prix Ganay, the Prix d'Ispahan, taking 10.8 seconds to cover the last furlong (200 m), the Prix Foy and lastly the Prix de l'Arc de Triomphe, in which she beat Comtesse de Loir by only a head. In the first two races of the year she had beaten her old rival Dahlia, whom she had already defeated in the fillies' classics the year before.

Allez France raced seven more times as a five-year-old although she won only three races: the Prix Ganay for the second year running, the Prix Dollar and the Prix Foy, also for the second time. Allez France then attempted the Prix de l'Arc de Triomphe for the third time but was injured during the race and finished fifth. Though she recovered in time to run in the Champion Stakes at Newmarket she was beaten into second place by Rose Bowl and her magnificent career ended in an anti-climax when she was last of 11 in the National Thoroughbred Championship at Santa Anita.

Allez France	Sea Bird ◇ 1962	Dan Cupid ◇ 1956	Native Dancer	Polynesian	Unbreakable 4 / Black Polly 14
				Geisha	Discovery 23 / Miyako 5
			Vixenette	Sickle	Phalaris 1 / Selene 6
				Lady Reynard	Gallant Fox 4 / Nerva 4
		Sicalade ○ 1956	Sicambre	Prince Bio	Prince Rose 10 / Biologie 1
				Sif	Rialto 12 / Suavita 7
			Marmelade	Maurepas	Aethelstan 23 / Brocéliande 12
				Couleur	Biribi 27 / Colour Bar 2
	Priceless Gem ○ 1963	Hail to Reason ● 1958	Turn-to	Royal Charger	Nearco 4 / Sun Princess 9
				Source Soucrée	Admiral Drake 16 / Lavendula II 1
			Nothirdchance	Blue Swords	Blue Larkspur 8 / Flaming Swords 7
				Galla Colors	Sir Gallahad III 16 / Rouge et Noir 4
		Searching ○ 1952	War Admiral	Man o'War	Fair Play 9 / Mahubah 4
				Brushup	Sweep 8 / Annette K. 11
			Big Hurry	Black Toney	Peter Pan 2 / Belgravia 10
				La Troienne	Teddy 2 / Hélène de Troie 1

Breeder: Bieber-Jacobs Stable
Owner: M D. Wildenstein
Most important wins: Critérium des Pouliches, Poule d'Essai des Pouliches, Prix de Diane, Prix Vermeille, Prix Ganay (twice), Prix de l'Arc de Triomphe, Prix d'Ispahan, Prix d'Harcourt

Racing Career

Age	Starts	Wins
2	2	2
3	7	3
4	5	5
5	7	3
Total	21	13

ALLEZ FRANCE

NONOALCO

b.h. 1971 – No. 2 Fam. – foaled in the United States

Sired by the Canadian stallion Nearctic, Nonoalco has a particularly attractive conformation and is a tall horse (16.3 hands (1.70 m)). He was bought for the famous actress, Maria Felix, at the Keeneland Sales for $30,000, a ridiculously small amount compared with the prices that have been paid over the past few years. Nonoalco raced at two and three, and was at his best over 1 mile (1,600 m). In his first year he was beaten only once, by Mississipian in the Grand Criterium (Group I), but before that he had won the Prix Morny (Group I) and the Prix de la Salamandre (Group I), over distances of 6 furlongs (1,200 m) and 7 furlongs (1,400 m) respectively.

Nonoalco reached the high spot of his career at the age of three when he surprised many at Newmarket by winning the 2,000 Guineas (Group 1), skilfully ridden by Yves Saint-Martin, to beat Giacometti and Apalachee. In England he also ran in the Epsom Derby, but as was expected, did not stay a mile and a half, but back over 1 mile (1,600 m), he won the Prix Jacques Le Marois (Group I) at Deauville in France.

Nonoalco went to stud in 1975 and after one year in France was moved to Ireland. He has sired some good winners, mostly fillies, like Nonoalca, winner of two Group III races in France, Mesange Bleue who came to the fore in Italy by winning the Premio Dormello (Group III) and Melyno (1979), winner of the Poule d'Essai des Poulains (Group I). As yet he has failed to sire the top class animal on which all hopes of continuing his bloodline have been based, and he was exported to Japan in 1981.

				Polymelus	3
			Phalaris	Bromus	1
		Pharos		**Chaucer**	1
			Scapa Flow	Anchora	13
	Nearco ● 1935			Rabelais	14
			Havresac II	Hors Concours	8
		Nogara		Spearmint	1
Nearctic ● 1954			Catnip	Sibola	4
				Bayardo	10
			Gainsborough	Rosedrop	2
		Hyperion		**Chaucer**	1
			Selene	Serenissima	6
	Lady Angela ◇ 1944			Tracery	19
			Abbots Trace	Abbots Anne	4
		Sister Sarah		Swynford	1
Nonoalco			Sarita	Molly Desmond	14
				Teddy	2
			Sir Gallahad III	Plucky Liège	16
		Roman		Buchan	16
			Buckup	Look Up	20
	Hasty Road ○ 1951			Display	2
			Discovery	Ariadne	23
		Traffic Court		Broomstick	16
			Traffic	Traverse	3
Seximée ◇ 1966				**Sir Gallahad III**	16
			Fighting Fox	Marguerite	4
		Crafty Admiral		War Admiral	11
			Admiral's Lady	Boola Brook	8
	Jambo ◇ 1959			Equipoise	5
			Shut Out	Goose Egg	16
		Bank Account		Balladier	3
			Balla Tryst	Twilight Tryst	2

Breeder: F.B. Mars
Owner: M.F. Berger
Most important wins: Prix Morny, Prix de la Salamandre, 2,000 Guineas, Prix Jacques de Marois, Prix du Rond-Point

Racing Career		
Age	Starts	Wins
2	4	3
3	6	4
Total	10	7

GRUNDY

ch.h. 1972 – No. 8 Fam. – foaled in Ireland

Grundy was an average-sized horse (15.3 hands (1.62 m)), with an elegant conformation, attractive limbs, well-developed muscles and a broad, deep chest. He raced in Ireland and England at the age of two and three, winning over distances ranging from 6 furlongs (1,200 m) to 1½ miles (2,400 m). As a two-year-old he was unbeaten in his four races, which included the William Hill Dewhurst Stakes at Newmarket and the Champagne Stakes at Doncaster.

In his first race as a three-year-old, he was second in the Clerical Medical Greenham Stakes (Group III) at Newbury, to an average horse named Mark Anthony, and in the 2,000 Guineas he was beaten by Bolkonski, but after this defeat he gained four brilliant successes in the Irish 2,000 Guineas, the Epsom Derby, ahead of Nobiliary, the Irish Sweeps Derby and the King George VI and Queen Elizabeth Diamond Stakes in a record-breaking finish with Bustino. The last race of his career was the Benson and Hedges Gold Cup in which he came only fourth behind Dahlia, Card King and Star Appeal.

Grundy went to stud in 1976 and although he has already sired several Group race winners, including the Oaks heroine Bireme and the Ascot Gold Cup winner Little Woy, has still not produced a horse with good enough qualities to satisfy the expectations placed on him, and he was sold to Japan in the autumn of 1983 in a deal which provoked great controversy.

					Polymelus	3
				Phalaris	Bromus	1
			Fairway		Chaucer	1
				Scapa Flow	Anchora	13
		Honeyway ● 1941			Tracery	19
				Papyrus	Miss Matty	16
			Honey Buzzard		White Eagle	5
				Lady Peregrine	Lisma	9
	Great Nephew ○ 1963				Gainsborough	2
				Hyperion	Selene	6
			Admiral's Walk		Roi Hérode	1
				Tabaris	Tip-toe	1
		Sybil's Niece ◇ 1951			Pharos	13
				Nearco	Nogara	4
			Sybil's Sister		Abbots Trace	4
				Sister Sarah	Sarita	14
Grundy					Rabelais	14
				Rialto	La Grêlée	12
			Wild Risk		Blandford	3
				Wild Violet	Wood Violet	3
		Worden ◇ 1949			Solario	26
				Sind	Mirawala	14
			Sans Tares		Teddy	2
				Tara	Jean Gow	13
	Word From Lundy ○ 1966				**Nearco**	4
				Nasrullah	Mumtaz Begum	9
			Princely Gift		Blue Peter	20
				Blue Gem	Sparkle	13
		Lundy Princess ○ 1960			Flamboyant	16
				Flamingo	**Lady Peregrine**	9
			Lundy Parrot		Friar Marcus	20
				Waterval	Lilaline	8

Breeder: The Overbury Stud
Owner: Carlo Vittadini
Most important wins: William Hill Dewhurst Stakes, Champagne Stakes, Irish 2,000 Guineas, Derby, Irish Sweeps Derby, King George VI and Queen Elizabeth Diamond Stakes

Racing Career		
Age	**Starts**	**Wins**
2	4	4
3	7	4
Total	11	8

EXCELLER

b.h. 1973 – No. 21 Fam. – foaled in the United States

Exceller was bought as a yearling by the Texan oil tycoon Nelson Bunker Hunt for $25,000, even though there were rumours that he was not sound. These fears were nevertheless fully allayed through his racing career which lasted until he was five and saw him win over distances ranging from 1 mile 1 furlong (1,800 m) to 1 mile 7½ furlongs (3,100 m). He went into training in France and at Evry won his first two-year-old race, the only win he had that year. In his three-year season he won the Prix du Lys and had two brilliant successes in the Grand Prix de Paris and the Prix Royal Oak, both over the demanding distance of 1 mile 7½ furlongs (3,100 m). As a four-year-old Exceller won the Grand Prix de Saint-Cloud and the Coronation Cup at Epsom, and in the King George VI and Queen Elizabeth Diamond Stakes he finished third behind The Minstrel and Orange Bay. He then moved to America where he won the Canadian International Championship Stakes at Woodbine over a distance of 1 mile 5 furlongs (2,600 m) while in the Washington D.C. International, run in heavy going, he had to be satisfied with third place.

Having become acclimatized in America, Exceller had a notable season as a five-year-old, when he won seven races from ten starts. After winning the Arcadia Handicap (Group III) at Santa Anita, he took the Hollywood Gold Cup over 1 mile 2 furlongs (2,000 m) in a time of 1 minute 59.2 seconds, the Sunset Handicap (also at Hollywood Park) and the Jockey Club Gold Cup at Belmont Park. In this last race, after having been 20 lengths behind the group at one stage, he headed Seattle Slew near the line and won by a nose. This was, without any doubt, Exceller's greatest achievement.

In the same year he won other Group I races, the Hollywood Invitational Turf Handicap over 1½ miles (2,400 m), the San Juan Capistrano Invitational Handicap over 1 mile 6 furlongs (2,800 m) at Santa Anita and the Oak Tree Invitational Handicap over 1½ miles (2,400 m) on the same course. As a six-year-old, Exceller appeared four more times on the track but failed to win though he was placed in good company in his last race, the Century Handicap, when he broke a bone and was retired to the Gainesway Stud in Kentucky. Despite his unsuccessful last year he was, without doubt, a high-class racehorse.

Exceller	Vaguely Noble ○ 1965	Vienna ◇ 1957	Aureole	**Hyperion**	Gainsborough 2 / Selene 6
				Angelola	Donatello II 14 / Feola 2
			Turkish Blood	Turkhan	**Bahram** 16 / Theresina 6
				Rusk	Manna 22 / Baby Polly 14
		Noble Lassie ○ 1956	**Nearco**	Pharos	Phalaris 1 / Scapa Flow 13
				Nogara	Havresac II 8 / Catnip 4
			Belle Sauvage	Big Game	**Bahram** 16 / Myrobella 6
				Tropical Sun	**Hyperion** 6 / Brulette 1
	Too Bold • 1964	Bald Eagle ○ 1955	**Nasrullah**	**Nearco**	Pharos 13 / Nogara 4
				Mumtaz Begum	Blenheim 1 / Mumtaz Mahal 9
			Siama	Tiger	**Bull Dog** 16 / Starless Moment 13
				China Face	Display 2 / Sweepilla 4
		Hidden Talent ○ 1956	Dark Star	Royal Gem II	Dhoti 2 / French Gem 1
				Isolde	**Bull Dog** 16 / Fiji 3
			Dangerous Dame	**Nasrullah**	**Nearco** 4 / Mumtaz Begum 9
				Lady Kells	His Highness 2 / Anyway 21

Breeder: Mrs C.W. Engelhard
Owner: N.B. Hunt
Most important wins: Grand Prix de Paris, Prix Royal Oak, Grand Prix de Saint Cloud, Coronation Cup, Hollywood Gold Cup, Sunset Handicap, Jockey Club Gold Cup, Canadian International Championship Stakes, Hollywood Invitational Turf Handicap, San Juan Capistrano Invitational Handicap, Oak Tree Invitational Handicap

Racing Career		
Age	**Starts**	**Wins**
2	4	1
3	6	4
4	9	3
5	10	7
6	4	0
Total	33	15

ALLEGED

b.h. 1974 – No. 2 Fam. – foaled in the United States

Alleged was bought as a yearling for $34,000 and was trained by Vincent O'Brien when he raced in Europe, winning over distances from 7 furlongs (1,400 m) to 1½ miles (2,400 m). He made his debut in Ireland, winning his only race at the age of two over 7 furlongs (1,400 m) at The Curragh. As a three-year-old, after winning the Gallinule Stakes (Group II) and the Royal Whip Stakes (Group III) in Ireland, Alleged spreadeagled his rivals in the Great Voltigeur Stakes at York. He then suffered the only defeat in his career in the Doncaster St. Leger when he was beaten by Dunfermline, a filly owned and bred by Queen Elizabeth II. Alleged promptly redeemed himself by winning the Prix de l'Arc de Triomphe at Longchamp,

where Balmerino, Crystal Palace and Dunfermline followed him home.

As a four-year-old he ran three more races, repeating the success of the previous year in the Royal Whip, winning the Prix Prince d'Orange (Group III) and confirming his merit in the Prix de l'Arc de Triomphe, which he won for the second year running as his great grandsire, Ribot, had done before him. In this second Arc success Alleged went to the front early in the home straight and won by 3 lengths from the filly Trillion, with another filly, Dancing Maid, third in a field of 18.

Alleged went to stud in 1979 and though he cannot yet be properly evaluated as a stallion he has already sired a number of promising winners.

				Bellini	2
		Ribot	Tenerani	Tofanella	6
	Tom Rolfe ○ 1962		Romanella	El Greco	14
				Barbara Burrini	4
		Pocahontas	Roman	Sir Gallahad III	16
				Buckup	20
Hoist the Flag ○ 1968			How	**Princequillo**	1
				The Squaw II	9
		War Admiral	Man o'War	Fair Play	9
				Mahubah	4
	Wavy Navy ○ 1954		Brushup	Sweep	8
				Annette K	11
		Triomphe	Tourbillon	Ksar	3
				Durban	13
			Melibee	Firdaussi	1
				Metairie	5
Alleged		**Princequillo**	Prince Rose	Rose Prince	11
				Indolence	10
	Prince John ◇ 1953		Cosquilla	Papyrus	16
				Quick Thought	1
		Not Afraid	Count Fleet	Reigh Count	2
				Quickly	6
			Banish Fear	Blue Larkspur	8
				Herodiade	14
Princess Pout ○ 1966		Determine	Alibhai	Hyperion	6
				Teresina	6
			Koubis	Mahmoud	9
	Determined Lady • 1959			Brown Biscuit	5
		War Admiral	Man o'War	4	
		Tumbling		Brushup	11
			Up the Hill	Jacopo	22
				Gentle Tryst	2

Breeder: Mrs June McKnight
Owner: R.E. Sangster
Most important wins: Prix de l'Arc de Triomphe (twice), Gallinule Stakes, Great Voltigeur Stakes, Royal Whip Stakes (twice)

Racing Career

Age	Starts	Wins
2	1	1
3	6	5
4	3	3
Total	10	9

THE MINSTREL

Racing Career		
Age	Starts	Wins
2	3	3
3	6	4
Total	9	7

THE MINSTREL

ch.h. 1974 – No. 8 Fam. – foaled in Canada

The Minstrel is a three-quarters brother to the great Nijinsky as he has the same sire and his dam Fleur was half-sister to Nijinsky. He is an average-sized horse (15.3 hands (1.61 m)) with a neat appearance and good conformation.

He raced in Ireland and England making nine appearances spread over two seasons. The Minstrel won all three starts in his first year of racing and was rated equal fourth with Gairloch, on 8 st 13 lb (56.5 kg) in the Free Handicap after victories in the Group I William Hill Dewhurst Stakes and one Group III (Larkspur Stakes). J.O. Tobin (by Never Bend), Godswalk (by Dancer's Image) and Padroug (by Sir Ivor) were put above him.

As a three-year-old The Minstrel won the 2,000 Guineas Trial Stakes (Group III) at Ascot, and was then placed in the English and Irish 2,000 Guineas. At Newmarket he was unable to live up to his position of favourite and came third behind Nebbiolo and Tachypous, while at The Curragh he was beated by Pampapaul. However, in the Epsom Derby The Minstrel produced a very brave finish in the last furlong to beat Hot Grove by a neck in a field of 22. After this brilliant success he also won the Irish Derby and in July he beat Orange Bay by short head in the King George VI and Queen Elizabeth Diamond Stakes. In 1978 The Minstrel went to stud.

Breeder: E.P. Taylor
Owner: R.E. Sangster
Most important wins: William Hill Dewhurst Stakes, Derby, Irish Sweeps Derby, King George VI and Queen Elizabeth Diamond Stakes

The Minstrel	Northern Dancer ○ 1961	Nearctic ● 1954	Nearco	Pharos	Phalaris 1 / Scapa Flow 13
				Nogara	Havresac II 8 / Catnip 4
			Lady Angela	Hyperion	Gainsborough 2 / Selene 6
				Sister Sarah	Abbots Trace 4 / Sarita 14
		Natalma ○ 1957	Native Dancer	Polynesian	Unbreakable 4 / Black Polly 14
				Geisha	Discovery 23 / Miyako 5
			Almahmoud	Mahmoud	Blenheim 1 / Mah Mahal 9
				Arbitrator	Peace Chance 10 / Mother Goose 2
	Fleur ○ 1964	Victoria Park ○ 1957	Chop Chop	Flares	Gallant Fox 4 / Flambino 17
				Sceptical	Buchan 16 / Clodagh 2
			Victoriana	Windfields	Bunty Lawless 23 / Nandi 11
				Iribelle	Osiris II 2 / Belmona 10
		Flaming Page ○ 1959	Bull Page	Bull Lea	Bull Dog 16 / Rose Leaves 9
				Our Page	Blue Larkspur 8 / Occult 4
			Flaring Top	Menow	Pharamond II 6 / Alcibiades 8
				Flaming Top	Omaha 17 / Firetop 8

LE MOSS

ch.h. 1975 – No. 1 Fam. – foaled in Ireland

Le Moss is a full brother to Levmoss, winner of the Prix de l'Arc de Triomphe, and Sweet Mimosa (Prix de Diane) and he was one of the greatest stayers of our time. In an age when the aim of breeding and race programming is becoming increasingly orientated towards pure speed, a horse of this type could seem anachronistic. In actual fact this is not the case, since where there is stamina there is also very often consistency and quality, and it does not always follow that the offspring of a long-distance horse need necessarily inherit the characteristics of their sire since it is equally important to bear in mind the importance that the choice of brood mare can have.

Le Moss was bought as a yearling at Goff's sales and his racing career lasted four years, from two to five, and included wins over distances of between 1 mile 6 furlongs (2,800 m) and 2 miles 5 furlongs (4,200 m) taking the greatest English long-distance races. He was unplaced in the only race he ran as a two-year-old but the following year he won the Matthew Dawson Stakes over 1 mile 6 furlongs (2,800 m) at Newmarket, the Queen's Vase (Group III) over 2 miles (3,200 m) at Ascot, the March Stakes over 1 mile 7 furlongs (3,000 m) at Goodwood and the Tennent Trophy Handicap over 1 mile 6 furlongs (2,800 m) at Ayr, before finishing second to Julio

Mariner in the Doncaster St. Leger. As a four-year-old Le Moss won the Lymm Stakes over 2 miles (3,200 m) at Haydock Park and triumphed in the Ascot Gold Cup (Group I) over 2½ miles (4,000 m), beating Buckskin by 7 lengths, the Goodwood Cup (Group II) over 2 miles 5 furlongs (4,200 m) by 7 lengths from Arapahos and the Doncaster Cup (Group III) over 2 miles 2 furlongs (3,600 m), before finishing unplaced in the Jockey Club at Newmarket.

As a five-year-old he repeated his successes of the previous year in all three major Cup races: at Ascot he beat Ardross by three-quarters of a length; at Goodwood he beat the same rival by just a neck and at Doncaster he won, once more by a neck, in their third encounter. He ended the season, and his racing days, by running second, beaten half a length, in the Prix Gladiateur at Longchamps. Le Moss had an outstanding racing career which also illustrated his temperament as a great fighter. Timeform's assessment, as high as 135 lb, is evidence of his unquestionable value. He was bought back by the McGrath family, who had bred him, and in 1981 he began his career as a stallion at the Brownstown Stud in Ireland.

Le Moss	Le Levanstell ○ 1957	Le Lavandou ○ 1944	Djebel	Tourbillon	Ksar 3 / Durban 13
				Loïka	Gay Crusader 1 / Coeur à Coeur 5
			Lavande	Rustom Pasha	**Son-in-Law** 5 / Cos 2
				Livadia	Epinard 4 / Lady Kroon 4
		Stella's Sister ◇ 1950	Ballyogan	**Fair Trial**	Fairway 13 / Lady Juror 9
				Serial	**Solario** 26 / Booktalk 2
			My Aid	Knight of the Garter	**Son-in-Law** 5 / Castelline 4
				Flying Aid	Flying Orb 22 / Aideen 7
	Feemoss ○ 1960	Ballymoss ◇ 1954	Mossborough	Nearco	Pharos 13 / Nogara 4
				All Moonshine	Bobsleigh 3 / Selene 6
			Indian Call	Singapore	Gainsborough 2 / Tetrabbazia 8
				Flittemere	Buchan 16 / Keysoe 2
		Feevagh ○ 1951	Solar Slipper	Windsor Slipper	Windsor Lad 19 / Carpet Slipper 5
				Solar Flower	**Solario** 26 / Serena 10
			Astrid Wood	Bois Roussel	Vatout 3 / Plucky Liège 16
				Astrid	**Fair Trial** 9 / Ethereal 1

Breeder: McGrath Trust Co.
Owner: Carlo D'Alessio
Most important wins: Ascot Gold Cup (twice), Goodwood Cup (twice), Doncaster Cup (twice)

Racing Career

Age	Starts	Wins
2	1	0
3	5	4
4	5	4
5	4	3
Total	15	11

AFFIRMED

ch.h. 1975 – No. 23 Fam. – foaled in the United States

Affirmed was an average-sized horse (16 hands (1.63 m)) with a perfect conformation and tough, solid build, bred by Louis Wolfson, founder of the Harbor View Farm near Ocala in Florida. He raced from two to four and during his career on the track won races over almost all distances between 5½ furlongs (1,100 m) and 1½ miles (2,400 m).

He began by winning a maiden race at Belmont Part after which he took the Youthful Stakes over 5½ furlongs (1,100 m) on the same track. Nearly three weeks later he was beaten for the first time in his life by Alydar who for the rest of Affirmed's career was to be his toughest rival. After this defeat Affirmed won four races in a row: the Hollywood Juvenile Championship (Group II) over 6 furlongs (1,200 m), the Sanford Stakes (Group II) at Saratoga over the same distance with a time of 1 minute 9 seconds, the Hopeful Stakes (Group I) on the same track over 6½ furlongs (1,300 m), beating Alydar by half a length, and the Futurity Stakes (Group I) at Belmont Park over 7 furlongs (1,400 m) beating the same opponent by just a nose. Just under a month later Alydar squared

his account by beating Affirmed by a length and a quarter in the Champagne Stakes, again at Belmont Park but this time over a mile. In the last race of his first year, the Laurel Futurity (Group 1) over 8½ furlongs (1,700 m), Affirmed came out on top again by beating Alydar by just a neck, with the third horse 10 lengths behind.

As a three-year-old Affirmed won a 6½ furlong (1,300 m) race at Santa Anita and on the same course he later took two important races, the San Felipe Handicap (Group II), and the Santa Anita Derby (Group I), in which he beat Balzac by eight lengths. Just two weeks later Affirmed achieved another important victory in the Hollywood Derby (Group I), after which he took the American Triple Crown by beating Alydar in all three of the important races which make up the Crown. In the Kentucky Derby over 1 mile 2 furlongs (2,000 m) the distance between him and his regular opponent was quite clear-cut (1½ lengths), in the Preakness Stakes it was a neck and in the Belmont Stakes (1½ miles (2,400 m)) just a head. At Saratoga in the Travers Stakes, Affirmed was once again the first to reach the post ahead of his

formidable opponent, but this time he was put down to second place after hampering Alydar, who was awarded the race. That same year Affirmed also won the Jim Dandy Stakes (Group III) at Saratoga over 1 mile 1 furlong (1,800 m) and finished second in the Marlboro Cup Handicap, beaten by that great champion, Seattle Slew. In the Jockey Club Gold Cup, won by Exceller narrowly from Seattle Slew, Affirmed finished unplaced for the first and only time in his career. This was due to the fact that his saddle had slipped at the start and his jockey was unable to ride him.

As a four-year-old Affirmed won seven races including the Jockey Club Gold Cup (Group I) at Belmont Park, where he beat Spectacular Bid and Coastal, the Hollywood Gold Cup (Group I) ahead of Sirlad,

the Santa Anita Handicap (Group I), the Californian Stakes (Group I) at Hollywood, the Woodward Stakes (Group 1) at Belmont Park, in which he again beat Coastal, and the Charles H. Strub Stakes (Group I) at Santa Anita. Affirmed's career was of the highest standard and apart from winning 14 Group I races, he was also declared Two-year-old Champion in 1977, Horse of the Year and Three-year-old Champion in 1978 and Horse of the Year and Handicap Champion in 1979.

Affirmed had his eccentricities and fixations, and apart from not allowing anyone but his groom, Juan Alaniz, into his box, he would not tolerate the saliva which dirtied his muzzle after training gallops or races and adopted the habit of wiping himself clean on his groom's trousers and refusing to have his saddle removed or receive applause from the public until he had completed this operation. Affirmed also beat the prize money record, earning the sums of $2,393,818. He went to stud in 1980.

				Unbreakable	4
			Polynesian	Black Polly	14
		Native Dancer		Discovery	23
	Raise a Native ◊ 1961		Geisha	Miyako	5
				Teddy	2
		Raise You	Case Ace	Sweetheart	1
Exclusive Native ◊ 1965				American Flag	7
			Lady Glory	Beloved	8
				Pennant	8
		Shut Out	Equipoise	Swinging	5
	Exclusive ◊ 1953		Goose Egg	Chicle	31
				Oval	16
				Friar Rock	9
		Good Example	Pilate	Herodias	14
			Parade Girl	Display	2
Affirmed				Panoply	10
			Sir Gallahad III	**Teddy**	2
		Fighting Fox		Plucky Liège	16
	Crafty Admiral ○ 1948		Marguerite	Celt	1
				Fairy Ray	4
			War Admiral	Man o'War	4
		Admiral's Lady		Brushup	11
			Boola Brook	Bull Dog	16
Won't Tell You ○ 1962				Brookdale	8
			Ambrose Light	Pharos	13
		Volcanic		La Roseraie	7
	Scarlet Ribbon ○ 1957		Hot Supper	Gallant Fox	4
				Big Dinner	20
			Mahmoud	Blenheim	1
		Native Valor		Mah Mahal	9
			Native Gal	**Sir Gallahad III**	16
				Native Wit	23

AFFIRMED

Breeder: Harbor View Farm
Owner: Harbor View Farm
Most important wins: Hopeful Stakes, Futurity Stakes, Laurel Futurity, Santa Anita Derby, Hollywood Derby, Kentucky Derby, Preakness Stakes, Belmont Stakes, Jockey Club Gold Cup, Hollywood Gold Cup, Santa Anita Handicap, Californian Stakes, Woodward Stakes, Charles H. Strub Stakes

Racing Career		
Age	**Starts**	**Wins**
2	9	7
3	11	8
4	9	7
Total	29	22

TROY

b.h. 1976 – No. 1 Fam. – foaled in Ireland

Troy was sired by the miler Petingo out of La Milo, dam of seven winners. He appeared on the racetrack at two and three winning eight races over distances of between 7 furlongs (1,400 m) and 1½ miles (2,400 m), never finishing lower than third in all his races. After running second in his first race as a two-year-old, he won the the Plantation Stakes at Newmarket and the Lanson Champagne Stakes at Goodwood, both over a distance of 7 furlongs (1,400 m) but in the Royal Lodge Stakes (Group II) he came second to Ela-Mana-Mou whom he had beaten in a previous race.

As a three-year-old Troy reached his highest peak, triumphing in the Epsom Derby. He dominated the finish and was 7 lengths ahead of the runner-up, Dickens Hill, with 3 lengths back to third-placed Northern Baby and three-quarters of a length to Ela-Mana-Mou. After this brilliant success he also won the Irish Derby and carried off both the King George VI and Queen Elizabeth Diamond Stakes and the Benson and Hedges Gold Cup. Earlier in the year, before the Derby, he also won in England, the classic Trial Stakes (Group III) over 1 mile 2 furlongs (2,000 m) at

Sandown and the Predominate Stakes over 1½ miles (2,400 m) at Goodwood. Troy's final race was in the Prix de l'Arc de Triomphe in which he was an honourable third to Three Troikas and Le Marmot. In 1980 Troy went to stud in England as the property of a syndicate. His success as a stallion was awaited with great interest, but unfortunately he died in 1983, before any of his offspring were even old enough to appear on the track. Those who represented him posthumously showed enough to suggest that he is a major loss to racing.

				Phalaris	1
			Fairway	Scapa Flow	13
		Fair Trial		Son-in-Law	5
	Petition		Lady Juror	Lady Josephine	9
	• 1944			**Gainsborough**	2
			Artist's Proof	Clear Evidence	14
		Art Paper		Fairy King	8
Petingo			Quire	Queen Carbine	16
○ 1965				Blenheim	1
			Donatello II	Delleana	14
		Alycidon		**Hyperion**	6
	Alcazar		Aurora	Rose Red	1
	◇ 1957			Pharos	13
			Nearco	Nogara	4
		Quarterdeck		The Recorder	9
			Poker Chip	Straight Sequence	22
Troy				Bayardo	10
			Gainsborough	Rose Drop	2
		Hyperion		Chaucer	1
	Hornbeam		Selene	Serenissima	6
	◇ 1953			**Nearco**	4
			Nasrullah	Mumtaz Begum	9
		Thicket		Bois Roussel	16
			Thorn Wood	Point Duty	1
La Milo				Chateau Bouscaut	7
◇ 1963			Chanteur II	La Diva	12
		Pinza		**Donatello II**	14
			Pasqua	Pasca	3
	Pin Prick			**Nearco**	4
	○ 1955		Royal Charger	Sun Princess	9
		Miss Winston		Foxlaw	2
			East Wantleye	Tetrill	1

Breeder: Ballymacoll Stud Farm Ltd
Owner: Sir Michael Sobell
Most important wins: Derby, Irish Sweeps Derby, King George VI and Queen Elizabeth Diamond Stakes, Benson and Hedges Gold Cup

Racing Career		
Age	Starts	Wins
2	4	2
3	7	6
Total	11	8

TROY

133

SPECTACULAR BID

gr.h. 1976 – No. 2 Fam. – foaled in the United States

Spectacular Bid was not accepted for the Keeneland Summer Sales as his female line was not considered to be sufficiently consistent and so he was sent to the Keeneland Fall Sales where he was bought by Harry Meyerhoff's Hawksworth Farm for $37,000. He raced from two to four, in which time he won 26 out of his 30 starts, over distances between 7 furlongs (1,400 m) and 1 mile 2 furlongs (2,000 m).

As a two-year-old he won the Champagne Stakes (Group I) over a mile at Belmont Park, the Laurel Futurity (Group I) over 8¼ furlongs (1,700 m) the Heritage. Stakes (Group II) over the same distance at Keystone, the World's Playground Stakes (Group III) over 7 furlongs (1,400 m) at Atlantic City, and the Young American Stakes over 8½ furlongs (1,700 m) at Meadowlands, in addition to two other races at Pimlico.

As a three-year-old Spectacular Bid carried off other brilliant successes by winning the Florida Derby over 1 mile 1 furlong (1,800 m) at Gulfstream Park, the Flamingo Stakes at Hialeah Park over the same distance, the Blue Grass Stakes again over 1 mile 1 furlong (1,800 m) at Keeneland, the Kentucky Derby over 1 mile 2 furlongs (2,000 m) at Churchill Downs, even after a slow start, the Preakness Stakes at Pimlico over 1 mile 1½ furlongs (1,900 m) and the Marlboro Cup Handicap over 1 mile 1 furlong (1,800 m) at Belmont Park, all Group I races; the Meadowlands Cup (Group II) over 1 mile 2 furlongs (2,000 m) and the Hutcheson Stakes over 7 furlongs (1,400 m).

His bid for the Triple Crown came to an unsatisfactory and rather sour end in the Belmont Stakes when Spectacular Bid could finish only third, starting at 3 to 10, behind Coastal and Golden Act. He also won at Delaware over 8½ furlongs (1,700 m) and ended the year with a second in the Jockey Club Gold Cup.

As a four-year-old he was unbeaten, including a walk-over for the Woodward Stakes at Belmont Park, the Santa Anita Handicap over 1 mile 2 furlongs (2,000 m), carrying top weight of 9 st 4 lb (59 kg), the Californian Stakes at Hollywood Park over 1 mile 1 furlong (1,800 m), the Amory L. Haskell Stakes, again over 1 mile 1 furlong (1,800 m), at Monmouth Park and the Charles H. Strub Stakes over 1 mile 2 furlongs (2,000 m) at Santa Anita, all Group I races; the Mervyn Leroy Handicap (Group II) over 8½ furlongs (1,700 m) at Hollywood Park, the San Fernando Stakes (Group II) at Santa Anita, the Malibu Stakes (Group II) on the same track and the Washington Park Stakes (Group III) at Arlington Park.

Spectacular Bid had had an exceptional racing career winning 14 Group I races, five Group IIs and three Group IIIs, in addition to the titles of Two-year-old Champion in

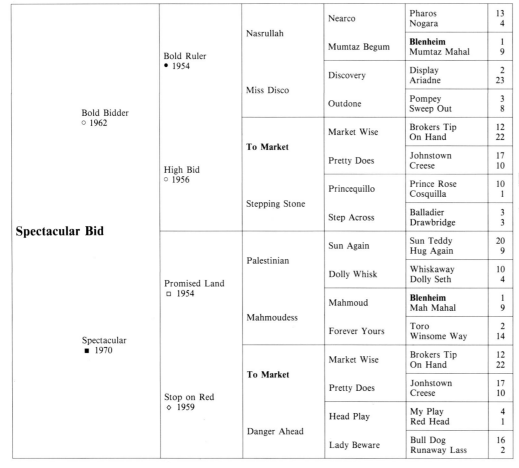

				Pharos	13
			Nearco	Nogara	4
		Nasrullah		Blenheim	1
	Bold Ruler • 1954		Mumtaz Begum	Mumtaz Mahal	9
			Discovery	Display	2
		Miss Disco		Ariadne	23
Bold Bidder ∘ 1962			Outdone	Pompey	3
				Sweep Out	8
			Market Wise	Brokers Tip	12
		To Market		On Hand	22
	High Bid ∘ 1956		Pretty Does	Johnstown	17
				Creese	10
			Princequillo	Prince Rose	10
		Stepping Stone		Cosquilla	1
Spectacular Bid			Step Across	Balladier	3
				Drawbridge	3
			Sun Again	Sun Teddy	20
		Palestinian		Hug Again	9
			Dolly Whisk	Whiskaway	10
	Promised Land ◻ 1954			Dolly Seth	4
			Mahmoud	Blenheim	1
		Mahmoudess		Mah Mahal	9
			Forever Yours	Toro	2
				Winsome Way	14
Spectacular ■ 1970			Market Wise	Brokers Tip	12
		To Market		On Hand	22
			Pretty Does	Jonhstown	17
	Stop on Red ◇ 1959			Creese	10
			Head Play	My Play	4
		Danger Ahead		Red Head	1
			Lady Beware	Bull Dog	16
				Runaway Lass	2

Racing Career

Age	Starts	Wins
2	9	7
3	12	10
4	9	9
Total	30	26

SPECTACULAR BID

1978, Three year-old Champion in 1979 and Veteran Champion and Horse of the Year in 1980. Spectacular Bid exceeded the $2,000,000 mark in prize money by the end of his career and was syndicated in 40 shares as a stallion with a value of $22,000,000. His sire, Bold Bidder, headed the 1974 stallions' list in the United States. He did not race as a two-year-old, won seven races as a three-year-old and at four years old proved himself Champion Handicap horse and had career figures of 13 out of his 33 starts. Spectacular Bid went to stud in 1981.

Breeders: Mrs W. Gilmore and Mrs W. M. Jason
Owner: Hawksworth Farm
Most important wins: Champagne Stakes (USA), Laurel Futurity, Florida Derby, Flamingo Stakes, Preakness Stakes, Kentucky Derby, Blue Grass Stakes, Marlboro Cup Handicap, Woodward Stakes, Santa Anita Handicap, Californian Stakes, Amory L. Haskell Stakes, Charles H. Strub Stakes

b.h. 1978 – No. 21 Fam. – foaled in Great Britain

Glint of Gold, a son of Mill Reef, was the winner of the first Italian Derby to be made open to all horses, regardless of the country in which they were foaled or trained. It was said that second rate English and French horses would come to win the classic and when Glint of Gold won many thought that he was one such horse. In fact, as a two-year-old this horse had won the Sandwich Maiden Stakes at Ascot, had been second to Cocaine in the Acomb Stakes and beaten Bold Brigadier in Milan's Gran Criterium, while as a three-year-old, before running in the Derby in Italy, he had won the Warren Stakes from Belloc and Cocaine. His overall performance was distinctly above average but nevertheless, it was not enough to quell the doubts in the minds of those who were of the opinion that the Italian Derby had, as forecast, been won by a mediocre horse. Subsequent events involving Glint of Gold have proved these pessimistic assessments to be wrong.

In the Epsom Derby he was second to Shergar, admittedly beaten by 10 lengths, but he won the Grand Prix de Paris and the Great Voltigeur Stakes, and was second in the Doncaster St. Leger to Cut Above with Shergar only fourth. After wins in England, Italy and France, Glint of Gold ended his second year's racing in Germany by winning the Preis von Europa, 1½ miles (2,400 m), in Cologne. As a four-year-old he won the John Porter Stakes and was second in the Jockey Club Stakes to Ardross who had fought so well against Le Moss in the English Cup races two years earlier. Glint of Gold was second in the Coronation Cup to Baster Sun, and in the Hardwicke Stakes to Critique, before winning the Grand Prix de Saint-Cloud. After third place in the King George VI and Queen Elizabeth Diamond Stakes, Glint of Gold paid another visit to Germany and won the Grosser Preis von Baden.

His career was consistent and successful in the highest class. He never came lower than third place and finished second six times, in addition to ten wins. His contemporary, Shergar, (who was kidnapped in 1983), won the English and Irish Derbies but overall Glint of Gold was not that far behind him. The fact that a top class horse won the "open" Italian Derby was the best reply that a horse could have given to those petty protectionists who see horse racing in a very narrow perspective and exclusively related to their own interests.

Glint of Gold					
Mill Reef ○ 1968	Never Bend ○ 1960	Nasrullah	Nearco	Pharos	13
				Nogara	4
			Mumtaz Begum	Blenheim	1
				Mumtaz Mahal	9
		Lalun	Djeddah	Djebel	5
				Djezima	13
			Be Faithful	Bimelech	1
				Blood Root	19
	Milan Mill ○ 1962	Princequillo	Prince Rose	Rose Prince	11
				Indolence	10
			Cosquilla	Papyrus	16
				Quick Thought	1
		Virginia Water	Count Fleet	Reigh Count	2
				Quickly	6
			Red Ray	**Hyperion**	6
				Infra Red	22
Crown Treasure ○ 1973	Graustark ◊ 1963	Ribot	Tenerani	Bellini	2
				Tofanella	6
			Romanella	El Greco	14
				Barbara Burrini	4
		Flower Bowl	Alibhai	**Hyperion**	6
				Teresina	6
			Flower Bed	Beau Père	3
				Boudoir III	4
	Treasure Chest ○ 1962	Rough'n Tumble	Free for All	Questionnaire	2
				Panay	1
			Roused	Bull Dog	16
				Rude Awakening	1
		Iltis	War Relic	Man o'War	4
				Friar's Carse	1
			We Hail	Balladier	3
				Clonaslee	21

Breeder: P. Mellon
Owner: P. Mellon
Most important wins: Gran Criterium, Italian Derby, Grand Prix de Paris, Preis von Europa, Grand Prix de Saint-Cloud, Grosser Preis von Baden, Great Voltigeur Stakes

Racing Career		
Age	Starts	Wins
2	3	2
3	7	5
4	7	3
Total	17	10

RACING COLOURS

Any individual or company intending to race horses on the recognized racecourses must request proper authorization from the responsible organizations, and their colours. This authorization can be obtained either under one's own name or, in some countries, under an assumed name. An assumed name cannot however be granted to bookmakers, their partners and business associates, horseracing agencies (the same above-mentioned conditions applying) and trainers. This restriction extends also to relatives and first-degree kinsmen. All these people are therefore obliged to race their horses under their own name. In the request for the authorization, the colours and the design chosen for the jacket and cap must be indicated, and the combination of hoops, stripes, sash, checks etc. must be different from those already registered.

An owner in possession of racing colours issued in any one country can also race his horses abroad, but should he stay for longer than 30 days he must request authorization from the authorities of the host nation. This does not apply in Great Britain, where a declaration of colours to the overnight declarations office by the time fixed for declaration of runners in the conditions of the race is acceptable in lieu of registration. Some owners may use different colours from the ones they use in their own country for horses permanently posted abroad.

In the history of racing, the practice of making jockeys wear coloured shirts to enable the judges to distinguish the various competitors during the race dates back over 200 years and was first used in England. At first the colours used were the most common, such as red, yellow, blue or green but it could be that in one race several competitors were wearing the same colour of shirt. For this reason in 1762 the Jockey Club decided to make it compulsory for the owners to adopt distinctive colours and the first list of such colours was issued to come into force for the second October meeting at Newmarket that autumn.

In illustrating some of the most important colours we have also included those of stables no longer racing but which have helped in the past to enliven and identify interest in the most important events in the racing calendar.

GREAT BRITAIN

Her Majesty Queen Elizabeth the Queen Mother

Her Majesty the Queen

Anne Duchess of Westminster

The Hon. Sir John Astor

Lord Derby

H.J. Joel

Sir Reginald Macdonald-Buchanan

Lady Macdonald-Buchanan

The Hon. J.P. Philipps

Lady Sassoon

Michael Sobell

Lady Zia Wernher

Lord Allendale

Lord Carnarvon

Mrs. D. Thompson

E.R. Courage

L.B. Holliday

G.A. Oldham

William Hill

W.H. Gollings

Lord Leverhulme

Lady Weir

H.D.H. Wills

Sir Humphrey de Trafford

Lord Rosebery

W.H. Whitbread

FRANCE

Aga Khan

Marcel Boussac

François Dupré

Comte François
de Ganay

Baron G. de Waldner

Baron Louis
de la Rochette

Baron Guy de Rothschild

Jean Stern

Mme Léon Volterra

A. Weisweiller

D. Wildenstein

Mme Cino del Duca

Lady Granard

Mme R.B.
Strassburger

Comte de Rivaud

Comte L. de Kérouara

M. Mahmoud Fustok

Paul Duboscq

Ernest Masurel

ITALY

Razza Dormello-Olgiata

Razza Spineta

Carlo Vittadini

Ettore Tagliabue

Scuderia Cieffedi

Scuderia Mantova

Scuderia Miani

Razza del Soldo

Razza Ticino

Razza della Sila

Nob. G. De Montel

Razza di Vedano

Razza Ascagnano

Razza Montalbano

Maurizio Bongianni

GERMANY

Gestüt Asta

M. Gräfin Batthyany

Gestüt Niederrhein

Gestüt Röttgen

Gestüt Zoppenbroich

Gestüt Charlottenhof

Gestüt Schlenderhan

Gestüt Waldfried

Gestüt Fährhof

H. Pferdmenges

Gestüt Fohlenhof

Gestüt Harzburg

Gestüt Atlas

Gestüt Bona

Gestüt Buschhof

Gestüt Ebbesloh

W. Eichholz

Gestüt Werne

BELGIUM

Haras de la Rochette

Baron Lunden

IRELAND

The President of Ireland

Major Dermont
McCalmont

Raymond Guest

B. Kerr

C. W. Engelhard

UNITED STATES

Mrs. Gladys Phipps
(Wheatley Stable)

C.T. Chenery
(Meadow Stable)

Mrs. Ethel D. Jacobs

Paul Mellon

A.G. Vanderbilt

C.V. Whitney

George D. Widener

Louis E. Wolfson
(Harbor View Farm)

Nelson B. Hunt

John W. Galbreath
(Darby Dan Farm)

Mrs. Lucille P. Markey
(Calumet Farm)

Ogden Phipps

Hawksworth Farm

Robert Sangster

Mrs. Edith W. Bancroft

Mrs. Gerard Smith

Rex C. Ellsworth

Jack J. Dreyfus
(Hobeau Farm)

Mrs. Richard C. Du Pont
(Bohemia Stable)

Robert J. Kleberg jr.
(King Ranch)

Mrs. Ewart Johnston

John M. Olin

Harry F. Guggenheim
(Cain Hoy Stable)

Antony Imbesi

Charles E. Mather, II
(Avonwood Stable)

Michael Ford
(Ford Stable)

John E. du Pont
(Foxcatcher Farms)

William Haggin Perry

Cortright Wetherill
(Happy Hill Farm)

CANADA

E.P. Taylor
(Windfields Farm)

Max Bell of Calgary
(Golden West Farm)

Bill Beasley

Saul Wagman

JAPAN

Kokichi Hashimoto

Yuji Kuribayashi

Yuzaku Kato

Kazuo Fujii

ARGENTINA

Mazaichi Nagata

Ignacio Correas

Fernando de
Alzaga Unzué

Coronel Jorge
Castro Madero

SOUTH AFRICA

Felix de Alzaga Unzué

P. Dolt

M. et Mme
Oppenheimer

A.R. & G.A. Ellis

AUSTRALIA

André Ozoux

Sir Frank Packer &
Mr. L.K. Martin

P.G., A.J., K. Stiles

Brian H. Crowley

T.L. Baillieu

SOVIET UNION

Haras de
Dnepropetrovsky

POLAND

Janow Podlaski

THE WORLD'S FLAT RACING COURSES

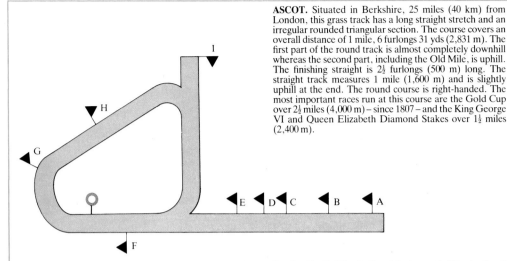

ASCOT. Situated in Berkshire, 25 miles (40 km) from London, this grass track has a long straight stretch and an irregular rounded triangular section. The course covers an overall distance of 1 mile, 6 furlongs 31 yds (2,831 m). The first part of the round track is almost completely downhill whereas the second part, including the Old Mile, is uphill. The finishing straight is 2½ furlongs (500 m) long. The straight track measures 1 mile (1,600 m) and is slightly uphill at the end. The round course is right-handed. The most important races run at this course are the Gold Cup over 2½ miles (4,000 m) – since 1807 – and the King George VI and Queen Elizabeth Diamond Stakes over 1½ miles (2,400 m).

A – 1 mile (1,600 m). **B** – 7 furlongs (1,400 m). **C** – 6 furlongs (1,200 m). **D** – 2½ miles (4,000 m). **E** – 5 furlongs (1,000 m). **F** – 2 miles (3,200 m). **G** – 1½ miles (2,400 m). **H** – 1 mile 2 furlongs (2,000 m). **I** – Old Mile (1,600 m).

CHESTER. On this course, 179 miles (288 km) from London, races have been run since 1512, when England was under the rule of Henry VIII. The racecourse has a flat, irregular round grass track covering 1 mile 67 yds (1,667 m) with a finishing straight of just 230 yds (210 m). The course is left-handed.

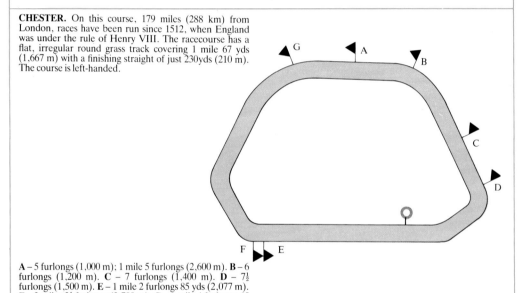

A – 5 furlongs (1,000 m); 1 mile 5 furlongs (2,600 m). **B** – 6 furlongs (1,200 m). **C** – 7 furlongs (1,400 m). **D** – 7½ furlongs (1,500 m). **E** – 1 mile 2 furlongs 85 yds (2,077 m). **F** – 2 miles 2½ furlongs (3,700 m). **G** – 1 mile 4 furlongs 65 yds (2,460 m).

DONCASTER. In Yorkshire, 163 miles (262 km) from London, this course has an irregular round grass track, and measures 1 mile 7⅞ furlongs (3,142 m) overall. The straight track is 1 mile (1,600 m) long. The width of the track varies from 60 ft (18 m) to 88 ft (27 m). The course is left-handed. The most important race run here is the St. Leger over 1 mile 6 furlongs 137 yds (2,925 m), which dates back to 1776.

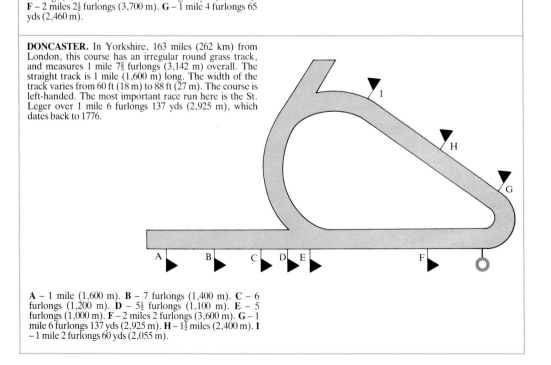

A – 1 mile (1,600 m). **B** – 7 furlongs (1,400 m). **C** – 6 furlongs (1,200 m). **D** – 5½ furlongs (1,100 m). **E** – 5 furlongs (1,000 m). **F** – 2 miles 2 furlongs (3,600 m). **G** – 1 mile 6 furlongs 137 yds (2,925 m). **H** – 1½ miles (2,400 m). **I** – 1 mile 2 furlongs 60 yds (2,055 m).

F our centuries have passed since the very first racecourses, if they can be so called, began to appear in England. Initially, they generally tended merely to be fenced tracks, very different from our modern-day conception of a racecourse. From then on these venues, which were to help bring about the evolution of horse racing as a sport, have continued to develop and increase in numbers attracting interest from all corners of the world. Today, especially in some countries, fabulous complexes have been constructed, where modern technical equipment (for preparing the turf for racing) is combined with infrastructures to provide the spectator with every comfort. The tracks can be grass, sand or dirt and their development, like their layout, has differed greatly from country to country.

Some racecourses have perfectly flat tracks whereas others have gradients that are occasionally quite steep. Another important factor is their capacity for sub-surface drainage, enabling the ground to maintain a soft springy surface by a rapid downflow of the rain or irrigation water. We have tried to give a general picture of some of the world's most important racecourses in the form of diagrams, ignoring the stands and spectator facilities, and concentrating on the courses and starts over which the races are run. Not all these diagrams are to scale since some, especially the English ones, are in schematic form and so on occasion fail to take account of actual proportions, particularly as regards the position of the starts.

EDINBURGH. Situated in Musselburgh, 6 miles (10 km) from Edinburgh. A flat oval grass track, the circular part covering 1 mile 2 furlongs (2,000 m), plus an additional 2 furlongs (400 m) chute, the site of the start for the 5 furlongs (1,000 m) and 1 mile 7 furlongs (3,000 m) races. The last furlong (200 m) before the winning post is uphill and the course is right-handed.

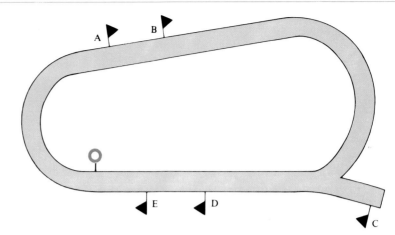

A – 1 mile (1,600 m). **B** – 7 furlongs (1,400 m). **C** – 5 furlongs (1,000 m); 1 mile 7 furlongs (3,000 m). **D** – 1½ miles (2,400 m). **E** – 1 mile 3 furlongs (2,200 m).

EPSOM. 15 miles (24 km) outside London. The racecourse is named after the nearby town which took its name from a Latin inscription found on a fragment of a Roman tombstone: (PRINC)EPS O.M., the first part of which (PRINC) was missing. The grass track is in a very irregular circle and the longest stretch, the Derby Track, measures 1½ miles (2,400 m). The first 5 furlongs (1,000 m) are on an uphill gradient, but the rest of the track goes downhill to the finishing straight which is 4 furlongs (800 m) long and slopes upwards towards the end. The straight track measures 5 furlongs (1,000 m). The most important races run here are the Derby (since 1780) and the Oaks (since 1779) over a distance of 1½ miles (2,400 m). For these, as in most other races, the course is left-handed, but the Great Metropolitan Handicap over 2¼ miles (3,600 m) starts at the finishing post and results in the horses running along the straight in both directions.

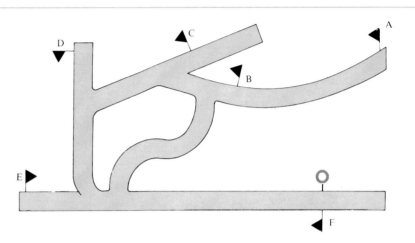

A – 1 mile 4 furlongs (2,400 m) – (Derby). **B** – 1 mile 2 furlongs (2,000 m). **C** – 7 furlongs (1,400 m). **D** – 6 furlongs (1,200 m). **E** – 5 furlongs (1,000 m). **F** – 2 miles 2 furlongs (3,600 m).

GOODWOOD. 70 miles (112 km) from London. The grass track covers 2 miles (3,200 m) overall and has a very unusual, shape, the only one of its kind. The straight course is 6 furlongs (1,200 m) long. For races over 2 miles 3 furlongs (3,800 m) and 2 miles 5 furlongs (4,200 m) the horses run in both directions along the straight. The most important race run here is the Sussex Stakes over 1 mile (1,600 m), which dates back to 1841.

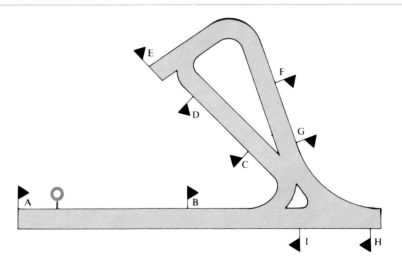

A – 2 miles 5 furlongs (4,200 m). **B** – 2 miles 3 furlongs (3,800 m). **C** – 1 mile 6 furlongs (2,800 m). **D** – 1 mile 2 furlongs (2,000 m). **E** – 1½ miles (2,400 m). **F** – 1 mile (1,600 m). **G** – 7 furlongs (1,400 m). **H** – 6 furlongs (1,200 m). **I** – 5 furlongs (1,000 m).

HAYDOCK PARK. 188 miles (302 km) from London. This grass track is almost oval in shape and covers 1 mile 5 furlongs (2,600 m) with a finishing straight of 4 furlongs (800 m). The course is almost flat and left-handed. The straight track measures 5 furlongs (1,000 m) which, just before it meets the main circuit, is joined by the short chute, site of the 6-furlong (1,200 m) start.

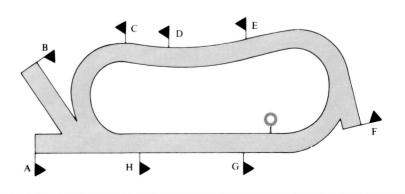

A – 5 furlongs (1,000 m). **B** – 6 furlongs (1,200 m). **C** – 7 furlongs 40 yds (1,436 m). **D** – 1 mile 40 yds (1,636 m). **E** – 1 mile 2 furlongs 131 yds (2,120 m). **F** – 1½ miles (2,400 m). **G** – 1 mile 6 furlongs (2,800 m). **H** – 2 miles 28 yds (3,226 m).

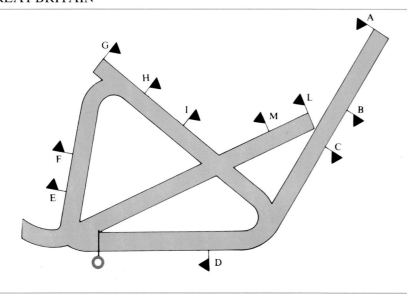

KEMPTON PARK. 18 miles (29 km) from London, this is a triangular-shaped course covering an overall distance of 1 mile 6 furlongs (2,800 m). The "Jubilee Course" which measures 1 mile 2 furlongs (2,000 m) joins the main track about 3 furlongs (600 m) before the finishing straight which is about 3½ furlongs (700 m) in length. The straight course is 6 furlongs (1,200 m) long and completely separate from the rest of the circuit. The course is right-handed.

A – 1 mile 2 furlongs – Jubilee Course (2,000 m). **B** – 1 mile – Jubilee Course (1,600 m). **C** – 7 furlongs – Jubilee Course (1,400 m). **D** – 2 miles (3,200 m) **E** – 1½ miles (2,400 m). **F** – 1 mile 3 furlongs (2,200 m). **G** – 1 mile 1 furlong (1,800 m). **H** – 1 mile (1,600 m). **I** – 7 furlongs (1,400 m). **L** – 6 furlongs (1,200 m). **M** – 5 furlongs (1,000 m).

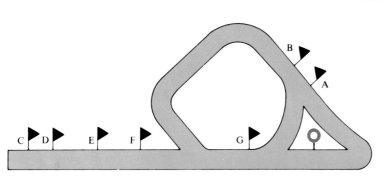

LINGFIELD PARK. 27 miles (43 km) from London, this course covers an overall distance of over 2 miles (3,200 m). The straight course is 7 furlongs 140 yds (1,528 m) long and joins the circular track just under 4 furlongs (800 m) from the winning post. The straight course is not consistently level but slopes steadily downwards, especially in the second half. The first half of the round course is flat, after which comes a slight climb, and a steep descent to the final turn. The course is left-handed.

A – 1 mile 2 furlongs (2,000 m). **B** – 1 mile 1 furlong (1,800 m). **C** – 7 furlongs 140 yds (1,528 m). **D** – 7 furlongs (1,400 m). **E** – 6 furlongs (1,200 m); 2 miles (3,200 m). **F** – 5 furlongs (1,000 m). **G** – 1½ miles (2,400 m).

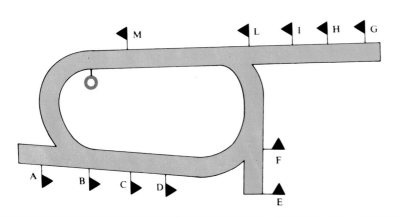

NEWBURY. This racecourse, 53 miles (85 km) from London, has a left-handed track covering an overall distance of just under 2 miles (3,200 m). The finishing straight is almost 5 furlongs (1,000 m) long and the straight course 1 mile (1,600 m).

A – 1 mile 5 furlongs 55 yds (2,655 m). **B** – 1½ miles (2,400 m). **C** – 1 mile 3 furlongs (2,200 m). **D** – 1 mile 2 furlongs (2,000 m). **E** – 1 mile (1,600 m). **F** – 7 furlongs 60 yds (1,454 m). **G** – 1 mile (1,600 m). **H** – 7 furlongs (1,400 m). **I** – 6 furlongs (1,200 m). **L** – 5 furlongs (1,000 m). **M** – 2 miles (3,200 m).

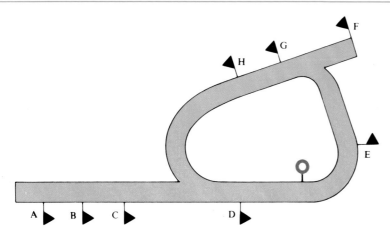

NEWCASTLE. Situated in Northumberland and 269 miles (432 km) from London, this left-handed racecourse has a 1 mile 6 furlongs (2,800 m) circular track. The straight course is 7 furlongs (1,400 m) long.

A – 7 furlongs (1,400 m). **B** – 6 furlongs (1,200 m). **C** – 5 furlongs (1,000 m). **D** – 2 miles (3,200 m). **E** – 1½ miles 60 yds (2,454 m). **F** – 1 mile 2 furlongs (2,000 m). **G** – 1 mile 1 furlong (1,800 m). **H** – 1 mile (1,600 m).

NEWMARKET. An unusual feature of this racecourse, situated in Suffolk, 90 miles (145 km) from London, is that it has two tracks which are completely separate and used at different times of the year. The July Course is used in June, July and August and the other, the Rowley Mile Course, in the remaining months. The two courses share an initial stretch of approximately 6 furlongs (1,200 m), which is downhill and called the "Beacon Course." The Rowley Mile Course covers 2 miles 2 furlongs (3,600 m) and has a finishing straight of 1 mile 2 furlongs (2,000 m), the last 2 furlongs (400 m) of which is downhill for the first half and climbs uphill for the rest of the way. The July Course covers almost 2 miles (2,965 m) and after 2 furlongs (400 m) slopes more steeply downhill, climbing uphill again in the final stretch. The main race on the July Course is the July Cup (first run in 1876). The following races are run on the Rowley Mile Course: the 2,000 Guineas (first run in 1809) and the 1,000 Guineas (first run in 1814), both over 1 mile (1,600 m); the Cambridgeshire over 1 mile 1 furlong (1,800 m) and the Cesarewitch over 2 miles 2 furlongs (3,600 m), both first run in 1839; the Jockey Club Stakes over 1 mile 6 furlongs (2,800 m) and the Middle Park Stakes over 6 furlongs (1,200 m).

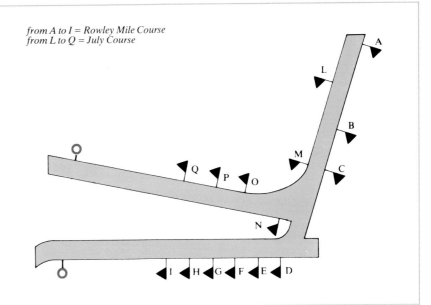

from A to I = Rowley Mile Course
from L to Q = July Course

A – 2 miles 2 furlongs (3,600 m). **B** – 1 mile 6 furlongs (2,800 m). **C** – 1½ miles (2,400 m). **D** – 1 mile 2 furlongs (2,000 m). **E** – 1 mile 1 furlong (1,800 m). **F** – 1 mile (1,600 m). **G** – 7 furlongs (1,400 m). **H** – 6 furlongs (1,200 m). **I** – 5 furlongs (1,000 m). **L** – 1 mile 6 furlongs 171 yds (2,965 m). **M** – 1 mile 2 furlongs (2,000 m). **N** – 1 mile (1,600 m). **O** – 7 furlongs (1,400 m). **P** – 6 furlongs (1,200 m). **Q** – 5 furlongs (1,000 m).

SALISBURY. Situated 84 miles (135 km) from London. It has a track on which races over 1½ miles (2,400 m) and 1¾ miles (2,800 m) are first run left-handed and then right-handed. The last 5 furlongs (1,000 m) before the finishing post are on a slight uphill slope.

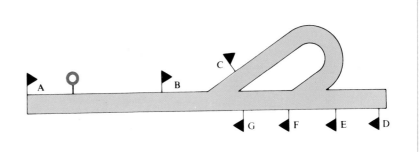

A – 1 mile 6 furlongs (2,800 m). **B** – 1½ miles (2,400 m). **C** – 1 mile 2 furlongs (2,000 m). **D** – 1 mile (1,600 m). **E** – 7 furlongs (1,400 m). **F** – 6 furlongs (1,200 m). **G** – 5 furlongs (1,000 m).

SANDOWN PARK. This circuit, situated in Surrey, 13 miles (21 km) from London, has a finishing straight of 1,000 yards (914 m). The ground is fairly even until the final stretch where there is a steady uphill climb to the winning post. The overall length of this right-handed course is 1 mile 5 furlongs 33 yds (2,630 m). The straight course, rises for its entire length of 5 furlongs (1,000 m) and is separate from the finishing straight. The main race run on this course is the Eclipse Stakes over 1 mile 2 furlongs (2,000 m), first run in 1886.

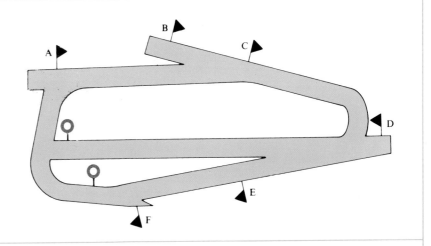

A – 1 mile 2 furlongs (2,000 m). **B** – 1 mile (1,600 m). **C** – 7 furlongs (1,400 m). **D** – 5 furlongs (1,000 m). **E** – 2 miles (3,200 m). **F** – 1 mile 6 furlongs (2,800 m).

WINDSOR. This racecourse is in Berkshire, 22 miles (35 km) from London. The figure of eight circuit is fairly even and covers an overall distance of 1½ miles (2,400 m). The course for 6-furlong (1,200 m) and 5-furlong (1,000 m) races is slightly curved for the first 2 furlongs (400 m) after which it is practically straight.

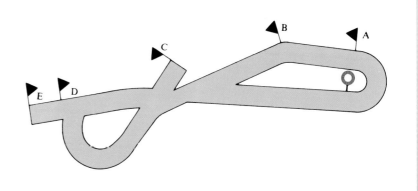

A – 1 mile 3 furlongs 150 yds (2,337 m). **B** – 1 mile 2 furlongs 22 yds (2,020 m). **C** – 1 mile 70 yds (1,664 m). **D** – 5 furlongs (1,000 m). **E** – 6 furlongs (1,200 m).

GREAT BRITAIN – IRELAND – FRANCE

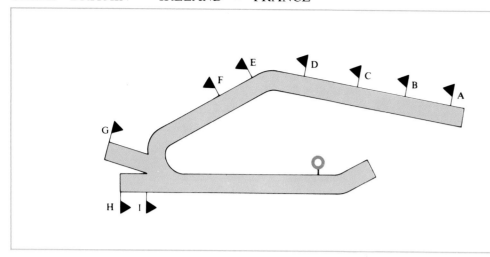

YORK. Situated 188 miles (302 km) from London, this 2-mile (3,200 m) circuit is gently undulating except for the finishing straight which is perfectly flat. The straight course measures 6 furlongs (1,200 m) and the short chute with the 7-furlong (1,400 m) start joins onto the track at the crook of the last bend. The course is left-handed.

A – 2 miles (3,200 m). **B** – 1 mile 6 furlongs (2,800 m). **C** – 1½ miles (2,400 m). **D** – 1 mile 2 furlongs 110 yds (2,100 m). **E** – 1 mile 1 furlong (1,800 m). **F** – 1 mile (1,600 m). **G** – 7 furlongs (1,400 m). **H** – 6 furlongs (1,200 m). **I** – 5 furlongs (1,000 m).

IRELAND

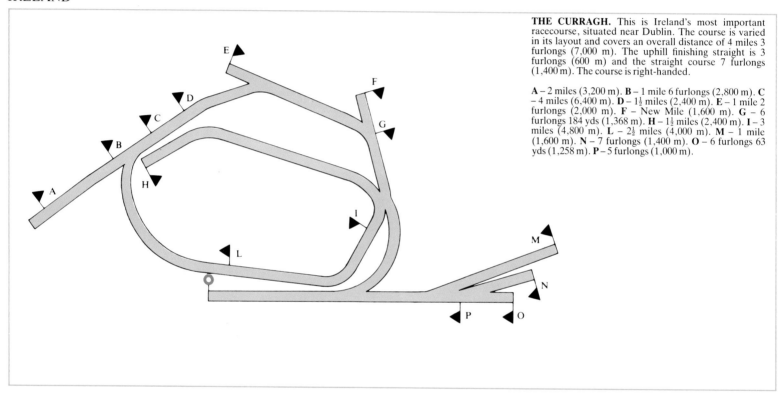

THE CURRAGH. This is Ireland's most important racecourse, situated near Dublin. The course is varied in its layout and covers an overall distance of 4 miles 3 furlongs (7,000 m). The uphill finishing straight is 3 furlongs (600 m) and the straight course 7 furlongs (1,400 m). The course is right-handed.

A – 2 miles (3,200 m). **B** – 1 mile 6 furlongs (2,800 m). **C** – 4 miles (6,400 m). **D** – 1½ miles (2,400 m). **E** – 1 mile 2 furlongs (2,000 m). **F** – New Mile (1,600 m). **G** – 6 furlongs 184 yds (1,368 m). **H** – 1½ miles (2,400 m). **I** – 3 miles (4,800 m). **L** – 2½ miles (4,000 m). **M** – 1 mile (1,600 m). **N** – 7 furlongs (1,400 m). **O** – 6 furlongs 63 yds (1,258 m). **P** – 5 furlongs (1,000 m).

FRANCE

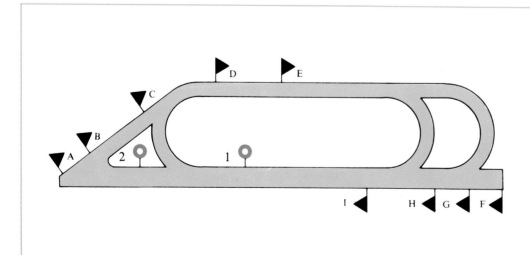

BELLERIVE. This racecourse is situated at Vichy. Depending on whether the grass circuit is measured on the inside or the outside of the bend it covers approximately 7 furlongs (1,400 m), middle course, or about 1 mile 2 furlongs (2,000 m), outer course. The finishing straight has two different winning posts 1½ furlongs (300 m) apart. The straight 5-furlong (1,000 m) course finishes at the second post and both courses are right-handed.

A – 1 mile 1 furlong (1,800 m – middle course, 2nd post); 7½ furlongs (1,500 m – middle course). **B** – 1 mile 2 furlongs (2,000 m). **C** – 1 mile 1 furlong (1,800 m). **D** – 1 mile (1,600 m). **E** – 7 furlongs (1,400 m). **F** – 1 mile 3 furlongs (2,200 m – middle course); 1 mile 6 furlongs (2,800 m); 1 mile 7½ furlongs (3,100 m – 2nd post); 5 furlongs (1,000 m – straight course, 2nd post). **G** – 1½ miles (2,400 m – middle course, 2nd post); 1 mile 7 furlongs (3,000 m – 2nd post). **H** – 1 mile 2 furlongs (2,000 m – middle course); 1 mile 5 furlongs (2,600 m). **I** – 1 mile 1 furlong (1,800 m – middle course); 1½ miles (2,400 m).

150

CHANTILLY. Situated 22½ miles (36 km) from Paris, this racecourse has a grass circuit covering about 1 mile 3½ furlongs (2,300 m) and four different finishing posts. After the third post on the extension of the finishing extension the 1½ mile (2,400 m) Prix du Jockey-Club track begins. The new course with the 7-furlong (1,400 m) start joins the circuit at the point where the latter intersects the Prix du Jockey-Club track. The courses are right-handed.

A – 5½ furlongs (1,100 m – straight course – 4th post). **B** – 5 furlongs (1,000 m – straight course – 4th post). **C** – 1½ miles (2,400 m – Jockey Club Course). **D** – 1 mile 3 furlongs (2,200 m – Jockey Club Course). **E** – 1 mile 2½ furlongs (2,100 m – Jockey Club Course). **F** – 1 mile 2 furlongs (2,000 m – Jockey Club Course). **G** – 2 miles 4½ furlongs (4,100 m and 1 mile 1 furlong (1,800 m – circuit)). **H** – 2½ miles (4,000 m – circuit). **I** – 1 mile (1,600 m – circuit). **L** – 7 furlongs (1,400 m – new course). **M** – 2 miles 2 furlongs (3,600 m – circuit). **N** – 5½ furlongs (1,100 m – straight course, 2nd post); 7 furlongs (1,400 m – straight course, 3rd post). **O** – 5 furlongs (1,000 m – straight course, 3rd post). **P** – 6 furlongs (1,200 m – straight course, 3rd post).

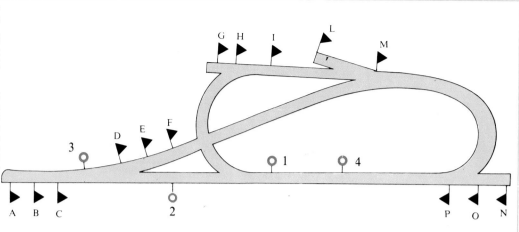

CAGNES-SUR-MER is situated on the Côte d'Azur and has a grass track which is used for both flat races and steeplechases. The oval course has three concentric curves which converge in the finishing straight and so the length of the track varies according to the route taken, from 1 mile (1,600 m – inner course), to 1 mile 2 furlongs (2,000 m – middle course, and 1½ miles (2,400 m) – outer course). For steeplechases the two diagonal tracks which join the inner course are also used. The straight course measures five furlongs (1,000 m) and all the courses are left-handed. There is a trotting course inside the flat racing course.

A – 5 furlongs (1,000 m – straight course). **B** – 1 mile 3 furlongs (2,200 m – inner course); 1 mile 5 furlongs (2,600 m – middle course); 1 mile 7 furlongs (3,000 m – outer course). **C** – 1½ miles (2,400 m – middle course); 1 mile 6 furlongs (2,800 m – outer course). **D** – 1 mile 2 furlongs (2,000 m – outer course); 1 mile (1,600 m – middle course). **E** – 1 mile 1½ furlongs (1,900 m – outer course); 7½ furlongs (1,500 m – middle course). **F** – 8½ furlongs (1,700 m – outer course); 6½ furlongs (1,300 m – middle course). **G** – 1 mile (1,600 m – outer course).

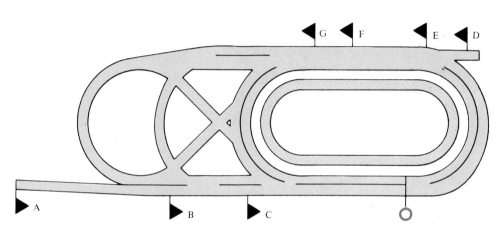

DEAUVILLE. A right-hand grass circuit of 1 mile 3½ furlongs (2,300 m) with a long extension to the finishing straight enabling races to be run on the straight course up to a distance of 1 mile (1,600 m).

A – 1 mile 2 furlongs (2,000 m). **B** – 1 mile (1,600 m). **C** – 7½ furlongs (1,500 m). **D** – 7 furlongs (1,400 m). **E** – 1 mile (1,600 m – straight course). **F** – 7½ furlongs (1,500 m – straight course). **G** – 7 furlongs (1,400 m – straight course). **H** – 6½ furlongs (1,300 m – straight course). **I** – 6 furlongs (1,200 m – straight course). **L** – 5½ furlongs (1,100 m – straight course); 2 miles 1 furlong (3,400 m). **M** – 5 furlongs (1,000 m – straight course). **N** – 2 miles (3,200 m). **O** – 1 mile 7 furlongs (3,000 m). **P** – 1 mile 6 furlongs (2,800 m). **Q** – 1 mile 5½ furlongs (2,700 m). **R** – 1 mile 4½ furlongs (2,500 m).

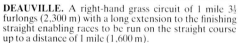

EVRY. A grass circuit which branches into two separate courses in the middle: the large course (1½ miles 151 yds (2,538 m)) and the inner course (1 mile 1 furlong 154 yds (1,940 m)). There is also a middle course of 1 mile 2½ furlongs (2,100 m) and a 6½-furlong (1,300 m) separate straight course. All courses are left-handed.

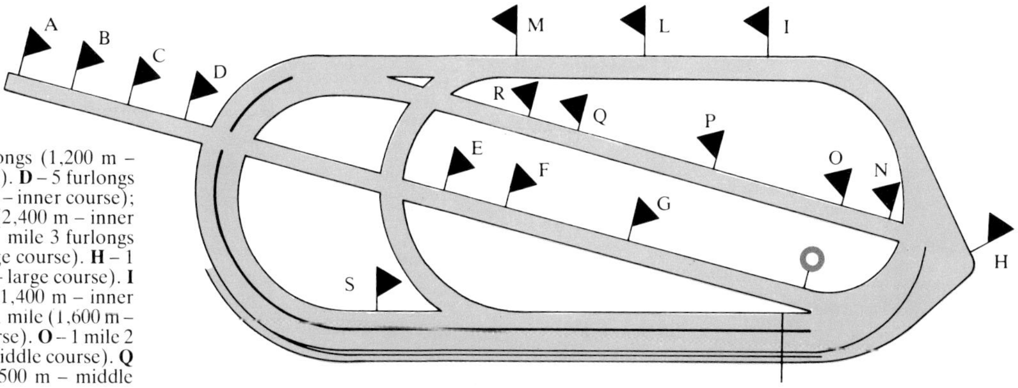

A – 6½ furlongs (1,300 m – straight course). **B** – 6 furlongs (1,200 m – straight course). **C** – 5½ furlongs (1,100 m – straight course). **D** – 5 furlongs (1,000 m – straight course). **E** – 1 mile 4½ furlongs (2,500 m – inner course); 1 mile 7½ furlongs (3,100 m – large course). **F** – 1½ miles (2,400 m – inner course); 1 mile 7 furlongs (3,000 m – large course). **G** – 1 mile 3 furlongs (2,200 m – inner course); 1 mile 6 furlongs (2,800 m – large course). **H** – 1 mile 1 furlong (1,800 m – inner course); 1½ miles (2,400 m – large course). **I** – 1 mile 2 furlongs (2,000 m – large course); 7 furlongs (1,400 m – inner course). **L** – 1 mile 1 furlong (1,800 m – large course). **M** – 1 mile (1,600 m – large course). **N** – 1 mile 2½ furlongs (2,100 m – middle course). **O** – 1 mile 2 furlongs (2,000 m – middle course). **P** – 1 mile (1,600 m – middle course). **Q** – 1 mile (1,600 m – middle course). **R** – 7½ furlongs (1,500 m – middle course). **S** – 1 mile 5 furlongs (2,600 m – inner course).

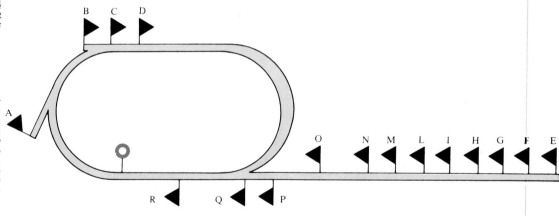

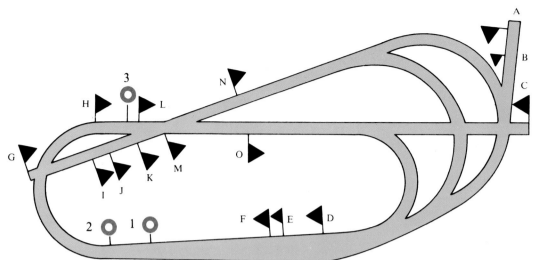

LONGCHAMP. This racecourse, which was opened in 1859 and restructured in 1966, is situated in the heart of Paris, in the Bois de Boulogne on the plain once called the Sablons. The grass course is flat in the straight in front of the stands and around the first bend, then it climbs up to the Porte de Boulogne, at which point it begins to slope steadily downhill into the final bend.

A – 7 furlongs (1,400 m – new course, 2nd post); 2 miles 1 furlong (3,400 m – new course and small course); 2 miles 1½ furlongs (3,500 m – new course and small course, 2nd post); 2 miles 3 furlongs (3,800 m – new course and middle course); 2½ miles (4,000 m – new course and large course). **B** – 6½ furlongs (1,300 m – new course); 2 miles 1 furlong (3,400 m – new course and small course); 2 miles 1½ furlongs (3,500 m – new course and small course, 2nd post). **C** – 5 furlongs (1,000 m – straight course). **D** – 1 mile 7½ furlongs (3,100 m – middle course, 2nd post); 2 miles (3,200 m – large course); 2 miles ½ furlong (3,300 m – large course, 2nd post); 1 mile 5½ furlongs (2,700 m – small course, 2nd post). **E** – 1 mile 5 furlongs (2,600 m – small course, 2nd post); 1 mile 7 furlongs (3,000 m – middle course); 1 mile 7½ furlongs (3,100 m – middle course, 2nd post); 2 miles (3,200 m – large course); 2 miles ½ furlong (3,300 m – large course, 2nd post). **F** – 1 mile 6 furlongs (2,800 m – middle course); 1 mile 7 furlongs (3,000 m – large course). **G** – 1 mile 2 furlongs 153 yds (2,141 m – middle course); 1 mile 3 furlongs 43 yds (2,239 m – middle course, 2nd post); 1½ miles (2,400 m – large course); 1 mile 4½ furlongs (2,500 m – large course, 2nd post). **H** – 1 mile (1,600 m – small course); 1 mile ½ furlong (1,700 m – small course, 2nd post). **I** – 1 mile 2 furlongs (2,000 m – middle course); 1 mile 2½ furlongs (2,100 m – middle course, 2nd post); 2 miles 6 furlongs (4,800 m – middle course and large course). **J** – 1 mile 3 furlongs (2,200 m – large course); 1 mile 3½ furlongs (2,300 m – large course, 2nd post). **K** – 1 mile 2½ furlongs (2,100 m – large course); 1 mile 3 furlongs (2,200 m – large course, 2nd post). **L** – 7½ furlongs (1,500 m – small course); 1 mile (1,600 m – small course, 2nd post). **M** – 7½ furlongs (1,500 m – small course, 2nd post); 1 mile 1 furlong (1,800 m – middle course, 2nd post). **N** – 1 mile (1,600 m – middle course); 1 mile ½ furlong (1,700 m – middle course, 2nd post); 1 mile 1 furlong 45 yds (1,841 m – large course); 1 mile 1 furlong 154 yds (1,940 m – large course, 2nd post); 2 miles 2½ furlongs (3,700 m – middle course and small course). **O** – 2½ miles (4,000 m – small course and large course).

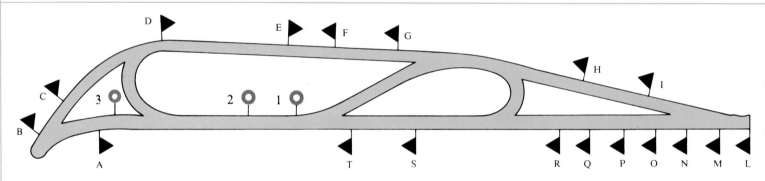

MAISONS-LAFFITTE. Situated 10 miles (16 km) from Paris. Although this grass course is in a circuit it extends a long way beyond this. The long finishing straight has three winning posts enabling races of up to 1 mile 2 furlongs (2,000 m) to be run on the straight course. This course is both right-handed (finishing at the second post) and left-handed (finishing at the first post). The third post is for races on the straight stretch of 1 mile (1,600 m), 1 mile 1 furlong (1,800 m) and 1 mile 2 furlongs (2,000 m). The course also has a chute, diagonal to the two straights.

A – 1½ miles (2,400 m – right-hand chute). **B** – 1 mile 5 furlongs (2,600 m). **C** – 1 mile 4½ furlongs (2,500 m). **D** – 1 mile 2½ furlongs (2,100 m). **E** – 1 mile (1,600 m). **F** – 7 furlongs (1,400 m – left-handed). **G** – 1 mile (1,600 m – left-handed). **H** – 1 mile 3 furlongs (2,200 m – left-handed). **I** – 1½ miles (2,400 m – left-handed). **L** – 1 mile (1,600 m – straight course); 1 mile 2 furlongs (2,000 m – straight course, 3rd post). **M** – 7½ furlongs (1,500 m – straight course). **N** – 7 furlongs (1,400 m – straight course); 1 mile 1 furlong (1,800 m – straight course, 3rd post). **O** – 6½ furlongs (1,300 m – straight course). **P** – 6 furlongs (1,200 m – straight course); 1 mile (1,600 m – straight course, 3rd post). **Q** – 5½ furlongs (1,100 m – straight course). **R** – 5 furlongs (1,000 m – straight course). **S** – 2 miles (3,200 m). **T** – 1 mile 7 furlongs (3,000 m).

SAINT-CLOUD. Situated on the outskirts of Paris, this grass racecourse is almost triangular in shape and has three bends, only the last being fairly sharp. The course is about 1 mile 3 furlongs (2,200 m) in length and there is a branch of the finishing straight where the start for the 1 mile 4½ furlong (2,500 m) race is situated. The course is left-handed.

A – 1 mile 2½ furlongs (2,100 m). **B** – 1 mile 2 furlongs (2,000 m). **C** – 1 mile (1,600 m). **D** – 7½ furlongs (1,500 m). **E** – 7 furlongs (1,400 m). **F** – 6½ furlongs (1,300 m). **G** – 6 furlongs (1,200 m). **H** – 1 mile 4½ furlongs (2,500 m). **I** – 1½ miles (2,400 m). **L** – 1 mile 6 furlongs (2,800 m).

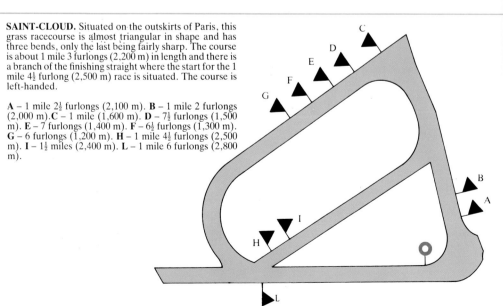

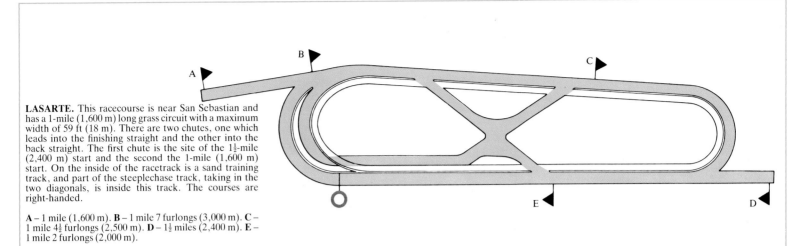

LASARTE. This racecourse is near San Sebastian and has a 1-mile (1,600 m) long grass circuit with a maximum width of 59 ft (18 m). There are two chutes, one which leads into the finishing straight and the other into the back straight. The first chute is the site of the 1½-mile (2,400 m) start and the second the 1-mile (1,600 m) start. On the inside of the racetrack is a sand training track, and part of the steeplechase track, taking in the two diagonals, is inside this track. The courses are right-handed.

A – 1 mile (1,600 m). **B** – 1 mile 7 furlongs (3,000 m). **C** – 1 mile 4½ furlongs (2,500 m). **D** – 1½ miles (2,400 m). **E** – 1 mile 2 furlongs (2,000 m).

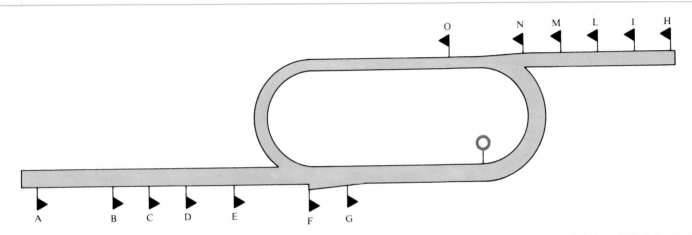

LA ZARZUELA. This grass course which covers a distance of approximately 1 mile 128 yds (1,717 m) is in Madrid. The finishing straight is 2 furlongs 63 yds (457 m) long and 148 ft (45 m) wide. The straight course is 6 furlongs 26 yds (1,457 m) long and the first part, before it joins the finishing straight, is 115 ft (35 m) wide. A chute for the 1 mile 1 furlong (1,800 m) start runs into the back stretch. The course is left-handed.

A – 6 furlongs (1,200 m). **B** – 5 furlongs (1,000 m). **C** – 4½ furlongs (900 m). **D** – 4 furlongs (800 m). **E** – 1½ miles (2,400 m). **F** – 1 mile 3 furlongs (2,200 m). **G** – 1 mile 2½ furlongs (2,100 m). **H** – 1 mile 1 furlong (1,800 m). **I** – 1 mile ½ furlong (1,700 m). **L** – 1 mile (1,600 m). **M** – 7½ furlongs (1,500 m). **N** – 7 furlongs (1,400 m). **O** – 6 furlongs (1,200 m).

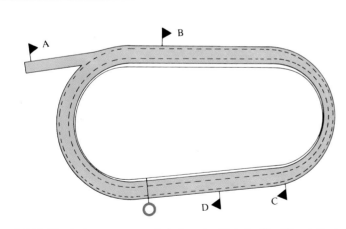

LIVORNO. The Ardenza racecourse is dedicated to Federico Caprilli and situated on the outskirts of Leghorn. The oval grass course is 6 furlongs (1,200 m) long and has a minimum width of 39 ft (12 m) around the last bend which is also sharper than the course's other bend. The finishing straight is about 1½ furlongs (300 m) long. The course is particularly sharp so, given the awkward position of the starts in relation to the bends, the horse with the draw number nearest the rails has a great advantage. The course is right-handed.

A – 5 furlongs (1,000 m); 1 mile 3¼ furlongs (2,250 m). **B** – 1 mile 1 furlong 164 yds (1,950 m). **C** – 7 furlongs 164 yds (1,550 m); 1 mile 5½ furlongs (2,700 m). **D** – 6¾ furlongs (1,350 m).

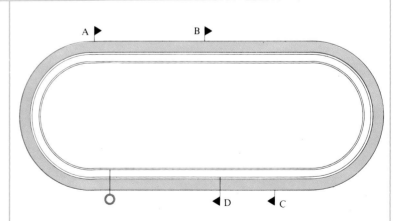

VARESE. The Bettole racecourse, north of Milan, has an oval grass track of 6½ furlongs (1,300 m) and is approximately 65½ ft (20 m) wide. The finishing straight measures about 1,149 ft wide (350 m). There is a wood shaving training track parallel to and inside the racing track. The course is right-handed.

A – 5 furlongs (1,000 m); 1 mile 3½ furlongs (2,300 m). **B** – 1 mile 2½ furlongs (2,100 m). **C** – 1 mile (1,600 m). **D** – 7¾ furlongs (1,550 m); 1 mile 6 furlongs (2,800 m).

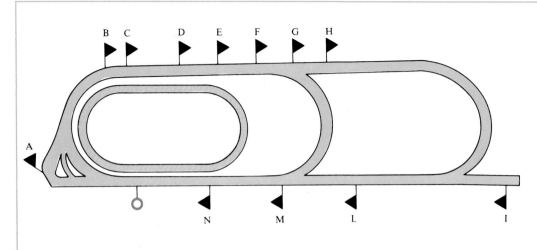

AGNANO. This racecourse is just outside Naples and near the town of Terme di Agnano. The round grass horseracing track is about 1½ miles (2,400 m) on the large outer track with a finishing straight of about 4¼ furlongs (850 m) whereas round the inner track it measures 8¼ furlongs (1,650 m) with a finishing straight of about 2 furlongs. The straight course is 5 furlongs (1,000 m) long and after a downhill stretch climbs gently upwards to the point where the tracks cross until 164 yds (150 m) from the finishing post. The 5-furlong (1,000 m) trotting track is inside the racing track.

A – 7½ furlongs (1,500 m – small course); 1 mile 3¼ furlongs (2,250 m – large course). **B** – 1 mile 2 furlongs (2,000 m – large course). **C** – 6 furlongs (1,200 m – small course); 1 mile 1 furlong 164 yds (1,950 m – large course). **D** – 1 mile 1 furlong (1,800 m – large course). **E** – 8½ furlongs (1,700 m – large course). **F** – 1 mile (1,600 m – large course). **G** – 7½ furlongs (1,500 m – large course). **H** – 7 furlongs (1,400 m – large course). **I** – 5 furlongs (1,000 m – straight course). **L** – 1 mile 3 furlongs (2,200 m – small course). **M** – 1 mile 2 furlongs (2,000 m – small course). **N** – 1 mile 1 furlong (1,800 m – small course); 1 mile 5 furlongs (2,600 m – large course).

CAPANNELLE. Situated on the Via Appia, this course is 7½ miles (12 km) from the center of Rome. It was built in 1881 and restructured in 1926 and has two flat racing tracks, one outer grass circuit and an inner sand track. The grass course, 98 ft (30 m) wide, measures 1 mile 5 furlongs (2,600 m) round the outside and 1 mile 2½ furlongs (2,100 m) round the inside. The Derby course measures 1½ miles (2,400 m) and the straight course is 6 furlongs (1,200 m) long. The finishing straights are 4¼ furlongs (850 m – big course) and 3 furlongs (600 m – small course). The course undulates and in the homestretch falls slightly downhill (1:500 (0.2%)) while the first bend climbs uphill for its entire length. The sand course is 65½ ft (20 m) wide and 1 mile (1,600 m) long round the inside (with a straight of 2 furlongs (400 m) and 1 mile 2 furlongs (2,000 m) round the outside with a finishing straight of 3 furlongs (600 m). The race course also has a steeplechase circuit within the flat racing tracks, which is 1 mile (1,600 m) long and 79 ft (24 m) wide. The courses are right-handed.

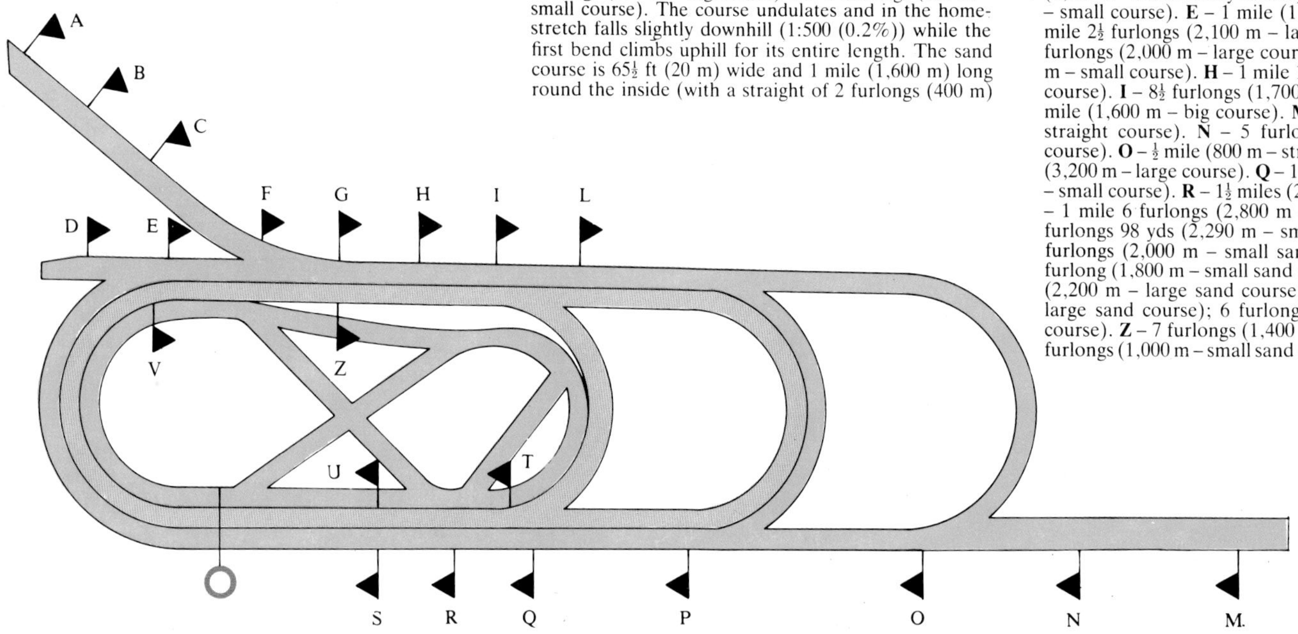

A – 1½ miles (2,400 m – Derby course). **B** – 1 mile 1 furlong (1,800 m – small Derby course). **C** – 1 mile 3 furlongs (2,200 m – large Derby course); 8½ furlongs (1,700 m – small course). **D** – 8½ furlongs (1,700 m – small course). **E** – 1 mile (1,600 m – small course); 1 mile 2½ furlongs (2,100 m – large course). **F** – 1 mile 2 furlongs (2,000 m – small course). **G** – 7 furlongs (1,400 m – small course). **H** – 1 mile 1 furlong (1,800 m – large course). **I** – 8½ furlongs (1,700 m – large course). **L** – 1 mile (1,600 m – big course). **M** – 6 furlongs (1,200 m – straight course). **N** – 5 furlongs (1,000 m – straight course). **O** – ½ mile (800 m – straight course). **P** – 2 miles (3,200 m – large course). **Q** – 1 mile 4½ furlongs (2,500 m – small course). **R** – 1½ miles (2,400 m – small course). **S** – 1 mile 6 furlongs (2,800 m – large course); 1 mile 3 furlongs 98 yds (2,290 m – small course). **T** – 1 mile 2 furlongs (2,000 m – small sand course). **U** – 1 mile 1 furlong (1,800 m – small sand course); 1 mile 3 furlongs (2,200 m – large sand course). **V** – 1 mile (1,600 m – large sand course); 6 furlongs (1,200 m – small sand course). **Z** – 7 furlongs (1,400 m – large sand course); 5 furlongs (1,000 m – small sand course).

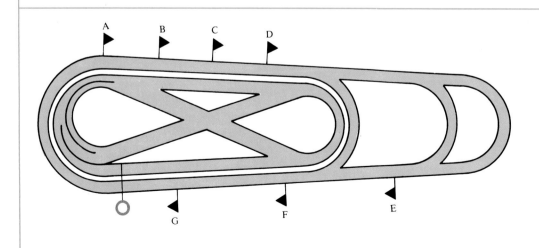

CASCINE. This racecourse is situated in the Cascine, Florence and has an oval grass track which measures 1 mile 1½ furlongs (1,900 m) round the outside, with a straight of about 3¼ furlongs (650 m). Round the middle circuit it measures 8½ furlongs (1,700 m) with a finishing straight of 2¾ furlongs (550 m), and the inner circuit has a length of 7 furlongs (1,400 m) with a homestretch of 383 yds (350 m). The width of the track is 79 ft (24 m) around the bends and across the straight opposite the finishing stretch, and at the finish measures 65½ ft (20 m) across. The big 6-furlong 97 yds (1,289 m) figure of eight steeplechase track is inside the small track.

A – 6½ furlongs (1,300 m – middle course); 7½ furlongs (1,500 m – large course). **B** – 1 mile 3½ furlongs (2,300 m – small course). **C** – ½ mile (800 m – small course). **D** – 5 furlongs (1,000 m – middle course); 6 furlongs (1,200 m – large course). **E** – 1½ miles (2,400 m – large course). **F** – 8½ furlongs (1,700 m – small course); 1 mile 2 furlongs (2,000 m – middle course); 1 mile 3 furlongs (2,200 m – large course). **G** – 7½ furlongs (1,500 m – small course); 1 mile 1 furlong (1,800 m) – middle course); 1 mile 2 furlongs (2,000 m – large course).

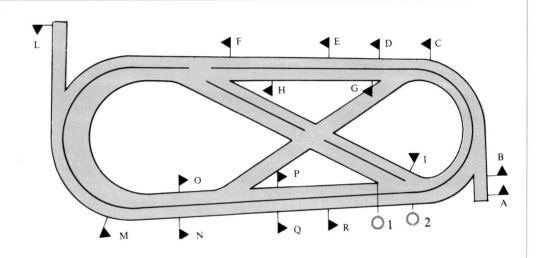

SAN SIRO. Situated on the outskirts of Milan, this racecourse was built in 1888 and restructured in 1920. The flat oval grass track measures, depending on the bends covered, 1 mile 6 furlongs (2,800 m – big outer bends), 1½ miles (2,400 m – big bend), 1 mile 2 furlongs (2,000 m – middle bend), 1 mile 1½ furlongs (1,900 m – inner middle bend) and 1 mile (1,600 m – small bend). The circuit that includes the big outer bends is the Gran Premio track but for the other races the only difference is the second bend since the first bend is always the inner one.

A – 1 mile 2 furlongs (2,000 m – inner middle course). **B** – 1 mile (1,600 m – small course); 1 mile 2 furlongs (2,000 m – middle course); 1½ miles (2,400 m – large course). **C** – 7½ furlongs (1,500 m – small course). **D** – 1 mile 1 furlong (1,800 m – inner middle course). **E** – 7 furlongs (1,400 m – small course); 1 mile 1 furlong (1,800 m – middle course); 1 mile 3 furlongs (2,200 m – large course). **F** – 8½ furlongs (1,700 m – inner middle course). **G** – 8½ furlongs (1,700 m – middle course). **H** – 1 mile (1,600 m – inner middle course). **I** – 1 mile (1,600 m – middle course); 1 mile 2 furlongs (2,000 m – large course). **L** – 7½ furlongs (1,500 m – inner middle course). **M** – 7½ furlongs (1,500 m – middle course). **N** – 7 furlongs (1,400 m – middle course); 1 mile 1 furlong (1,800 m – large course). **O** – 5 furlongs (1,000 m – straight course, 1st post); 6 furlongs (1,200 m – straight course, 2nd post); 7 furlongs (1,400 m – straight course, 3rd post). **P** – 1½ miles (2,400 m – small course). **Q** – 1 mile 3 furlongs (2,200 m – small course). **R** – 1 mile 2 furlongs (2,000 m – small course); 1½ miles (2,400 m – middle course); 1 mile 6 furlongs (2,800 m – large course); 2 miles (3,200 m – Gran Premio track). **S** – 1 mile 1 furlong (1,800 m – small course); 1 mile 3 furlongs (2,200 m – middle course); 1 mile 5 furlongs (2,600 m – large course); 1 mile 7 furlongs (3,000 m – Gran Premio track).

TURIN. This racecourse has two concentric oval grass tracks. The big outer track is 1 mile 2 furlongs (2,000 m) long and 98 ft (30 m) wide, while the small inner one measures 1 mile 1 furlong (1,800 m) and is 82 ft (25 m) wide. The course has two different finishing posts so the homestretch can therefore be 2 furlongs 55 yds (450 m) or 2 furlongs 142 yds (530 m) long. The small course has just one post, 2 furlongs 22 yds (420 m) down. Two diagonals meet to form a figure of eight course.

A – 1 mile 1½ furlongs (1,900 m – large course, 2nd post). **B** – 1 mile 1 furlong (1,800 m – large course). **C** – 1 mile (1,600 m – large course). **D** – 7½ furlongs (1,500 m – large course). **E** – 7 furlongs (1,400 m – large course). **F** – 6 furlongs (1,200 m – large course). **G** – 6½ furlongs (1,300 m – small course). **H** – 5½ furlongs (1,100 m – small course). **I** – 1 mile (1,600 m – large course); 7½ furlongs (1,500 m – small course). **L** – 5 furlongs (1,000 m – large course, 2nd post). **M** – 1 mile 5 furlongs (2,600 m – large course, 2nd post). **N** – 1½ miles (2,400 m – large course). **O** – 1 mile 3 furlongs (2,200 m – small course). **P** – 1 mile 2 furlongs (2,000 m – small course). **Q** – 1 mile 3 furlongs (2,200 m – small course). **R** – 1 mile 2½ furlongs (2,100 m – large course).

BADEN-BADEN. This racecourse has one round grass course with two tracks: the first follows the inner bend and is 1 mile 2 furlongs (2,000 m) long; the second follows the outer bend and measures 1 mile 4½ furlongs (2,500 m). Inside the flat-racing course is a steeplechase course with 17 jumps which crosses and goes beyond the main course. There is also a round course for hurdle-racing which has eight flights. Still farther inside is a sand training track. The course is left-handed.

A – 1 mile 2 furlongs (2,000 m – large course). **B** – 7 furlongs (1,400 m – small course). **C** – 1 mile 1 furlong (1,800 m – large course). **D** – 1 mile (1,600 m – large course). **E** – 6 furlongs (1,200 m); 2 miles (3,200 m – small course). **F** – 5 furlongs (1,000 m). **G** – 1 mile 6 furlongs (2,800 m – small course). **H** – 1 mile 4½ furlongs (2,500 m – small course). **I** – 1½ miles (2,400 m – small course). **L** – 1 mile 3 furlongs (2,200 m – small course).

155

WEST GERMANY

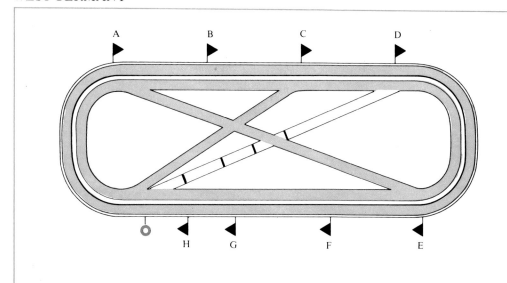

BREMEN. This racecourse has an oval grass track of 1 mile 2 furlongs (2,000 m) with a finishing straight of approximately 3 furlongs (600 m). The course is right-handed. The 11-jump steeplechase course is inside the flat-racing course and between these two is a training course. The steeplechase course takes in the two diagonals. A third diagonal is used for a steeplechase schooling course. Outside the grass flat-racing course is a sand exercise track.

A – 1 mile (1,600 m). **B** – 7 furlongs (1,400 m). **C** – 6 furlongs (1,200 m). **D** – 5 furlongs (1,000 m). **E** – 1 mile 5 furlongs (2,600 m). **F** – 1½ miles (2,400 m). **G** – 1 mile 3 furlongs (2,200 m). **H** – 1 mile 2½ furlongs (2,100 m).

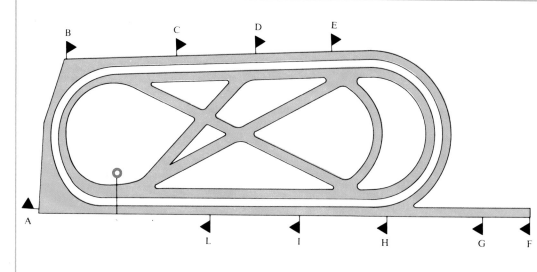

DORTMUND. This racecourse has a long grass circuit covering a distance of 1 mile 3 furlongs (2,200 m). The straight course is 5 furlongs (1,000 m) long. The courses are right-handed. There is a steeplechase course inside the flat-racing course with 15 obstacles and three diagonals. Between the two courses is an exercise track.

A – 1 mile 2 furlongs 55 yds (2,050 m). **B** – 1 mile 1 furlong (1,800 m). **C** – 1 mile (1,600 m). **D** – 7 furlongs (1,400 m). **E** – 6 furlongs (1,200 m). **F** – 5 furlongs (1,000 m). **G** – 1 mile 7 furlongs (3,000 m). **H** – 1 mile 6 furlongs (2,800 m). **I** – 1 mile 5 furlongs (2,600 m). **L** – 1½ miles (2,400 m).

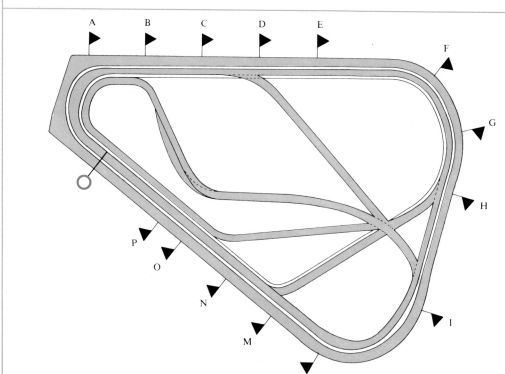

DÜSSELDORF. This racecourse is an almost triangular-shaped grass circuit covering a distance of 1 mile 1½ furlongs (1,900 m) with three bends and is right-handed. Inside this course is the 16-jump steeplechase course and between the two is a grass training track. Inside the steeplechase course is a sand exercise track.

A – 8½ furlongs (1,700 m). **B** – 1 mile (1,600 m); 2 miles 1½ furlongs (3,500 m). **C** – 7½ furlongs (1,500 m); 2 miles 1 furlong (3,400 m). **D** – 7 furlongs (1,400 m). **E** – 6½ furlongs (1,300 m); 2 miles (3,200 m). **F** – 1 mile 7 furlongs (3,000 m). **G** – 5 furlongs (1,000 m). **H** – 1 mile 6 furlongs (2,800 m). **I** – 1 mile 5 furlongs (2,600 m). **L** – 1½ miles (2,400 m). **M** – 1 mile 3½ furlongs (2,300 m). **N** – 1 mile 3 furlongs (2,200 m). **O** – 1 mile 2½ furlongs (2,100 m). **P** – 1 mile 2 furlongs 55 yds (2,050 m).

FRANKFURT. This 8¾ furlong (1,750 m) racecourse has a round grass track with a rather short finishing straight measuring just over 1¾ furlongs (350 m). The course is left-handed. There is a 13-fence steeplechase course inside this course and between the two is a 1-mile (1,600 m) steeplechase circuit running concentric to the main one. Inside the latter is a sand training track.

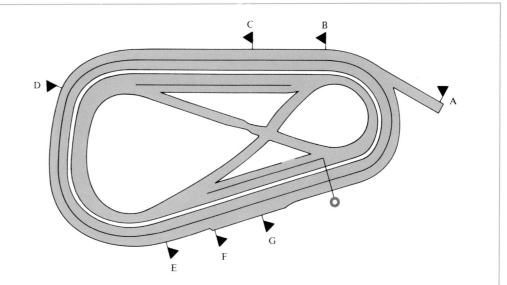

A – 1 mile (1,600 m). **B** – 6¾ furlongs (1,350 m). **C** – 6 furlongs (1,200 m). **D** – 1 mile 4½ furlongs (2,500 m). **E** – 1 mile 2½ furlongs (2,100 m). **F** – 1 mile 2 furlongs (2,000 m). **G** – 1 mile 1½ furlongs (1,900 m).

GELSENKIRCHEN-HORSTER. This racecourse has a grass track with two circuits. The first follows the big bend and is 1 mile 4½ furlongs (2,500 m) long, and the second follows the small bend (new course) which is 1 mile 1 furlong 164 yds (1,950 m) long. The course is right-handed. Inside the flat-racing course is a 13-fence steeplechase course and between the two is a sand training track.

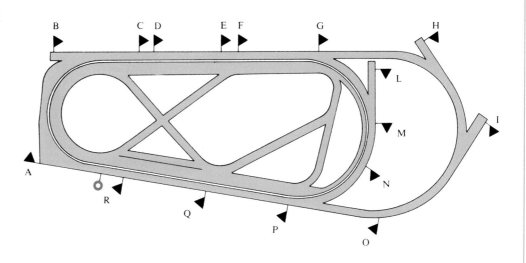

A – 1 mile 1 furlong (1,800 m – small course). **B** – 1 mile (1,600 m – small course). **C** – 7 furlongs (1,400 m – small course). **D** – 1 mile 1 furlong (1,800 m – large course). **E** – 6 furlongs (1,200 m – small course). **F** – 1 mile (1,600 m – large course). **G** – 7 furlongs (1,400 m – large course). **H** – 6 furlongs (1,200 m). **I** – 5 furlongs (1,000 m). **L** – 1 mile 6 furlongs (2,800 m – small course). **M** – 1 mile 5½ furlongs (2,700 m – small course). **N** – 1 mile 5 furlongs (2,600 m – small course). **O** – 1 mile 7 furlongs (3,000 m – large course). **P** – 1½ miles (2,400 m – small course). **Q** – 1 mile 3 furlongs (2,200 m – small course). **R** – 1 mile 2 furlongs (2,000 m – small course).

HAMBURG-HORN. Hamburg's racecourse has a grass circuit 1 mile 2 furlongs (2,000 m) long which is right-handed. Inside it is a 17-fence steeplechase course, with many intersections and diagonal tracks, which crosses and goes beyond the boundaries of the flat-racing course in the second half of the straight opposite the home straight and then rejoins the main circuit on the penultimate bend.

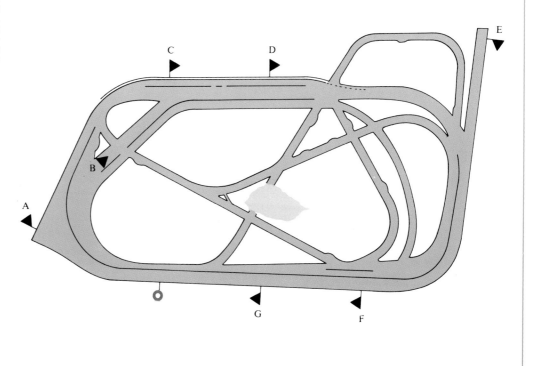

A – 1 mile 1 furlong (1,800 m). **B** – 1 mile (1,600 m). **C** – 7 furlongs (1,400 m). **D** – 6 furlongs (1,200 m). **E** 5 furlongs (1,000 m). **F** – 1½ miles (2,400 m). **G** – 1 mile 3 furlongs (2,200 m).

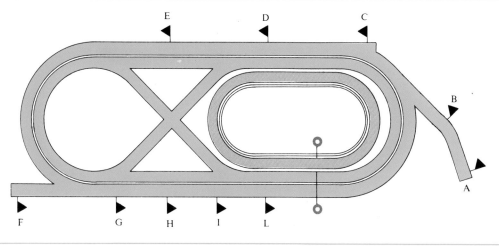

HANNOVER. The course has a grass circuit of 1 mile 1 furlong (1,800 m). Inside the flat-racing course is a figure of eight steeplechase course with 13 fences and within this is a trotting course. The course is left-handed.

A – 1 mile 175 yds (1,760 m). **B** – 2 miles 1 furlong (3,400 m); 1 mile (1,600 m). **C** – 7 furlongs (1,400 m); 2 miles (3,200 m). **D** – 6 furlongs (1,200 m); 1 mile 7 furlongs (3,000 m). **E** – 5 furlongs (1,000 m); 1 mile 6 furlongs (2,800 m). **F** – 1½ miles (2,400 m). **G** – 1 mile 3 furlongs (2,200 m). **H** – 1 mile 2½ furlongs (2,100 m). **I** – 1 mile 2 furlongs (2,000 m); 2 miles 3 furlongs (3,800 m). **L** – 1 mile 1½ furlongs (1,900 m).

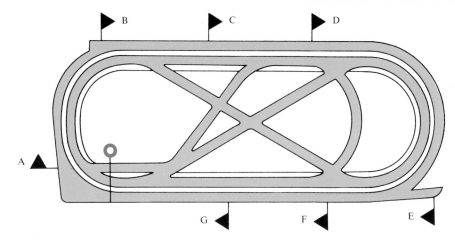

KREFELD. This oval grass circuit covers a distance of 1 mile 1 furlong (1,800 m) within which is a training course. Inside these two is the 13-fence steeplechase course which although in a figure of eight has various other tracks. Inside this there is another practice track. The course is right-handed.

A – 1 mile (1,600 m). **B** – 7 furlongs (1,400 m); 2 miles (3,200 m). **C** – 6 furlongs (1,200 m). **D** – 5 furlongs (1,000 m); 1 mile 6 furlongs (2,800 m). **E** – 1½ miles (2,400 m). **F** – 1 mile 3 furlongs (2,200 m). **G** – 1 mile 2 furlongs (2,000 m).

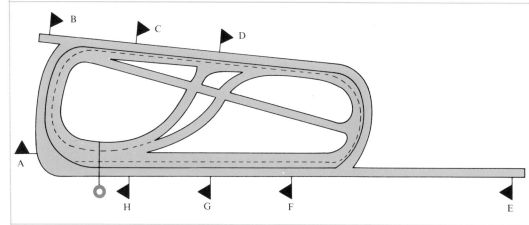

KÖLNER. Flat racing on this course is staged on a grass circuit 1 mile 1¾ furlongs (1,950 m) long. The straight course measures 5 furlongs (1,000 m) and the course is right-handed. Inside the flat racing track is a 13-fence steeplechase course.

A – 1 mile 1 furlong 66 yds (1,860 m). **B** – 1 mile (1,600 m). **C** – 7 furlongs (1,400 m). **D** – 6 furlongs (1,200 m). **E** – 5 furlongs (1,000 m); 1 mile 6 furlongs 164 yds (2,950 m). **F** – 1½ miles (2,400 m). **G** – 1 mile 3 furlongs (2,200 m). **H** – 1 mile 2 furlongs (2,000 m).

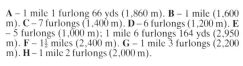

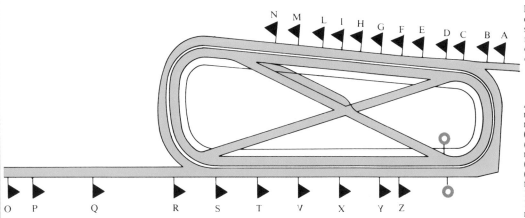

MÜNCHEN-RIEM. Munich's racecourse has a grass circuit covering 1 mile 1 furlong 142 yds (1,930 m). The straight course measures 5 furlongs (1,000 m). In the middle of the flat-racing course is a 14-fence steeplechase course in a figure of eight. Inside this is a training course. The course is left-handed.

A – 8½ furlongs (1,700 m). **B** – 2 miles 2 furlongs (3,600 m). **C** – 1 mile (1,600 m). **D** – 2 miles 1½ furlongs (3,500 m). **E** – 7½ furlongs (1,500 m). **F** – 2 miles 1 furlong (3,400 m). **G** – 7 furlongs (1,400 m). **H** – 2 miles ½ furlong (3,300 m). **I** – 6½ furlongs (1,300 m). **L** – 2 miles (3,200 m). **M** – 6 furlongs (1,200 m). **N** – 1 mile 7½ furlongs (3,100 m). **O** – 1 mile 7 furlongs (3,000 m). **P** – 5 furlongs (1,000 m). **Q** – 1 mile 6 furlongs (2,800 m). **R** – 1 mile 5 furlongs (2,600 m). **S** – 1 mile 4½ furlongs (2,500 m). **T** – 1½ miles (2,400 m). **V** – 1 mile 3½ furlongs (2,300 m). **X** – 1 mile 3 furlongs (2,200 m). **Y** – 1 mile 2½ furlongs (2,100 m). **Z** – 2 miles 3 furlongs (4,000 m).

MÜLHEIM. This racecourse is situated close to the German town of the same name. It has a grass flat-racing course which covers an overall distance of 1 mile 1 furlong (1,800 m) and is right-handed. It is oval in shape and surrounded by a sand training track. There are two concentric steeplechase courses within the flat-racing course, taking in the two diagonals.

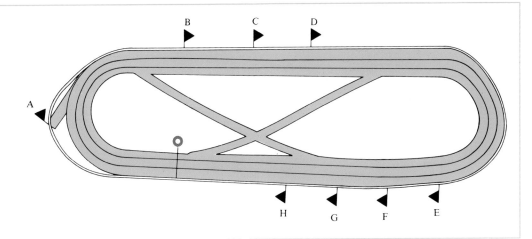

A – 1 mile (1,600 m). **B** – 7 furlongs (1,400 m); 2 miles (3,200 m). **C** – 6 furlongs (1,200 m); 1 mile 7 furlongs (3,000 m). **D** – 1 mile 6½ furlongs (2,900 m). **E** – 1½ miles (2,400 m). **F** – 1 mile 3½ furlongs (2,300 m). **G** – 1 mile 3 furlongs (2,200 m). **H** – 1 mile 2½ furlongs (2,100 m).

EXHIBITION PARK. This racecourse, in British Columbia, near Vancouver, has a sand track measuring 5 furlongs 69 yds (1,063 m) with an inner 4-furlong (800 m) grass circuit. The main course is 65 ft (20 m) wide and measures 170 yds (156 m) from the start of the finishing straight to the post. The course is left-handed. Seats 7,500.

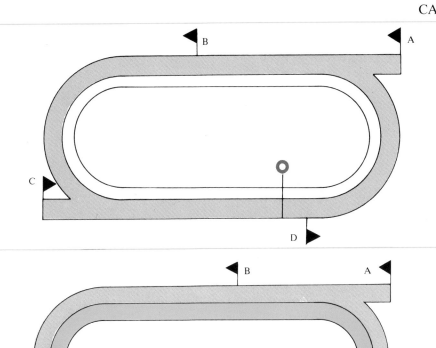

A – 1 mile 1 furlong (1,800 m). **B** – 1 mile (1,600 m). **C** – 6½ furlongs (1,300 m). **D** – 5 furlongs (1,000 m).

FORT ERIE. The racecourse is in Ontario, 6 miles (9.5 km) from Buffalo. It has two tracks, one outer sand track and a grass one in the middle. The sand track is 1 mile (1,600 m) long and oval in shape. It is 85 ft (26 m) wide along the finishing straight and 65 ft (20 m) along the back straight. The total distance from the end of the last bend to the finishing post is 354 yds (323 m). Inside and concentric to the sand track is a grass course 7 furlongs (1,400 m) long. The courses are all left-handed. The grandstand seats 7,200 and the Club House seats 1,800.

A – 6½ furlongs (1,300 m). **B** – 5 furlongs (1,000 m). **C** – 1 mile 2 furlongs (2,000 m). **D** – 1 mile (1,600 m).

WOODBINE PARK. Situated on the outskirts of Toronto, Ontario, this racecourse has two racing circuits, one outer sand track and a concentric grass track which lies inside it except for the section containing the 2-mile (3,200 m), the 1½ mile (2,400 m) and 1-mile 2-furlongs (2,000 m) starts. The oval sand track is 1 mile (1,600 m) long and 105 ft (32 m) wide along the finishing straight and 85 ft (26 m) wide across the back straight. There is a distance of 325 yds (297 m) between the last bend and the finishing post. The grass course is 7 furlongs (1,400 m) long and 85 ft (26 m) wide. The grandstand seats 10,000 and the Club House 3,000.

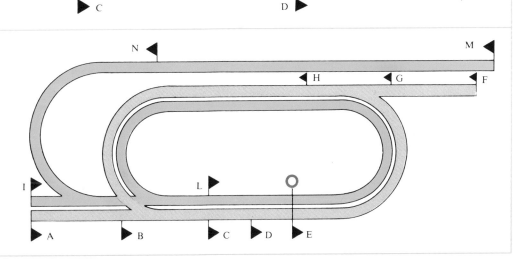

A – 1 mile 3 furlongs (2,200 m). **B** – 1 mile 2 furlongs (2,000 m). **C** – 1 mile 1 furlong (1,800 m). **D** – 8½ furlongs (1,700 m). **E** – 1 mile (1,600 m). **F** – 7 furlongs (1,400 m). **G** – 6 furlongs (1,200 m). **H** – 5 furlongs (1,000 m). **I** – 1 mile 2 furlongs (2,000 m). **L** – 1 mile (1,600 m). **M** – 2 miles (3,200 m). **N** – 1½ miles (2,400 m).

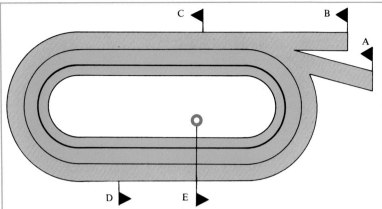

ARLINGTON PARK. This racecourse in Illinois lies 23 miles (37 km) from the center of Chicago. It has one outer oval sand track which has two concentric grass tracks inside. The sand track covers an overall distance of 1 mile 1 furlong (1,800 m) and along the finishing straight has a width of 101 ft (30.8 m). On this track the distance from the last bend to the finishing post is 342 yds (313 m). The grass tracks measure 1 mile (1,600 m) and 7 furlongs (1,400 m) respectively. The courses are left-handed. Seats a total number of 30,598.

A – 1 mile (1,600 m). **B** – 7 furlongs (1,400 m). **C** – 5 furlongs (1,000 m). **D** – 1 mile 2 furlongs (2,000 m). **E** – 1 mile 1 furlong (1,800 m).

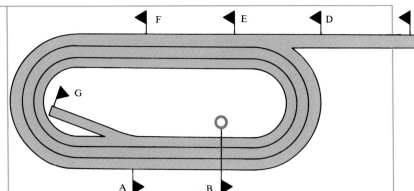

AQUEDUCT. This racecourse, in New York State, is 12 miles (19 km) from New York itself and has two sand tracks and one grass course. The outermost sand track is oval-shaped and covers a distance of 1 mile 1 furlong (1,800 m), and is 100 ft (30.48 m) wide along the finishing straight and 110 ft (35.2 m) across the opposite straight, narrowing, however, to 100 ft (30.48 m) at the end. The distance from the last bend to the finishing post is 385 yds (35.2 m). The inner sand track is also oval-shaped and is 1 mile (1,600 m) long and 90 ft (27.4 m) wide along the finishing straight. The grass course is 7 furlongs 14 yds (1,413 m) long. The courses are left-handed.

A – 1 mile 2 furlongs (2,000 m). **B** – 1 mile 1 furlong (1,800 m). **C** – 1 mile (1,600 m). **D** – 7 furlongs (1,400 m). **E** – 6 furlongs (1,200 m). **F** – 5 furlongs (1,000 m). **G** – 1 mile 1 furlong (1,800 m).

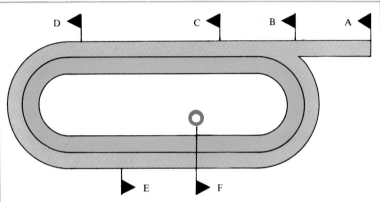

ATLANTIC CITY. This racecourse, 14 miles (22.5 km) from Atlantic City and 46 miles (74 km) from Philadelphia, has an outer sand track and a concentric inner grass track. The sand track is oval in shape and covers a distance of 1 mile 1 furlong (1,800 m). The width of this track is 100 ft (30.48 m) and the distance from the last bend to the finishing post is 316 yds (289 m). The grass course is 1 mile (1,600 m) long and 100 ft (30.48 m) wide. The courses are left-handed. Seats a total of 16,000.

A – 7 furlongs (1,400 m). **B** – 6 furlongs (1,200 m). **C** – 5 furlongs (1,000 m). **D** – 1½ miles (2,400 m). **E** – 1 mile 2 furlongs (2,000 m). **F** – 1 mile 1 furlong (1,800 m).

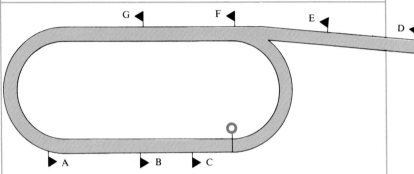

CHURCHILL DOWNS. This racecourse is on the outskirts of Louisville, Kentucky, and has an oval-shaped track 1 mile (1,600 m) long. The track is 80 ft (24.3 m) wide along the finishing straight and slightly narrower (79 ft (24 m)) across the opposite straight. The distance from the Derby start and the finishing post is 440 yds (402 m) whereas from the last bend to the finishing post it is 411 yds (390 m). The course is 120 ft (36.5 m) wide at the Derby start and left-handed. Seats a total of 45,000.

A – 1 mile 2 furlongs (2,000 m). **B** – 1 mile 1 furlong (1,800 m). **C** – 8½ furlongs (1,700 m). **D** – 1 mile (1,600 m). **E** – 7 furlongs (1,400 m). **F** – 6 furlongs (1,200 m). **G** – 5 furlongs (1,000 m).

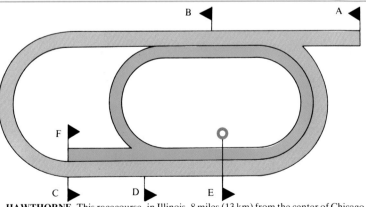

HAWTHORNE. This racecourse, in Illinois, 8 miles (13 km) from the center of Chicago, has two tracks, the outer one being of sand and the inner one of grass. The sand track is 1 mile (1,600 m) long and oval in shape. It is 75 ft (22.8 m) wide along the finishing straight, but around the finishing post broadens to 82 ft (25 m). The opposite straight is 75 ft (22.8 m) wide. The distance between the last bend and the finishing post is 2 furlongs (400 m). The grass course covers a distance of approximately 6 furlongs (1,200 m) and has a chute for the 1-mile (1,600 m) start. The courses are left-handed. Seats a total of 15,000.

A – 6½ furlongs (1,300 m). **B** – 5 furlongs (1,000 m). **C** – 1 mile 2 furlongs (2,000 m). **D** – 1 mile 1 furlong (1,800 m). **E** – 1 mile (1,600 m). **F** – 1 mile (1,600 m).

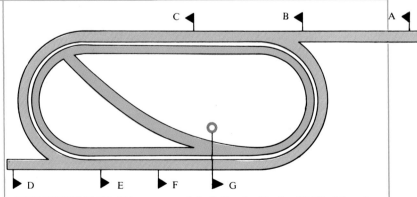

HOLLYWOOD PARK. This racecourse is in California, 11 miles (17.5 km) from Los Angeles and 8 miles (13 km) from Hollywood. It has two tracks, one outer oval sand track and an inner grass course with one diagonal. The sand track is 1 mile (1,600 m) long and 80.5 ft (24.5 m) wide across the straight opposite the winning straight, which is 90.5 ft (27.5 m) wide. The track measures 323 yds (295 m) from the start of the finishing straight to the post. The grass course is 7¼ furlongs (1,450 m) long and both courses are left-handed. Seats a total of 28,897.

A – 7 furlongs (1,400 m). **B** – 6 furlongs (1,200 m). **C** – 5 furlongs (1,000 m). **D** – 1 mile 2 furlongs (2,000 m). **E** – 1 mile 1 furlong (1,800 m). **F** – 8½ furlongs (1,700 m). **G** – 1 mile (1,600 m).

BELMONT PARK. This racecourse is in New York and 20 miles (32 km) from New York City. It has one sand track, two grass courses and an outer training track positioned at a tangent. The sand track is 1½ miles (2,400 m) long, oval-shaped and 88 ft (26.8 m) wide along the finishing straight and 80 ft (24 m) wide across the back straight. This track measures 366 yds (334 m) from the start of the finishing straight to the post. The outermost grass course covers a distance of 1 mile 2 furlongs 119 yds (2,109 m) whereas the innermost track is 1 mile 1 furlong 143 yds (1,131 m). The courses are left-handed. Seats 30,000.

A – 1½ miles (2,400 m). B – 1 mile 2 furlongs (2,000 m). C – 1 mile (1,600 m). D – 7 furlongs (1,400 m). E – 6 furlongs (1,200 m). F – 8½ furlongs (1,700 m). G – 1 mile (1,600 m). H – 1½ miles (2,400 m). I – 1 mile 2 furlongs (2,000 m).

A – 7 furlongs (1,400 m). B – 6 furlongs (1,200 m). C – 5 furlongs (1,000 m). D – 1½ miles (2,400 m). E – 1 mile 2 furlongs (2,000 m). F – 1 mile 1 furlong (1,800 m). G – 8½ furlongs (1,700). H – 1 mile (1,600 m). I – 1 mile 6 furlongs (2,800 m). L – 1½ miles (2.400 m). M – 1 mile 2 furlongs (2,000 m).

SANTA ANITA PARK. This racecourse is 10 miles (17 km) from the center of Los Angeles and has an outer sand track with a grass course inside it. The oval sand track is 1 mile (1,600 m) long and varies in width from 80 to 85 ft (24–26 m), wider along the finishing straight. At the 1¼-mile (2,000 m) start the course is 125 ft (38 m) wide. The distance between the end of the last bend and the finishing post is 330 yds (301 m). In addition to following a round path inside and concentric to the sand track (which is 9/10 of a mile (1,440 m) in length), a 5¾ furlong (1,150 m) stretch of the grass course runs outside the main ring and descends from a hill, at the top of which is the 1¾-mile (2,800 m) start. The 1½-mile (2,400 m) and 1¼-mile (2,000 m) starts are also to be found along this stretch. The courses are left-handed.

HIALEAH PARK. Six miles (9.5 km) from the center of Miami in Florida, this racecourse has two tracks, an outer sand track and a concentric grass course inside. The sand track covers a distance of 1 mile 1 furlong (1,800 m) and is oval-shaped. It is 80 ft (24 m) wide and the distance from the last bend to the finishing post is 358 yds (327 m). The grass track is just under 1 mile long (1,564 m) and 90 ft (27.4 m) wide. The distance from the last bend to the finishing post on this course is 325 yds (297 m). The courses are left-handed. The grandstand seats 13,000 and the Club House 7,000.

A – 7 furlongs (1,400 m). B – 5 furlongs (1,000 m). C – 1½ miles (2,400 m). D – 1 mile 2 furlongs (2,000 m). E – 1 mile 1½ furlongs (1,900 m). F – 1 mile 1 furlong (1,800 m).

LAUREL RACECOURSE. Situated in Maryland State, 20 miles (32 km) from both Baltimore and Washington, this racecourse has two tracks, one outer sand track, on the inside of which runs a concentric grass course. The sand track covers a distance of 1 mile 1 furlong (1,800 m) and has a width of 86 ft (26 m) along the finishing straight and 70 ft (21 m) across the back straight. The distance from the end of the last bend to the finishing post is 338 yds (309 m). The grass course is 1 mile (1,600 m) long and 80 ft (24 m) wide. Here, the distance from the start of the finishing straight to the normal post is 330 yds (301 m) and 410 yds (375 m) to the auxiliary post. The courses are left-handed.

A – 1 mile (1,600 m). B – 7 furlongs (1,400 m). C – 6 furlongs (1,200 m). D – 5 furlongs (1,000 m). E – 1 mile 3 furlongs (2,200 m). F – 1 mile 2 furlongs (2,000 m). G – 1 mile 1 furlong (1,800 m).

PIMLICO. This racecourse is in Maryland, 40 miles (64 km) from Washington and 5 miles (8 km) from Baltimore. It has two tracks, the outer one of sand and the inner one of grass. The sand track is oval-shaped and 1 mile (1,600 m) long. The width of the straight is 69 ft (21 m) and the distance between the last bend and the finishing post is 384 yds (351 m). The grass course is inside and concentric to the sand track and is 7 furlongs (1,400 m) in length. The courses are left-handed. The grandstand seats 8,702, the old grandstand 7,342 and the Club House 2,778.

A – 6 furlongs (1,200 m). B – 5 furlongs (1,000 m). C – 1 mile 2 furlongs (2,000 m). D – 1 mile (1,600 m).

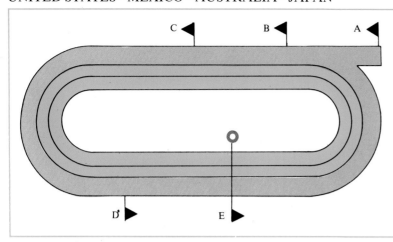

SARATOGA. The racecourse is in Saratoga County in New York State and has one outer sand track with two inner grass courses concentric to it. The oval sand track covers a distance of 1 mile 1 furlong (1,800 m) and is 100 ft (30.48 m) wide. The distance between the last bend and the finishing post is 381 yds (348 m). The grass courses measure 1 mile 33 yds (1,638 m – the outer one) and 7 furlongs 101 yds (1,492 m – the inner one). The courses are left-handed. The grandstand seats 7,365 and the Club House 1,500.

A – 7 furlongs (1,400 m). **B** – 5 furlongs (1,000 m). **C** – 1 mile 2 furlongs (2,000 m). **D** – 1 mile 1 furlong (1,800 m). **E** – 1 mile 1 furlong (1,800 m).

MEXICO

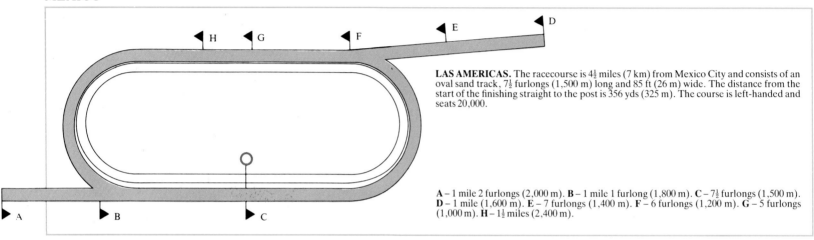

LAS AMERICAS. The racecourse is 4½ miles (7 km) from Mexico City and consists of an oval sand track, 7½ furlongs (1,500 m) long and 85 ft (26 m) wide. The distance from the start of the finishing straight to the post is 356 yds (325 m). The course is left-handed and seats 20,000.

A – 1 mile 2 furlongs (2,000 m). **B** – 1 mile 1 furlong (1,800 m). **C** – 7½ furlongs (1,500 m). **D** – 1 mile (1,600 m). **E** – 7 furlongs (1,400 m). **F** – 6 furlongs (1,200 m). **G** – 5 furlongs (1,000 m). **H** – 1½ miles (2,400 m).

AUSTRALIA

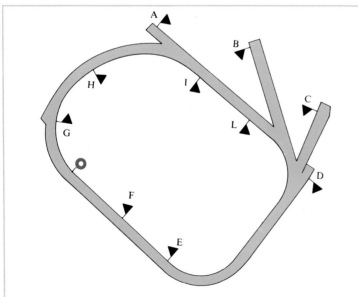

RANDWICK. The racecourse is near Sydney in the state of New South Wales. Its grass course is an irregular round shape which in fact has three bends, two of which are sharper. The circumference of the track is 1 mile 3 furlongs (2,213 m). The finishing straight is 460 yds (420 m) long, 98 ft (30 m) wide. The course is right-handed.

A – 1 mile (1,600 m). **B** – 7 furlongs (1,400 m). **C** – 6 furlongs (1,200 m). **D** – 5 furlongs (1,000 m). **E** – 1 mile 5 furlongs (2,600 m). **F** – 1½ miles (2,400 m). **G** – 1 mile 2 furlongs (2,000 m). **H** – 1 mile 1 furlong (1,800 m). **I** – 7 furlongs (1,400 m). **L** – 6 furlongs (1,200 m).

JAPAN

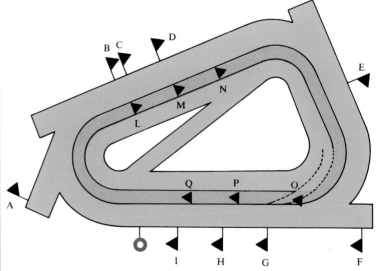

HANSHIN. The racecourse is in Takarazuka City, 12½ miles (20 km) from Kobe and Osaka. It has two tracks, an outer grass course, 1 mile 124 yds (1,712 m) long, 82 ft (25 m) wide, with a 390-yd (356 m) finishing straight, and an inner sand track of the same width but 7 furlongs 146 yds (1,536 m) long with a homestretch of 387 yds (354 m). The courses are right-handed. There is a long steeplechase course, 65½ ft (20 m) wide, and 6 furlongs 200 yds (1,383 m) long with a 342-yd (313 m) long diagonal inside the flat-racing course.

A – 1 mile (1,600 m). **B** – 6½ furlongs (1,300 m). **C** – 1 mile 7 furlongs (3,000 m). **D** – 6 furlongs (1,200 m). **E** – 1½ miles (2,400 m). **F** – 1 mile 3 furlongs (2,200 m). **G** – 1 mile 2 furlongs (2,000 m). **H** – 1 mile 1½ furlongs (1,900 m). **I** – 1 mile 1 furlong (1,800 m). **L** – 6 furlongs (1,200 m). **M** – 5½ furlongs (1,100 m). **N** – 5 furlongs (1,000 m). **O** – 1 mile 1½ furlongs (1,900 m). **P** – 1 mile 1 furlong (1,800 m). **Q** – 8½ furlongs (1,700 m).

KYOTO. Twelve miles (20 km) from Kyoto and 24 miles (40 km) from Osaka, this racecourse has two tracks: an outer grass course and an inner sand track. The grass course measures 1 mile 1½ furlongs (1,911 m) round the outer bend and 1 mile 1 furlong (1,802 m) round the inner one, with a width of 82–114 ft (25–35 m), depending on the stretch. The finishing straights measure 440 yds (406 m) and 374 yds (342 m) respectively. The oval sand track is concentric to the grass course and is 1 mile 28 yds (1,626 m) long, 82–88 ft (25–27 m) wide. The courses are right-handed.

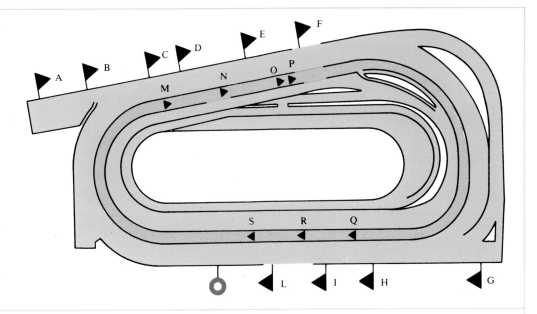

A – 7½ furlongs (1,500 m – small course); 1 mile (1,600 m – large course). **B** – 7 furlongs (1,400 m – small course); 7½ furlongs (1,500 m – large course). **C** – 7 furlongs (1,400 m – large course). **D** – 6 furlongs (1,200 m – small course). **E** – 5½ furlongs (1,100 m – small course). **F** – 1 mile 7 furlongs (3,000 – large course). **G** – 1½ miles (2,400 m – large course). **H** – 1 mile 3 furlongs (2,200 m – large course). **I** – 1 mile 2 furlongs (2,000 m – small course). **L** – 1 mile 1 furlong (1,800 m – small course); 1 mile 2 furlongs (2,000 m – large course). **M** – 6 furlongs (1,200 m). **N** – 5½ furlongs (1,100 m). **O** – 5 furlongs (1,000 m). **P** – 1 mile 5 furlongs (2,600 m). **Q** – 1 mile 1½ furlongs (1,900 m). **R** – 1 mile 1 furlong (1,800 m). **S** – 8½ furlongs (1,700 m).

NAKAYAMA. This racecourse is in Funabashi City, 18 miles (30 km) from Tokyo. It has an outer grass course of which the longer course, running round a wide bend adjacent to the opposite straight, measures 1 mile 1 furlong 82 yds (1,875 m), while the inner course covers a distance of 8½ furlongs (1,699 m). The grass course varies in width from 65½ ft (20 m) to 105 ft (32 m), depending on the course being followed, and the finishing straight is 339 yds (310 m) long. Concentric to and inside the grass course is a sand track which is 7 furlongs 170 yds (1,556 m) long, 65½ ft (20 m) wide, with a finishing straight of 336 yds (308 m). The racecourse also has a steeplechase course with two parallel diagonals. The round circuit is 7 furlongs 55 yds (1,450 m) long whereas the two diagonals measure 700 yds (640 m) and 630 yds (576 m). The steeplechase course is 56–98 ft (17–30 m) wide. The training courses are positioned between the sand track and the steeplechase course. The courses are right-handed.

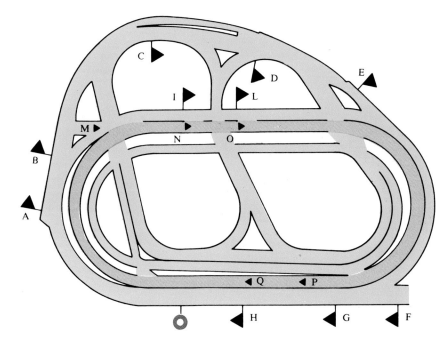

A – 1 mile (1,600 m). **B** – 2 miles (3,200 m). **C** – 6 furlongs (1,200 m). **D** – 5 furlongs (1,000 m). **E** – 1 mile 4½ furlongs (2,500 m – small course). **F** – 2½ miles (4,000 m – small and large courses); 1 mile 3½ furlongs (2,300 m – large course). **G** – 1 mile 2 furlongs (2,000 m – small course). **H** – 1 mile 2 furlongs (2,000 m – large course). **I** – 5 furlongs (1,000 m). **L** – 5 furlongs (1,000 m). **M** – 6 furlongs (1,200 m). **N** – 1 mile 5 furlongs (2,600 m). **O** – 1 mile 4½ furlongs (2,500 m). **P** – 1 mile 1 furlong (1,800 m). **Q** – 8½ furlongs (1,700 m).

TOKYO. This racecourse is in Fuchu City, 17 miles (27 km) from the heart of Tokyo. There are two racetracks: one inner sand track of about 1 mile 1½ furlongs (1,900 m) long, 81–87 ft (25–27 m) wide, with a finishing straight of 521 yds (477 m), and an outer grass course, 1 mile 2½ furlongs (2,100 m) long with a finishing straight of 555 yds (508 m). There is a third course, for steeplechases, within these two. In the last 273 yds (250 m) and after the winning post up to the 1-mile 1-furlong (1,800 m) post, the track is absolutely flat. The grass course also has a wider outer bend than the one on which the 1-mile 2-furlong (2,000 m) start is located. The starts for the 1-mile 1-furlong (1,800 m) and 8½-furlong (1,700 m) races are in the space between the two bends (on the grass and sand tracks respectively). The courses are left- and right-handed.

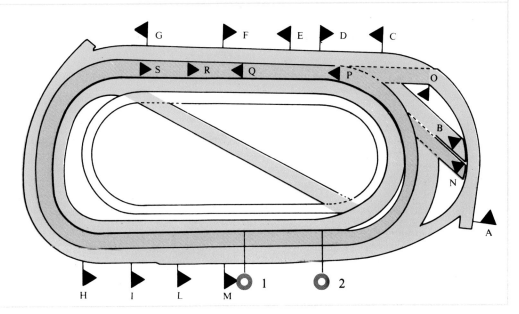

A – 1 mile 2 furlongs (2,000 m). **B** – 1 mile 1 furlong (1,800 m). **C** – 1 mile (1,600 m). **D** – 5 furlongs* (1,000 m). **E** – 7 furlongs (1,400 m). **F** – 6 furlongs* (1,200 m). **G** – 6 furlongs (1,200 m). **H** – 1 mile 5 furlongs (2,600 m). **I** – 1 mile 4½ furlongs (2,500 m). **L** – 1½ miles (2,400 m). **M** – 1 mile 3½ furlongs (2,300 m). **N** – 8½ furlongs (1,700 m). **O** – 1 mile (1,600 m). **P** – 7 furlongs (1,400 m). **Q** – 6 furlongs (1,200 m). **R** – 5 furlongs* (1,000 m). **S** – 5½ furlongs (1,100 m).

*first post.

CHAMPIONSHIP RECORDS

CHAMPIONSHIP RECORDS   ENGLISH TRIPLE CROWN WINNERS
2000 Guineas - Derby Stakes - St. Leger Stakes

Horse	Year of birth	Sire	Owner	Starts	Wins	Other Important Wins
West Australian	♂ ○ 1850	Melbourne	J. Bowes	11	10	Ascot Gold Cup
Gladiateur	♂ ○ 1862	Monarque	C.te F. de Lagrange	19	16	Grand Prix de Paris, Prix Royal Oak, Ascot Gold Cup
Lord Lyon	♂ ○ 1863	Stockwell	Mr. R. Sutton	21	17	Craven Stakes, Stockbridge Cup
Ormonde	♂ ○ 1883	Bend Or	Duke of Westminster	16	16	Champion Stakes, Dewhurst Stakes, Rous Memorial Stakes, Hardwicke Stakes, St. James's Palace Stakes
Common	♂ ● 1888	Isonomy	F. Johnstone	5	4	St. James's Palace Stakes
Isinglass	♂ ○ 1890	Isonomy	H. Mc Calmont	12	11	Ascot Gold Cup, Eclipse Stakes, Middle Park Stakes, Jockey Club Stakes, Newmarket Stakes, New Stakes, Princess of Wales's Stakes
Galtee More	♂ ○ 1894	Kendal	Mr. J. Gubbins	12	10	Middle Park Stakes
Flying Fox	♂ ○ 1896	Orme	Duke of Westminster	11	9	New Stakes, Eclipse Stakes, Criterion Stakes, Jockey Club Stakes, Princess of Wales's Stakes
Diamond Jubilee	♂ ○ 1897	St. Simon	Prince of Wales	13	6	Eclipse Stakes, Newmarket Stakes
Rock Sand	♂ ● 1900	Sainfoin	J. Miller	20	16	Woodcote Stakes, Coventry Stakes, Hardwicke Stakes, Champagne Stakes, Jockey Club Stakes, Dewhurst Stakes, Princess of Wales's Stakes, St. James's Palace Stakes, Chesterfield Stakes
Pommern	♂ ○ 1912	Polymelus	S. Joel	10	7	Richmond Stakes, Imperial Produce Stakes
Gay Crusader	♂ ○ 1914	Bayardo	Mr. Fairie	10	8	Newmarket Gold Cup, Champion Stakes, Criterion Stakes, Ascot Gold Cup
Gainsborough	♂ ○ 1915	Bayardo	Lady J. Douglas	9	5	Ascot Gold Cup
Bahram	♂ ○ 1932	Blandford	Aga Khan	9	9	Middle Park Stakes, Gimcrack Stakes, St. James's Palace Stakes
Nijinsky	♂ ○ 1967	Northern Dancer	C.W. Engelhard	13	11	Irish Sweeps Derby, King George VI and Queen Elizabeth Stakes, Dewhurst Stakes

AMERICAN TRIPLE CROWN WINNERS
Kentucky Derby - Preakness Stakes - Belmont Stakes

Horse	Year of birth	Sire	Owner	Starts	Wins	Other Important Wins
Sir Barton	♂ ○ 1916	Star Shoot	J. K. L. Ross	31	13	Withers Stakes, Maryland Handicap, Saratoga Handicap
Gallant Fox	♂ ○ 1927	Sir Gallahad III	W. Woodward	17	11	Saratoga Cup, Lawrence Realization Stakes, Jockey Club Gold Cup, Wood Memorial Stakes, Arlington Classic Stakes
Omaha	♂ ◇ 1932	Gallant Fox	W. Woodward	22	9	Arlington Classic Stakes
War Admiral	♂ ● 1934	Man o'War	S. D. Riddle	26	21	Pimlico Special, Saratoga Handicap, Saratoga Cup, Jockey Club Gold Cup, Washington Handicap

(American Triple Crown winners continued)

Horse	Year of birth	Sire	Owner	Starts	Wins	Other Important Wins
Whirlaway	♂ ◇ 1938	Blenheim	W. Wright	60	32	Saratoga Special, Hopeful Stakes, Breeders' Futurity, Travers Stakes, American Derby, Lawrence Realization Stakes, Jockey Club Gold Cup, Washington Handicap
Count Fleet	♂ • 1940	Reigh Count	John Hertz	21	16	Champagne Stakes, Pimlico Futurity, Wood Memorial Stakes, Withers Stakes
Assault	♂ ◇ 1943	Bold Venture	R. J. Kleberg Jr.	33	16	Experimental Free Handicap, Wood Memorial, Suburban Handicap, Brooklyn Handicap
Citation	♂ ○ 1945	Bull Lea	Calumet Farm	45	32	Futurity Stakes, Pimlico Futurity, Flamingo Stakes, Derby Trial, American Derby, Jockey Club Gold Cup, Gold Cup (Belmont Park), Hollywood Gold Cup, Pimlico Special (walk-over)
Secretariat	♂ ◇ 1970	Bold Ruler	Meadow Stable	21	16	Hopeful Stakes, Futurity Stakes, Laurel Futurity, Marlboro Cup Invitational Handicap, Man o' War Stakes, Canadian International Championship Stakes
Seattle Slew	♂ • 1974	Bold Reasoning	Karen Taylor	17	14	Champagne Stakes, Wood Memorial Stakes, Flamingo Stakes, Marlboro Cup, Woodward Stakes
Affirmed	♂ ◇ 1975	Exclusive Native	Harbor View Farm	29	22	Hopeful Stakes, Futurity Stakes, Laurel Futurity, Santa Anita Derby, Hollywood Derby, Jockey Club Gold Cup, Hollywood Gold Cup, Santa Anita Handicap, Californian Stakes, Woodward Stakes, Charles H. Strub Stakes

SOME OF THE WORLD'S MAJOR FLAT RACES

Great Britain

April — General Accident 1,000 Guineas – Rowley Mile (1,600 m) – Group I – 3-year-old fillies – Newmarket

April — General Accident 2,000 Guineas – Rowley Mile (1,600 m) – Group I – 3-year-olds – Newmarket

June — Ever Ready Derby Stakes – 1½ miles (2,400 m) – Group I – 3-year-olds – Epsom

June — Coronation Cup – 1½ miles (2,400 m) – Group I – 4-year-olds and upwards – Epsom

June — Gold Seal Oaks Stakes – 1½ miles (2,400 m) – Group I – 3-year-old fillies – Epsom

June — St. James's Palace Stakes – Old Mile (1,600 m) – Group II – 3-year-olds – Ascot

June — Coventry Stakes – 6 furlongs (1,200 m) – Group II – 2-year-olds – Ascot

June — Prince of Wales's Stakes – 1 mile 2 furlongs (2,000 m) – Group II – 3-year-olds and upwards – Ascot

June — Gold Cup – 2½ miles (4,000 m) – Group I – 3-year-olds and upwards – Ascot

June — King's Stand Stakes – 5 furlongs (1,000 m) – Group I – 3-year-olds and upwards – Ascot

June — Hardwicke Stakes – 1½ miles (2,400 m) – Group II – 4-year-olds and upwards – Ascot

July — Norcros July Cup – 6 furlongs (1,200 m) – Group I – 3-year-olds and upwards – Newmarket

July — King George VI and Queen Elizabeth Diamond Stakes – 1½ miles (2,400 m) – Group I – 3-year-olds and upwards – Ascot

July — Swettenham Stud Sussex Stakes – 1 mile (1,600 m) – Group I – 3-year-olds and upwards – Goodwood

August — Yorkshire Oaks – 1½ miles (2,400 m) – Group I – 3-year-old fillies – York

August — Benson and Hedges Gold Cup – 1 mile 2½ furlongs (2,100 m) – Group I – 3-year-olds and upwards – York

August — Gimcrack Stakes – 6 furlongs (1,200 m) – Group II – 2-year-olds – York

September — Holsten Pils St. Leger Stakes – 1 mile 6 furlongs 127 yds (2,920 m) – Group I – 3-year-olds – Doncaster

September — Tattersalls Cheveley Park Stakes – 6 furlongs (1,200 m) – 2-year-old fillies – Newmarket

October — Middle Park Stakes – 6 furlongs (1,200 m) – Group I – 2-year-olds – Newmarket

October — William Hill Dewhurst Stakes – 7 furlongs (1,400 m) – Group I – 2-year-olds – Newmarket

October — Dubai Champion Stakes – 1 mile 2 furlongs (2,000 m) – Group I – 3-year-olds and upwards – Newmarket

October William Hill Futurity (ex Observer Gold Cup) – 1 mile (1,600 m) – 2-year-olds – Doncaster

Ireland

May Goffs Irish 1,000 Guineas – 1 mile (1,600 m) – Group I – 3-year-old fillies – The Curragh
May Airlie/Coolmore Irish 2,000 Guineas – 1 mile (1,600 m) – Group I – 3-year-olds – The Curragh
May Gallinule Stakes – 1½ miles (2,400 m) – Group II – 3-year-olds – The Curragh
June Irish Sweeps Derby – 1½ miles (2,400 m) – Group I – 3-year-olds – The Curragh
July Irish Guinness Oaks – 1½ miles (2,400 m) – Group I – 3-year-old fillies – The Curragh
September Joe McGrath Memorial Stakes – 1 mile 2 furlongs (2,000 m) – Group I – 3-year-olds and upwards – Leopardstown
October Jefferson Smurfit Memorial Irish St. Leger – 1 mile 6 furlongs (2,800 m) – Group I – 3-year-olds and upwards – The Curragh

France

April Prix Greffulhe – 1 mile 2½ furlongs (2,100 m) – Group II – 3-year-olds – Longchamp
April Poule d'Essai des Poulains – 1 mile (1,600 m) – Group I – 3-year-old colts – Longchamp
April Prix Noailles – 1 mile 3 furlongs (2,200 m) – Group II – 3-year-olds – Longchamp
May Poule d'Essai des Pouliches – 1 mile (1,600 m) – Group I – 3-year-old fillies – Longchamp
May Prix Ganay – 1 mile 2½ furlongs (2,100 m) – Group I – 4-year-olds and upwards – Longchamp
May Prix Hocquart – 1½ miles (2,400 m) – Group II – 3-year-olds – Longchamp
May Prix Lupin – 1 mile 2½ furlongs (2,100 m) – Group I – 3-year-olds – Longchamp
May Prix Saint-Alary – 1 mile 2 furlongs (2,000 m) – Group I – 3-year-old fillies – Longchamp
June Prix du Jockey Club – 1½ miles (2,400 m) – Group I – 3-year-olds – Chantilly
June Prix de Diane Hermes – 1 mile 2½ furlongs (2,100 m) – Group I – 3-year-old fillies – Chantilly
June Grand Prix de Paris – 1 mile 7 furlongs (3,000 m) – Group I – 3-year-olds – Longchamp
June Prix d'Ispahan – 1 mile 1¼ furlongs (1,850 m) – Group I – 3-year-olds and upwards – Longchamp
July Grand Prix de Saint-Cloud – 1 mile 4½ furlongs (2,500 m) – Group I – 3-year-olds and upwards – Saint Cloud
July Prix Robert Papin – 5½ furlongs (1,100 m) – Group I – 2-year-olds – Maisons-Laffitte
August Prix Jacques le Marois – 1 mile (1,600 m) – Group I – 3-year-olds and upwards – Deauville
August Prix Morny – 6 furlongs (1,200 m) – Group I – 2-year-olds – Deauville
September Prix du Moulin de Longchamp – 1 mile (1,600 m) – Group I – 3-year-olds and upwards – Longchamp
September Trusthouse Forte Prix Vermeille – 1½ miles (2,400 m) – Group I – 3-year-old fillies – Longchamp
September Prix de la Salamandre – 7 furlongs (1,400 m) – Group I – 2-year-olds – Longchamp
October Prix de l'Abbaye de Longchamp – 5 furlongs (1,000 m) – straight course – Group I – 2-year-olds and upwards – Longchamp
October Trusthouse Forte Prix de l'Arc de Triomphe – 1½ miles (2,400 m) – Group I – 3-year-olds and upwards – Longchamp
October Prix Marcel Boussac (Critérium des Pouliches) – 1 mile (1,600 m) – Group I – 2-year-old fillies – Longchamp
October Grand Critérium – 1 mile (1,600 m) – Group I – 2-year-olds – Longchamp
October Prix de la Forêt – 7 furlongs (1,400 m) – Group I – 2-year-olds and upwards – Longchamp
October Prix Royal-Oak – 1 mile 7½ furlongs (3,100 m) – Group I – 3-year-olds and upwards – Longchamp

Italy

April Premio Emanuele Filiberto – 1 mile 2 furlongs (2,000 m) – Group II – 3-year-olds – San Siro
April Premio Regina Elena – 1 mile (1,600 m) – Group I – 3-year-old fillies – Capannelle
April Premio Coppa d'Oro di Milano – 1 mile 7 furlongs (3,000 m) – Group III – 4-year-olds and upwards – San Siro
May Derby Italiano – 1½ miles (2,400 m) – Group I – 3-year-olds – Capannelle
May Premio Presidente della Repubblica – 1 mile 2 furlongs (2,000 m) – Group I – 3-year-olds and upwards – Capannelle
May Gran Premio d'Italia – 1½ miles (2,400 m) – Group I – 3-year-olds – San Siro
June Gran Premio di Milano – 1½ miles (2,400 m) – Group I – 3-year-olds and upwards – San Siro
September Criterium Nazionale – 6 furlongs (1,200 m) – Group III – 2-year-olds – San Siro
September St. Leger Italiano – 1 mile 6 furlongs (2,800 m) – Group II – 3-year-olds – San Siro
October Gran Criterium – 1 mile (1,600 m) – Group I – 2-year-olds – San Siro
October Gran Premio del Jockey Club – 1½ miles (2,400 m) – Group I – 3-year-olds and upwards – San Siro
November Premio Tevere – 1 mile (1,600 m) – Group II – 2-year-olds – Capannelle

Germany

July Deutsches Derby – 1½ miles (2,400 m) – Group I – 3-year-olds – Hamburg Horn
September Grosser Preis von Baden – 1½ miles (2,400 m) – Group I – 3-year-olds and upwards – Baden Baden
October Preis von Europa – 1½ miles (2,400 m) – Group I – 3-year-olds and upwards – Cologne

United States

March Florida Derby – 1 mile 1 furlong (1,800 m) – Group I – 3-year-olds – Gulfstream Park
April Santa Anita Derby – 1 mile 1 furlong (1,800 m) – Group I – 3-year-olds – Santa Anita
May Kentucky Oaks – 1 mile 1 furlong (1,800 m) – Group I – 3-year-old fillies – Churchill Downs
May Kentucky Derby – 1 mile 2 furlongs (2,000 m) – Group I – 3-year-olds – Churchill Downs
May Preakness Stakes – 1 mile 1½ furlongs (1,900 m) – Group I – 3-year-olds – Pimlico
June Belmont Stakes – 1½ miles (2,400 m) – Group I – 3-year-olds – Belmont Park
June Hollywood Gold Cup Handicap – 1 mile 2 furlongs (2,000 m) – Group I – 3-year-olds and upwards – Hollywood Park
July Swaps Stakes – 1 mile 2 furlongs (2,000 m) – Group I – 3-year-olds – Hollywood Park
September Futurity Stakes – 7 furlongs (1,400 m) – Group I – 2-year-olds – Belmont Park
October Man o'War Stakes – 1 mile 3 furlongs (2,200 m) – Group I – 3-year-olds and upwards – Belmont Park
October Jockey Club Gold Cup Stakes – 1½ miles (2,400 m) – Group I – 3-year-olds and upwards – Belmont Park
October Laurel Futurity – 1 mile ½ furlong (1,700 m) – Group I – 2-year-olds – Laurel
November Washington D.C. International – 1½ miles (2,400 m) – Group I – 3-year-olds and upwards – Laurel

Japan

April Satsuki Shou (Japanese 2,000 Guineas) – 1 mile 2 furlongs (2,000 m) – Group I – 3-year-olds – Nakayama
May Yuushun Hinba (Japanese Oaks) – 1½ miles (2,400 m) – Group I – 3-year-old fillies – Tokyo
November Kikuka Shou (Japanese St. Leger) – 1 mile 7 furlongs (3,000 m) – Group I – 3-year-olds – Kyoto
November Japan Cup – 1½ miles (2,400 m) – Group I – 3-year-olds and upwards – Tokyo
December Arima Kinen (Nakayama Grand Prix) – 1 mile 4½ furlong (2,500 m) – Group I – 3-year-olds and upwards – Nakayama

The calendar may vary from one year to the next

THE QUARTER HORSE

The Quarter Horse was developed by the early settlers in Virginia and Carolina who needed a horse with the characteristics and performance to suit their particular requirements. They began the selection process by crossbreeding horses of Andalusian and English thoroughbred stock that they had brought over from England. These were English horses which already had the characteristics of the thoroughbred, but could not be defined as such since the breed had not yet been officially established. The products of this crossbreeding were used for races over a quarter of a mile (which is how the breed gets its name) along the main road of the village. This practical, selective breeding resulted in the creation of a fast, lively and agile horse with very quick reflexes which proved very useful to the cowboys who were quick to recognize its natural ability for this type of work. These characteristics still make it the ideal horse for rodeos, sporting displays reviving the spirit of the America of a bygone era.

Apart from being an excellent racehorse in its own special area, the quarter horse is also very suitable for polo, jumping and hunting, and its very versatile nature makes it a top class horse for sporting events. The American Quarter Horse Association, set up in 1941 at Fort Worth, with its headquarters at Amarillo in Texas, currently keeps a record of over 800,000 regularly registered horses, not only in the United States but in 40 other countries. On the whole, the quarter horse is a sturdy powerfully-built horse with an exceptionally well-balanced temperament. It has a dolichomorphic constitution and its height at the withers varies from 15.1 to 15.9 hands (1.54–1.62 m). It is a docile-natured horse but, at the same time, energetic and lively. Various colours can be found: bay, dark bay, black, grey, chestnut, burnt chestnut, dun, golden chestnut, light-brown, grey brown, palomino, blue roan and strawberry roan.

The quarter horse has a broad head and straight profile, large lively eyes, broad forehead, pointed ears, wide nostrils and slightly protruding jaws. It has a slightly arched, well-conformed muscular neck, well-placed withers, a straight dorsolumbar line, short muscular back, strong loins, muscular sloping croup, tail attached low down, well-developed long sloping shoulders and a roomy deep chest. The legs are solid and muscular with broad clean joints, well-defined tendons, short cannon and pastern bones, very well-developed hindquarters and hard well-conformed hooves.

THE RACES

These typically American horse shows attract large audiences at about a hundred tracks dotted all over the United States. The races cover various distances ranging from 300 yards (274 m) to 350 yards (320 m), 400 yards (365 m) and 440 yards (402 m) – the most traditional distance. There are also heats over 550 yards (502 m) and 870 yards (795 m). The spectacular circus connected with these shows is truly enthralling. Before each race, the contestants file past, each accompanied by another horse mounted by a rider dressed in fox-hunting livery. A trumpet sounds, calling the horses to the starting line and the contestants take their places in the stalls. When the stalls open, the horses shoot off like bullets from a gun, a group of three or four arriving almost simultaneously a few seconds later.

The visual effect of these races is vaguely reminiscent of greyhound races and very often the order of arrival can be determined only after examining the photo finish. The ceremony leading up to the race is probably to compensate for the short duration of the competition, but whoever watches this type of spectacle is almost sure to leave with a favourable impression. The most important race, which takes place at the Los Alamitos racetrack in California, is the Fabergé Special Effort Futurity, held in August over 440 yards (402 m) with a prize in 1982 of $1,200,000, equivalent to about £800,000. At this racecourse all races are run on a straight track with the starting point in the chute that joins on to the finishing straight, except for the 870-yard (795 m) races which start in the stretch in front of the stands.

The speeds attained in these races are quite remarkable, the maximum being reached in the 440-yard races. The track record at Los Alamitos over this distance is held by Dash for Cash with a time of 21'17". The time usually taken to cover this distance is 21'65", equivalent to 53"8/10 over 1,000 meters. This speed increases from the 300-yard (273 m) races (1'33"3/mile (0.58 km)) culminating, as already stated in the traditional distance of 440 yards (402 m) whereas beyond this it drops as low as 1'26"9/mile (54" – to 1,000 in the 550-yard races and 1'33"3/mile (58" – still to the kilometer) in the 870-yard (795 m) races.

DASH FOR CASH

ch.h. 1973

There are many interesting features in the pedigree of this horse. In 1970, Dash for Cash's sire, Rocket Wrangler, was the two-year-old Quarter Horse Champion as well as winner of the All American Futurity, the Rainbow Futurity and the New Mexico State Fair Stakes. He was out of Go Galla Go, a mare by Go Man Go, in his turn rated World Champion for two years running by the American Quarter Horse Association. Although Dash for Cash's male line includes champions of this caliber, his female line is just as interesting for different reasons, since his dam was a thoroughbred sired by the stallion To Market (sire of stakes winners and himself a stakes winner) and he belonged to a family that had produced a large number of winners. Find a Buyer in fact produced winners both amongst quarter horses and thoroughbreds and her third dam, Imperatrice, produced Somethingroyal, the dam of Secretariat. Dash for Cash's origins are, therefore, perfectly respectable, 13 of his 16 ancestors in the fourth remove being English thoroughbreds.

The racing career of this exceptional horse lasted from two to four and as well as his 21 wins, over distances of between 300 yds (274 m) and 440 yds (402 m) (some of which were very important), he boasts some exceptionally prestigious titles: World Champion in 1976 and 1977, Three-year-old and Three-year-old Entire Horse Champion in 1976 and Aged Horses Champion and Entire Aged Horse Champion in 1977. Dash for Cash suffered only four defeats in his career, two in the first year and two in the second. The first was when he was second (a neck behind the winner) in the Sunland Futurity Trial and again in the Classic, the Sunland Park Fall Futurity, in which he was unplaced for the first and only time in his life. As a three-year-old Dash for Cash met with two more defeats on the Ruidoso track, the first in the Rainbow Derby and the other in the American Derby. He finished second in both races half a length behind the winner.

When his brilliant racing career was over Dash for Cash was syndicated for two and a half million dollars, B. F. Phillips Jr remaining the majority shareholder. In his new role as a stallion, he was as successful as he was on the track and in his first three years at stud he sired some very able performers, mostly fillies. Those of his offspring (111 performers up to 9 February 1983) of greatest credit to him are: Baby Hold On (ch.m. 1978) winner of the Alamo Q.H.B.A. Futurity; Queen for Cash (ch.m. 1978) Three-year-old Filly Champion, winner of the Lassie Handicap and the Miss Princess Handicap at Los Alamitos; Dash Again (ch.m. 1979) winner of the Kindergarten Futurity; Justanold Love (ch.m. 1979) winner of the Juvenile Invitational Handicap at Los Alamitos and the All American Derby at Ruidoso the following year; Dashingly (ch.m. 1979) winner of the Skoal Dash For Cash Futurity and the Golden State Futurity at Los Alamitos; Make Mine Cash (ch.m. 1980) who took the Fabergé Special Effort Futurity ($933,546), the most important of the Two-year-old Classic races; Cashcan (ch.m. 1980) winner of the Northeast Kansas Futurity; and Katchina Doll (ch.m. 1980) winner of the Ed Burke Memorial Futurity with two other daughters of Dash for Cash, Deal In Cash and Profit Plan, third and fifth places.

These were truly exceptional results which would lead one to hope for more high-quality offspring in the future, including similarly accomplished males as well. It is a curious fact that all Dash for Cash's best products that have appeared on the track so far are the same colour as himself – "sorrel" (chestnut).

Dash For Cash				
Rocket Wrangler ◊ 1968	Rocket Bar *	Three Bars	Percentage Myrtle Dee	
		Golden Rocket	Cartago Morshion	
	Go Galla Go	Go Man Go	Top Deck Lightfoot Sis	
		La Galla Win	Direct Win * La Gallina V	
Find a Buyer * ◊ 1966	To Market	Market Wise	Brokers Tip On Hand	
		Pretty Does	Johnstown Creese	
	Hide and Seek	Alibhai	Hyperion Teresina	
		Scattered	Whirlaway Imperatrice	

* English thoroughbred

Breeders: B.F. Phillips Jr & King Ranch Inc.
Owners: B. F. Phillips Jr & King Ranch Inc.
Most Important Wins: Lubbock Downs Futurity, Sunland Country Futurity, Jet Deck Handicap, Los Alamitos Derby, Champion of Champions Invitational (twice), Vessels Maturity, Los Alamitos Championship

Racing Career

Age	No. of Races	Starts	Wins	Placings
2	10	10	8	1
3	11	11	9	2
4	4	4	4	0
Total	25	25	21	3

Steeplechasing

GREAT STEEPLECHASES

The Aintree Grand National is the oldest steeplechase still run today, dating back to 1837 when it was instituted as the Grand Liverpool Chase, later (1847) assuming its current name. France's most important race is the Grand Steeple-Chase de Paris, run at Auteuil since 1847, but steeplechases took place in France as early as 1830 in the Bièvre valley, in the Bois de Boulogne, while steeplechases were being run regularly (for a small élite) as early as 1836 at the Croix de Berny on a type of racecourse which even then followed a set route. In 1863 the Société Générale des Steeple-Chase de France was founded (one of its patrons being Joachim Murat) and steeplechasing began firstly at Vincennes and later, under the leadership of the Prince de Sagan, at the new Auteuil racecourse.

In the United States, the oldest steeplechase is the Maryland Hunt Cup, dating back to 1894, while other important races include My Lady's Manor Stakes at Monkton and the Belmont Park Grand National Steeplechase, both over a three-mile (4.8 km) course. In Italy, the most important race is the Gran Premio di Merano, instituted in 1935 and relatively young in comparison with the other great European and American competitions. As early as 1854, however, the Gran Steeple-Chase di Roma (in effect a cross-country race) was run in Italy, while a "race with hurdles" is known to have been staged in Turin (Piazza d'Armi) in 1841 over 1½ miles 59 yds (2,466 m).

VARIOUS TYPES OF STEEPLECHASES

Like flat races, steeplechases are divided into weight for age races (where the weight is determined in relation to the horse's age by a special table), conditions races, handicaps, beginners' races, maiden, selling races or claiming races. In descending handicaps the maximum weight is 12 st 7 lb (79¼ kg) for jockeys' races and 13 st (83 kg) for amateurs and ladies' races, whereas in ascending handicaps the minimum weight is 9 st 4 lb (60 kg) for jockeys and 10 st 2 lb (65 kg) for amateurs and ladies.

In races that are open to both professionals and amateurs, the weight limits (minimum and maximum) are those set for amateurs and ladies. In the case of descending handicaps the above-mentioned limits can, in exceptional cases, be raised at the handicapper's discretion to 13 st (83 kg) and 13 st 8 lb (88 kg) respectively. According to their particular characteristics, races involving jumping over obstacles are divided into hurdle races, steeplechases, cross-countries and hunter trials.

Hurdle races take place over a set course, the obstacles being natural or artificial hedges, both fixed and movable. In this type of race there must be at least eight obstacles in the first 1 mile 4½ furlongs (2,500 m) plus an additional jump every further 1½ furlongs (300 m). The minimum distance for hurdle races is 1 mile 4½ furlongs (2,500 m) for three-year-olds, at which age horses can begin hurdling. In other types of races involving jumping over obstacles the minimum age is four and 1 mile 5 furlongs (2,600 m) the minimum distance for horses of four and over.

Steeplechases also take place over a marked out course, but here, in addition to hedges, there are also other types of obstacles of varying difficulty. In steeplechases, there must be at least nine obstacles in the first 1 mile 7 furlongs (3,000 m), six of which can be chosen from the compulsory obstacles and the other from the optional ones, plus at least one obstacle every further 1½ furlongs (300 m). In steeplechases, the first and last obstacles must be an ordinary hedge or big hedge, and two consecutive obstacles must not be the same. The minimum distance for steeplechases is 1 mile 7 furlongs (3,000 m). In English and American steeplechases, the rules are less definite and the obstacles take the form of large hedges, fences and the ever-present water-jump, without some of the obstacles typical of French and Italian steeplechases, such as walls and large beams.

Cross-countries, unlike steeplechases and hurdle races, take place partly over a steeplechase course and partly outside the course on a different track over different sized obstacles, both natural and artificial. In a cross-country race there must be at least 12 obstacles in the first 1 mile 7 furlongs (3,000 m) plus another every further 1½ furlongs (300 m). The last obstacle must be an ordinary or a large hedge. The minimum distance is 2 miles 1½ furlongs (3,500 m), which can be reduced to 1 mile 4½ furlongs (2,500 m) in races for apprentices, amateurs or ladies, or the forces.

Hunter trials are races run completely across country over varied ground and scattered with natural or artificial obstacles. In all these types of races each obstacle (even hedges) must have a minimum frontage of 38 ft (12 m), the side wings of the obstacles must be directed towards the obstacle itself and be a minimum of 16 ft (5 m) long and 1½ ft (0.5m) higher than the obstacle at its highest part. Furthermore, all the obstacles must be sturdy enough so as to force the horse to jump over them rather than allow him to crash through them. The ordinary and large hedges must be clipped in a rounded shape for obstacles that can be jumped either way, whereas those jumped just one way must be slanting towards the horse. In steeplechases the distance between one obstacle and the other cannot be greater than 1½ furlongs (300 m) and the final obstacle must be in the finishing straight, about 1 furlong (200 m) from the post.

The compulsory obstacles in steeplechases are the bullfinch (embankment between hedges), talus (railed embankment) and oxer (ditch between hedges), wall, water-jump, hedge (natural or artificial, fixed or movable), large quickset or artificial hedge, large hedge preceded by ditch, large beam (open ditch) and large hedge preceded by railed ditch (rails, ditch and fence), known simply as "fence." In addition to these, there are other optional obstacles such as the large railed hedge (double beam), railed ditch or watercourse (brook), bank and large beam.

In cross-country racing, in addition to the obstacles used in hurdle racing and steeplechasing, other obstacles characteristic of hunter trials are also allowed. Some of the obstacles typical of hunter trials are the small bank, the large bank, the hurdle, the hurdle cage and the large beam with hedge and hurdle. In cross-countries and hunter trials, the obstacles must be marked by two flags or two wicker balls (red on the right-hand side and white on the left) while the obligatory courses are marked by four large black and white chequered flags crossed in pairs either side. In hunter trials yellow flags are set up along the route to indicate the direction of the race. In this type of competition composite obstacles, made up of several elements, are considered as a single unit and so in the case of a horse's refusal to jump just one element, it must be re-jumped in conjunction with the others.

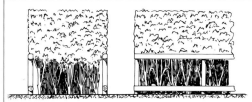

Quickset or natural hedge. This is fixed and must have the following conformation, consistency and dimensions: branches with green leaves, minimum height of 3 ft 7 in (1.1 m), minimum width of 3 ft 7 in (1.1 m); a wooden container 2 ft (1.6 m) in the ground, made of sturdy wooden beams (or horizontal chestnut-wood poles) well nailed in from the front on to vertical wooden posts, 6 ft 6 in (2 m) apart. The container must not have sharp corners and the posts must be driven well into the ground. To achieve the proper consistency of a quickset hedge, it may be necessary to reinforce it from within (up to a height of 3 ft (0.90 m) with a hardy strain of heather and preferably with branches of a suitable kind of wood. In France, the minimum dimensions for the hedge are a height of 3 ft 5 in (1.05 m) and width of 3 ft 3 in (1 m), while the wooden box must be at least 1 ft 7 in (1.5 m) high.

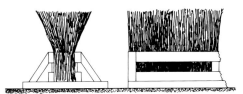

Movable artificial hedge (brush fence). This can be jumped from only one direction and is made up of various movable boxes, with sturdy feet resting on the ground, at least 3 ft 3 in (1.00 m) away from the part to be jumped by the horse, and butted together so as to form a single obstacle, well-anchored to the ground. The movable brush must have no sharp corners and be made so that it cannot be knocked over. This brush must be a minimum of 2 ft 7 in (0.8 m) wide and, if possible, be used only for the final hedge in the race.

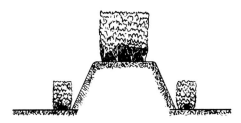

Embankment between hedges (bullfinch). Covered in turf, it is 3 ft (1.9 m) high, 4 ft 11 in (1.5 m) wide at the bottom and 2 ft 7 in (0.8 m) wide at the top. The hedge on top is quickset, 1 ft 4 in (0.4 m) high, 1 ft 4 in (0.4 m) wide, and can be marked by a 10 in (0.25 m) white bar. There are two small hedges, placed closely one in front and the other behind the embankment, 1 ft 4 in (0.4 m) high and 1 ft 4 in (0.4 m) wide, which can be marked by an 8 in (0.2 m) high white bar. It must be possible to jump the bullfinch from either side. In France, the minimum height of the embankment is reduced to 2 ft 1 in (0.65 m) while the hedge on top is at least 1 ft 3 in (0.7 m) high and 2 ft 1 in (0.65 m) wide. The small hedges must be no less than 10 in (0.25 m) wide.

Railed embankment (talus). Covered in turf, it is 3 ft 7 in (1.1 m) high, 5 ft 10 in (1.8 m) wide at the base and 3 ft 3 in (1 m) wide at the top. The 1 ft 7 in (0.5 m) tall, 1 ft 7 in (0.5 m) wide hedge on top is quickset and must be secured by a white bar 10 in (0.25 m) of the way up. The talus is railed on both sides by two large beams painted white and with a diameter of 4 in (0.1 m). It must be possible to jump the talus from both sides.

Large bank. A deep, dry ditch, 4 ft 7 in (1 4 m) wide and 2 ft (0.6 m) deep with sloping sides. The bank measures 49 ft 2 in (15 m) (first and second walls at an angle of 35° and 4 ft (1.2 m) high) and in the middle is 6 ft 2 in (1.9 m). The bank must be 3 ft 3 in (1 m) high and 41 ft (12.5 m) long, 3 ft 7 in (1.1 m) high in the middle.

Bank. A 4 ft (1.2 m) wide, dry ditch with a solid quickset hedge in front and behind, 2 ft 3 in (0.7 m) and 2 ft 2 in (0.6 m) high respectively and 2 ft (0.6 m) wide, placed 8 in (0.2 m) from the edge of the ditch. There is a slope 65 ft 7 in (20 m) long; a brick wall painted white and topped by well-compacted turf, all of which is 3 ft (0.9 m) high; a 65 ft 7 in (20 m) long slope; a 4 ft (1.2 m) wide, dry ditch with a quickset framed hedge in front and behind, 2 ft (0.6 m) and 2 ft 3 in (0.7 m) high respectively, 2 ft (0.6 m) wide and 8 in (0.2 m) away from the ditch. The hedge frame must be painted white and both ditches be 2 ft (0.6 m) deep and have sloping sides.

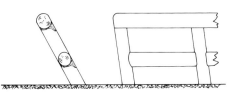

Large beam. Two white cross members with a minimum diameter of 9⅘ in (0.4 m) apart. The top beam must be padded with material and the obstacle must be 3 ft (0.9 m) high, set at an angle of 35°. In France this angle is 30°.

Ditch between hedges (oxer). A ditch between two large hedges clipped sloping towards the approaching horse. The first is 4 ft (1.2 m) high at the front and 4 ft 3 in (1.3 m) at the back; the second 4 ft 3 in (1.3 m) at the front and 4 ft 7 in (1.4 m) at the back. Both of these large hedges are 3 ft (0.9 m) wide. The first hedge must be well-secured by a 2 ft 3 in (0.7 m) frame with white rails. The ditch must be 2 ft (0.6 m) deep and 3 ft 7 in (1.1 m) wide. If it is to be a two-way jump, both hedges must be clipped into a rounded shape and be at least 4 ft 1 in (1.25 m) high. In France, the hedges must be a minimum of 2 ft 5 in × 2 ft 5 in (0.75 × 0.75 m) and the width of the ditch must be no less than 4 ft 1 in (1.25 m).

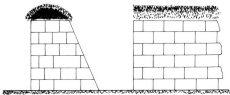

Big hedge with ordinary hedge in front and behind. Like the one described above but with a hedge set 1 ft (0.3 m) in front and another the same distance behind. These thick quickset hedges are supported by a small white bar 10 in (0.25 m) from the base and are clipped flat.

Large hedge with ditch and large beam in front (open ditch). A large, quickset or artificial hedge with the same characteristics as the one previously described and a 4 ft (1.2 m) wide, 2 ft (0.6 m) deep, steep-sided ditch in front. The ditch must be a distance of 8 in (0.2 m) from the hedge and on the side opposite the hedge there must

be a large beam with crossmembers at least 10 in (0.25 m) in diameter, or else a large sloping board of natural unpainted wood, set at a slight angle to the ground and placed 4 in (0.1 m) from the edge of the ditch. In France, the minimum dimensions of the large hedge are 4 ft 3 in (1.30 m) × 4 ft 3 in (1.30 m), the ditch must not be less than 3 ft 3 in (1 m) wide and the distance from the hedge to the ditch must be 4 in (0.1 m), while the height of the large beam is set at a minimum of 1 ft 9 in (0.55 m).

Wall. Can be built of brick, stone or beaten earth blocks, is 4 ft (1.2 m) wide at the base, 2 ft 3 in (0.7 m) at the top and 2 ft 7 in (0.8 m) high. It must have 1 ft (0.3 m) of well beaten earth on top, covered with turf. Positioned 4 in (0.1 m) away, in front and behind, is a 1 ft 1 in (0.35 m) high, 1 ft (0.3 m) wide hedge, supported half way up by a white rail and sloping on both sides at an angle of 30°.

Water-jump. A stretch of water at least 9 ft 10 in (3 m) wide, preceded by an upright green hedge clipped flat and positioned 1 ft (0.3 m) from the edge of the ditch. This hedge, which must not be higher than 2 ft (0.6 m) so as to enable the stretch of water to be seen, must be 2 ft 3 in (0.7 m) wide. Should brushes be used, the frame must be well-anchored to the ground and have a rail 1 ft (0.3 m) from the ground. The brush can be moved away from the edge of the ditch to increase the total width of the obstacle up to a maximum of 14 ft 9 in (4.5 m).

Hurdle. Three rows of solid chestnut-wood poles, securely nailed on to sturdy upright posts 6 ft 6 in (2 m) apart and driven well into the ground, using curved nails hammered in from the direction in which the jump is to be approached. Hurdles can vary in height from 3 ft (0.9 m) to 4 ft (1.2 m).

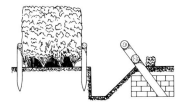

Railed ditch or watercourse (brook). Large beam set at an angle of 35° with two or three crossmembers, the obstacle being 2 ft 3 in (0.7 m) high. An 8 ft 2 in (2.5 m) wide ditch with or without water. In France, the minimum width of the ditch is 7 ft 10 in (2.4 m).

Large quickset or artificial hedge. Height 4 ft 7 in (1.4 m), width 4 ft (1.2 m), fixed 2 ft 3 in (1.7 m) of the way up. The fixed part, as in ordinary hedges, is in the form of a sturdy 4 in (0.1 m) diameter beam or chestnut-wood poles painted white.

Large hedge with railed ditch in front (rails, ditch and fence, commonly known as "fence"). A big, quickset or artificial hedge with the same characteristics as the one previously described, and a white wooden railing, positioned on the side opposite the hedge, 4 in (0.1 m) from the edge of the ditch, 2 ft (0.6 m) high and set at an angle of 35°. This railing must comprise two or three small cross members one above the other, 4 in (0.1 m) apart and 4 in (0.1 m) in diameter.

Large railed hedge (or double beam). An obstacle which can be jumped from either side. The beams which contain the hedge are set at an angle of 35° and rest

against the hedge itself. The 2 ft 7 in (0.8 m) beams are made up of two cross members, the top one being padded and 10 in (0.25 m) in diameter, set 1 ft 4 in (0.4 m) apart, joined together lengthwise and crosswise and painted white. The double beam is 5 ft (1.5 m) wide at the bottom. The large quickset hedge between the two beams is 3 ft 3 in (1 m) wide and 4 ft 3 in (1.3 m) high. In France, the beams must not be less than 2 ft 9 in (0.85 m) high and must have three cross members; the hedge can be no smaller than 3 ft 9 in (1.15 m) high and 3 ft 3 in (1 m) wide; and as a whole the obstacle must be at least 5 ft 6 in (1.7 m) wide at the base.

GRAND NATIONAL STEEPLECHASE

Aintree – 4½ miles

The Grand National Steeplechase is a handicap race for horses of six years old and over, which has been run since 1839 at the Aintree racecourse near Liverpool. There were two earlier races at nearby Maghulls. The distance of the race is 4½ miles (7,238 m) and the course includes 16 obstacles which must all be jumped twice, except the last two, which are tackled only on the first lap.

The total number of obstacles to be jumped, therefore, is 30 and the most awesome of these are Becher's Brook (6th and 22nd) 4 ft 10 in (1.47 m) high and 3 ft 3 in (0.99 m) wide with a natural brook 5 ft 6 in (1.67 m) across; Valentine's Brook (9th and 25th) 5 ft (1.52 m) high, the same width as the previous jump and with a similar brook; the open ditch (15th obstacle), also called "The Chair" since a course judge used to sit at that point; and the water-jump (16th obstacle). The open ditch is 5 ft 2 in (1.57 m) high and 3 ft 9 in (1.14 m) wide with a 2 ft 6 in (0.76 m) deep, 6 ft (1.82 m) wide ditch, preceded by a big 1 ft 5 in (0.45 m) high beam on the bank. The water-jump is also very demanding, being 14 ft 9 in (4.50 m) wide (with a 12 ft 3 in (3.73 m) stretch of water) and 2 ft 6 in (0.76 m) deep with a 2 ft 6 in (0.76 m) high and equally wide hedge in front. Becher's Brook takes its name from Captain Becher who, while riding his horse, Conrad, in the very first race ever to be staged, fell at this obstacle and took cover in the brook, until the other runners had passed. Valentine's Brook, on the other hand, has its name connected with a bet made by a Mr. Power, owner and rider of Valentine, in the 1840 Grand National. He said that his horse would jump the obstacle in question before any of the others, which is precisely what happened although Valentine could not quite maintain his effort and finished third. The distance between the start and the first obstacle is 471 yds (451.7 m).

From its institution to the present day only seven horses are listed as having won the Grand National twice at Liverpool and only one, Red Rum (1973, 1974, 1977) managed to win this great race three times. One dual winner was Manifesto, winner in 1897 and 1899 and third in 1900, 1902 and 1903, while Red Rum was also second in 1975 and 1976. The name of Peter Simple appears in so many Grand National records that the horse appears to be the most regular contestant there has ever been in the race and twice a winner, in 1849 and 1853. But there are too many doubts that the Peter Simple of 1841 is the same horse as the Peter Simple of 1853, not least because the contemporary descriptions refer to one Peter Simple as being grey, while the later bearer of that name was a bay horse. They were clearly therefore different horses.

The race with the greatest number of runners was that of 1929 which had 66 participants while in 1928 only one of the 42 competitors, Tipperary Tim, reached the post unscathed and he was followed by a single adversary, Billy Barton, who after having fallen at the last fence was remounted to finish second. The record time held by Golden Miller who in 1934, carrying 12 st 12 lb (76.96 kg) took 9' 20⅖" to complete the course, was broken in 1973 by Red Rum with a time of 9' 1.9" but under a very different weight – 10 st 5 lb (65.7 kg). Golden Miller won the race in the final flat stretch by five lengths beating Delaneige, who led at the last.

After winning the race in 1934, Golden Miller ran in another three Grand Nationals: in 1935, 1936 and 1937. In 1935, carrying top weight of 12 st 7 lb (79.375 kg), he unseated his jockey at the fence after Valentine's Brook; in 1936 he fell at the very first obstacle, and in 1937 he refused to jump the 12th. Although he failed in his attempts to win the Grand National twice, Golden Miller proved his excellence by taking the Cheltenham Gold Cup five times.

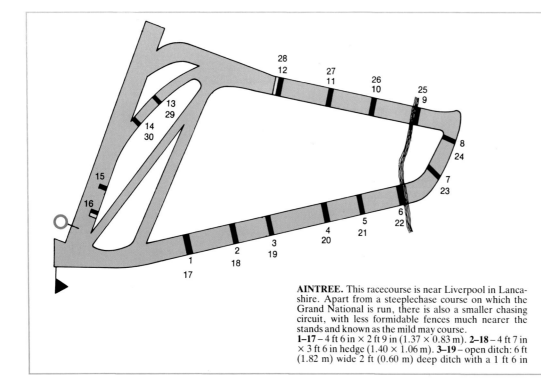

AINTREE. This racecourse is near Liverpool in Lancashire. Apart from a steeplechase course on which the Grand National is run, there is also a smaller chasing circuit, with less formidable fences much nearer the stands and known as the mild may course.
1–17 – 4 ft 6 in × 2 ft 9 in (1.37 × 0.83 m). **2–18** – 4 ft 7 in × 3 ft 6 in hedge (1.40 × 1.06 m). **3–19** – open ditch: 6 ft (1.82 m) wide 2 ft (0.60 m) deep ditch with a 1 ft 6 in (0.45 m) high beam in front positioned on the bank; 4 ft 11 in × 3 ft hedge (1.50 × 0.9 m). **4–20** – 4 ft 10 in × 3 ft hedge (1.47 × 0.90 m). **5–21** – 5 ft hedge (1.52 × 1.06 m). **6–22** – Becher's Brook: 4 ft 10 in × 3 ft 3 in hedge (1.47 × 0.99 m); 5 ft 6 in (1.67 m) wide brook. **7–23** – 4 ft 6 in × 2 ft 9 in hedge (1.37 × 0.83 m). **8–24** – The Canal Turn: 5 ft × 3 ft 3 in hedge (1.52 × 0.99 m). **9–25** – Valentine's Brook: 5 ft × 3 ft 3 in hedge (1.52 × 0.99 m); 5 ft 6 in (1.67 m) wide brook. **10–26** – 5 ft × 3 ft hedge (1.52 × 0.91 m). **11–27** – open ditch: 6 ft (1.82 m) wide 2 ft (0.6 m) deep ditch with 1 ft 5 in (0.45 m) high beam positioned on the bank. **12–28** – 5 ft × 3 ft hedge (1.52 × 0.91 m); 5 ft 6 in (1.67 m) wide 4 ft (1.22 m) deep ditch. **13–29** – 4 ft 7 in × 3 ft hedge (1.40 × 0.91 m). **14–30** – 4 ft 6 in × 3 ft hedge (1.37 × 0.91 m). **15** – The Chair (open ditch): 5 ft 2 in × 3 ft 9 in hedge (1.57 × 1.14 m); 6 ft (1.82 m) wide 2 ft 6 in (0.76 m) deep ditch with a 1 ft 6 in (0.45 m) high beam positioned on the bank. **16** – Water-jump: 2 ft 6 in × 2 ft 6 in hedge (0.76 × 0.76 m); 12 ft 3 in (3.73 m) wide 2 ft 6 in (0.76 m) deep stretch of water; overall width of the obstacle 14 ft 9 in (4.5 m).

METATERO

GRAND STEEPLE-CHASE DE PARIS

Auteuil – 3 miles 4 furlongs 188 yds (5,800 m)

The Grand Steeple-Chase de Paris, which has been run, apart from some war years, since 1874 at Auteuil, is France's most important steeplechase and also the one to offer the biggest prize. From 1874 to 1889 this race, which began as a handicap, was run over a distance of 3 miles 5 furlongs 178 yds (6,000 m) increased from 1890 to 1923 to 4 miles 74 yds (6,500 m) and from 1924 to 1925 to as much as 4 miles 2 furlongs 72 yds (6,900 m). This distance was reduced between 1926 and 1968 to 4 miles 74 yds (6,500 m) and once again between 1971 and 1980 (in 1969 and 1970 the race was run over 3 miles 7 furlongs 75 yds (6,300 m)). Since 1981 it has been run over 3 miles 4 furlongs 188 yds (5,800 m).

The Grand Steeple-Chase de Paris is now a weight for age race open to horses of five years old and upwards (in the past it was also open to four-year-olds) where the youngest carry 9 st 10 lb (62 kg) while for those aged six or more the weight is 10 st 1 lb (64 kg). The course is very demanding with 23 obstacles, beginning in front of the water-jump in front of the stands and going on, after a hedge, to a double barrier, a bullfinch, an oxer, a water-jump (in front of the stands) after which the route winds along the inner steeplechase track. The stands water-jump is cleared for a second time and then the middle course begins, after which the runners move to the outer steeplechase course.

The Grand Steeple-Chase de Paris is one of those races which have now become legend. The first winner was Miss Hungerford, ridden by M. Rolly and owned by M.F. Bennett, who beat 17 other competitors. The race was not run between 1915 and 1918 nor in 1940.

Throughout its history, only one horse has ever managed to win it three years in succession – Hyères III (1964, 1965, 1966) ridden on all three occasions by J. Daumas. Another five horses have managed to win twice, but of these only three for two years in succession: Wild Monarch (1878, 1879), Dandolo (1904, 1908), Ingré (1937, 1939), Lindor (1946, 1947) and Huron (1969, 1970). From 1943 to the present day, the only trainer who has ever had five successes is A. Adèle who first won with Sidéré in 1958 and, after the double with Huron, won again in 1973 with Giguin (owned by the actress Maria Felix) and in 1977 with Corps à Corps. Also from 1943 to the present day, J. Daumas, who rode Hyères, was the only jockey who won the race five times. After winning in 1959 riding Xanthor and in 1961 on Cousin Pons, he achieved his brilliant hat-trick with Hyères III.

In 1982, the race was won by Metatero, ridden by B. Jollivet, and trained by A. Fabre who had won the two previous races with Fondeur and Isopani. Although Metatero took the Gold Cup in 1981, a special French listed race run in several heats, he was considered a bit of a hack, but after this triumph he bounced back into the limelight, so much that he was considered the best French steeplechaser of the time. Metatero was bred for jumping since his sire, Orvilliers, had won the Grande Course de Haies d'Auteuil, in 1968.

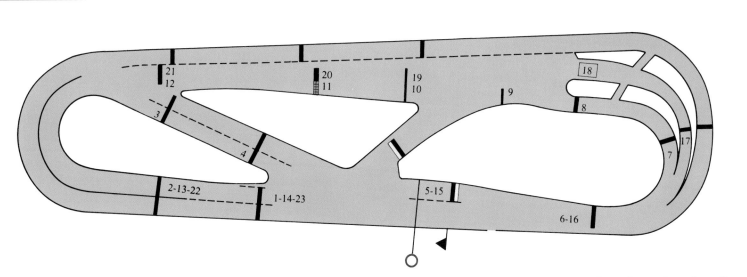

AUTEUIL. The racecourse is in the heart of Paris and has a grass course used solely for steeplechases. There is also an outer 1½ mile hurdle-race course.

1 – hedge. 2 – double barrier. 3 – bullfinch. 4 – oxer. 5 – stands water-jump. 6 – pavillon hedge. 7 – hedge (inner steeplechase course). 8 – earth talus. 9 – brook. 10 – big open ditch. 11 – stone wall. 12 – hedge. 13 – double barrier. 14 – hedge. 15 – stands water-jump. 16 – pavillon hedge. 17 – small open ditch. 18 – earth props. 19 – rail, ditch and fence. 20 – new open ditch. 21 – hedge. 22 – double barrier. 23 – last hedge.

GRANDE COURSE DE HAIES D'AUTEUIL

Auteuil – 3 miles 1½ furlongs (5,100 m)

This is one of Europe's most important hurdle races run at Auteuil since 1874, when it began as a handicap. Today it is run over 3 miles 1½ furlongs (5,100 m) and is open to horses of five and over, but in the past four-year-olds could also take part and the course was 109 yds (100 m) shorter. It is a weight for age race, where five-year-olds carry 9 st 10 lb (62 kg) and the older horses 10 st 1 lb (64 kg), and starts in front of the last hedge at the initial intersection point continuing left-handed in the direction of the Auteuil bend and round the outside course. In all there are 16 hedges, eight for each of the two laps round.

The Grand Course de Haies d'Auteuil was not run during the First World War (from 1915 to 1918 inclusive) nor in 1940. So far only four horses have managed to win this prestigious race twice (all two years running). These were Evohé (1937, 1938), Wild Risk (1944, 1945), Hardatit (1972, 1973) and Paiute (1979, 1980), but no horse has managed to win it three times. While on the subject of Wild Risk (b.h. 1940), it should be said that despite the fact that this horse was a jumper, he was also renowned as a stallion by siring excellent horses such as Worden II, a great sire of brood mares, and Le Fabuleux (ch. 1961).

Another outstanding winner of this race was born and bred in Italy. This was Nigra (ch.h. 1944 by Bozzetto) who triumphed in 1949, carrying the colours of Ettore Tagliabue and ridden by Pericle Mercury. The only horse to win both France's most important jump races was Loreto who won the Grande Course de Haies d'Auteuil in 1958 and the Grand Steeple-Chase de Paris in 1963. In 1982 the winner was World Citizen, ridden by N. Peguy and owned by Daniel Wildenstein whose colours are often at the forefront not only in the great steeplechases but also in most prestigious flat races.

1-9 – pavillon hedge. 2-10 – Auteuil bend hedge. 3-11 – Porte d'Auteuil hedge. 4-12 – rails, ditch and hedge. 5-13 – new open ditch hedge. 6-14 – Passy hedge. 7-15 – penultimate hedge. 8-16 – last hedge.

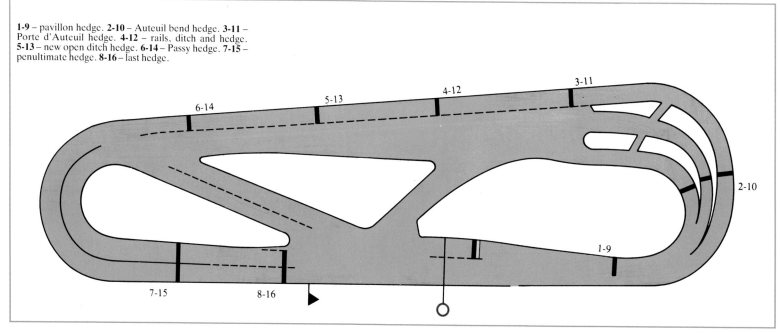

MARYLAND HUNT CUP

Glydon – 4 miles (6,436 m)

This is in practice a hunter trial for amateur riders and is run at Worthington Valley, Glydon near Baltimore over a distance of 4 miles (6,436 m). The Maryland Hunt Cup is a weight-for-age race for horses of four years old and over and the only weight allowances are for maidens over timber. Another unusual aspect of this race is that until 1971 it did not offer prize money but only a silver cup for the owner of the winner and a small trophy for the winning jockey. The race is held in April in a large oval basin with uneven contours, in the middle of the valley, and attracts a massive number of enthusiasts.

The extremely varied course involves jumping 22 typically American cross-country obstacles, 18 of which are post-and-rail jumps with four or five poles, three board fences and one (the penultimate jump) made up of a board fence and a 6½ ft (2 m) brook with natural sides. The poles of these obstacles are not nailed to the posts but wedged in, making the course more difficult since the obstacles are 4 ft 3 in (1.3 m) high, whilst three of them are 4 ft 9 in (1.45 m) and one (the 16th) as high as 4 ft 11 in (1.5 m). The 21st obstacle is a 6 ft 10 in (2.1 m) wide water-jump, or rather a brook, with a 3 ft (0.9 m) high board fence in front, which in itself is extremely difficult to negotiate.

Seven horses in the race's history have managed to win it three times: Garry Owen (1901, 1902, 1907), Princeton (1903, 1905, 1906), Blockade (1938, 1939, 1940), Winton (1942, 1946, 1947), Prince Pep (1949, 1950, 1952), Jay Trump (1963, 1964, 1966) and Mountain Dew (1962, 1965, 1967). The only horse to have won the Maryland Hunt Cup for three years running was Blockade who in 1938 also set the race record with the exceptional time of 8'44". This record stood for more than 20 years and even when in 1960 it was beaten by Fluctuate, it was by only a fifth of a second (8'43"⅘). In 1963, Jay Trump made a further improvement on the record by bringing it to 8'42"⅕ and in 1971 Landing Party set the current limit with a time of exactly 8'42".

Another horse who achieved victory three times was Winton who, considering that the race was not run from 1943 to 1945, can claim a more remarkable achievement than Blockade since he won the last race before the war and the first after it. But yet another horse reigns supreme over this race – Mountain Dew – since he was the only one to come very close to winning it for a fourth time, finishing amongst the first three for eight years running from 1961 to 1968. Mountain Dew not only won three times but was also second in 1963, 1964 and 1966 and third in 1961 and 1968.

Among the curious things that have happened throughout the history of the Maryland Hunt Cup, Tom Clark's five second places in 1897, 1898, 1899, 1901 and 1903 deserve a mention. He won the race in 1900. Another remarkable occurrence was when Ben Nevis II, Perfect Cast and Moon Meeting were first, second and third respectively in 1977 and in exactly the same order in 1978. Two years later, Ben Nevis crossed the Atlantic to win the Grand National at Aintree, following in the footsteps of Jay Trump who achieved the same feat in 1965. The degree of difficulty and very testing nature of this race is shown by the fact that in one year only Landslide managed to complete the course, and on another three occasions only one rival followed the winner past the post when Brose Hover was second to Soissons in 1931, Prince Vins was second to Mountain Dew in 1967 and Blaze Miller was runner-up behind Cancottage in 1981. In 1982 the title went to Tong, who had previously won in the United States the Elkridge-Harford Point to Point (1979) and the Virginia Gold Cup (1980), but showed his true worth by winning the Maryland Hunt Cup.

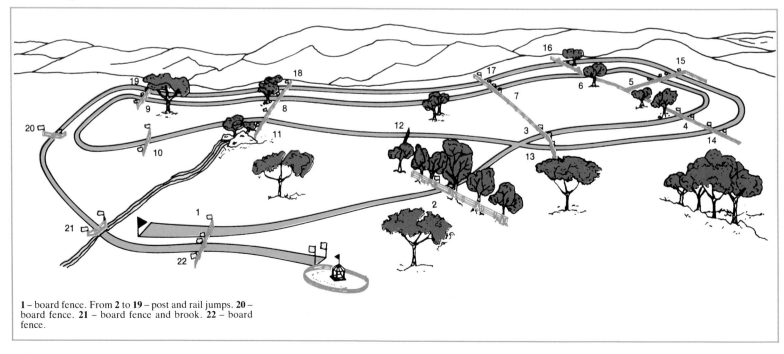

1 – board fence. From 2 to 19 – post and rail jumps. 20 – board fence. 21 – board fence and brook. 22 – board fence.

GRAN PREMIO DI MERANO

Maia Bassa – 3 miles 193 yds (5,000 m)

Unquestionably Italy's most important steeplechase, run every year in September at the Maia Bassa racecourse in the splendid setting provided by this delightful little town in the South Tyrol. It is held over 3 miles 193 yds (5,000 m) and covers a very demanding course. Its capacity for drawing large crowds is due both to the participation of foreign horses, which give the race an international flavour that places it amongst the most important competitions of this type in Europe, and to the interest it arouses by being linked with the now traditional Lotteria Nazionale (National Sweepstake).

The race was inaugurated in 1935 when it was won by Roi de Trèfle, a seven-year-old owned by S. Guthmann, but was not run during and immediately after the Second World War (from 1943 to 1947). It recommenced in 1948 when it was won by Gong from the Italian stud-farm Razza del Soldo.

In 1951 the race was carried off by Nagara, owned by J.P. Phillips, who that year had won the Grand Steeple-Chase de Paris. Another horse that won both these races, though not in the same year, was Bosnap, winner in 1956 at Merano and in the following year at Auteuil. Throughout the history of the Gran Premio di Merano only one horse has managed to win the race three times. This was Aègior who won for the first time in 1955 carrying the colours of M. Roy, repeating this success in 1959 and 1961 when, however, he ran under the colours of A. Galdi.

Another horse whose track performance at Merano did him credit was Spegasso from the Scuderia Mantova who not only won in 1958 but was also second in 1960 and third in 1956 and 1959. The only horse to win the Gran Premio di Merano two years running was Trapezio who was successful in 1975 and 1976. Of all these horses, however-

er, one in particular deserves individual attention – Cogne. He was a son of Tommaso Guidi and apart from winning this important race twice (in 1967 and 1969) he was second three times (1963, 1968 and 1971), third twice (1970 and 1972), fourth once (1974) and fifth once. When Cogne (defending the Aurora Stud colours) ran in this race for the last time, he was 16 years old and 11 years had passed since the day he first ran in it.

In 1982 the race was won in a photo-finish by the five-year-old Guidsun just ahead of Prince Pamir, who had lost the race the previous year. But this time science came to Prince Pamir's aid as the results of tests carried out for drugs showed that Guidson had been doped. He was disqualified and so Prince Pamir finally succeeded in winning the Gran Premio di Merano, a success which he deserved.

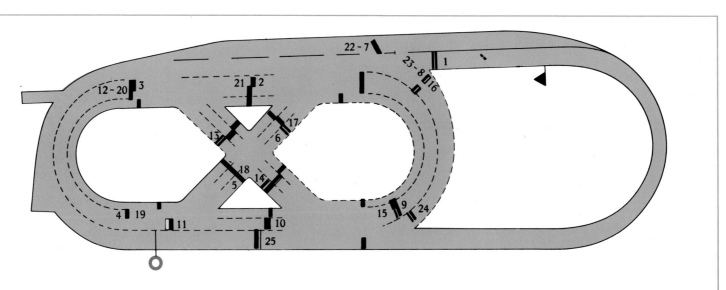

MERANO. The Maia Bassa racecourse is less than half a mile from the center of this small Tyrolean town and has a grass circuit for flat racing, varying in width from 65½ to 82 ft (20–25 m) with an overall length of 1 mile 2 furlongs (2,000 m). The finishing straight measures 711 yds (650 m). There is another smaller flat-racing course, also grass, with a length of 7 furlongs (1,400 m) and a finishing straight of 383 yds (350 m). Inside the flat courses, which are marked off by natural hedges rather than rails, are the hurdle courses, the steeplechase track and the cross-country course. The overall length of the courses, both flat and obstacles is 3 miles 193 yds (5,000 m).

1 – hedge. **2** – wall (21). **3** – double beam (12–20). **4** – hedge. **5** – talus (18). **6** – wall (17). **7** – large vertical hedge (22). **8** – large embankment (16–23). **9** – low hedge (15). **10** – large railed hedge. **11** – water-jump. **12** – double beam (in opposite direction to 3). **13** – large bank. **14** – large brook. **15** – low hedge (in opposite direction to 9). **16** – large embankment (in opposite direction to 8). **17** – wall (in opposite direction to 6). **18** – talus (in opposite direction to 5). **19** – hedge (in opposite direction to 4). **20** – double beam (same direction as 12). **21** – wall (in opposite direction to 2). **22** – large vertical hedge (same direction as 7). **23** – large embankment . **24** – large hedge. **25** – hedge.

CHAMPIONSHIP RECORDS

GRAND NATIONAL STEEPLECHASE
Aintree – 4½ miles

Year	Winner	Jockey	Runners	Year	Winner	Jockey	Runners
1837	The Duke	Mr. H. Potts	6	1883	Zoedone	Count C. Kinsky	10
1838	Sir Henry	T. Oliver	10	1884	Voluptuary	E.P. Wilson	15
1839	Lottery	J. Mason	17	1885	Roquefort	E.P. Wilson	19
1840	Jerry	Mr. Bretherton	12	1886	Old Joe	T. Skelton	23
1841	Charity	Mr. Powell	11	1887	Gamecock	W. Daniels	16
1842	Gaylad	T. Oliver	15	1888	Playfair	Mawson	20
1843	Vanguard	T. Oliver	16	1889	Frigate	T. Beasley	20
1844	Discount	Crickmere	22	1890	Ilex	A. Nightingall	16
1845	Cure All	Loft	15	1891	Come Away	H. Beasley	21
1846	Pioneer	Taylor	22	1892	Father O'Flynn	Capt. E.R. Owen	25
1847	Matthew	L. Wynne	26	1893	Cloister	Dollery	15
1848	Chandler	Capt. Little	30	1894	Why Not	A. Nightingall	14
1849	Peter Simple	T. Cunningham	24	1895	Wild Man from Borneo	J. Widger	19
1850	Abd-El-Kader	C. Green	32	1896	The Soarer	D.M.G. Campbell	28
1851	Abd-El-Kader	T. Abbott	21	1897	Manifesto	T. Kavanagh	28
1852	Miss Mowbray	A. Goodman	24	1898	Drogheda	J. Gourley	25
1853	Peter Simple	T. Oliver	21	1899	Manifesto	G. Williamson	19
1854	Bourton	Tasker	21	1900	Ambush II	A. Anthony	16
1855	Wanderer	J. Hanlon	20	1901	Grudon	A. Nightingall	24
1856	Freetrader	G. Stevens	21	1902	Shannon Lass	D. Read	21
1857	Emigrant	C. Boyce	28	1903	Drumcree	P. Woodland	23
1858	Little Charley	W. Archer	16	1904	Moifaa	A. Birch	26
1859	Half Caste	C. Green	20	1905	Kirkland	F. Mason	27
1860	Anatis	Mr. Thomas	19	1906	Ascetic's Silver	Hon. A. Hastings	23
1861	Jealousy	J. Kendall	24	1907	Eremon	A. Newey	23
1862	The Huntsman	H. Lamplugh	13	1908	Rubio	H.B. Bletsoe	24
1863	Emblem	G. Stevens	16	1909	Lutteur III	G. Parfrement	32
1864	Emblematic	G. Stevens	25	1910	Jenkinstown	R. Chadwick	25
1865	Alcibiade	Capt. Coventry	23	1911	Glenside	Mr. J. Anthony	26
1866	Salamander	A. Goodman	30	1912	Jerry M.	E. Piggott	24
1867	Cortolvin	J. Page	23	1913	Covertcoat	P. Woodland	22
1868	The Lamb	Mr. Edwards	21	1914	Sunloch	W.J. Smith	20
1869	The Colonel	G. Stevens	22	1915	Ally Sloper	Mr. J. Anthony	20
1870	The Colonel	G. Stevens	23	1916	Vermouth	J. Reardon	21
1871	The Lamb	Mr. Thomas	25	1917	Ballymacad	E. Driscoll	19
1872	Casse Tête	J. Page	25	1918	Poethlyn	E. Piggott	17
1873	Disturbance	J.M. Richardson	28	1919	Poethlyn	E. Piggott	22
1874	Reugny	J.M. Richardson	22	1920	Troytown	Mr. J. Anthony	24
1875	Pathfinder	Mr. Thomas	18	1921	Shaun Spadah	F. Rees	35
1876	Regal	J. Cannon	19	1922	Music Hall	L. Rees	32
1877	Austerlitz	F.G. Hobson	16	1923	Sergeant Murphy	Capt. G. Bennett	28
1878	Shifnal	J. Jones	12	1924	Master Robert	R. Trudgill	30
1879	The Liberator	G. Moore	18	1925	Double Chance	Maj. J.P. Wilson	33
1880	Empress	T. Beasley	14	1926	Jack Horner	W. Watkinson	30
1881	Woodbrook	T. Beasley	13	1927	Sprig	T. Leader	37
1882	Seaman	Lord Manners	12	1928	Tipperary Tim	W.P. Dutton	42

CHAMPIONSHIP RECORDS

(Grand National Steeplechase continued)

Year	Winner	Jockey	Runners
1929	Gregalach	R. Everett	66
1930	Shaun Goilin	T. Cullinan	41
1931	Grakle	R. Lyall	36
1932	Forbra	J. Hamey	36
1933	Kellsboro' Jack	D. Williams	34
1934	Golden Miller	G. Wilson	30
1935	Reynoldstown	Mr. F. Furlong	27
1936	Reynoldstown	Mr. F. Walwyn	35
1937	Royal Mail	E. Williams	33
1938	Battleship	B. Hobbs	36
1939	Workman	T. Hyde	37
1940	Bogskar	M. Jones	30
1946	Lovely Cottage	Capt. R. Petre	34
1947	Caughoo	E. Dempsey	57
1948	Sheila's Cottage	A.P. Thompson	43
1949	Russian Hero	L. McMorrow	43
1950	Freebooter	J. Power	49
1951	Nickel Coin	J. Bullock	36
1952	Teal	A.P. Thompson	47
1953	Early Mist	B. Marshall	31
1954	Royal Tan	B. Marshall	29
1955	Quare Times	P. Taaffe	30
1956	E.S.B.	D.V. Dick	29
1957	Sundew	F.T. Winter	35
1958	Mr. What	A. Freeman	31
1959	Oxo	M. Scudamore	34
1960	Merryman II	G. Scott	26
1961	Nicolaus Silver	H. Beasley	35
1962	Kilmore	F.T. Winter	32
1963	Ayala	P. Buckley	47
1964	Team Spirit	G.W. Robinson	33
1965	Jay Trump	Mr. C. Smith jr.	47
1966	Anglo	T. Norman	47
1967	Foinavon	J. Buckingham	44
1968	Red Alligator	B. Fletcher	45
1969	Highland Wedding	E.P. Harty	30
1970	Gay Trip	P. Taaffe	28
1971	Specify	J. Cook	38
1972	Well To Do	G. Thorner	42
1973	Red Rum	B. Fletcher	38
1974	Red Rum	B. Fletcher	42
1975	L'Escargot	T. Carberry	31
1976	Rag Trade	J. Burke	32
1977	Red Rum	T. Stack	42
1978	Lucius	B.R. Davies	37
1979	Rubstic	M. Barnes	34

Year	Winner	Jockey	Runners
1980	Ben Nevis II	Mr. C. Fenwick Jr.	30
1981	Aldaniti	R. Champion	39
1982	Grittar	D. Saunders	39
1983	Corbiere	B. de Haan	41
1984	Hallo Dandy	N. Doughty	40

Substitute race run at Gatwick from 1916 to 1918; no race from 1941 to 1945.

GRAND STEEPLE-CHASE DE PARIS
(Auteuil – 3 miles 4 furlongs 180 yd (5,800m))

Year	Winner	Age	Weight (kg)
1874	Miss Hungerford	a	70 1/2
1875	La Veine	5	77
1876	Ventriloque	4	63 1/2
1877	Congress	a	80
1878	Wild Monarch	a	72 1/2
1879	Wild Monarch	a	74 1/2
1880	Recruit II	a	58
1881	Maubourguet	a	73
1882	Whisper Low	4	65 3/4
1883	Too Good	4	67
1884	Varaville	6	64
1885	Redpath	a	67
1886	Boissy	5	66
1887	La Vigne	4	64
1888	Parasang	a	68
1889	Le Torpilleur	4	66
1890	Royal Meath	6	72 1/2
1891	Saïda	5	70
1892	Fleurissant	4	62 1/2
1893	Skedaddle	4	62 1/2
1894	Lontch	4	62 1/2
1895	Styrax	5	70
1896	Valois	5	70
1897	Solitaire	5	70
1898	Marise	5	70

CHAMPIONSHIP RECORDS

(Grand Steeple-Chase de Paris continued)

Year	Winner	Age	Weight (kg)
1899	Tancarville	4	62 1/2
1900	Mélibée	4	62 1/2
1901	Calabrais	6	72 1/2
1902	Gratin	a	72 1/2
1903	Veinard	5	70
1904	Dandolo	5	70
1905	Canard	4	62 1/2
1906	Burgrave II	4	62 1/2
1907	Grosse Mère	4	62 1/2
1908	Dandolo	9	76
1909	Saint Caradec	4	62 1/2
1910	Jerry M	a	72 1/2
1911	Blagueur II	6	72 1/2
1912	Hopper	5	70
1913	Ultimatum	4	62 1/2
1914	Lord Loris	6	72 1/2
1919	Troytown	6	70 1/2
1920	Coq Gaulois	5	66
1921	Roi Belge	6	67
1922	Héros XII	7	67
1923	L'Yser	8	68
1924	Master Bob	10	68
1925	Silvo	9	69
1926	Portmore	11	69
1927	The Coyote	7	69
1928	Maguelonne	6	69
1929	Le Touquet	7	69
1930	Le Fils de la Lune	7	69
1931	La Frégate	5	68
1932	Duc d'Anjou	4	60
1933	Millionnaire II	7	69
1934	Agitato	7	69
1935	Fleuret	7	69
1936	Potentate	7	69
1937	Ingré	5	68
1938	Hève	8	69
1939	Ingré	7	74
1941	Kerfany	6	64
1942	Symbole	6	64
1943	Kargal	6	64
1944	Hahnhof	7	64
1945	Boum	6	64
1946	Lindor	5	62
1947	Lindor	6	69
1948	Ridéo	6	64
1949	Bouzoulou	6	64

Year	Winner	Age	Weight (kg)
1950	Méli Mélo	8	64
1951	Nagara	9	64
1952	Tournay	5	62
1953	Pharamond III	7	64
1954	Orléans	7	65
1955	Farfatch	5	62
1956	Nécor	8	64
1957	Bonosnap	6	64
1958	Sidéré	7	64
1959	Xanthor	9	64
1960	Kingcraft	10	64
1961	Cousin Pons	5	62
1962	Mandarin	11	64
1963	Loreto	9	64
1964	Hyères III	6	64
1965	Hyères III	7	67
1966	Hyères III	8	67
1967	Cacao	6	64
1968	Haroué	6	64
1969	Huron	5	63
1970	Huron	6	67
1971	Pot d'Or	5	62
1972	Morgex	6	64
1973	Giquin	6	64
1974	Chic Type	7	64
1975	Air Landais	5	62
1976	Piomares	5	62
1977	Corps à Corps	5	62
1978	Mon Filleul	5	62
1979	Chinco	7	64
1980	Fondeur	7	64
1981	Isopani	7	64
1982	Metatero	9	64
1983	Jasmin II	8	64

Not run from 1915 to 1918 and in 1940. Variations in the distance: from 1874 to 1889 3 miles 5 furlongs 178 yds. (6,000 m); from 1890 to 1923, from 1926 to 1968 and from 1971 to 1980 4 miles 64 yds. (6,500 m); in 1924 and 1925 4 miles 2 furlongs 61 yds (6,900 m); in 1969 and 1970 3 miles 7 furlongs 66 yds (6,300 m); since 1981 3 miles 4 furlongs 180 yds (5,800 m).

a = aged

CHAMPIONSHIP RECORDS

GRANDE COURSE DE HAIES D'AUTEUIL

(Auteuil – 3 miles 1 furlong 74 yds (5,100 m))

Year	Winner	Age	Weight (kg)	Year	Winner	Age	Weight (kg)
1874	Jackal	6	72	1924	Arrowhead	4	60
1875	Borély	5	68 1/2	1925	Rocking Chair	6	68
1876	Vichnou	5	73	1926	Histoire de Rire	4	60
1877	Miss Lizzie	4	67	1927	Lannilis	4	60
1878	Patriarche	4	65 3/4	1928	Don Zuniga	4	60
1879	Paul's Cray	4	69	1929	Largo	4	60
1880	Doublon	6	72	1930	Le Bouif	6	67
1881	Seaman	5	68 1/2	1931	Baoulé	4	60
1882	Marc Antony	5	66	1932	Pour le Roi	4	60
1883	Beatus	5	68 1/2	1933	Lands End	4	60
1884	Baudres	4	67	1934	Lord Byron	4	60
1885	Newmarket	5	70	1935	Robin des Bois	5	65
1886	Jannock	a	62 1/2	1936	Cérélealiste	5	65
1887	Kersage	5	65	1937	Evohé II	8	66
1888	Aladdin	6	68 1/2	1938	Evohé II	9	69
1889	Vanille	5	68 1/2	1939	Royal Kidney	6	66
1890	Saint Claude	4	62 1/2	1941	Short	4	60
1891	Augure	5	68	1942	Lycoming	4	61
1892	Le Gourzy	5	68	1943	Ludovic le More	5	65
1893	Ranville	5	68	1944	Wild Risk	4	60
1894	Vertige	5	68	1945	Wild Risk	5	68
1895	Charlatan	5	68	1946	Vatelys	6	66
1896	Count Schomberg	4	62 1/2	1947	Le Papillon	5	65
1897	Soliman	5	68	1948	Septième Ciel	6	66
1898	Grandlieu	4	62 1/2	1949	Nigra	5	65
1899	Kérym	6	70	1950	Amati	4	60
1900	General Peace	6	70	1951	Verdi	4	60
1901	Monsieur Piperlin	4	62 1/2	1952	Prince Hindou	6	66
1902	Bébé	4	62 1/2	1953	Frascati	4	60
1903	Nivolet	4	62 1/2	1954	Sicié	4	60
1904	Hipparque	4	62 1/2	1955	Elégant	4	60
1905	Karakoul	6	70	1956	Méhariste	5	65
1906	Fragilité	6	70	1957	Romantisme	7	66
1907	Chi lo sa	4	62 1/2	1958	Loreto	4	60
1908	Ingénu	4	62 1/2	1959	Friendship	8	66
1909	Hérisson II	5	68	1960	Poutje Elday	4	60
1910	Blagueur II	5	68	1961	Choute	5	61
1911	Carpe Diem	4	62 1/2	1962	Miror	6	61
1912	Balscadden	5	68	1963	Ouf	5	62
1913	Galafron	4	62 1/2	1964	Santo Pietro	5	62
1914	Lilium	5	68	1965	Ketch	5	62
1919	Saint Tudwal	5	70	1966	Pansa	7	64
1920	Chaud	4	60	1967	Rivoli	6	64
1921	Forearm	5	66	1968	Orvilliers	5	62
1922	Fauche Le Pré	4	60	1969	Gopal	5	62
1923	Onyx II	4	60	1970	Samour	5	62

CHAMPIONSHIP RECORDS

(Grand Course de Haies d'Auteuil continued)

Year	Winner	Age	Weight (kg)
1971	Le Pontet	6	64
1972	Hardatit	6	64
1973	Hardatit	7	64
1974	Baby Taine	5	62
1975	Mazel Tov	5	62
1976	Les Roseaux	7	64
1977	Top Gear	5	62
1978	Roselier	5	62
1979	Paiute (IRE)	6	64
1980	Paiute (IRE)	7	64
1981	Bison Futé	5	62
1982	World Citizen	5	62
1983	Melinoir	5	62

Not run from 1915 to 1918 and in 1940. Variations in the distance: from 1874 to 1968 3 miles 192 yds (5,000 m).

MARYLAND HUNT CUP
(Glyndon – 4 miles over timber)

Year	Winner	Age	Jockey	Weight (lb)
1894	Johnny Miller	—	J. McHenry	—
1895	Sixty	—	G. Elder	—
1896	Kingsbury	—	T.D. Whistler	160
1897	Little Giant	—	G. Elder	160
1898	The Squire	—	W.P. Stewart	160
1899	Reveller	—	J. Piper	160
1900	Tom Clark	—	G. Brown Jr.	—
1901	Garry Owen	—	J. Spencer Jr.	—
1902	Garry Owen	a	J. Spencer Jr.	—
1903	Princeton	a	W. Walters	—
1904	Landslide	6	R.C. Stewart	—
1905	Princeton	a	S. Watters	—
1906	Princeton	a	W. Watters	165
1907	Garry Owen	a	J. Spencer Jr.	165

(Maryland Hunt Cup continued)

Year	Winner	Age	Jockey	Weight (lb)
1908	Judge Parker	5	G. Nicholas	160
1909	Sacandaga	7	A. Devereux	165
1910	Sacandaga	8	A. Devereux	165
1911	Pebbles	a	J. Leiper Jr.	150
1912	Conbe	5	G. Blakiston Jr.	160
1913	Zarda	a	G. Willing Jr.	165
1914	Rutland	a	G. Mather	165
1915	Talisman	a	J. Spencer Jr.	165
1916	Bourgeois	a	G. Brown Jr.	165
1917	Brosseau	a	G. Mather	165
1918	Marcellinus	a	E.M. Cheston	165
1919	Chuckatuck	a	J. Spencer Jr.	165
1920	Oracle II	a	A. White	165
1921	Mazarin	a	G. Thompson	165
1922	Oracle II	a	R. Belmont	165
1923	Red Bud	a	C. Burton	165
1924	Daybreak	a	J. Ewing	165
1925	Burgoright	a	J. Bowen Jr.	165
1926	Billy Barton	a	A.G. Ober Jr.	165
1927	Bon Master	a	F. Bonsal Jr.	165
1928	Bon Master	a	F. Bonsal Jr.	165
1929	Alligator	a	C. Plum	165
1930	Brose Hover	a	C. Burton	165
1931	Soissons	8	J.T. Skinner	165
1932	Trouble Maker	9	N. Lang	165
1933	Captain Kettle	9	C.R. White	165
1934	Captain Kettle	10	C.R. White	165
1935	Hotspur II	12	S. Janney Jr.	165
1936	Inshore	7	H. Frost Jr.	165
1937	Welbourne Jake	7	J. Harrison	165
1938	Blockade	9	J. Colwill	165
1939	Blockade	10	J. Colwill	165
1940	Blockade	11	J. Colwill	165
1941	Coq Bruyere	12	R. Hamilton	165
1942	Winton	8	S. Janney Jr.	165
1946	Winton	12	S. Janney Jr.	165
1947	Winton	13	S. Janney Jr.	165
1948	Peterski	12	E. Bennett	155
1949	Pine Pep	9	D.M. Smithwick	165
1950	Pine Pep	10	D.M. Smithwick	165
1951	Jester's Moon	8	W.H. Dixon	165
1952	Pine Pep	12	D.M. Smithwick	165
1953	Third Army	7	P.D. Reid	165
1954	Marchized	7	D.M. Smithwick	165
1955	Land's Corner	11	B.H. Murray	165
1956	Lancrel	11	F. Bonsal Jr.	165

CHAMPIONSHIP RECORDS

(Maryland Hunt Cup continued)

(Gran Premio di Merano continued)

Year	Winner	Age	Jockey	Weight (lb)
1957	Ned's Flying	10	E. Weymouth	165
1958	Ned's Flying	11	P. Fanning	165
1959	Fluctuate	12	C. Smith Jr.	165
1960	Fluctuate	13	D.M. Smithwick	165
1961	Simple Samson	10	C. Smith Jr.	165
1962	Mountain Dew	7	J. Fisher III	165
1963	Jay Trump	6	C. Smith Jr.	165
1964	Jay Trump	7	C. Smith Jr.	165
1965	Mountain Dew	10	J. Fisher III	165
1966	Jay Trump	9	C. Smith Jr.	165
1967	Mountain Dew	12	J. Fisher III	165
1968	Haffaday	7	L. Neilson III	165
1969	Landing Party	7	J.R.S. Fisher	165
1970	Morning Mac	8	R. Hannum	165
1971	Landing Party	9	J.R.S. Fisher	165
1972	Early Earner	11	J. Martin Jr.	165
1973	Morning Mac	11	R. Hannum	165
1974	Burnmac	9	L. Neilson III	165
1975	Jacko	12	R. Jones Jr.	165
1976	Fort Devon	10	R. Hannum	165
1977	Ben Nevis II	9	C. Fenwick Jr.	165
1978	Ben Nevis II	10	C. Fenwick Jr.	165
1979	Dosdi	10	C. Fenwick Jr.	165
1980	Cancottage	10	J. Slater	165
1981	Cancottage	11	J. Slater	165
1982	Tong	8	H.T. Mc Knight	165
1983	Cancottage	13	Mrs. Miles Valentine	165

Not run from 1943 to 1945.
Variations in the distance: 4½ miles (7,240 m) in 1895; distance not specified in 1896; 4 miles 1 furlong (6,638 m) in 1900 and 1901.
In 1948 this race was won by Carolina who was however disqualified.
a = aged

GRAND PREMIO DI MERANO
(International Steeplechase – Maia Bassa – 3 miles 193 yds (5,000 m)

Year	Winner	Age	Jockey	Weight (kg)	
1935	Roi de Trèfle	7	H. Hawes	65	17
1936	Horizon	8	A. Kalley	68	17
1937	Hayer	4	M. Bonaventure	60	20
1938	Empressor	4	L. Miliano	63	10
1939	Isoletta	4	J. Menichetti	61	16

Year	Winner	Age	Jockey	Weight (kg)	Runners
1940	Moenio	4	P. Mercuri	60 1/2	20
1941	Valperga	7	L. Miliano	73	13
1942	Tabula Rasa	9	A. Lorenzetti	70	21
1948	Gong	4	F. Palagi	60	10
1949	Ermellino	5	D. Murray	64	8
1950	Le Radar	4	P. Delfarguiel	69	9
1951	Nagara	9	P. Hieronimus	73 1/2	11
1952	El Krim	5	L. Gaumondy	69 1/2	12
1953	Montlouvier	5	C. Maire	69 1/2	9
1954	Lokifepsscht	4	A. Carangio	65	18
1955	Aègior	5	M. Rion	67	16
1956	Bonosnap	5	P. Peraldi	70	11
1957	Bergette	5	R. Mantelin	71 1/2	13
1958	Spegasso	7	C. Ferrari	67 1/2	11
1959	Aègior	9	L. Celli	73	14
1960	Zambo II	9	N. Coccia	68 1/2	13
1961	Aègior	11	R. Feligioni	67 1/2	13
1962	Blacklock	4	L. Baldisseri	65	14
1963	Dragon Vert	6	N. Coccia	73 1/2	13
1964	Loupiot	5	M. Geffroy	67	14
1965	Crême Anglaise	4	N. Coccia	62	17
1966	Conte Biancamano	8	A. Baseggio	69	15
1967	Cogne	9	A. Mattei	72	19
1968	Pigalle	4	A. Baseggio	63 1/2	15
1969	Cogne	11	F. Capasso	72	15
1970	Tatti Jacopo	4	A. Mattei	63 1/2	11
1971	Mister Magoo	4	P. Costes	65 1/2	18
1972	Whispin	5	A. Donati	68 1/2	16
1973	Willipas	6	J. Linxe	69 1/2	17
1974	Chivas Regal	6	G. Morazzoni	68 1/2	13
1975	Trapezio	4	F. Saggiomo	65 1/2	14
1976	Trapezio	5	F. Saggiomo	70	16
1977	Red Chief	5	G.A. Colleo	64	13
1978	The Champ	10	D. Gray	67	19
1979	Ryan's Daughter	6	P. Santoni	71	17
1980	Cartum	4	A. Chelet	65	16
1981	Amado	4	P. Labordiere	64	18
1982	Prince Pamir	6	P. Cadeddu	70 1/2	16
1983	Guidsun	6	P.P. Alberelli	65 1/2	20

Not run from 1943 to 1947.

Trotting

TROTTING RACES

Trotting races are every bit as exciting as flat races and are often easier for the spectator to follow since most race courses, at least in Europe, have tracks covering shorter distances of 4–5 furlongs (800–1,000 m). The types of races are the same as those on the flat except "class races" where the horses that take part are all able to trot a set distance at the same speed. Trotting races are usually over distances in the region of 1 mile (1,600 m) and 1 mile 2 furlongs (2,000 m) but there are competitions, especially in France, over distances of 1½ miles (2,400 m) and even further. In the handicaps, the advantage given by the more able competitors to those who are less talented is not based on an increase in weight (as in flat racing), which would be senseless, but by increasing the distance to be covered. These increases range from a minimum of 21.8 (20 m) to 109.3 yds (100 m) and even 131 yds (120 m).

The current trend after the introduction of breaking from a movable starting gate, where the horses are lined up behind a car with two unfolded barriers which close up after breaking, is to reduce the number of handicaps in order to base the programmes on class races where the horses obviously start from the same mark. In trotting races there are competitions reserved for amateurs and ladies and there are many owners in this sport who train and drive their own horses, even in professional races.

In France, in addition to traditional harnessed trotting races, in which the driver sits in a very light two-wheeled cart (sulky) weighing between 33 lb and 55 lb (15–25 kg), there are also mounted trotting races which are just as exciting and spectacular. In trotting races, the competitor whose horse breaks into a gallop if not held back, and loses ground in an attempt to regain control, is disqualified for persistent breaking as are horses that break as they cross the finishing line. Horses that fall into irregular gaits such as pacing and the broken trot are also disqualified.

The American public is attracted to pacer races since with these horses there is practically no possibility of breaking and even less of falling into irregular gaits. Pacing is faster than trotting and differs from the latter in that the horse's legs move in lateral pairs, i.e. first raising the fore and hind feet on one side simultaneously and then those on the other. In trotting, on the other hand, the horse's legs move in diagonal pairs (first the fore foot on one side and the hind foot on the opposite side and then vice versa). Trotters and pacers are broken in at the age of about 18–20 months and after being gradually made to use the bit and harness they are first harnessed to a light cart and a gig (small one-horse training carriages) and then to a sulky.

Like flat-racers they begin racing at two years old, but a trotter's career is usually longer and more intense. The age limits for horses taking part in trotting races vary all over the world and some countries do not in fact have any limit. In Italy, for example, the age limit for mares and geldings is seven and ten for stallions.

Another difference between trotting and flat racing lies in the fact that in trotting races the trainer and driver are one and the same whereas in flat races, apart from a few rare exceptions, the trainer and jockey are two different people. The origins of trotting racing do not go back nearly as far in history as those of flat racing, although in France trotting races appear to have taken place as early as 1600. In order to fix the dates with greater certainty, we must look to Russia where trotting races were held in 1775, even before the creation of the Orlov breed (1778).

In Italy, the first trotting races were held in 1808 in the Prato della Valle in Padua, with money and medals as prizes for the winners. In these races, instead of the present-day sulky, another type of small one-horse carriage, the "Padovanella," was used. Their original weight of 661 lb (300 kg) was reduced in 1842 to 522 lb (237 kg) and again in 1869 to 249 lb (113 kg).

It was in 1869 that the fantastic Vandalo (ro. 1862) began his remarkable career. He remained active until he was 20 years old, running in 226 races and winning 200. In Italy there was virtually no stud farming until 1880, and the competitions took place in the streets of many towns and villages. In the period that followed, however, from 1881–1900, a great many Orlov and American breeds were imported, especially by Senator Vincenzo Stefano Breda, who from the brood mare Orlov Vertlawaya and the American stallion Elwood Medium got Conte Rosso the winner of the Austrian and Berlin Derbies in 1885. After the First World War Italian trotting racing suddenly gained much popularity due to the construction of the San Siro race course in Milan and the Villa Glori race course in Rome and because of Count Paolo Orsi Mangelli's great enthusiasm, both as a breeder and stable owner.

In France the first trotting races date back to 1836 and were held on the track at Cherbourg race course. Subsequent development has been remarkable, partly because in France trotter breeding became a subject of particular interest, integrating perfectly with the agricultural economy of France as a whole but especially with that of the region of Normandy.

In America races have taken place on the roads since the early 19th century, but the first track for official races was instituted in 1825 in Long Island. The first known race in America, however, dates back to 18 June 1806 in New Haven, Connecticut and was won by Janhey who trotted the mile in 2'59". This was, however, an isolated event as until 1815 horse racing was prohibited by strict laws in virtually all the Northern States on the grounds of immorality. Only after 1815 did the authorities become more tolerant and in 1830 these repressive laws were finally abolished. From that moment on American trotting has never looked back and from the first record over the mile, set in 1845 by an old grey mare, Lady Suffolk, with a time of 2'29½" (1'33" 9/km), until today it has progressed in a manner which in those days would have been almost impossible to imagine.

THE STANDARD-BRED

AMERICAN TROTTER

Both pacers and trotters come under the description of Standardbred. Pacing is a gait not normally found in horses and is faster than the trot, for which reason it is considered to be against the rules in trotters' races, and results in the disqualification of the transgressor. In America, however, there are races for pacers and for this reason breeders are encouraged to try to establish the perfect pacer through crossbreeding horses which show a natural disposition towards such a gait. The importance of trotters, however, is far greater than that of pacers which are really specializd horses within the same breed.

The progenitor of the American Trotter was an English thoroughbred stallion named Messenger (gr. 1780), imported into the United States in 1788. He had a determining influence, either directly or through his descendants, on American breeding. A stallion from Norfolk, named Bellfounder (1817), also made an important contribution to the creation of the breed. He was imported into America in 1822 with the aim of introducing a different bloodline so as to avoid excessive inbreeding.

Messenger was a descendant in the direct male line of Sampson who was of primary importance in the formation of trotter breeds. Hambletonian 10 descends in the third generation and direct male line from Messenger and it is from this famous horse that all existing American Trotters are descended in the direct male line. The other strains which have been involved in the creation of the breed, such as the Mambrinos (also descended from Messenger), the Clays (which did not have a natural aptitude for trotting) and the Morgans (descended from Justin Morgan) are no longer represented since their direct male line has failed to survive into the present day.

On examination of Hambletonian 10's pedigree, it is very easy to see the importance of Messenger to whom Hambletonian 10 is inbred $3 \times 4 \times 4 \times 4 \times 5 \times 6$. Three of the 1,300 horses sired by Hambletonian 10 have founded today's four bloodlines: Happy Medium (from whom descend the lines headed by Peter the Great), Electioneer (important now only as regards pacers, now that the Bingen Line has become extinct) and George Wilkes from whom the stallion lines of Axworthy and McKinney descend – the latter being of vital importance for the evolution of the French Trotter. Prince Hall, sire of the great Mistero (1940), and De Sota (1934 by Peter Volo), can both be traced back to Peter the Great.

However, other nations, apart from Italy, such as Germany, Sweden, the Soviet Union and even France have also used the American trotter to improve and add to their respective stock. A determining rôle in the origins of the American trotter was played by some English thoroughbred horses (Sampson, Messenger, Orville and Diomed) who have passed down their natural ability for trotting. By comparing these origins with those of the French trotter and the Orlov we can see similarities which lead us to consider any mating between horses belonging to different "breeds" as true "outcrossing," rather than "crossbreeding," between horses of the same blood, (i.e. those that carry the same original blood).

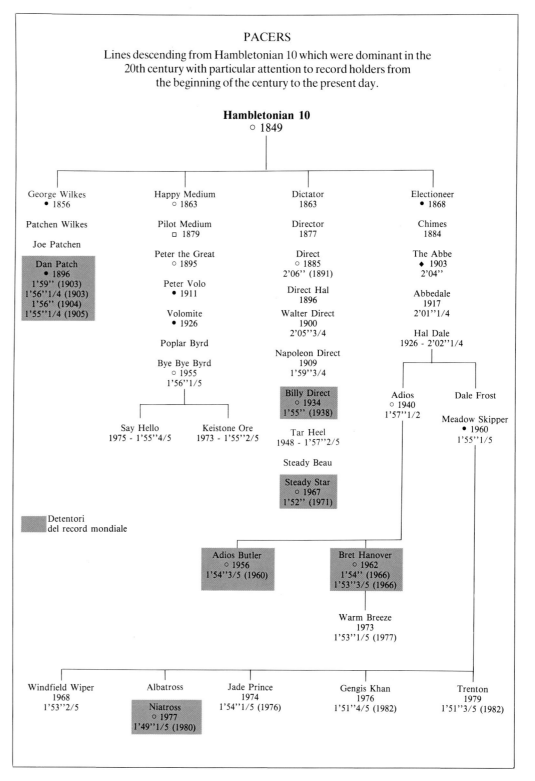

PACERS

Lines descending from Hambletonian 10 which were dominant in the 20th century with particular attention to record holders from the beginning of the century to the present day.

Hambletonian 10
○ 1849

George Wilkes ● 1856
Patchen Wilkes
Joe Patchen
Dan Patch ● 1896 1'59'' (1903) 1'56''1/4 (1903) 1'56'' (1904) 1'55''1/4 (1905)

Happy Medium ○ 1863
Pilot Medium □ 1879
Peter the Great ○ 1895
Peter Volo ● 1911
Volomite ● 1926
Poplar Byrd
Bye Bye Byrd ○ 1955 1'56''1/5
Say Hello 1975 - 1'55''4/5
Keistone Ore 1973 - 1'55''2/5

Dictator 1863
Director 1877
Direct ○ 1885 2'06'' (1891)
Direct Hal 1896
Walter Direct 1900 2'05''3/4
Napoleon Direct 1909 1'59''3/4
Billy Direct ○ 1934 1'55'' (1938)
Tar Heel 1948 - 1'57''2/5
Steady Beau
Steady Star ○ 1967 1'52'' (1971)

Electioneer ● 1868
Chimes 1884
The Abbe ♦ 1903 2'04''
Abbedale 1917 2'01''1/4
Hal Dale 1926 - 2'02''1/4
Adios ○ 1940 1'57''1/2
Dale Frost
Meadow Skipper ● 1960 1'55''1/5

Detentori del record mondiale

Adios Butler ○ 1956 1'54''3/5 (1960)
Bret Hanover ○ 1962 1'54'' (1966) 1'53''3/5 (1966)
Warm Breeze 1973 1'53''1/5 (1977)

Windfield Wiper 1968 1'53''2/5
Albatross 1974
Niatross ○ 1977 1'49''1/5 (1980)
Jade Prince 1974 1'54''1/5 (1976)
Gengis Khan 1976 1'51''4/5 (1982)
Trenton 1979 1'51''3/5 (1982)

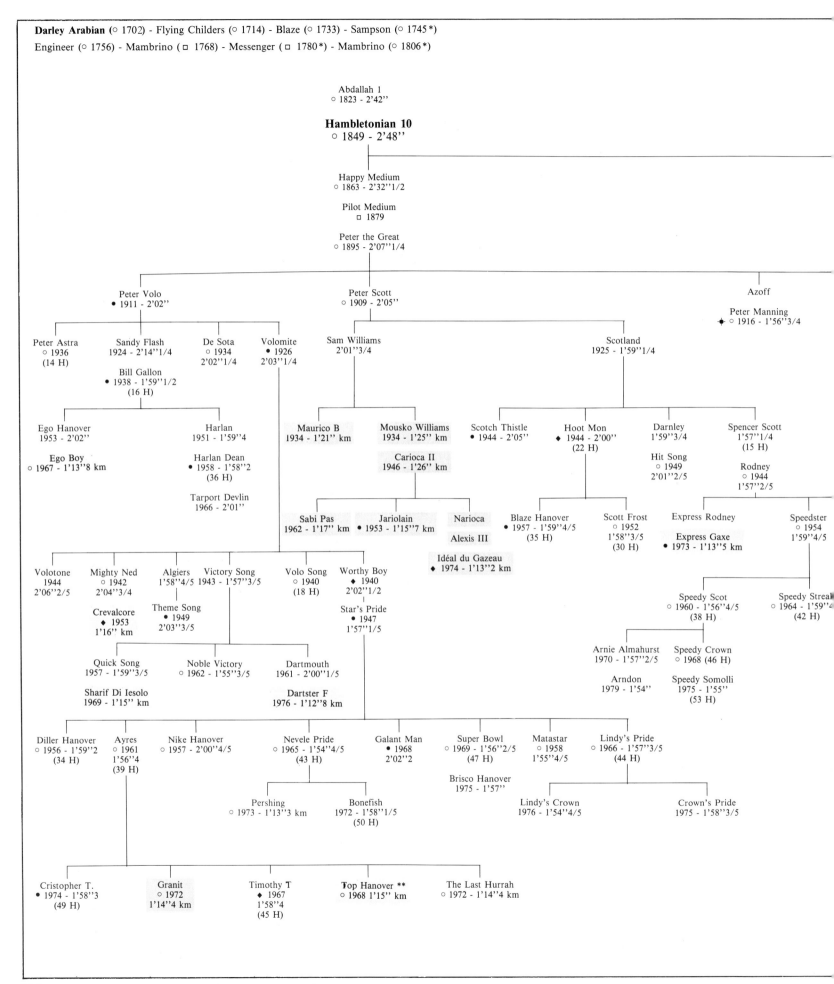

Darley Arabian (○ 1702) - Flying Childers (○ 1714) - Blaze (○ 1733) - Sampson (○ 1745 *)

Engineer (○ 1756) - Mambrino (□ 1768) - Messenger (□ 1780 *) - Mambrino (○ 1806 *)

Abdallah 1
○ 1823 - 2'42''

Hambletonian 10
○ 1849 - 2'48''

Happy Medium
○ 1863 - 2'32''1/2

Pilot Medium
□ 1879

Peter the Great
○ 1895 - 2'07''1/4

Peter Volo
● 1911 - 2'02''

Peter Scott
○ 1909 - 2'05''

Azoff

Peter Manning
◆ ○ 1916 - 1'56''3/4

Peter Astra
○ 1936
(14 H)

Sandy Flash
1924 - 2'14''1/4

De Sota
○ 1934
2'02''1/4

Volomite
● 1926
2'03''1/4

Sam Williams
2'01''3/4

Scotland
1925 - 1'59''1/4

Bill Gallon
● 1938 - 1'59''1/2
(16 H)

Ego Hanover
1953 - 2'02''

Harlan
1951 - 1'59''4

Maurico B
1934 - 1'21'' km

Mousko Williams
1934 - 1'25'' km

Scotch Thistle
● 1944 - 2'05''

Hoot Mon
◆ 1944 - 2'00''
(22 H)

Darnley
1'59''3/4

Spencer Scott
1'57''1/4
(15 H)

Ego Boy
○ 1967 - 1'13''8 km

Harlan Dean
● 1958 - 1'58''2
(36 H)

Carioca II
1946 - 1'26'' km

Hit Song
○ 1949
2'01''2/5

Rodney
○ 1944
1'57''2/5

Tarport Devlin
1966 - 2'01''

Sabi Pas
1962 - 1'17'' km

Jariolain
● 1953 - 1'15''7 km

Narioca

Blaze Hanover
● 1957 - 1'59''4/5
(35 H)

Scott Frost
○ 1952
1'58''3/5
(30 H)

Express Rodney

Speedster
○ 1954
1'59''4/5

Alexis III

Express Gaxe
● 1973 - 1'13''5 km

Idéal du Gazeau
◆ 1974 - 1'13''2 km

Volotone
1944
2'06''2/5

Mighty Ned
○ 1942
2'04''3/4

Algiers
1'58''4/5

Victory Song
1943 - 1'57''3/5

Volo Song
○ 1940
(18 H)

Worthy Boy
◆ 1940
2'02''1/2

Speedy Scot
○ 1960 - 1'56''4/5
(38 H)

Speedy Streak
○ 1964 - 1'59''4
(42 H)

Crevalcore
◆ 1953
1'16'' km

Theme Song
● 1949
2'03''3/5

Star's Pride
● 1947
1'57''1/5

Quick Song
1957 - 1'59''3/5

Noble Victory
○ 1962 - 1'55''3/5

Dartmouth
1961 - 2'00''1/5

Arnie Almahurst
1970 - 1'57''2/5

Speedy Crown
○ 1968 (46 H)

Sharif Di Iesolo
1969 - 1'15'' km

Dartster F
1976 - 1'12''8 km

Arndon
1979 - 1'54''

Speedy Somolli
1975 - 1'55''
(53 H)

Diller Hanover
○ 1956 - 1'59''2
(34 H)

Ayres
○ 1961
1'56''4
(39 H)

Nike Hanover
○ 1957 - 2'00''4/5

Nevele Pride
○ 1965 - 1'54''4/5
(43 H)

Galant Man
● 1968
2'02''2

Super Bowl
○ 1969 - 1'56''2/5
(47 H)

Matastar
○ 1958
1'55''4/5

Lindy's Pride
○ 1966 - 1'57''3/5
(44 H)

Pershing
○ 1973 - 1'13''3 km

Bonefish
1972 - 1'58''1/5
(50 H)

Brisco Hanover
1975 - 1'57''

Lindy's Crown
1976 - 1'54''4/5

Crown's Pride
1975 - 1'58''3/5

Cristopher T.
● 1974 - 1'58''3
(49 H)

Granit
○ 1972
1'14''4 km

Timothy T
◆ 1967
1'58''4
(45 H)

Top Hanover **
○ 1968 1'15'' km

The Last Hurrah
○ 1972 - 1'14''4 km

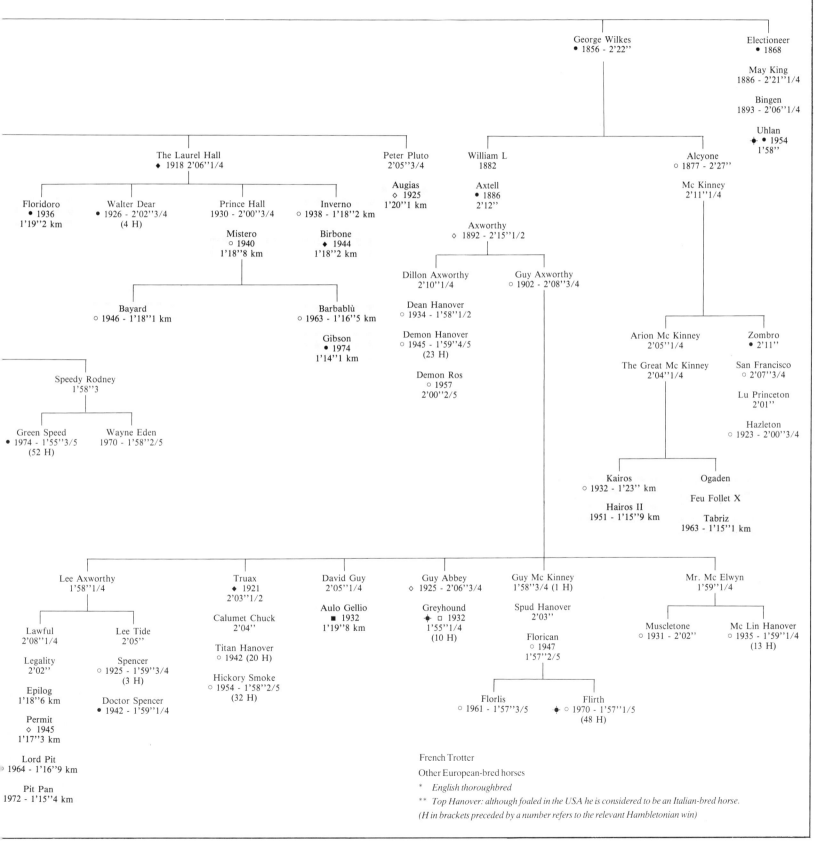

George Wilkes
● 1856 - 2'22''

Electioneer
● 1868

May King
1886 - 2'21''1/4

Bingen
1893 - 2'06''1/4

Uhlan
◆ ● 1954
1'58''

The Laurel Hall
◆ 1918 2'06''1/4

Peter Pluto
2'05''3/4

William L
1882

Alcyone
○ 1877 - 2'27''

Mc Kinney
2'11''1/4

Augias
◇ 1925
1'20''1 km

Axtell
● 1886
2'12''

Floridoro
● 1936
1'19''2 km

Walter Dear
● 1926 - 2'02''3/4
(4 H)

Prince Hall
1930 - 2'00''3/4

Inverno
○ 1938 - 1'18''2 km

Axworthy
◇ 1892 - 2'15''1/2

Mistero
○ 1940
1'18''8 km

Birbone
◆ 1944
1'18''2 km

Dillon Axworthy
2'10''1/4

Guy Axworthy
○ 1902 - 2'08''3/4

Bayard
○ 1946 - 1'18''1 km

Barbablù
○ 1963 - 1'16''5 km

Dean Hanover
○ 1934 - 1'58''1/2

Gibson
● 1974
1'14''1 km

Demon Hanover
○ 1945 - 1'59''4/5
(23 H)

Arion Mc Kinney
2'05''1/4

Zombro
● 2'11''

Demon Ros
○ 1957
2'00''2/5

The Great Mc Kinney
2'04''1/4

San Francisco
○ 2'07''3/4

Speedy Rodney
1'58''3

Lu Princeton
2'01''

Hazleton
○ 1923 - 2'00''3/4

Green Speed
● 1974 - 1'55''3/5
(52 H)

Wayne Eden
1970 - 1'58''2/5

Kairos
○ 1932 - 1'23'' km

Ogaden

Feu Follet X

Hairos II
1951 - 1'15''9 km

Tabriz
1963 - 1'15''1 km

Lee Axworthy
1'58''1/4

Truax
◆ 1921
2'03''1/2

David Guy
2'05''1/4

Guy Abbey
◇ 1925 - 2'06''3/4

Guy Mc Kinney
1'58''3/4 (1 H)

Mr. Mc Elwyn
1'59''1/4

Lawful
2'08''1/4

Lee Tide
2'05''

Calumet Chuck
2'04''

Aulo Gellio
■ 1932
1'19''8 km

Greyhound
◆ □ 1932
1'55''1/4
(10 H)

Spud Hanover
2'03''

Muscletone
○ 1931 - 2'02''

Mc Lin Hanover
○ 1935 - 1'59''1/4
(13 H)

Legality
2'02''

Spencer
○ 1925 - 1'59''3/4
(3 H)

Titan Hanover
○ 1942 (20 H)

Florican
○ 1947
1'57''2/5

Epilog
1'18''6 km

Doctor Spencer
● 1942 - 1'59''1/4

Hickory Smoke
○ 1954 - 1'58''2/5
(32 H)

Permit
◇ 1945
1'17''3 km

Florlis
○ 1961 - 1'57''3/5

Flirth
◆ ○ 1970 - 1'57''1/5
(48 H)

Lord Pit
○ 1964 - 1'16''9 km

Pit Pan
1972 - 1'15''4 km

French Trotter

Other European-bred horses

*   English thoroughbred

** Top Hanover: although foaled in the USA he is considered to be an Italian-bred horse.

(H in brackets preceded by a number refers to the relevant Hambletonian win)

MESSENGER

gr.h. 1780

This English throroughbred is considered to be the foundation sire of the American trotter since all the horses of this breed carry his original blood. From Messenger through Mambrino and Abdallah I we come to Hambletonian 10 from whom all existing American trotters descend in direct male line. If, on the other hand, we go back from Messenger through his sire Mambrino (not to be confused with Messenger's son of the same name) and his grandsire Engineer, we come to Sampson (by Blaze) who played a major rôle in passing down the aptitude for trotting. In 1788 Messenger was imported into the United States, having completed his racing career in England, in which from the age of three to five, he had won eight of his 14 starts and only once finished unplaced.

In America he made his debut as a stallion in Philadelphia and covered various types of brood mares, from English thoroughbreds to half-breeds and even draught mares, getting strong, courageous foals with a varying range of abilities. His importance in the formation of the American trotter is very great indeed if we consider that two dynasties descend from him: the Mambrino dynasty (now extinct in the direct male line) and the Hambletonian which founded this breed, considered to be America's greatest ever "zootechnical invention."

Messenger				
	Mambrino □ 1768	Engineer ○ 1756	Sampson ○ 1745	Blaze ○ 1733 / Hip Mare
			Young Greyhound Mare	Young Greyhound / Curwen Bay Barb Mare
		Cade Mare □ 1751	Cade ○ 1734	Godolphin Arabian ● 1724 / Roxana
			Little John Mare	Little John / Favourite
	Turf Mare ◆ 1774	Turf ○ 1760	Matchem ○ 1748	Cade / Partner Mare
			Ancaster Starling Mare	Ancaster Starling / Romp
		Figurante's Sister ○ 1761	Regulus ○ 1739	Godolphin Arabian ● 1724 / Grey Robinson
			Starling Mare ◆ 1753	Starling / Fox Mare

HAMBLETONIAN 10

b.h. 1849

All existing American trotters descend from Hambletonian 10. He was not a handsome horse with his heavy head and features showing no signs of distinction whatever. On the other hand, he had a solid bone structure and very well-developed muscles, especially in his hindquarters which gave him a great spring and considerable length of stride, characteristics which he handed down to his descendants.

He was foaled on 5 May 1849 in Sugar Loaf, County Orange, at the farm of Jonas Seely who, in the autumn of that year, sold him and his dam, Charles Kent Mare, to William Rysdyk of Chester. The following year the new owner decided to put all his horses up for auction but, dissatisfied with tthe prices offered for the first lot, he withdrew the rest, one of which was Hambletonian 10. Though Hambletonian never took part in official competitions it seems that at the age of three he set a time of 2'48" in a trial run over a mile. He began his career as a stallion at the age of only two and continued serving until the age of 27, dying on 27 March 1876.

His production at stud was exceptional, for he sired 1,325 horses including 130 stallions and 80 mares (all dams of trotters). He himself sired 40 trotters and it appears that in one year (1864) he managed

Hambletonian 10 (2'48")					
	Abdallah 1 ○ 1823	Mambrino ○ 1806*	Messenger □ 1780	Mambrino □ 1768	Engineer ○ 1756 / Cade Mare □ 1751
				Turf Mare ◆ 1774	Turf ○ 1760 / Figurante's Sister ○ 1761
			Sour-crout Mare	Sour-crout ○ 1786	Highflyer ○ 1774 / Jewel ○ 1775
				Whirligig Mare	Whirligig ○ 1763 / Old Slamerkin
		Amazzonia ◇ 1810	Dove	Saratoga	Messenger □ 1780* / —
				Expedition Mare	Expedition ◇ 1795* / Messenger Mare
			Fagdown	Messenger □ 1780*	Mambrino □ 1768 / Turf Mare ◆ 1774
				—	— / —
	Charles Kent Mare ○ 1834	Bellfounder ○ 1817	Old Bellfounder ○ 1797	Pretender ◆ 1788	Fire Away ◇ 1780 / Joseph Andrews Mare
				Smuggler Mare	Smuggler ● 1786 / —
			Velocity	Haphazard ● 1797*	Sir Peter ○ 1783 / Herwey
				—	— / —
		One Eye ○ 1815	Hambletonian ○ 1804*	Messenger □ 1780	Mambrino □ 1768 / Turf Mare ◆ 1774
				Pheasant ● 1790	Shark ● 1771 / Medley Mare
			Silvertail □ 1802	Messenger □ 1780*	Mambrino □ 1768 / Turf Mare ◆ 1774
				Black Jin	— / —

* English thoroughbred

196

Messenger

Hambletonian 10

to cover 217 brood mares, an excessive performance by today's standards. Hambletonian's pedigree shows a 3 × 4 × 4 × 4 × 5 × 6 inbreeding to Messenger and the two direct male lines, that of his sire, Abdallah, and dam, Charles Kent Mare, can be traced back to Sampson and Old Shales respectively, both of whom were sired by Blaze. In fact, Charles Kent Mare's sire, Bellfounder, is a descendant of Fire Away, sired by Driver who in turn was by Old Shales.

Moreover, Old Bellfounder, the sire of Bellfounder in the direct male line on his dam's side, descends from Old Shales. The dam of Driver (mentioned above) was by Foxhunter who descends from Sampson, and Old Shales was out of a mare by Sampson, which represents a very close inbreeding (1 × 3) to Blaze. Thus it is easy to understand the importance of Blaze, through Old Shales and, above all, Sampson, in the formation of trotter breeds.

Hambletonian 10 created four stallion lines through his progeny Happy Medium (b. 1863), George Wilkes (dk.b. 1856) and Electioneer (dk.b. 1868), two of which descended from George Wilkes, through Alcyone and William L respectively.

Breeder: Jonas Seely
Owner: W. Rysdyk
Racing Career: did not take part in official competitions

AXWORTHY

ch.b. 1892

His sire, Axtell, was bred by C.W. Williams, an important egg and butter retailer and a self-made man. Spurred on by his great passion for horses, he purchased Lou (b. 1880), Axtell's dam, deciding to have her as a brood mare and so he chose for her a stallion by the name of William L who covered her for just a few dollars. William L by the great George Wilkes, one of Williams's favourite stallions and from this union Axtell was born.

Axtell was trained and driven by his breeder who wanted to try his hand at this rôle as well. There was certainly no lack of results: Axtell lowered the male two-year-old record from 2'26" to 2'23" and won all the races he entered that year. At the age of three Axtell was still unbeaten and at four he broke the world record, which then stood at 2'18", three times, first trotting at 2'15"½ and then at 2'14" and finally at 2'12". This last performance was also a record for horses of all ages where the previous best was 2'13"½. The very evening of the day when Axtell achieved this victory at Terre Haute in Indiana, C.W. Williams sold him for 105,000 dollars to a syndicate which included amongst its members Col. J. Conley of Chicago and W.P. Jiams of Terre Haute.

Axtell became a stallion (in actual fact his previous owner had already used him for this purpose when he was still training) at a covering fee of 1,000 dollars, which was a truly exceptional sum for those days considering that it was double the going rate for St. Simon in England. Col. Conley,

the organizer of the syndicate which he had started for Axtell, was a friend of A.B. Darling, the owner of a large New York hotel and also a member of the "Sealskins Brigade" for "street drivers" in the city. Darling was asked by Col. Conley to choose two of his brood mares to be covered by the new stallion. One of the brood mares selected was Marguerite whose second dam, Old Daisy, Darling had used in street races while he also owned her sire, Kentucky Prince. Marguerite's first foal was born in 1891, but died at the age of two while the second (1892) was Axworthy, a chestnut with a small triangular star on his forehead.

Axworthy had a distinctive appearance and an attractive though rather large head with eyes whose expression denoted great intelligence. Although he had a good overall conformation and a long top line, he, like his sire, had ugly hocks. In action however, he had a great length of stride, with considerable spring from his hindquarters. Axworthy could not, however, be classed as a great racehorse, especially since having run very well indeed as a two-year-old, the following year he suffered such serious leg problems that he was sold at the Kellogg Sales to a Mr Shults, who used him for breeding.

His results as a stallion were surprising and won him a position of importance as one of the most successful sires of all times. Axworthy sired 59 stallions and 191 Standardbreds, 26 of which ran over the mile in 2'10" and 2 in 2'05" and the dams of 449

foals, 114 of which trotted at 2'10" and 31 at 2'05", but his best products were Guy Axworthy (b.h. 1902) and Dillon Axworthy (b.h. 1910).

Guy Axworthy, whose record over the mile was 2'08", was the outstanding stallion seen this century, siring many fine horses, in particular Guy McKinney (b.h. 1923) the first winner of the Hambletonian. Guy Axworthy produced a total of 454 trotters (44 with a record of 2'05" and four with one of 2'00"), including 110 stallions and the dams of 674 trotters of which 113 ran over the mile in 2'05" and 11 in 2'00".

Dillon Axworthy's personal record was 2'10" and he sired 199 trotters (18 of which had a record of 2'05" and one of 2'00") including 12 stallions and the dams of 342 trotters, 44 of which ran at 2'05" and 3 at 2'00". The most notable of Dillon Axworthy's progeny on the track was Dean Hanover (b.h. 1934) who trotted at 1'58"½. At stud he was not so successful although he did produce three 2'00" horses and a valuable broodmare in Misty Hanover (b. 1941), dam of Hickory Smoke (1'58"⅖), Hickory Pride (2'01"⅖) and Hickory Fire (2'04"⅗). Dean Hanover also sired Mimi Hanover (1945 – 2'09"), in turn dam of Speedster (1954 – 1'59"⅘), Magnolia Hanover (1944 – 2'13"⅕, Nevele Pride's second dam) and Goddess Hanover (1943 – 2'05"⅖, Ayres's second dam). This was a truly exceptional collection of brood mares whose contribution has proved a determining factor in the improvement of the breed.

Axworthy (2'15"1/2)	Axtell • 1886 (2'12")	William L. ○ 1882	George Wilkes • 1856 (2'22")	Hambletonian 10 (2'48") / Dolly Spanker (2'27")
			Lady Bunker 1873	**Mambrino Patchen** ♦ 1862 / Lady Dunn
		Lou ○ 1880	Mambrino Boy 1868 (2'26"1/2)	**Mambrino Patchen** ♦ 1862 / Roving Nelly
			Bird Mitchell	Mambrino Royal / Morgan Mare
	Marguerite ○ 1876	Kentucky Prince ○ 1870	Clark Chief 1861	Mambrino Chief • 1844 / Little Nora
			Kentucky Queen	Morgan Eagle / Blytes Whip Mare
		Young Daisy □ 1870	Strideaway 1863 (2'31")	Black Hawk Telegraph / Pocahontas (2'17"1/2) *
			Old Daisy	— / —

* Pacer

Breeder: A.B. Darling
Owner: A.B. Darling
Driver: A.B. Darling

Racing Career			
Age	No. of Races	Wins	Placings
2	2	0	2
3	3	2	1
Total	2	2	3

PETER THE GREAT

b.h. 1895

When Peter the Great was foaled his breeder named him after Peter V. Johnston, the trainer who looked after the horses in his stables and who was also given the task of breaking him in and preparing him for the Futurity Stakes for which he had already been entered. Johnston's task was not easy due to the horse's problematic temperament and when preparations were at a reasonably advanced stage the horse was stricken by a form of influenza which forced him to remain inactive for over a month. After this interruption his trainer patiently resumed even though he virtually had to start again from scratch. When the horse left for Lexington, Johnston held out very little hope but, despite the lack of confidence, Peter the Great did very well to finish second in both races behind the unbeaten favourite, Janie T.

After this he was sent to Michigan where he spent the whole winter out at grass. When the time came to resume training for the Three-year-old Futurity Stakes, Peter the Great had forgotten everything he had learned the previous year and his trainer had again to start everything from the very beginning. The programme was modified and preparations were made for the Kentucky Futurity, in which Peter the Great won all three heats, breaking the existing record in the last one with a time of 2'12''½.

At the beginning of 1899, Peter the Great was sold to J. Malcolm Forbes of Boston and was handed over to the young Henry Titer for training. The reason behind his breeder's decision to sell was that Peter V. Johnston had decided, at the age of 57, to withdraw from sporting activities. The new owner moved the horse to his stud farm and used him as a stallion until the end of spring. When the time came to resume training Titer encountered great difficulties in preparing the trotter, especially as regards finding the correct balance.

Peter the Great ran his first four-year-old race at Hartford. He was beaten in the first heat but won the other three, with speeds of 2'08'', 2'09''¼ and 2'09''½ respectively. After this brilliant performance he was transferred to New York where, on the new Empire City track, he won his two heats in 2'07''¼ and 2'08''¼. On 26 September he won the two heats of a race at Louisville, without arousing much excitement in the more modest times of 2'11'' in the first and 2'10'' in the second. On 5 October at Lexington, he took part in the Transylvania Trot, winning the first heat in 2'05''¼. In the second he was placed under considerable pressure by Charley Heer but still managed to win through in 2'08''¼. In the third he broke and was relegated to third place. In the fourth heat he was perfectly controlled but, after having led up to the finish straight he broke twice, the second time at the post causing him to be disqualified even though he had arrived first.

In the fifth heat the tactics were the same as in the previous one and the horse repeated his mistakes, this time only a furlong (200 m) from the post. He came third in both the sixth and the seventh heats which were for the winners of the first five. The following week he was re-entered for the Ashland Cup. He was beaten by Tommy Britton, who won in 2'09''¾, and won the second in 2'12''¾. The first two matches used up the energy of the two contestants and the other three competitors were carried off by Bonnatella who won, surprisingly, in 2'12''½, 2'12''½ and 2'12''¾.

In the Spring of 1900, Peter the Great was again used as a stallion and when Titer decided to resume training, the horse would have nothing to do with racing and so it was announced that training for the Grand Circuit would be postponed. However, Peter the Great was eventually withdrawn from racing altogether and Forbes, instead of blaming the trainer or criticizing himself for having misused the horse, took it out on the poor animal, treating him in a way which was unworthy of such a great champion.

In the spring of 1903, Sadie Mac, a daughter of Peter the Great and Fanella, won the Kentucky Futurity in 2'06''¼ but despite this Forbes put the stallion up for sale at Madison Square Garden in New York, where he was bought for $5,000 by Peter Duryea. The purchaser was in partnership with W.E. Stokes who disapproved of the transaction but ended up accepting co-ownership of the horse. In their stud farm in Lexington (Patchen Wilkes Farm), Peter the Great revealed himself as a real star, at a fee of $100.

When Duryea's and Stokes's company was wound up Duryea took over ownership of the horse and sold him in 1916 for $50,000 to Fletchen, the owner of Laurel Hall Farm in Indianapolis. As agreed, Peter the Great served for a further two years in Kentucky at Forkland Farm, but in 1918 was transferred to a new stud where he served for four seasons. He was withdrawn from activity in 1922 because he had become impotent and died a year later on 25th March 1923 at the age of 28, with his head in the hands of Jacob Councilman, the man to whom he had been entrusted and of whom Peter the Great was very fond. The feeling was mutual to such an extent that Councilman wrote in his will that on his death he wanted to be cremated and have his ashes scattered on Peter the Great's grave.

Peter the Great's stud career can be summarized as follows: he was the sire of 189 stallions and 498 trotters, as well as 163 pacers, while his daughters produced 812

Pilot Medium □ 1879	Happy Medium ○ 1863 (2'32''1/2)	Hambletonian 10 ○ 1849 (2'48'')	Abdallah 1 ○ 1823 Charles Kent Mare ○ 1834
		Princess ○ 1846 (2'30'')	Andrus' Hambletonian Isaiah Wilcox Mare
	Tackey □ 1859 (2'26'')	Pilot Jr. □ 1844	Old Pacing Pilot ♦ 1826 ** Nancy Pope ◇ 1838
		Jenny Lind	Bellfounder ○ 1817 —
Peter the Great (2'07''1/4)			
Santos ♦ 1887	Grand Sentinel ○ 1873 (2'27''1/4)	Sentinel ○ 1863 (2'29''3/4)	Hambletonian 10 ○ 1849 Lady Patriot ○ 1850
		Maid of Lexington	Mambrino Pilot (2'27''1/2) Brownlock *
*English thoroughbred ** Pacer*	Shadow ♦ 1870 (2'27'')	Octoroon **	Morgan Joe Brown Mare
		Swallow	Joe Hooker Sam Johnson Horse Mare

200

PETER THE GREAT

trotters. Peter the Great's most famous sons were : Peter Scott (b. 1909) sire of 15 stallions and 88 trotters; Peter Volo (dk.b. 1911) sire of 69 stallions and 377 trotters 7 of which had a record of 2'00''; Peter the Brewer (b. 1918) sire of 17 stallions and 143 trotters; The Laurel Hall (dk.b. 1918) sire of 10 stallions and 96 trotters in the USA and 95 trotters in Italy; and Azoff, sire of the great Peter Manning (b.g. 1916 – 1'56''¾).

Breeder: Mr Streeter
Owner: Mr Streeter – J. Malcolm Forbes
Driver: P.V. Johnston – H. Titer
Most important wins: Kentucky Futurity (1898)

Racing Career			
Age	No. of Races	Wins	Placings
2	1	0	1
3	1	1	0
4	5	3	2
Total	7	4	3

VOLOMITE

dk.b.h. 1926

Peter the Great produced two great stallions which are the foundation sires of almost all modern American trotters – excluding the lines descending from Axworthy. One was Peter Volo who won several important races including the Kentucky Futurity (2'03''½) in 1914, setting his personal record at 2'02'', and proved even more valuable at stud. In his career as a stallion Peter Volo produced 533 Standardbreds (89 with a record of 2'05'' and 10 of 2'00'') including 68 stallions and the dams of 1003 Standardbreds (127 trotting at 2'05'' and 6 at 2'00''). Peter Volo also produced three Hambletonian winners, but it is Volomite who stands out both as a racehorse and above all as perpetuator of the paternal line.

Volomite (15.5 hands (1.58 m)) had a slender, elegant conformation with very attractive limbs, probably derived from his maternal granddam, who was a thorough-

bred. In the 1929 Hambletonian he was beaten in both heats by Walter Dear, his training companion, preferred by W. Cox and driven by W.H. Leese, but Volomite's personal record of 2'03''¼ is evidence of his ability.

It was, however, at stud that Volomite really showed his true value, producing 609 Standardbreds (33 with a record of 2'00'', 11 of which were trotters) who produced 154 stallions and the dams of 567 horses, 18 of which had a record of 2'00'' (15 being trotters). This was an exceptional record and, equally important, Volomite produced four winners of the Hambletonian – in 1943 three of his offspring filled the first three places. In addition, he produced horses such as Worthy Boy, sire of the great Star's Pride and Mighty Ned, twice winner of the Prix d'Amérique carrying the colours of Count Paolo Orsi Mangelli, and among the pacers Poplar Byrd (1'59''⅗).

			Pilot Medium □ 1879	Happy Medium (2'32''1/2) Tackey (2'26'')
		Peter the Great ○ 1895 (2'07''1/4)		
	Peter Volo • 1911 (2'02'')		Santos ◆ 1887	Grand Sentinel (2'27''1/4) Shadow (2'27'')
			Nervolo ○ 1896 (2'04''1/4) **	Colbert (2'07''1/2) ** Nelly D.
		Nervolo Belle ○ 1906		
Volomite (2'03''1/4)			Josephine Knight ◇ 1890	Batterton Mambrino Beauty ◇ 1881
			Zombro • 1892 (2'11'')	Mc Kinney (2'11''1/4) Whisper
		San Francisco ○ 1903 (2'07''3/4)		
	Cita Frisco ○ 1915		Oniska ○ 1898	Nutwood Wilkes (2'16''1/2) Bay Line
			Mendocino ○ 1889 (2'19''1/2)	Electioneer • 1868 Mano ◇ 1883
*English thoroughbred ** Pacer		Mendocita ○ 1899		
			Esther ○ 1877 *	Express ○ 1853 Coliseum • 1869

Breeder: Walnut Hall Farm
Owner: Walnut Hall Farm
Drivers: W. Cox – (W.H. Leese*)
Most important wins: Junior Kentucky Futurity (1928), Horseman Futurity (1929), Matron Stake (1929), Charter Oak Stake (1929)
Occasional driver

Racing Career

Age	No. of Races	Wins	Placings
2	15	4	4
3	24	15	5
Total	39	19	9

VOLOMITE

GREYHOUND

gr.g. 1932

Because of his extraordinary feats Greyhound was nicknamed "the Grey Cyclone." His sire was Guy Abbey, the runner-up in the 1928 Hambletonian, and his dam Elizabeth was full sister to the stallion Peter the Brewer. This represents a combination of two very important bloodlines: that of Axworthy (through Guy Axworthy, sire of Guy Abbey) and Peter the Great (sire of Elizabeth). Greyhound's pedigree is quite impressive but despite this, perhaps because of the colours of his coat, he was gelded as a foal, a move which was later much regretted.

When he was born Greyhound had a slender form like that of a greyhound, which is clearly how he acquired his name. He was bought as a yearling at the Indianapolis auctions by E.J. Baker who handed him over to Sep Palin for training. Greyhound ran his first race at the age of two in Columbus, winning with a time of 2'17". In that year he won six consecutive races, setting his first record, that for two-year-old geldings, clocking a time of 2'04"¾ in the second heat of the Horseman Futurity. At three he was unbeaten in all eight races (winning 18 of their 20 heats), including the most important three-year-old race, the Hambletonian where he won both heats (2'02"¼ and 2'02"¾). As a four-year-old he was beaten by Tara at Goshen where the track was full of bends and short straights, and he won only one of the four heats.

From that day Greyhound was unbeaten until he retired from racing in 1940 at the age of eight when he was still in his prime. That year he had won seven races taking 14 out of 15 heats and finishing second in the other. However, before he was taken to his owner's home at Northbrook, Greyhound demolished the world mounted trot record with a time of 2'01"¾, knocking 3½ seconds off the previous record held by

Hollywood Boris. Mrs Frances Dodge Johnson was in the saddle on this occasion. This was the last of a long series of world records set by Greyhound, who was above all a horse of great records. The most important was without doubt the absolute world record of 1'55"¼, which he set in Lexington at the age of six, beating his own time of 1'56" which he had set the year before on the same track. The previous best time was recorded by Peter Manning who clocked 1'56"¾ in 1922. The most remarkable thing is that this record was to stand until 1969 when, after 31 years, it was broken by Nevele Pride.

In 1935 at Springfield he broke the three-year-old three-heat race record (2'06", – 2'06", – 2'03"¼), as well as the general three-year-old gelding record (2'00"). In 1936, with a time of 1'57"½, he set the four-year-old horse and four-year-old gelding race record. In the same year, with times of 2'02" and 1'57"¼, he broke the two-heat race record and, with times of 2'01", 2'00"¼, 2'00", the three-heat race record on the one mile track at Goshen. In 1937, with a time of 1'56" he set the five-year-old record and with 1'05"¾ the half mile track record, again at Goshen. In the same year, he also set the one and a half mile record with a time of 3'02"½ at Indianapolis, beating the 3'12"½ set up by Peter Manning. In Indianapolis in 1939, it was the turn of the two-mile record in 4'06" and the pairs record (with Rosalind) in 1'58"¼. Some of these records still remain unbroken 40 years later.

Breeder: Henry Knight
Owner: Col. E.J. Baker – Hotel Baker Stable
Trainer-driver: S. Palin
Most important wins: Horseman Futurity (two-year-olds – 1934), Horseman Futurity (three-year-olds – 1935), Hambletonian Stake (1935), Stallion Stake (1935)

GREYHOUND

				Axtell ● 1886 (2'12'')
			Axworthy (2'15''1/2)	Marguerite ○ 1876
		Guy Axworthy ○ 1902 (2'08''3/4)		
			Lillian Wilkes (2'17''3/4)	Guy Wilkes (2'15''1/4)
	Guy Abbey ◇ 1925 (2'06''3/4)			Flora *
			The Abbe (2'10''1/2) **	Chimes (2'30''3/4)
		Abbacy ◇ 1918 (2'04''1/4)		Nettie King
Greyhound (1'55''1/4)			Regal Mc Kinney	Mc Kinney (2'11''1/4)
				Princess Royal (2'20'')
			Pilot Medium □ 1879	Happy Medium (2'32''1/2)
		Peter the Great ○ 1895 (2'07''1/4)		Tackey (2'26'')
			Santos ◆ 1887	Grand Sentinel (2'27''1/4)
	Elizabeth □ 1923			Shadow (2'27'')
			Zombro ● 1892 (2'11'')	Mc Kinney (2'11''1/4)
		Zombrewer □ 1905 (2'04''1/4) **		Whisper
* English thoroughbred ** Pacer			Mary Bales □ 1894 (2'26''1/4)	Montjoy ○ 1887
				Molly J. □ 1888

Racing Career

Age	No. of Races	Wins	Placings
2	18	12	2
3	20	18	1
4	17	15	2
5	12	12	0
6	10	10	0
7	*only heats against the clock in trials and exhibition races*		
8	15	14	1
Total	83	71	6

MIGHTY NED

b.h. 1942

He was a horse of considerable size, moved easily and was extremely powerful. He was imported into Italy in 1945 from the United States where he had finished fourth overall in the 20th Hambletonian won by Titan Hanover. Mighty Ned had a few problems with his hocks and he also suffered from trouble with his feet which caused his new Italian owner, Mr Tondini, so much worry and disappointment that he sold Mighty Ned to Count Paolo Orsi Mangelli. Mighty Ned was unshod and put out to grass in order to be retained, some time later, on the dirt track next to the Budrie Stud Farm. Once his foot had healed, the horse returned to his former self and won his first European race in Turin in October 1947 with a time of 2'12" 7/mile (1'22"5/km), beating Austin Hanover. Later on, Mighty Ned won the Premio d'Inverno in 2'10" 9/mile (1'21"37/km).

In 1948 his performance in Italian long distance racing was outstanding. In Rome on the Villa Gloria racecourse in February, he won the Premio Viminale over 1½ miles 118 yd (2,520 m) and although burdened by a stiff handicap against Giaur Brivio and set to give even greater advantage to the other Italian horses lined up at the first tape, 100 m ahead of him, he caught up with the bunch with an impressive and unforgettable burst of speed as he came out of the first bend. He went on from there to lead the field and won by a wide margin in 1'56" 1/mile (1'21"2/km) ahead of Giaur Brivio. Also in 1948, he triumphed in France in the Prix d'Amérique in 2'15" 1/mile (1'24"/km) over 1 mile 5 furlongs (2,600 m) and the same year he also won the Prix d'Europe at Enghien. In 1949 he made another attempt at the Prix d'Amérique in Paris but was unable to make up the 27.3 yd (23 m) handicap that he had to accept for having won the race the previous year and came second behind Venutar. In Italy, he still played an important rôle on the racecourses in Rome, Milan, Modena and Cesena.

In 1950 he repeated his success in the European Championship in Cesena but this time he won only two heats with a time of 2'8"5/mile (1'19"9/km), beating Scotch Thistle in both. In 1951 he returned to Paris to win his second Prix d'Amérique in 2'13"/mile (1'22"7/km) from Scotch Thistle, but gave a disappointing performance in Naples in the Gran Premio Lotteria in which he had to be content with winning the consolation final. That same year he was second in the European Championship won by Birbone in three heats (3rd – 1st – 2nd) while Mighty Ned, who had finished fourth in the first heat and third in the second, won the third.

In 1952 Mighty Ned was sent to stud and produced excellent results: in fact he produced 342 trotters, 85 of which had records of 2'8"7/mile (1'20"/km), 21 of 2'5"5/mile (1'18/km) and one of 2'2"/mile (1'16"/km). The most illustrious of his offspring were Glaudio (1963 – 2'1"8/mile (1'15"7/km)), Crevalcore (1953 – 2'2"2/mile (1'16"/km)), Gualdo (1957 – 2'3"4/mile (1'16"/km)), Blera (1960 – 2'3"8/mile (1'37"/km)), Checco Prà (1952 – 2'5"1/mile (1'17"8/km)), Qualto (1960 – 2'5"7/mile (1'18"/km)), Fra Diavolo (1951 – 1'49"5/mile (1'8"1/km)), Alfredo (1958 – 1'50"/mile (1'18"4/km)) and Valganna (1961 – 2'6"3/mile (1'18"5/km)). Mighty Ned died in 1970 at the age of 28.

Breeder: Walnut Hall Farm
Owners: Joseph Burke – Count P. Orsi Mangelli
Drivers: T. Berry – A. Finn – V. Antonellini
Most important wins: Reading Fair Futurity (1945), Premio d'Inverno (1947), Prix d'Europe (1948), Prix d'Amérique (1948 – 1951), Gran Premio della Fiera (1948 – 1949), Premio Ghirlandina (1949), Campionato Europeo (1949 – 1950)

		Peter the Great ○ 1895 (2'07"1/4)	Pilot Medium □ 1879 Santos ◆ 1887
	Peter Volo ● 1911 (2'02")		
Volomite ● 1926 (2'03"1/4)		Nervolo Belle ○ 1906	Nervolo (2'04"1/4)** Josephine Knight ◊ 1890
		San Francisco ○ 1903 (2'07"3/4)	Zombro (2'11") Oniska
	Cita Frisco ○ 1915		
Mighty Ned (2'04"3/4)		Mendocita ○ 1899	Mendocino (2'19"1/2) Esther ○ 1877*
		Axworthy ◊ 1892 (2'15"1/2)	Axtell ● 1886 (2'12") Marguerite ○ 1876
	Guy Axworthy ○ 1902 (2'08"3/4)		
Nedda Guy ○ 1928 (2'03"1/2)		Lillian Wilkes (2'17"3/4)	Guy Wilkes (2'15"1/4) Flora*
		Atlantic Espress (2'07"3/4)	Bellini (2'13"1/4) Expressive (2'12"1/2)
	Nedda ○ 1916 (1'58"1/4)		
*English thoroughbred **Pacer*		Pleasant Thoughts (2'21")	Prodigal (2'16") Extasy (2'10"1/2)**

Racing Career			
Age	No. of Races	Wins	Placings
3 (USA)	17	4	9
4	–	–	–
5	5	5	0
6	15	11	3
7	14	7	4
8	4	2	1
9	6	2	1
Total	61	31	18

STAR'S PRIDE

STAR'S PRIDE

dk.b.h. 1947

In the 1950 Hambletonian at Goshen, Star's Pride was beaten by Lusty Song in two heats finishing second in both. That year Florican also competed in this American three-year-old classic and came fourth, so that the two greatest stallions of the latter half of the 20th century were decisively beaten. That same year, however, Star's Pride won the Kentucky Futurity, which is just as prestigious as the Hambletonian, even though the latter, which can be considered as the American Trotting Derby always holds that special fascination which is peculiar to this type of competition all over the world. However, even though Star's Pride's performance on the trace was excellent, as a stallion it was truly extraordinary.

The very fact that eight of his progeny triumphed in the classic that he himself had been unable to win was proof enough. In the United States he produced a total of 629 trotters, 42 of which set a record of 2'00", in addition to the dams of 679 trotters (29 at 2'00"). The best of the progeny of Star's Pride were Ayres and Nevele Pride, the latter in particular for having broken Greyhound's world record, with a time of 1'54"⅘, which had stood for more than 30 years. There was also Nike Hanover, winner of the Prix d'Amérique in 1964, carrying the colours of the Manuela Stud; Lindy's Pride (b. 1966 – 1'57"⅗) and Super Bowl (b. 1969 – 1'56"⅖), winners of the 1969 and 1972 Hambletonian.

Breeder: Henry Warwick
Owners: E.R. Harriman – L.B. Sheppard
Drivers: Harry Pownall Sr – J. Simpson Sr
Most important wins: Kentucky Futurity (1950), Matron Stallion (1950), The Historic (1950), Trotting Derby (1951), McConnel Memorial (1951), The Titan (1951)

Racing Career			
Age	No. of Races	Wins	Placings
2	13	4	6
3	26	12	12
4	28	14	10
5	12	6	6
Total	79	36	34

			Peter Volo • 1911 (2'02")	**Peter the Great** (2'07"1/4) Nervolo Belle ○ 1906
		Volomite • 1926 (2'03"1/4)	Cita Frisco ○ 1915	**San Francisco** (2'07"3/4) Mendocita ○ 1899
	Worthy Boy ◆ 1940 (2'02"1/2)		Peter The Brewer (2'02"1/2)	**Peter the Great** (2'07"1/4) Zombrewer (2'04"1/4) *
		Warwell Worthy ○ 1932 (2'03"3/4)	Alma Lee (2'04"3/4)	Lee Worthy (2'02"1/2) Jeane Revere (2'06"3/4)
Star's Pride (1'57"1/5)			Guy Axworthy (2'08"3/4)	**Axworthy** (2'15"1/2) Lillian Wilkes (2'17"3/4)
		Mr.Mc Elwyn ○ 1921 (1'59"1/4)	Widow Maggie (2'24"1/2)	**Peter the Great** (2'07"1/4) Maggie Onward ○ 1898
	Stardrift • 1936 (2'03")		**San Francisco** (2'07"3/4)	Zombro • 1892 (2'11") Oniska ○ 1898
Pacer		Dillcisco ○ 1919 (2'06"1/2)	Dilworthy 1916 (2'15"1/2)	**Axworthy** (2'15"1/2) Dillon's Last 1909

NEVELE PRIDE

b.h. 1965

This horse was an exceptional trotter. During his racing career which lasted from the age of two to four he won the title of Horse of the Year three times. Nevele Pride was the result of classic breeding between Star's Pride and a brood mare, whose dam was Hoot Mon, and in 1967 he set the two-year-old mile record at 1'59''⅘.

In 1968 he took all the three-year-old Classics, carrying off the Du Quoin Hambletonian in just two heats and winning the Kentucky Futurity at Lexington. Previously he had won the Dexter Cup at Roosevelt Park, the Yonkers Trot at Yonkers in New York and the Colonial in Philadelphia's Liberty Bell Park. In a heat against the clock in 1969 at Indianapolis Nevele Pride recorded the most extraordinary achievement of his career by breaking the world

record, held by Greyhound since 1938, with the sensational time of 1'54''⅘. Only a week before, however, he had been beaten in the Roosevelt International Trot by the "Reine" of French trotters, the amazing Une de Mai, who had won this prestigious race (valued as a world championship event) in 2'2''7/mile (1'16''3/km).

At stud Nevele Pride was exceptional, siring 190 trotters (22 of which held 2'00'' records) including such high-caliber horses as Pershing and Bonefish, the latter being the winner of the 1975 Hambletonian. All things considered, Nevele Pride was perhaps the most extraordinary champion to be produced by American breeders since the Second World War and he certainly represents a milestone in world trotting racing.

Breeder: Mr & Mrs Edward Quin
Owners: Nevele Acres – Louis Resnick
Driver: Stanley Dancer
Most important wins: Horseman Stake (1967), Horseman Futurity (1968), Hambletonian Stake (1968), The Colonial (1968), Kentucky Futurity (1968), Yonkers Trot (1968), Dexter Cup (1968), American Trotting Championship (1969)

Racing Career			
Age	No. of Races	Wins	Placings
2	29	26	2
3	24	21	2
4	14	10	3
Total	67	57	7

Nevele Pride (1'54''4/5)	Star's Pride • 1947 (1'57''1/5)	Worthy Boy ♦ 1940 (2'02''1/2)	Volomite (2'03''1/4)	Peter Volo (2'02'') / Cita Frisco
			Warwell Worthy (2'03''3/4)	Peter The Brewer (2'02''1/2) / Alma Lee (2'04''3/4)
		Stardrift • 1936 (2'03'')	Mr.Mc Elwyn (1'59''1/4)	Guy Axworthy (2'08''3/4) / Widow Maggie (2'24''1/2)
			Dillcisco (2'06''1/2)	San Francisco (2'07''3/4) / Dilworthy
	Thankful • 1952 (2'03''2/5)	Hoot Mon ♦ 1944 (2'00'')	Scotland (1'59''1/4)	Peter Scott (2'05'') / Roya Mc Kinney (2'07''1/2)
			Missey ○ 1938	Guy Abbey (2'06''3/4) / Tilly Tonka (2'02''3/4)
		Magnolia Hanover • 1944 (2'13''1/5)	Dean Hanover (1'58''1/2)	Dillon Axworthy (2'10''1/4) / Palestrina (2'09''1/2)
			Melba Hanover (2'03''3/4)	Calumet Chuck (2'04'') / Isotta (2'09''3/4)

NEVELE PRIDE

SPEEDY CROWN

b.h. 1968

In 1957 Speedster finished unplaced in the 32nd Hambletonian, yet in a period of ten years two of his sons have taken this the classic American trotting race. In 1963 Speedy Scot won at Du Quoin beating Florlis (b.h. by Florican) in the third heat and in 1967 on the same track it was the turn of Speedy Streak, full brother to Speedy Scot, to win in just two heats. Of those two it was Speedy Scot who assumed the more important rôle at stud by siring Speedy Crown, winner of the 1971 Hambletonian, which he carried off by taking both heats, trotting at 1'57"2 in the first and 1'58"⅕ in the second.

Voted Trotter of the Year in 1971, Speedy Crown was a horse of exceptional qualities and his most thrilling season was as a four-year-old when he won ten of his 18 starts, coming second five times and third twice. His most convincing victory, apart from the Roosevelt International Trot, was the Challenge Cup where he beat the French mare Und de Mai and Fresh Yankee, trotting the distance of 1 mile 2 furlongs (2,011 m) in 2'31"⅕. However, although Speedy Crown was a great trotter he proved himself to be an even greater stallion. The 53rd Hambletonian, in 1978, was won by his son, Speedy Somolli, whose success meant that three successive generations from the same direct male line had won the Hambletonian, a treble without precedent. A further remarkable aspect of this victory was the world record set by Speedy Somolli and Florida Pro in the first two heats with the same time of 1'55". Not only was this a world record for three-year-olds, it was also a record for horses of all ages since Nevele Pride's record was set in a heat against the clock.

In the third heat Speedy Somolli beat Florida Pro, trotting at 1'57", thus ensuring his victory. Florida Pro was by Arnie Almahurst (b.h. 1970), also one of Speedy Scot's offspring. Speedy Crown's success as a stallion does not, however, end here. Up to now he has sired 119 winners, 45 of which hold the 2'00" record. One of them is Jazz Cosmos (b.h. 1979) who in the Kentucky Futurity at Lexington equalled the world record previously set by Speedy Somolli and Florida Pro, and beat horses like Speed Bowl, winner of the 1982 Hambletonian. That same year another of Speedy Crown's colts, T.V. Yankee, set the two-year-old world record with a time of 1'56" while one of his fillies, Ginger Belle, equalled the three-year-old world record, held since 1981 by Duchess Faye, with a time of 1'56"⅖. Speedy Crown has had an exceptional stud career which compares favourably with that of Speedy Scot's other son, Arnie Almahurst. Apart from having produced Florida Pro, this horse also sired Arndon (b.h. 1979) who in 1982 at Lexington trotted against the clock in 1'54" dead, beating Nevele Pride's previous absolute world record (1'54"⅘).

Speedy Crown (1'57"1/5)	Speedy Scot ○ 1960 (1'56"4/5)	Speedster ○ 1954 (1'59"4/5)	Rodney 1944 (1'57"2/5)	Spencer Scott (1'57"1/4) Earl's Princess Martha 1935
			Mimi Hanover 1945 (2'09")	Dean Hanover (1'58"1/2) Hanover Maid (2'02"1/4)
		Scotch Love • 1954 (2'04"3/5)	Victory Song (1'57"3/5)	Volomite (2'03"1/4) Evesong (2'08"3/4)
			Selka Scot (2'13"3/5)	**Scotland** (1'59"1/4) Selka Guy (2'21")
	Missile Toe ○ 1962 (2'05"2/5)	Florican ○ 1947 (1'57"2/5)	Spud Hanover (2'03")	Guy Mc Kinney (1'58"3/4) Evelyn the Great (2'08"3/4)
			Florimel (2'03"1/2)	Spencer (1'59"3/4) Carolyn (2'09")
		Worth A Plenty ○ 1954 (2'02"2/5)	Darnley (1'59"3/4)	**Scotland** (1'59"1/4) Fionne (2'07"3/4)
			Sparkle Plenty (2'07"3/5)	Worthy Boy (2'02"1/2) The Gem (2'08")

SPEEDY CROWN

Breeder: Mrs Howard Beissinger
Owner: Crown Stable
Driver: Howard Beissinger
Most important wins: Hambletonian Stake (1971), American National Stake (1971), Challenge Stake (1971), Gay Acres Stake (1971), Hanover Stake (1971), Roosevelt International Trot (1972), American Trotting Championship (1972), Maple Leaf Trotting Classic (1972)

	Racing Career		
Age	**No. of Races**	**Wins**	**Placings**
2	8	4	1
3	24	15	6
4	18	10	7
Total	50	29	14

PERSHING

b.h. 1973

Having raced as a two- and a three-year-old in the U.S.A. where he won only seven out of his 35 starts, Pershing, a son of Nevele Pride, was imported into Sweden by the KGB Stables. In the United States he set a personal record of 1'58" (1'13"3/km) but unfortunately fractured a leg which inevitably jeopardized his performance at the end of his first year of racing. Having undergone an operation he reappeared on the track at the age of three, fully recovered, but he finished unplaced in the Hambletonian.

After arriving in Europe in 1977, he achieved his first win at Solvalla over 1 mile 57 yd (1,600 m) trotting at 2'5"/mile (1'14"9/km). On 5 July in Hilversum, he won in 1'59"3/mile (1'14"2/km) beating Wiretapper and Speedy Volite, who in 1976 had won the Giants' Cup with an equally good time of 2'0"1/mile (1'14"7/km). A week later, he won the Elite-Rennen at Gelsenkirchen leading the field all the way and beating Granit, Equiléo and Bellino II in that order. In the Greyhound Rennen at Mönchengladbach he was second, just beaten by the French horse, Hadol du Vivier. In Munich he won the Preis der Besten beating Madison Avenue, while in the Giants' Cup at Hilversum he came second in the heat behind Bellino II, who also won the final in which Pershing could manage no better than fourth.

At the end of September Pershing returned to victory in the N.J. Koster Memorial in Copenhagen, going on to win the City of Vienna Grand Prix after just a month in Austria and in November he came fourth in the City of Gelsenkirchen Grand Prix. Seven days later, Pershing won the Grand Prix des Nations in Milan with a time of 2'1"6/mile (1'15"/km). On 1 May 1978 he won the Goldenes Bild Hufeisen at

Gelsenkirchen and on 28 May he won his heat in the Elitlopp from Hadol du Vivier: both horses recorded the same time, finishing in 1'58"2/mile (1'13"5/km). In the final Hadol du Vivier came off the better, winning in 1'59"/mile (1'14"/km) while Pershing was unplaced. In the Copenhagen Cup Pershing was again successful setting the European distance record (1 mile 2 furlongs (2,011 m) trotting at 1'59"3/mile (1'14"2/km). In July he won at Jagersro in Sweden with a time of 2'1"1/mile (1'15"3/km), over the mile in the Hugo Albergs Memorial and in December at Solvalla over 1 mile 5 furlongs 25 yd (2,640 m) in the C.Th. Ericsson Memorial (2'6"1/mile (1'18"4/km)); while in October, he repeated his success of the previous year in the City of Vienna Grand Prix. In 1979 Pershing won the Grosser Preis von Recklinghausen (1'59"/mile (1'14"/km)), the Goldenes Bild Hufeisen (2'03"/mile (1'14"6/km)), the Grote Prijs der Lage Landen, The Elite-Rennen, the Elitlopp, the European Championship at Cesena, the Grosser Preis von Dinslaken and the Grand Prix des Nations. He went to stud in 1980.

Breeder: Joseph T. Mendelson (USA)
Owner: J.T. Mendelson – KGB Stables
Drivers: H. Beissinger – Zeller Michae – Wm Herman – B. Lindstedt
Most important wins: Horseman Futurity (1976), Preis der Besten (1977), Grosser Preis der Stadt Wien (1977, 1978), Elite-Rennen (1977, 1979), Grand Prix des Nations (1977, 1979), Copenhagen Cup (1978), Hugo Albergs Memorial (1978), C.Th. Ericssons Memorial (1978), Grosser Preis der Stadt Gelsenkirchen (1978), Solvallas Jubileumspokal (1978, 1979), Grote Prijs der Lage Landen (1979), European Championship (1979), Gross Preis von Dinslaken (1979)

Racing Career

Age	No. of Races	Wins	Placings
2	16	2	8
3	19	5	6
4	26	13	12
5	31	18	8
6	27	18	8
Total	119	56	42

Pershing (1'13"3)	Nevele Pride ○ 1965 (1'54"4/5)	Star's Pride ● 1947 (1'57"1/5)	Worthy Boy 1940 (2'02"1/2) — **Volomite** (2'03"1/4), Warwell Worthy (2'03"3/4)
			Stardrift 1936 (2'03") — Mr.Mc Elwyn (1'59"1/4), Dillcisco (2'06"1/2)
		Thankful ● 1952 (2'03"2/5)	Hoot Mon 1944 (2'00") — **Scotland** (1'59"1/4), Missey ○ 1938
			Magnolia Hanover 1944 (2'13"1/5) — Dean Hanover (1'58"1/2), Melba Hanover (2'03"3/4)
	Flying Cloud ○ 1964 (2'04"1/5)	Florican ○ 1947 (1'57"2/5)	Spud Hanover 1936 (2'03") — Guy Mc Kinney (1'58"3/4), Evelyn the Great (2'08"3/4)
			Florimel 1938 (2'03"1/2) — Spencer (1'59"3/4), Carolyn (2'09")
		Flying Queen ○ 1960	Bombs Away (2'04"1/2) — **Volomite** (2'03"1/4), Iosola's Worthy (2'04"3/4)
			Torrid Scott (2'07")** — **Scotland** (1'59"1/4), Taurida Abbey

** Pacer

214

BRET HANOVER

Pacer – b.h. 1962

Bret Hanover's sire Adios is universally recognized as the sire of the modern pacer, and was one of the champions in the history of trotting racing. His sire had been unlucky in that his racing career developed at the height of the Second World War, yet in spite of this, he still made a name for himself racing from the age of two to seven and setting a record for the period of 1'57"½.

Adios was by Hal Dale who was a "free-legged" horse, that is, one of the race pacers who are capable of racing without hobbles, ugly contraptions attached to the horse's legs to ensure a regular gait. Although his racing career was extremely successful it was outshone by his performance as a stallion. Proof of this are the 78 2–minute record holders that he sired, while his total production included 132 stallions. Only a horse of such a high caliber could possible have sired Bret Hanover. In two years' racing, in addition to taking the pacer's Triple Crown by winning the Cane Pace at Yonkers in New York, the Little Brown Jug at the Delaware track (Ohio) and the Messenger Stake at the Roosevelt Raceway in New York, he won 38 consecutive races, and the grand sum of $514,274 (over £342,000) during his racing career.

Bret Hanover who was voted Horse of the Year in 1965, also set a series of records including the three-year-old pacers' world record over a mile track with a time of 1'55"/mile (1'11"5/km), the absolute world record in two heats for pacers of all ages over the half mile (804 m) with a time of 1'57" (1'12"7/km) and the absolute world record in two consecutive heats for pacers of all ages, also over the half-mile mile, with times of 1'57" and 1'57"⅕. These last two records were achieved on 23 September 1965 at Delaware. Just over a year later, on 7 October 1966 at Lexington, Bret Hanover also set the absolute world record for horses of all ages, with a time of 1'53"⅗ (1'10"6/km) over a mile, improving on the previous record of 1'54" that he himself had set that same year at Vernon. This record was broken in 1971 by Steady Star (b.h 1967) on the same track with a time of 1'52" and in 1980 by Niatross at the Roosevelt Raceway with a fantastic time of 1'49"⅕ (1'07"9/10/km).

Despite this, however, Bret Hanover's greatness remains unshaken, especially since he gave proof of his quality by producing Warm Breeze (1973), holder of the world speed record with a time of 1'53" achieved on 26 June 1977 on the one-mile track at the Golden Bear Raceway, crowning the career of a horse who as a colt had constantly suffered from one illness or another.

Breeder: Hanover Shoe Farm
Owner: Richard Downing
Driver: Frank Ervin
Most important wins: American National Stake (1964), Battle of Saratoga (1964), Goshen Cup (1964), Ohio Standardbred Futurity (1964), Reynolds Memorial (1964), Cane Pace (1965), Little Brown Jug (1965), Messenger Stake (1965), Matron Stake (1965)

Racing Career

Age	No. of Races	Wins	Placings
2	24	24	0
3	24	21	3
4	20	17	3
Total	68	62	6

Bret Hanover (1'53"3/5)				
Adios ○ 1940 (1'57"1/2)	Hal Dale 1926 (2'02"1/4)	Abbedale 1917 (2'01"1/4)	The Abbe ♦ 1903 (2'04")	
			Daisydale D. 1908 (2'15"1/4)	
		Margaret Hal (2'19"1/2)	Argot Hal (2'04"3/4)	
			Margaret Polk	
	Adioo Volo 1930 (2'05")	Adioo Guy (2'00"3/4)	Guy Dillon (2'23"1/2) *	
			Adioo ○ 1895	
		Sigrid Volo (2'04")	Peter Volo ● 1911 (2'02") *	
			Polly Parrot (2'13"1/4)	
Brenna Hanover ○ 1956 (2'01")	Tar Heel 1948 (1'57"2/5)	Billy Direct ○ 1934 (1'55")	Napoleon Direct (1'59"3/4)	
			Gay Forbes (2'07"3/4)	
		Leta Long (2'03"3/4)	Volomite (2'03"1/4) *	
			Rosette (2'06") *	
	Beryl Hanover 1947 (2'02")	Nibble Hanover (1'58"3/4) *	Calumet Chuck (2'04") *	
			Justissima (2'06"1/4) *	
		Laura Hanover (2'15"1/4) *	The Laurel Hall ♦ 1918 *	
			Miss Bertha Worthy (2'21") *	

* Trotter

NIATROSS

Pacer – b.h. 1977

When in 1971 Steady Star set the world pacer's record with a time of 1'52'', beating Bret Hanover's time of 1'53''⅗, it appeared that his record would be very difficult to beat. But nine years later Niatross managed to do so, knocking more than three seconds off the time and finishing a sensational 1'49'' (1'07''9/10/km). Apart from this important record Niatross' racing career is remarkable for the number and the importance of his victories and for the amount of prize money that he collected.

As a two-year-old Niatross was unbeaten in all 13 races, which included the Woodrow Wilson at Meadowlands, New York, the Kentucky Pacing Derby at Lousiville Downs and the International Stallion Stake at the Red Mile Racetrack in Lexington. The following year he was beaten only twice, in the Haswell Memorial at Saratoga where he finished up against the guard-rail, which totally eliminated all chances of victory, and in the preliminary heat of the Meadowlands Pace where he came fourth. Nevertheless seven days later he succeeded in winning the final of this race, which offers a prize of over one million dollars.

Niatross won no fewer that 23 other races apart from the Meadowlands Pace and the others were just as prestigious even though they offered less prize money. In 1980, Niatross won 24 races including the Hanover-Hempt at Vernon Downs (in 1979 he had won the two-year-old race), the Battle of the Brandywine at Wilmington, the Reynolds Memorial at Buffalo Raceway, the Cane Pace at Yonkers Raceway, the Gaines Memorial again at Vernon Downs, the Oliver Wendell Holmes at Meadowlands, the Prix d'Été at Blue Bonnets Raceway in Montreal, the James B Dancer Memorial at Freehold Raceway, the Little Brown Jug at Delaware, the Messenger Stake at Roosevelt Raceway and the Hanover Stake at Liberty Bell Park in Philadelphia.

Niatross could have ended his career at Hollywood with his success in the race dedicated to the memory of his sire, the Albatross Stake, but chose to add even further glory to his racing record with one last win in the American Pacing Classic in California. In just those two years Niatross proved himself to be a formidable champion, worthy of going down in history as one of the greatest Standardbreds of all time, having won all that a pacer could ever hope to win. When he retired his prize money added up to $2,019,213, almost £1,346,142.

Breeder: Niagara Acres
Owner: Niagara Acres – Clinton Galbraith – Niatross Stable.
Driver: C. Galbraith
Most important wins: Woodrow Wilson (1979), Kentucky Pacing Derby (1979), International Stallion Stake (1979), Battle of the Brandywine (1980), Cane Pace (1980), Meadowlands Pace (1980), Gaines Memorial (1980), Oliver Wendell Holmes (1980), Prix d'Été (1980), James B. Dancer Memorial (1980), Little Brown Jug (1980), Messenger Stake (1980), American Pacing Classic (1980)

Racing Career			
Age	No. of Races	Wins	Placings
2	13	13	0
3	26	24	0
Total	39	37	0

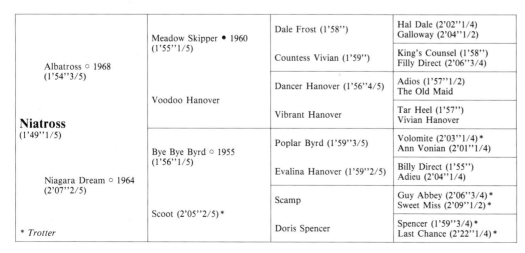

			Dale Frost (1'58'')	Hal Dale (2'02''1/4) Galloway (2'04''1/2)
	Meadow Skipper • 1960 (1'55''1/5)		Countess Vivian (1'59'')	King's Counsel (1'58'') Filly Direct (2'06''3/4)
Albatross ○ 1968 (1'54''3/5)		Voodoo Hanover	Dancer Hanover (1'56''4/5)	Adios (1'57''1/2) The Old Maid
			Vibrant Hanover	Tar Heel (1'57'') Vivian Hanover
Niatross (1'49''1/5)		Bye Bye Byrd ○ 1955 (1'56''1/5)	Poplar Byrd (1'59''3/5)	Volomite (2'03''1/4) * Ann Vonian (2'01''1/4)
			Evalina Hanover (1'59''2/5)	Billy Direct (1'55'') Adieu (2'04''1/4)
	Niagara Dream ○ 1964 (2'07''2/5)	Scoot (2'05''2/5) *	Scamp	Guy Abbey (2'06''3/4) * Sweet Miss (2'09''1/2) *
* *Trotter*			Doris Spencer	Spencer (1'59''3/4) * Last Chance (2'22''1/4) *

MISTERO

b.h. 1940

Mistero was the first trotter of international level to be produced by Italian breeders. His racing career began during the Second World War and continued into the years that immediately followed; he raced from 1942 to 1948. The following year, when he retired, two of his offspring, Bayard (1946 – 2'5''6/mile (1'18''1/km)) and Mandorlo (1946 – 2'11''6/mile (1'21''8/km), were already three years old and Mandorlo had won, admittedly in the absence of any better horses in his generation, the Italian Trotting Derby. In the spring of 1945, taking advantage of the suspension of racing, Mistero had covered a number of brood mares, including the dams of these two excellent horses. This instance of a champion whose sons embarked on their racing careers while he himself was still competing on the track was unique.

In 1948, at the age of eight, not only had Mistero set the Italian 1 mile 2½ furlongs (2,100 m) record in Milan with a time of 2'7''4/mile (1'19''2/km), a record that he was later to better at Ponte di Brenta trotting at 2'6''7/mile (1'18''8/km), but at the end of the year he topped the special prize money list. Mistero's career began when he was two and ran in two races, one of which he won in 2'22''2/mile (1'28''4/km). The following year his many wins included the Italian Trotting Derby, for which his driver was Ugo Bottoni.

The war restricted Mistero's sporting activities, which took place exclusively at the Villa Glori racecourse in Rome, where he was forced to concede a handicap of 65½ yds (60 m) to his rivals. On 4 November 1945 Mistero won the Premio Fondazione Breda in Bologna with a time of 2'16''2/mile (1'24''7/km). He first competed internationally in 1946, when he moved to France to contest the Prix d'Amérique which that year was run at Enghien and divided into two heats due to the excessive number of entrants. Mistero was second in his heat. After his usual very slow start he was beaten in the finishing straight by Quick Williams who called on his more powerful sprinting ability. This performance made Mistero favourite in the final, run on 3 February, but hampered by

the heavy going, he broke at the start. Brought back to the trot by the extremely capable Bottoni, he was soon back in the running and catching up on his rivals only to break once more, again when he was in a good position, and finishing fifth.

The following year, Romolo Ossani, to whom Mistero had been transferred for training, was successful where Ugo Bottoni had failed, for in January Mistero won the Prix d'Amérique from Quick Star, covering the 1 mile 5 furlongs (2,600 m) in 2'17''8/mile (1'25''7/km) with an extremely exciting run in which he gradually overtook all his rivals on the outside. That same year he won the Prix La Haye over 1 mile 6 furlongs 176 yds (2,975 m) at 2'13''3/mile (1'22''9/km) and the Prix d'Europe running the 1 mile 5½ furlongs (2,700 m) in 2'12''57/mile (1'22''2/km). In 1948, to crown a notable career, he won the Prix de Paris and the Prix de Copenhagen in France and set the record for Italian-born horses over 1 mile 2½ furlongs (2,100 m).

In 1949 he went to stud whilst his son, Bayard, was unbeaten in his ten races, including a defeat of his arch-rival Sagunto in an epic duel in the Gran Premio Nazionale. In Mistero's first year at stud the results were exceptional: 14 offspring, all trotters. Until his death in 1962, Mistero stood at the Allevamento San Bassiano, first at Rivolta d'Adda and then at Torlino Vimercati, even though it would definitely have been preferable for him to have returned to the Budrie where he was born. Besides Bayard and Mandorlo, the rest of his offspring have also proved to be quite outstanding: Barbablù (1963 – 2'3''/mile (1'16''5/km)), Urubù (1958 – 2'4''/mile (1'17''1/km)), Gebel (1952 – 2'4''5/mile (1'17''1/km)), Orco (1952 – 2'4''6/mile (1'17''5/km)), Dosso Bello (1946 – 2'5''8/mile (1'18''2/km)), Mister Taro (1953 – 2'5''8/mile (1'18''2/km)) and Bordo (1951 – 2'6''4/mile (1'18''6/km)). These names are only those of the most successful since in all Mistero sired 278 trotters. He also produced many fillies who besides being good racemares have also proved to be excellent brood mares, thus contributing to the improvement of Italian breeding.

Breeder: P. Orsi Mangelli
Owners: P. Orsi Mangelli – F. Mecheri – G. Pani – M. Gutman – Scuderia Fanfulla
Driver: V. Antonellini – U. Bottoni – R. Ossani
Most important wins: Italian Trotting Derby (1943), Premio Giovanardi (1943), Premio Italia (1943), Gran Premio Nazionale (1943), Gran Premio Napoli (1943), Premio d'Inverno (1946), Premio Encat (1946–1947), Prix d'Europe (1947), Prix d'Amérique (1947), Prix de Paris (1948), Prix de Copenhagen (1948), Premio della Repubblica (1948)

MISTERO

Mistero (1'18''8)	Prince Hall ◆ 1930 USA (2'00''3/4)	The Laurel Hall ◆ 1918 (2'06''1/4)	**Peter the Great** (2'07''1/4)	Pilot Medium □ 1879 Santos ◆ 1887
			Baby Bertha (2'04''1/4) *	Silk Cord ○ 1901 Bertha Derby ○ 1896
		Princess Etawah ○ 1916 (2'03''1/4)	Etawah ○ 1910 (2'03'')	Al Stanley ■ 1906 (2'08''1/4) Alicia Arion ○ 1901
			The Princess Helen * (2'10''1/4)	The Beau Ideal (2'15''1/2) Queen Regent Ideal ● 1897
	Naomi Guy ○ 1925 USA (2'07'')	Arion Guy ○ 1917 (1'59''3/4)	Guy Axworthy (2'08''3/4)	Axworthy (2'15''1/2) Lillian Wilkes (2'17''3/4)
			Margaret Parrish (2'06''1/4)	Vice Commodore (2'11'') Lady Leyburn (2'23''1/2)
		Hollyrood Naomi ○ 1915 (2'07'')	**Peter the Great** (2'07''1/4)	Pilot Medium □ 1879 Santos ◆ 1887
			Hollyrood Hebe	Zombro (2'11'') Redinda (2'07''1/4) *

* Pacer

Racing Career

Age	No. of Races	Wins	Placings
2	2	1	0
3	14	11	2
4	28	20	8
5	14	10	4
6	23	13	8
7	22	19	1
8	28	21	5
Total	131	95	28

MALE LINES OF THE FRENCH TROTTER DESCENDING FROM CONQUÉRANT AND GOING BACK TO THE GODOLPHIN ARABIAN WITH THEIR INFLUENCE ON ITALIAN BREEDING

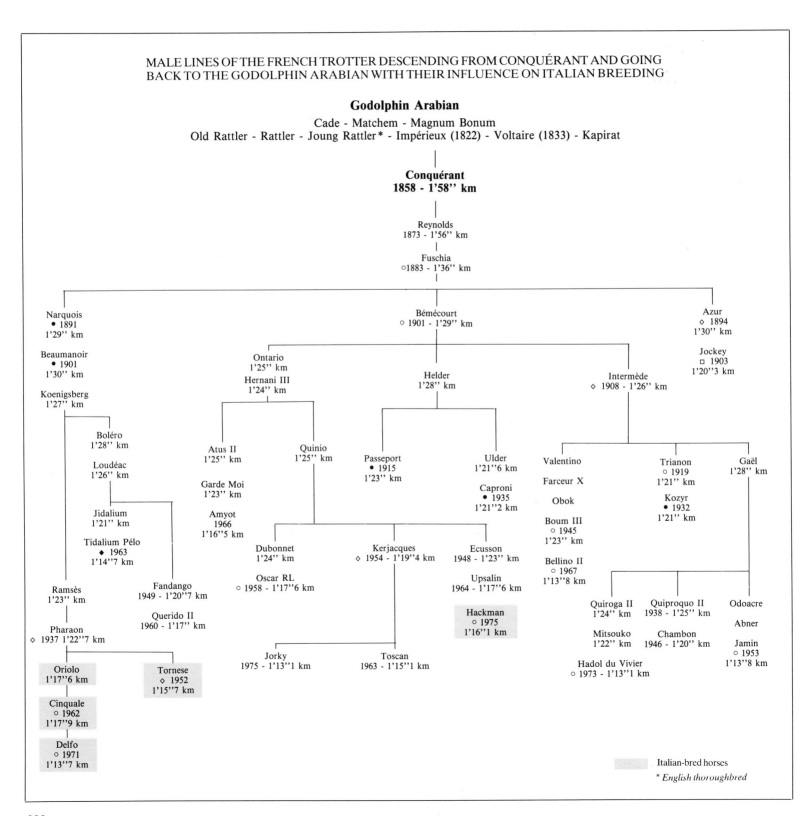

Godolphin Arabian

Cade - Matchem - Magnum Bonum
Old Rattler - Rattler - Joung Rattler* - Impérieux (1822) - Voltaire (1833) - Kapirat

Conquérant
1858 - 1'58'' km

Reynolds
1873 - 1'56'' km

Fuschia
○1883 - 1'36'' km

Narquois
● 1891
1'29'' km

Bémécourt
○ 1901 - 1'29'' km

Azur
◇ 1894
1'30'' km

Beaumanoir
● 1901
1'30'' km

Jockey
□ 1903
1'20''3 km

Koenigsberg
1'27'' km

Ontario
1'25'' km

Helder
1'28'' km

Intermède
◇ 1908 - 1'26'' km

Hernani III
1'24'' km

Boléro
1'28'' km

Loudéac
1'26'' km

Atus II
1'25'' km

Quinio
1'25'' km

Passeport
● 1915
1'23'' km

Ulder
1'21''6 km

Valentino

Trianon
○ 1919
1'21'' km

Gaël
1'28'' km

Garde Moi
1'23'' km

Caproni
● 1935
1'21''2 km

Farceur X

Kozyr
● 1932
1'21'' km

Jidalium
1'21'' km

Amyot
1966
1'16''5 km

Obok

Tidalium Pélo
◆ 1963
1'14''7 km

Dubonnet
1'24'' km

Kerjacques
◇ 1954 - 1'19''4 km

Ecusson
1948 - 1'23'' km

Boum III
○ 1945
1'23'' km

Ramsès
1'23'' km

Fandango
1949 - 1'20''7 km

Oscar RL
○ 1958 - 1'17''6 km

Upsalin
1964 - 1'17''6 km

Bellino II
○ 1967
1'13''8 km

Querido II
1960 - 1'17'' km

Quiroga II
1'24'' km

Quiproquo II
1938 - 1'25'' km

Odoacre

Pharaon
◇ 1937 1'22''7 km

Hackman
○ 1975
1'16''1 km

Mitsouko
1'22'' km

Chambon
1946 - 1'20'' km

Abner

Oriolo
1'17''6 km

Tornese
◇ 1952
1'15''7 km

Jorky
1975 - 1'13''1 km

Toscan
1963 - 1'15''1 km

Hadol du Vivier
○ 1973 - 1'13''1 km

Jamin
○ 1953
1'13''8 km

Cinquale
○ 1962
1'17''9 km

Delfo
○ 1971
1'13''7 km

Italian-bred horses

* *English thoroughbred*

THE FRENCH TROTTER

This horse is also know as the Norman Trotter since its most distant origins are closely interrelated with those of the Norman breed. The first official competitons for trotters were instituted in 1836 at Cherbourg racecourse in France, marking the beginning of a very tough practical selection process which has acted as a means of differentiating between the two breeds. The Norfolk (a breed which now no longer exists but gave rise to the hackney, its modern counterpart) initially played an important rôle in the formation of the French Trotter, as did half-bred English hunters, the Hackney and the English thoroughbred. A clever, tough selection process over difficult tracks and demanding distances, as still occurs in France today, led to the creation of a sturdy, solidly-built, fast trotter with considerable stamina.

Later on, American and Orlov blood was introduced. These are trotter breeds whose origins although not the same as those of the French trotter, have such similar beginnings that in the final analysis all three can be considered a variety of one single breed: "the racing trotter." More weight could be added to this theory because the boundaries between these breeds are becoming progressively more confused due to the repeated cross-breeding which has taken place, although the French Trotter is still quite different from the American from the point of view of its conformation and greater stamina.

The foundation sires of the French trotter were Conquérant (1858), Lavater (1867), Niager (1869) and Phaëton (1871). In the early twentieth century 95 per cent of horses of this breed descended from these five stallions. Afterwards, selection was directed solely towards the descendants of Conquérant, Phaëton and Normand, with clear predominance of the first two. From Conquérant descends Fuschia (1883) who together with Phaëton has impressed his distinctive stamp upon the breed.

All trotting breeds inherit their aptitude for trotting from Norfolk horses and the English thoroughbred Sampson (1745 by Blaze; who has made his presence felt in the French trotter on the female side of the pedigree, whereas in the American trotter he has greatly influenced the male side. Another English thoroughbred has, however, greatly contributed to the evolution of the French trotter as regards a natural disposition towards trotting. This is Orville (b.h. 1799), whose influence in this area has been of considerable importance.

The Stud Book for the breed was begun in 1922 and has been closed ever since 1941 as horses not in possession of the necessary qualifications may not be registered. The French trotter is also used in mounted trotting races, a spectacular special event which is very popular at French racecourses. While still on the subject of the by now frequent cross-breeding between the French and American trotter, it should be said that some authors maintain that the offspring thus obtained present the characteristics of a separate breed, calling it the Noram Trotter, but we refute this theory.

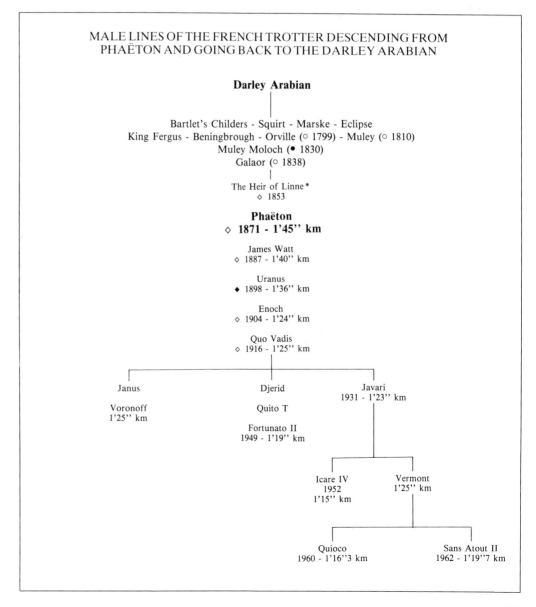

MALE LINES OF THE FRENCH TROTTER DESCENDING FROM PHAËTON AND GOING BACK TO THE DARLEY ARABIAN

Darley Arabian

Bartlet's Childers - Squirt - Marske - Eclipse
King Fergus - Beningbrough - Orville (○ 1799) - Muley (○ 1810)
Muley Moloch (● 1830)
Galaor (○ 1838)

The Heir of Linne*
◇ 1853

Phaëton
◇ 1871 - 1'45'' km

James Watt
◇ 1887 - 1'40'' km

Uranus
♦ 1898 - 1'36'' km

Enoch
◇ 1904 - 1'24'' km

Quo Vadis
◇ 1916 - 1'25'' km

Janus — Djerid — Javari
1931 - 1'23'' km

Voronoff
1'25'' km

Quito T

Fortunato II
1949 - 1'19'' km

Icare IV — Vermont
1952 — 1'25'' km
1'15'' km

Quioco — Sans Atout II
1960 - 1'16''3 km — 1962 - 1'19''7 km

223

PHAËTON

ch.h. 1871

Phaëton stands out among the five progenitors of the French Trotter because he was sired by an English thoroughbred, The Heir of Linne, who sired more than 20 trotters.

The names Selim (1802) and Orville (1799) both appear twice in The Heir of Linne's pedigree in the fourth remove. Further back the name Diomed (1777) appears twice and that of Sampson occurs six times amongst his ancestors. There is a strong concentration of trotter blood in

The Heir of Linne's pedigree and Selim himself is inbred to Blaze $5 \times 6 \times 7$. Phaëton's dam, La Crocus (or Ambition) is a daughter of Elisa, the dam of the other progenitor of the French trotter, the bay Conquérant.

When Phaëton trotted his gait was perfect, with well-stretched forelegs, but he had poor hocks, a defect which he passed on to some of his descendants. Among his most important offspring were James Watt (1877), who sired 231 trotters, and Harley

(1885) who produced 285 trotters. The former inherited Phaëton's ugly hocks but, through Uranus (1898) and Champaubert (1902), he started off two bloodlines which still continue today whereas Harley was unsuccessful in passing down to us a direct line of descendants.

During the formative years of the breed, the French trotter benefitted considerably by the meeting of the lines of Phaëton and Fuschia (b.h. 1883). The latter was the nephew, in the direct male line, of Conquérant since he was the son of Reynolds and Rêveuse who in turn was by Lavater and foaled the English thoroughbred, Sympathie. Fuschia was not a horse of distinction but had an extremely effective trot which he passed on to his numerous and accomplished descendants. In fact, through Rémécourt and Narquois he has created two lines which still play an extremely important rôle today even outside France.

Phaëton (1'45'')	The Heir of Linne ◇ 1853 **	Galaor ○ 1838	Muley Moloch • 1830	Muley ○ 1810 → **Orville** ○ 1799 / Eleanor ○ 1798
				Nancy ○ 1813 → Dick Andrews ○ 1797 / Spitfire ○ 1800
			Darioletta ○ 1822	Amadis ○ 1807 → Don Quixote ◇ 1784 / Fanny ○ 1796
				Selima ○ 1810 → **Selim** ◇ 1802 / Pot-8-o's Mare ◇ 1794
		Mrs. Walker ○ 1844	Jereed ○ 1834	Sultan ○ 1816 → **Selim** ◇ 1802 / Bacchante ○ 1809
				My Lady ○ 1818 → Comus ◇ 1809 / The Colonel's Dam ○ 1802
			Zinganee Mare ○ 1837	Zinganee ○ 1825 * → Tramp ○ 1810 / Folly ◇ 1808
				Orville Mare ○ 1812 → **Orville** ○ 1799 / Miss Grimstone ○ 1796
	La Crocus ◇ 1866	Crocus • 1858	Fireaway ○ 1852	Fireaway ○ 1844 → Shales ○ 1840 / Fireaway Mare
				Marshland Cob Mare → Marshland Cob / —
			Fireaway Phoenomenon Mare	Fireaway Phoenomenon → Fireaway / —
				Fireaway Mare → Fireaway
		Elisa ◇ 1853	Corsair ◇ 1845	J.G. Knox Corsair → Aughton Merrylegs
				Cleveland Mare → Cleveland • 1822 ** / —
			Elisa ○ 1831	Marcellus ○ 1819 ** → **Selim** ◇ 1802 / Briseis ○ 1804
				Jenny → Young Rattler ○ 1811 / Young Topper Mare

* or Priam o 1827
** English thoroughbred

Breeder: M. Lecuyer
Owner: M.L. Revel
Driver: M.L. Revel
Most important wins: Prix du Conseil Général de Caën (1875 – mounted trot)

Racing Career			
Age	No. of Races	Wins	Placings
3	5	1	3
4	6	3	3
Total	11	4	6

ROQUÉPINE

ROQUÉPINE

b.m. 1961

This exceptional mare dominated the world trotting scene from 1966 to 1968, during which period she won the Prix d'Amérique three times and the Grand Critérium de Vitesse de la Côte d'Azur and the Roosevelt International Trot twice. Those are the most prestigious international trotting competitions. Roquépine had easy wins in Rome, Milan, Naples, Turin, Copenhagen, New York, Cagnes-sur-Mer, Stockholm and Paris.

Her action was relaxed and natural and in racing she always showed the utmost concentration, which she demonstrated with sprints which often carried her into the lead in her races, but she adapted herself to any tactics, running just as well when restrained for a late challenger. Although arguably no great beauty she had the ideal conformation for a trotter. Roquépine was beaten in the 1966 Roosevelt International Trot by Arbro Flight as a result of questionable racing tactics: having been overtaken by the Canadian mare, she maintained the pressure all the way to the line in an exciting finish.

In the 1968 Grand Critérium de Vitesse at Cagnes-sur-Mer, she equalled her own record (set in 1966 in Stockholm) by winning the race in 3'4"7/mile (1'54"8/km)). When her career ended she was sent to the United States to be covered by two famous stallions: Star's Pride in 1970 and Ayres in 1971. From these two matings came Florestan and Granit who made names for themselves in Europe, though Granit was undoubtedly the better of the two. In Naples he set the track record with a time of 1'59"8/mile (1'45"5/km).

			Ontario (1'25")	Bémécourt (1'29") Epingle (1'29")
		Hernani III 1929 (1'24")		
			Odessa	Faucon II (1'35") Tenebreuse (1'31")
	Atus II ○ 1944 (1'25")			
			Cormontreuil (1'25")	Quarteron (1'25") Oriflamme
		Juignettes 1931		
Roquépine (1'15"3)			Quarantaine (1'30")	Kalmouk (1'33") Une Divorcée
			The Great Mc Kinney ○ 1922 USA (2'04"1/4)	Arion Mc Kinney (2'05"1/4) Virginia Dangler ○ 1908
		Kairos ○ 1932 (1'23")		
			Uranie ◇ 1920 (1'20"5)	Intermède (1'26") Pastourelle ◇ 1915
	Jalna IV ○ 1953 (1'21")			
			Karoly II (1'24")	Trianon (1'25") Braila
		Sa Bourbonnaise 1940 (1'23")		
			Bérésina II (1'29")	Nenni (1'29") Palatine

Breeder: H. Levesque
Owner: H. Levesque
Drivers: H. Levesque – J.R. Gougeon
Most important wins: Jubiliäumslob (1966), The United Nations Trot (1966), Solvallas Internationella Elitlopp (1966, 1967), Prix d'Amérique (1966, 1967, 1968), Grand Prix des Nations (1966, 1968), The Gotham Trot (1967), Preis von Deustschland (1967), Roosevelt International Trot (1967, 1968), Grand Critérium de Vitesse de la Côte d'Azur (1967, 1968), Gran Premio Lotteria Nazionale (1967) Gran Premio della Fiera (1967, 1968), Gran Premio Costa Azzurra (1967, 1968), Gran Premio Freccia d'Europa (1967, 1968), Premio Lido di Roma (1968)

Racing career in France			
Age	No. of races	Wins	Placings
3	9	3	4
4	12	5	1
5	14	5	4
6	7	5	2
7	9	5	0
8	5	0	4
Total	56	26	15

Success abroad: 22 wins (from 1966 until 1968)
Total no. of wins: 48

TIDALIUM PÉLO

dk.b.h. 1963

This trotter, with a physique more like that of a dinosaur than of a racehorse, was a late developer and achieved his most important successes from the age of six. In 1969 he won the Côte d'Azur Grand Prix (2'2''7/mile (1'16''3/km)) in Turin, beating Be Sweet and Agaunar. On 22 June of the same year he covered the 6 furlongs 136 yds (1,330 m) track at Argentan (Normandy), when beating Une de Mai, in a time of 2'02''/mile (1'14''7/km). In Munich Tidalium Pélo collected another important win in the Preis der Besten. In 1970 he won the Prix Cornulier in a mounted trotting race and was third in the Prix d'Amérique behind Toscan and Tony M. Tidalium Pélo also won the Prix de France, beating Une de Mai, and the Grand Prix in Hamburg (2'6''3/mile (1'8''4/km)) from Eileen Eden. The German horse Simmerl was also in the photo-finish in Hamburg, and both the photograph and the decision from it aroused so much controversy that there was a return race a week later. The result of the race was again in Tidalium Pélo's favour, and he won in 2'1''5/mile (1'15''5/km), beating the German and Italian-American horses. In the same year Tidalium Pélo also won the Prix d'Été over the 1 mile 5 furlongs 123 yds (2,725 m) track at Saint Vincent. The following year he was runner-up in the Prix de Cornulier to Uniflore, but triumphed in the Prix d'Amérique. In the Prix de Paris, despite a handicap of 54.68 yds (50 m) and a break at the start, he was second to Toscan. In Stockholm he won the heat and final of the Elitlopp (2'0''3–2'0''2/mile (1'14''8–1'14''7/km)) and in Munich the Bavaria Grand Prix. In 1972 he once again won the Prix de Cornulier and, for the second time running, the Prix d'Amérique, setting a track record with a time of 2'4''0/mile (1'17''1/km). In 1973, he was fourth in the Prix de Paris.

Tidalium Pélo's career was notable not so much for the number of wins, but for their importance and for the adversaries he ran against. The weakness of his legs, however, played an important part in his racing career, often compelling him to stay away from the tracks for long periods.

Breeder: R. Lemarié
Owner: R. Lemarié
Driver: J. Mary
Most important wins: Gran Premio Costa Azzurra (1969), Preis der Besten (1969), Prix de France (1970), Preis von Deutschland (1970, 1971), Prix de Cornulier (1970, 1972), Solvallas Internationella Elitlopp (1971), Grosser Preis von Bayern (1971), Prix d'Amérique (1971, 1972)

Racing career in France

Age	No. of races	Wins	Placings
2	10	1	4
3	15	2	5
4	12	5	4
5	12	7	3
6	13	5	5
7	7	4	3
8	12	3	6
9	5	2	1
10	3	0	1
Total	89	29	32

Successes abroad: 8 wins (from 1969 until 1971)
Total no. of wins: 37

		Boléro (1'28'')	**Koenigsberg** (1'27'')
	Loudéac 1933 (1'26'')		Odette (1'28'')
		Bonne Fortune (1'28'')	Jongleur (1'33'')
Jidalium ● 1953 (1'21'')			Querelleuse
		Enfant de Troupe (1'28'')	Quo Vadis (1'25'')
	Lyette 1933 (1'27'')		Olga
		Dona Sol (1'34'')	**Koenigsberg** (1'27'')
Tidalium Pélo (1'14''7)			Odessa
		Sam Williams (2'01''3/4) USA	Peter Scott (2'05'')
	Mousko Williams 1934 (1'25'')		Blitzie (2'01''1/4)
		Carlotta (1'32'')	Enoch (1'24'')
Hase Williams ◊ 1951			Junon
		Sam Williams (2'01''3/4) USA	Peter Scott (2'05'')
	Tanagra 1941 (1'31'')		Blitzie (2'01''1/4)
		Ernée (1'30'')	Ouistiti (1'22'')
			Glory USA

UNE DE MAI

UNE DE MAI

b.m. 1964

Known as "la Reine," this exceptional trotter really did reign over the international trotting scene like a queen, achieving her most important successes outside France. Her racing career was long and exacting since she continued racing on most of the tracks in Europe and America until the age of nine. She was an exceptionally beautiful mare with excellent conformation, capable of extraordinary power and a smooth and extremely effective trotting style.

Her international successes began in Italy in the 1968 Premio d'Europa, a classic for four-year-olds in Milan. From then on her wins followed rapidly one after the other but her most spectacular feats were winning the Grand Critérium de Vitesse at Cagnes-sur-Mer for five years running and the New York Roosevelt International Trot twice. In New York in 1969, she beat Nevele Pride, one of the best horses that the United States had bred, in a time of 2'2''7/mile (1'16''3/km). In the face of such results, the three wins in the Gran Premio Lotteria, the two in the Prix de Paris or the double success in the Gran Premio della Fiera, are of little importance in comparison. The only victory that eluded Une de Mai was the Prix d'Amérique, which almost seemed to have a jinx on her as the best she could achieve was second place in 1969 and third in 1971.

Une de Mai was sent to stud but did not produce a foal until 1977. She then had a filly by Quioco, but in the same year she died at the age of just 13.

Breeder: Hippolyte Bernereau
Owner: P. de Montesson
Driver: J.R. Gougeon
Most important wins: European Cup (1968), Gran Premio Continentale (1968), Premio d'Inverno (1969), Gran Premio Freccia d'Europa (1969–1970), Gran Premio Lotteria (1969–1970–1971), Grand Critérium de Vitesse de la Côte d'Azur (1969–1970–1971–1972–1973), Gran Premio della Fiera (1969–1970), Roosevelt International Trot (1969–1971), Premio Tor di Valle (1970), Gran Premio Costa Azzurra (1970–1971), Grand Prix des Nations (1970–1971), Prix de Paris (1970–1973), Prix de France (1972)

Racing career in France

Age	No. of races	Wins	Placings
2	4	0	3
3	13	7	1
4	14	7	7
5	11	5	5
6	12	5	4
7	12	8	3
8	10	6	2
9	10	3	5
10	4	0	3
Total	90	43	33

Success abroad: 31 wins (from 1968 until 1973)
Total no. of wins: 74

		Hernani III (1'24'')	Ontario (1'25'') Odessa
	Quinio 1938 (1'25'')		
		Germaine (1'29'')	Phoenix (1'29'') Lysistrata
Kerjacques ◇ 1954 (1'19''4)			
		Loudéac (1'26'')	Boléro (1'28'') Bonne Fortune (1'28'')
	Arlette III 1944 (1'22'')		
		Maggy II (1'35'')	Fidus (1'26'') Dédette II (1'34'')
Une de Mai (1'13''9)			
		Kairos (1'23'')	The Great Mc Kinney USA Uranie (1'20''5)
	Euripide 1948 (1'20'')		
		Staal D	Duc de Normandie II (1'24'') Bagatelle III
Luciole III ◇ 1955			
		Loudéac (1'26'')	Boléro (1'28'') Bonne Fortune (1'28'')
	Fleur de Mai F. 1949		
		Nuit de Mai (1'25'')	Enfant de Troupe (1'28'') Fleur de Mai (1'30'')

BELLINO II

b.h. 1967

Due to his massive build he was nicknamed The Dinosaur. He was foaled in Upper Savoy from parents who had already passed the age of 20 and his birth, as was often the case, was more a question of chance than the result of genetic engineering. His dam, Bella de Jour III became a brood mare late in life and after ten years of activity achieved very little.

She was bought by Maurice Macherat and covered by Boum III for the sake of convenience since the stallion was stabled nearby. Bellino II was foaled as a result of this union and as a colt lived up to his name (which meant "little beauty"), given him by mistake, however, being a corruption of Belluno. In fact, the breeder had intended to name the colt after Belluno, a small town in the Veneto region of Italy. As he grew up Bellino II began to show signs of increasingly less attractive and well-balanced traits. His massive build meant he was a clumsy mover. He was a voracious eater and did not need to train, but had to exercise for three hours in the morning and roughly the same amount of time in the afternoon. He slept for long periods in his box with a puppy on his back to keep him company.

Bellino II learned the skills of trotting from René Sala, a man who was totally dedicated to him and followed him step by step through his racing career. The fact that Bellino II did not need to train was undoubtedly unusual for a champion, but even more unusual was his inability to trot without being in a race. In fact, just the sound of the bell used by the starter to call the horses to the starting line, the electric atmosphere of the racecourse and the lure of the competition transformed him into a powerful machine capable of overwhelming any rival.

He was a late developer and made himself known for the first time as a four-year-old by winning eight of his 11 races, including the Prix des Centaures and the Prix des Élites. The following year he was third behind Bill D and Buffet in the Critérium des Cinq Ans and again won the Prix des Élites. As a six-year-old he won the Prix de Cornulier (mounted trot) but in 1974 his fortunes were mixed. He finished second in the mounted trotting race (Prix de Cornulier) behind Cette Histoire; he broke and was unplaced in the Prix d'Amérique; he also broke in the Prix de Paris before finishing third behind Timothy T and Cadsar and he won the Prix René Ballière.

In 1975, he showed excellent form, winning the Prix d'Amérique, the Prix de Cornulier, the Prix de Paris, the Grand Critérium de Vitesse de la Côte d'Azur, the Prix de l'Atlantique, the Premio Ghirlandina (1'59"/mile (1'14"/km)), the Prix René Vallière (for the second time) and the Premio Lido di Roma. In 1976, Bellino II continued this upward trend with another win in the Prix d'Amérique, the Prix de Cornulier, the Prix de Paris (giving as much as 82 yd (75m) to his opponents) and the Prix de France. To have won these four important races, which take place in quick succession, was a truly exceptional feat. There was more to come with successes in the Grand Critérium de Vitesse de la Côte d'Azur, the Prix de l'Atlantique (both for the second time running), the Côte d'Azur Grand Prix, the Gran Premio Lotteria Nazionale in Naples and the Prix René Ballière (for the third time).

In 1977, Bellino won the Prix d'Amérique for the third year running and was third in the Prix de Cornulier. In the Prix de France he was unable to give 89 ft (25m) to Eléazar and the other opponents, but in the Prix de Paris over 1 mile 7¾ furlongs (3,150 m) he gave 89 ft (25m) advantage to Eléazar and 163 ft (50m) to Dimitria. He then won the Prix de l'Atlantique (for the third time running), but in the Prix René Ballière was unable to beat Fakir du Vivier, in a photo finish with both recording the same time: 2'3"8/mile (1'17"/km). In Holland he won the Grote Prijs der Lage Landen but in Germany was only fourth in the Elite-Rennen, won by Pershing, while in the USA he was beaten by Delfo in the International Trot at the Roosevelt Raceway in New York. Seven days later, in the Challenge Cup, he again came third behind Kash Minbar and Delfo. But even Bellino II still had something in reserve to surprise everyone on his return to Europe. After finishing fourth in the Preis der Besten in Munich, he won the Giants' Cup in Holland, equalling the European record of Ego Boy and Flower Child with a time of 1'58"7/mile (1'13"8/km), and beating Pershing in the heat and Dauga in the final. Bellino II's racing career is unprecedented throughout trotting history and perhaps the only jewel missing from his crown is the International Trot in America, the win denied to him by Delfo.

Breeder: Maurice Macheret
Owner: Maurice Macheret
Drivers: R. Sala, J.R. Gougeon, (M. Gougeon*), (H. Filion*)
Most important wins: Prix de Cornulier (1973, 1975, 1976), Prix René Ballière (1974, 1975, 1976), Premio Lido di Roma (1975), Premio Ghirlandina (1975), Elite-Rennen (1975), Grand Critérium de Vitesse de la Côte d'Azur (1975, 1976), Prix d'Amérique (1975, 1976, 1977), Prix de Paris (1975, 1976, 1977), Prix de l'Atlantique (1975, 1976, 1977), Prix de France (1976), Gran Premio Lotteria Nazionale (1976), Gran Premio Costa Azzurra (1976), Prijs der Giganten (1977)
Occasional driver

Bellino II (1'13"8)				
Boum III ○ 1945 (1'23")	Obok 1936 (1'27")	Farceur X (1'24")	Valentino (1'27") Oriflamme	
		Siva (1'30")	Intermède (1'26") Gladys USA	
	Star Williams 1940 (1'28")	Sam Williams 1922 USA (2'01"3/4)	Peter Scott (2'05") Blitzie (2'06"1/4)	
		Impavide (1'27")	Valentino (1'27") Nalicante (1'32")	
Belle de Jour III ● 1945 (1'27")	Esix 1926 (1'24")	Ontario (1'25")	Bémécourt (1'29") Epingle (1'29")	
		Quatre à Quatre	Hoche (1'27") Kizil Kourgan	
	Danse Nuptiale 1925 (1'28")	Kalmouk (1'33")	Bémécourt (1'29") Quintille	
		Tempête (1'33")	Beaumanoir (1'30")* Cybèle (1'38")	

or Azur (1'30")

Racing career in France

Age	No. of races	Wins	Placings
3	20	6	5
4	11	8	1
5	10	5	5
6	8	4	3
7	9	2	4
8	11	8	2
9	10	9	1
10	8	3	4
Total	87	45	25

Success abroad: 10 wins from 1975 until 1977
Total no. of wins: 55

BELLINO II

HADOL DU VIVIER

b.h. 1973

He was bred at the Château du Vivier in Manche and like his half-brother, Fakir du Vivier, was bought at the age of three months by Henry Levesque for a ridiculously low price in a lot which also included four brood mares. He had a heavy bone structure, plenty of heart room and a short back and in general appearance resembled the American rather than the Norman trotter, even though it was possible to catch a glimpse of a certain coarseness which betrayed his origins. It is possible to trace American elements in Hadol. In addition to the presence, on the female side of the pedigree, of Zsiba, (daughter of the two American trotters The Havester and Petress Burton) and of Va Sylva (also with quite a lot of American blood), it appears that Hadol's great-grand-sire may have been Calument Delco and not Gaël, though this statement is merely hearsay and not based on any factual evidence.

Hadol du Vivier was extremely well-balanced both physically and mentally, and was always so calm and even-tempered that he came across as being rather cold in his attitude. His trot was perfect and well-balanced and characterized by a very easy movement. In 1976, at the age of three, Hadol du Vivier won the Prix Plazen, covering the 1 mile 3 furlongs 40 yds (2,250 m) in 2'9''3/mile (1'20''4/km) the Prix de l'Etoile (2'6''8/mile (1'18''8/km)) and the Critérium des Trois Ans. As a four-year-old he won the Prix Jules Thibault over 1 mile 3 furlongs 43 yds (2,250 m) in a time of 2'4''8/mile (1'19''4/km) and the Prix de Sélection (2'7''7/mile (1'19''4/km)). In the

same year, in Italy, he took the European Grand Prix with a time of 2'1''47/mile (1'15'5/km), beating Devasca, and also won the Critérium des Quatre Ans, the Greyhound Rennen in Mönchengladbach, the Critérium Continental, the Prix de l'Etoile (for the second time) and the Prix Guy le Gonidec.

His most important wins in 1978 were the Prix de Bourgogne in 2'3''5/mile (1'16''8/km) and the Prix René Ballière (2'5''5/mile (1'18''/km)) in France and the Elitlopp and the Elite Rennen abroad. In 1979 he won in the Prix de France (2'4''3/mile (1'17''3/km)), but was only third to high Echelon and Ebéazar in the Grand Critérium de Vitesse de la Côte d'Azur, at Cagnes-sur-Mer, second in the Grand Prix du Sud-Ouest in Bordeaux behind Eléazar and again second in Munich in the Grosser Preis von Bayern, won by Charme Asserdal. However, he did win the Aby Stora Pris in Sweden (2'1''4/mile (1'15''5/km)), the Giants' Cup in Holland (2'1''9/mile (1'15''8/km)), beating Charme Asserdal and Pershing, and the Grosser Preis der Stadt Gelsenkirchen (2'1''1/mile (1'15''3/km)).

In 1980, with a time of 1'59''2/mile (1'14''1/km), Hadol triumphed in the Grand Critérium de Vitesse de la Côte d'Azur ahead of Idéal du Gazeau, and was third in the Prix de France, behind Eléazar and Gadames. His overall performance as a trotter was excellent but his championship record lacks the most important win of all, especially for a French horse, the Prix d'Amérique.

Breeder: Jean-Yves Lécuyer
Owners: H. Levesque – H. de Bellevent – Mme H. Levesque
Driver: J.R. Gougeon
Most important wins: Critérium des Trois Ans (1976), European Grand Prix (1977), Greyhound Rennen (1977), Critérium des Quatre Ans (1977), Critérium Continental (1977), Elite-Rennen (1978), Prix René Ballière (1978), Prix de France (1979), Prijs der Giganten (1979), Grosser Preis der Stadt Gelsenkirchen (1979), Aby Stora Pris (1979), Grand Critérium de Vitesse de la Côte d'Azur (1980)

HADOL DU VIVIER

Racing Career			
Age	No. of Races	Wins	Placings
3	10	9	1
4	12	12	0
5	13	6	6
6	24	6	13
7	7	1	2
8	1	0	0
Total	67	34	22

IDÉAL DU GAZEAU

bl.h. 1974

No horse has had such an international racing career as Idéal du Gazeau, who won the most important European races and two of the most prestigious American ones. In France he dominated his generation by winning the Critérium des 3 Ans, des 4 Ans and des 5 Ans as well as the Critérium Continental. He twice won the Copenhagen Cup, the Roosevelt International Trot in New York, the Nations' Cup in Milan, the Gran Premio Costa Azzurra in Turin and the Elitlopp in Stockholm. For three years running (1980, 1981, 1982) Idéal du Gazeau took the list race, the Grand Circuit International, winning on the Danish, Dutch, Swedish, Finnish, German and Italian tracks as well as, of course, those in France where from 1979 to 1982 he was at the top of the special prize money list.

In 1977 and 1978 he set the national three- and four-year-old records over a distance of 1 mile 3 furlongs 70 yd (2,275 m) (tape start) with times of 2'5''8/mile (1'18''2/km) and 2'3''2/mile (1'16''6/km), records which are definitely not easy to beat on French tracks. In 1978 he achieved his first important victory at Helsinki, in Finland in the Kultakenkä (the Golden Horseshoe Cup), but Idéal du Gazeau's truly golden years were in 1980 and 1981. In 1980 he won the Prix Belgique, the Grand Prix du Sud-Ouest at Toulouse, the Elitlopp, the Copenhagen Cup, the Prix René Ballière, the Elite-Rennen and the European Championship at Cesena. In March that same year, however, he had to give best to Hadol du Vivier in the Grand Critérium de Vitesse de la Côte d'Azur and in May he was third in the Bavarian Grand Prix at Munich, beaten by Express Gaxe and Jorky who, however, were given the same time as he was (2'4''5/mile (1'17''4/km)).

In 1981 Idéal du Gazeau took one of the most coveted trotter prizes by winning the Prix d'Amérique; nor did he let the Grand Critérium de Vitesse de la Côte d'Azur slip away from him as he had done the year before. He also won the Gran Premio Costa Azzurra (for the second time), the Prix de l'Atlantique, the Grand Prix du Sud-Ouest at Agen, the Roosevelt International Trot (beating Jorky by a nose) and the Challenge Cup (dead heating with Jorky) in the United States, the Prix d'Europe at Enghien, the Aby Stora Pris at Gothenburg, the Finlandia Race in Helsinki, the Prijs der Giganten at Hilversum and the National Cup in Milan, where he took revenge on Jorky who had beaten him in June in the Copenhagen Cup and who eight days before (31 May) had won the Elitlopp in which Idéal du Gazeau, although having taken his heat with a time of 1'58''2/mile (1'13''5/km), was unplaced in the final.

At the beginning of 1982 it seemed that Idéal du Gazeau's career was on the decline for he was only second in the Prix de France and third in the Grand Critérium de Vitesse de la Côte d'Azur, both won by Hymour, but by winning the Grand Prix du Sud-Ouest, this time at Beaumont, for the third year running, the Elitlopp and the Nations' Cup in Europe and the Roosevelt International Trot in American he restored his international reputation. In the final of the Elitlopp he beat Dartster F (both credited with a time of 1'57''7/mile (1'13'2/km) after the latter had beaten him in the heat, trotting at 1'57''4/mile (1'13''/km).

If in this race Idéal du Gazeau had had the luck on his side that can play such an important role in all races, in the final of the Finlandia Race in September he had to admit defeat to Dartster F (1'58''9/mile (1'13''9/km)) who, like him had won his heat but in a time of 1'58''4/mile (1'13''6/km) against Idéal du Gazeau's 2'2''4/mile (1'16''1/km). At Hilversum the following month Idéal du Gazeau was beaten in the final race of the Giants' Cup by just 3/10 of a second by Ex Lee, after having come third in the first heat and having won the second. Idéal du Gazeau's racing career is not yet over. In 1983 he took the Prix d'Amérique for the second time (2'6''6/mile (1'18''7/km)), beating Lurabo, but after having made two bad moves in the Prix de France (in which he came fourth) and the Critérium de Vitesse (unplaced), he was beaten in Turin by Ghenderò in the Gran Premio Costa Azzurra.

Breeders: M.M. Henri Fradin and Guy Fradin
Owner: Jean Pierre Morin
Driver: Eugène Lefèvre
Most important wins: Critérium des 3 Ans (1977), Critérium des 4 Ans (1978), Critérium Continental (1978), Kultakenkä (1978), Critérium des 5 Ans (1979), Copenhagen Cup (1980, 1982), Elite-Rennen (1980), Solvallas Internationella Elitlopp (1980, 1982), Gran Premio Costa Azzurra (1980, 1981), European Championship (1980), Grand Prix du Sud-Ouest (1980, 1981, 1982), Prix d'Amérique (1981, 1983), Grand Critérium de Vitesse de la Côte d'Azur (1981), Roosevelt International Trot (1981, 1982), Aby Storia Pris (1981), Prijs der Giganten (1981), Grosser Preis Von Bayern (1982), Nations' Cup (1981, 1982).

IDÉAL DU GAZEAU

		Carioca II (1'26'')	Mousko Williams (1'25'') Quovaria (1'31'')	
	Narioca 1946 (1'20'')	Idole VI (1'29'')	Beaux Arts (1'22'') Emotion	
Alexis III ○ 1966 (1'18'')		Chambon (1'20'')	Quiproquo II (1'25'') Nomarchie	
	Olga II 1958	Tatiana (1'39'')	Hugues Capet (1'28'') Graziella (1'32'')	
Idéal du Gazeau (1'13''2)		Echec au Roi (1'22'')	Quick Williams (1'21'') Hollyanne (1'28'')	
	Loiron D 1955 (1'20'')	Sambre (1'29'')	Quo Vadis (1'25'') Galéjade (1'25'')	
Venise du Gazeau ◇ 1965 (1'25'')		Hoaro (1'23'')	Quiroga II (1'24'') Soulaines (1'34'')	
	Paquerette II 1959	Bari (1'31'')	Kairos (1'23'') Jenny W (1'29'')	

Racing career (until 4/9/83)			
Age	**No. of races**	**Wins**	**Placings**
2	3	2	1
3	6	5	1
4	11	9	2
5	8	6	2
6	20	10	7
7	18	15	2
8	19	10	7
9	12	3	6
Total	97	60	28

TORNESE

s.h 1952

Doubts about the sire of this great trotting champion appear to have been settled once and for all. In the pedigree Tabac Blond (ch. 1941 by Kozyr) should have in fact been replaced by Pharaon (ch. 1937). The doubts arose because of the extraordinary resemblance between the "Flying Chestnut," as Tornese was called, and Pharaon. There can be no objections to this nickname as the speed of his sprints, the pace which he was able to set in the race and his completely natural, easy trot, made it impossible to suggest a more suitable choice. It was a wonderful sight to watch him pass in front of the stands, his mane blowing in the wind, always fighting on courageously to reach the finishing post despite the fact that he suffered with a sandcrack (a split across the wall of the hoof) in his forefoot. It was for this reason that he did not begin racing until he was three, and then in a very low category, his first race being a selling race.

But the following year, Tornese showed his talent and landed a surprise win in the Grand Prix des Nations, driven as always by his trainer, M. Santi, and beating Smaragd and Oriolo. In 1957 he won the Gran Premio Lotteria Nazionale ahead of Gelinotte in the final and beat Oriole in the Premio UNIRE at San Siro in 2'5''5/mile (1'18''/km). The horse then changed trainers and went to Sergio Brighenti and his wins increased in number. He won on Italy's main racetracks, from Rome to Cesena, Naples, Florence, Modena and Milan. At San Siro he was beaten by Crevalcore in the Grand Prix des Nations in which Gelinotte and Icare IV also took part, but he won the Premio d'Inverno, beating Oriole who that year was his toughest opponent.

Tornese's golden year was 1958. After his unlucky attempt at the Prix d'Amérique in which he did not figure due to a worsening of his foot trouble, he was successful on all Italy's tracks: he won in Rome, Milan, Naples (repeating his success in the Gran Premio Lotteria Nazionale), Modena, Florence (in the Premio Duomo setting not only his personal record at 2'1''8/mile (1'15''7/km) but also the new Italian record), Trieste and Montecatini. After he had run second in the Grand Prix des Nations, Tornese was entrusted to G. Ossani. He won two races in Rome and then went to Milan for the Premio d'Inverno, but was unsuccessful as he had to concede 43.7 yds (40 m) to the younger horses.

In 1959 Tornese alternated positive results with disappointing heats. In the Prix d'Amérique in Paris he was third behind Jamin and Icare IV, whilst in Italy the duels with Crevalcore continued without respite. That year, his move to America resulted in fourth place in the New York Summer Festival won by Icare IV and second in the Roosevelt International Trot behind Jamin. In the Grand Prix des Nations in Milan, Tornese once again in the capable hands of S. Brighenti, achieved an important win ahead of Jamin and Icare IV.

In 1960 Tornese came second in the Prix d'Amérique which was won by Hairos but at Cagnes-sur-Mer he soon took revenge in the Grand Critérium de Vitesse de la Côte d'Azur, beating Hairos and Jamin. In Italy he ran with mixed fortune, winning the Gran Premio della Fiera but losing to Crevalcore in the European Championship. In 1961 he again came second in the Prix d'Amérique, won by Masina, but repeated the success of the previous year at Cagnes-sur-Mer (reaffirming his record of 2'1''8/mile (1'15''7/km)). Meanwhile rivalry with Crevalcore intensified often resulting in a third contestant winning the race.

In the United States he came fourth and second in the Roosevelt International Trot and the Challenge Cup respectively, both won by Hairos, but at the end of the year, Tornese won the Grand Circuit International. In 1962, at the age of ten, old Tornese was still playing a vital rôle on the racing scene. He won the Gran Premio Lotteria Nazionale, the European Championship in Cesena, the City of Montecatini Grand Prix and the Gran Premio Freccia d'Europa. Between 1957 and 1962 Tornese always appeared in the order of arrival in the European Championship (first four times and second twice) and he always got through to the final (six times in the final, first three times and second twice) of the Gran Premio Lotteria Nazionale in Agnano.

Tornese sired 45 trotters, four of which set records of 2'5''5/mile (1'18''/km). He died in 1966 without having had the possibility of siring the international-level horses expected of him.

Breeder: S. Manzoni
Owner: S. Manzoni – Portichetto Stud Farm
Trainers and Drivers: M. Santi – (S. Manzoni*) – S. Brighenti – (R. Miseroni*) – G. Ossani
*Occasional driver
Most important wins: Grand Prix des Nations (1956, 1959), Premio d'Inverno (1957), Gran Premio Lotteria Nazionale (1957, 1958, 1962), European Championship (1957, 1958, 1961, 1962), Gran Premio Freccia d'Europa (1957, 1958, 1962), Premio della Vittoria (1957, 1958), Premio Ghirlandina (1958, 1959), Premio Duomo (1958, 1960, 1961), Premio della Repubblica (1958, 1959, 1961), City of Montecatini Grand Prix (1958, 1960, 1962), Premio Tor di Valle (1959, 1960, 1961), Gran Premio della Fiera (1960), Grand Critérium de Vitesse de la Côte d'Azur (1960, 1961), Premio Encat (1960, 1961, 1962)

				Koenigsberg ◇ 1910 (1'27'')	Beaumanoir (1'30'')

		Ramsès ◇ 1917 (1'23'')	Koenigsberg ◇ 1910 (1'27'')	Beaumanoir (1'30'') Byzance (1'32'')
	Pharaon ◇ 1937 FR (1'22''7)		La Brinvillier ◇ 1911	**Bémécourt** (1'29'') **Devise** ◇ 1903 (1'39'')
		Babiole ◇ 1923 (1'27'')	Pro Patria ◇ 1915 (1'27'')	**Bémécourt** (1'29'') Hurgente (1'29'')
			Néva ◇ 1913	Danguel (1'29'') **Devise** ◇ 1903 (1'39'')
Tornese (1'15''7)		De Sota ○ 1934 USA (2'02''1/4)	Peter Volo 1911 (2'02'')	Peter the Great (2'07''1/4) Nervolo Belle ○ 1906
	Balboa ○ 1947 (1'28''8)		Symphonia 1924 (2'03'')	Guy Axworthy (2'08''3/4) Mary Tipton (2'17''1/4)
		Alma Mater ○ 1939 (1'25''8)	Spencer Mc Elwyn USA (2'04''1/4)	Spencer (1'59''3/4) Miss Mc Elwyn (2'04''1/2)
			Ave Roma 1932 (1'26''3)	David Guy USA Hollyrood Queen USA

Racing Career

Age	No. of Races	Wins	Placings
3	16	9	4
4	28	13	9
5	27	17	7
6	31	27	2
7	29	15	9
8	35	19	14
9	30	17	11
10	25	12	10
Total	221	129	66

DELFO

		Pharaon ◊ 1937 FR (1'22''7)	Ramsès ◊ 1917 (1'23'') Babiole (1'27'')
	Oriolo ◊ 1951 (1'17''6)		
		Heluan 1946	Floridoro (1'19''2) Finlandia (1'25''2)
Cinquale ○ 1962 (1'17''9)			
		Mc Lin Hanover 1935 USA (1'59''1/4)	Mr. Mc Elwyn (1'59''1/4) Ethelinda (2'02''1/4)
	Madrepora ○ 1954		
		Grande Gloria (1'26''3)	Great Night USA (1'22'') Macbeth (1'26'')
Delfo (1'13''7)			
		Florican 1947 (1'57''2/5)	Spud Hanover (2'03'') Florimel (2'03''1/2)
	Tribute ○ 1955 USA (2'03''2/5)		
		Victory Rose 1951	Victory Song (1'57''2/5) Rose Dean (2'04''3/4)
Lunda ○ 1962			
		Trooper Hanover 1942 USA (2'03''1/4)	Lawrence Hanover (2'00''3/4) Trudy Guy (2'09'')
	Saragozza ○ 1950		
		Avesella 1936 (1'24''4)	Brevere USA (2'03'') Maud Harvester (1'22''2)

Racing Career			
Age	No. of Races	Wins	Placings
2	9	2	4
3	29	9	9
4	20	7	7
5	29	8	7
6	25	9	7
7	17	4	3
8	19	6	6
Total	148	45	43

DELFO

b.h. 1971

Breeder: O. Ulivieri
Owner: R. Bacci – Del Borgo Stables – Del Triangolo – Stables Tritoy Stables – Little Toy Stables
Drivers: (R. Nesti) (A. Carrara) N. Bellei, S. Matarazzo Jr., S. Milani, S. Brighenti, V. Baldi, (J.R. Glougeon), (M.Ventura), A. Fontanesi
Most important wins: Premio T. Triossi (1975), Premio d'Inverno (1975, 1978), Gran Premio della Fiera (1975, 1979), European Championship (1976), Premio Tor di Valle (1976), Premio della Vittoria (1976), Premio UNIRE (1976, 1977), Roosevelt International Trot (1977), Premio Ghirlandina (1977), Premio Capannelle (1977, 1978), Australian Cup (1977, 1979)

This horse is one of the greatest champions produced by Italian breeders, even though Delfo's racing career has been rather unstable, and his performance erratic because of his delicate physical constitution and difficult character, inherited from his sire Cinquale, which has often led him to make mistakes at the starting post or at a critical moment in the race. To add to the complicated situation surrounding his racing, Delfo was subject to frequent changes of ownership and had several different handlers.

He made his debut as a two-year-old at Montecatini (driven by R. Nesti) where he finished second and achieved his first win at the end of November in Florence trotting at 2'23''2/mile (1'22''9/km). In 1974 Delfo was moved back to Nello Bellei who had started him off in racing, first with S. Matarazzo Jr. and then with S. Milani, although the horse failed to reveal his full potential. The following year Delfo, now driven by Sergio Brighenti, managed to win his first important race, he Gran Premio della Fiera beating Timothy T and Demonica Hanover, who had, however, given him 32.8 yds.

In 1975 he won the Premio Triossi (2'4''3/mile (1'17''3/km)) at Tor di Valle, the City of Turin Cup and the Premio San Gennaro. In the Premio d'Inverno in Milan he won in 2'7''2/mile (1'19''1/km), on a heavy track ahead of Dosson and Wayne Eden, proving to be Italy's best four-year-old. In 1976 in Padua, he won the Premio Ivone Grasetto in 2'00'' /mile (1'14''6/km) over a half mile track. Amongst Italian born horses only Carosic had ever done better when in Sweden (Solvalla), with a time of 1'59''2/mile (1'14''1/km) he came third behind Ego Boy and Flower Child in the Elitlopp, but at that time the track covered 5 furlongs (1,000 m).

In 1976 Delfo continued to give positive and negative results and his transfer to America, also because of an injury he received, failed to bear fruit. On his return to Italy, Delfo's breaks continued and so his owner decided to hand him over for training to Vivaldo Baldi. He broke again in the European Championship at Cesena in the first heat but came through in the second and in the two-horse final he beat Wayne Eden. In that same year Delfo won the Premio UNIRE in Milan, the Premio Due Torri and the Premio della Vittoria in

Bologna, while in the Premio D'Inverno be was unable to make up his handicap and was beaten in a photo finish by Scellino. But the year ended victoriously in Rome with the Premio Tor di Valle.

In 1977 Delfo made an attempt at the Prix d'Amérique: he raced off at the start but broke on the descent losing any chance of success. At Cagnes-sur-Mer in the Grand Critérium de Vitesse de la Côte d'Azur, he was second behind Eléazar who set the race record with a time of 2'6''/mile (1'15''/km). In the same year he won the Premio Capannelle, the heat of the Gran Premio Lotteria Nazionale in Naples and the Premio Ghirlandina in Modena. After two unplaced races in the Gran Premio della Fiera (driven by J.R. Gougeon) and the Premio Ovone Grassetto, the horse was again handed over to Sergio Brighenti. Delfo won the Gran Premio Regione Siciliana beating Granit, and the Premio UNIRE (2'1''8/mile (1'15''7/km), after which he suffered two defeats in the Premio Mirafiori in Turin and the Premio Toscana in Florence, driven on both occasions by M. Ventura.

He was third again in the Premio Duomo in Florence before he left for the United States where he achieved the most notable result of his career in the International Trot at the Roosevelt Raceway in New York, beating the French horse Bellino II and winning in 2'35''2. The success of this American transfer was completed when he came second behind Kash Minbar in the Challenge Cup in which he again beat Bellino II. On his return to Italy, after having broken in the City of Montecantini Grand Prix and won the Australia Cup in Rome, on 11 September on the same track at Tor di Valle, he ran a two-heat event over 1 mile (1,600 m) which served as a return race with Kash Minbar. He won both, the first in 2'l''/mile (1'14''7/km) and the second in 2'6''/mile (1'15''/km).

In 1978 Delfo had other important wins such as the Premio Capannelle and the Premio d'Inverno. In 1979 he won the Gran Premio della Fiera and in Rome won the Australian Cup. After this win Delfo was unplaced five times consecutively and in the race which was to have been his farewell to the track, driven by A. Fontanesi, he achieved no better than third place. Delfo went to stud in 1980.

PERMIT

ch.h. 1945

He was the first trotter born in Germany to succeed in making a name for himself in the international field. He was driven and trained by his owner and breeder, W. Heitmann, won the Matadoren-Rennen in Berlin for three years running, and in the Jubilee Cup in Stockholm he set his personal record at 2'4''3/mile (1'17''3/km) beating the Swedish horse Frances Bulwark. In Italy he was third in the 1951 Premio d'Inverno behind Mar Jonio and Opera but won that race the following year again beating Frances Bulwark.

In 1953, still in Italy, he won the Gran Premio della Fiera in 2'9''5/mile (1'20''5/km) from Karamazow and Birbone, while he was third in the Grand Prix des Nations behind Cancannière (2'11''1/mile (1'21''5/km)) and Mighty Fine. The best win of Permit's career, however, came in 1953 in Paris in the Prix d'Amérique which he won in 2'14'' /mile (1'23''3/km) from the Italo-American horse, Tryhussey. The same year he had a fourth attempt at the Matadoren-Rennen, which his sire Epilog had won in 1941, but he could do no better than second place behind Dietlinde.

In addition to racing, Permit also shone as a stallion, and produced a great number of high quality trotters including three winners of the German Derby. In 1978, two of his progeny, Lord Pit and Gerrol, filled the first two places respectively in the list of winning sires in Germany, a list headed by Epilog from 1950 to 1961 and by Permit from 1962 to 1968. In the same year the trotter Mister Permit, by Permit out of Micara, headed the prize money list. Lord Pit also headed the stallions list in 1979, was third in 1980 and second in1981. Lord Pit sired, amongst others, Pit Pan (out of Stella Allegro) who in 1981 trotted in Germany with a time of 2'1''3/mile (1'15''4/km).

Breeder: Stall Gutenberg
Owner: Stall Gutenberg
Driver: W. Heitmann
Most important wins: Elite-Rennen (1950, 1951), Gladiatoren-Rennen (1950, 1952), Matadoren-Rennen (1950, 1951, 1952), Premio d'Inverno (1952), Solvallas Jubileumspokal (1952), Graf Kalman Hunrady Gedenkrennen (1952), Gran Premio della Fiera (1953), Prix d'Amérique (1953)

Permit (1'17''3)	Epilog ● 1934 (1'18''6)	Legality 1927 (2'02'') - USA	Lawful (2'08''1/4)	Lee Axworthy (1'58''1/4) Sister Hattie (2'14''3/4)
			Rhein Lass	Bingen (2'06''1/4) Mokomo (2'28''3/4)
		Mary H. 1920 (1'20''8)	Issy Les Moulineaux FR (1'28''1)	Azur FR (1'30'') Algerienne FR (1'45'')
			Mary Mac (2'12''1/4) - USA	Constenaro (2'16''1/4) Bertine (2'21''1/4)
	Maienpracht ◇ 1938 (1'29''8)	The Great Midwest 1919 USA (2'16''1/2)	Peter the Great (2'07''1/4)	Pilot Medium □ 1879 Santos ◆ 1887
			Nervolo Belle ○ 1906	Nervolo (2'04''1/4) * Josephine Knight
		Maiennacht 1927 (1'27''8)	Harvest Day (1'21''9) - USA	Daystar 3J (2'05'') Harvest Girl (2'11''1/2)
			Maienlieb (1'24'')	Brilon USA (1'26''1/4) Mary Mac USA (2'12''1/4)

* Pacer

PERMIT

Racing Career			
Age	**No. of Races**	**Wins**	**Placings**
3	8	3	4
4	21	12	5
5	21	17	5
6	19	7	12
7	25	12	11
8	28	7	20
9	2	0	0
Total	124	58	57

CHAMPIONSHIP RECORDS

HAMBLETONIAN STAKE

Year	Winner	Origin	Driver	Second	Best Time
1926	Guy Mc Kinney	Guy Axworthy	N. Ray	Guy Dean	2'04''3/4
1927	Iosola's Worthy	Guy Axworthy	M. Childs	Nescopec	2'03''3/4
1928	Spencer	Lee Tide	W. Lessee	Guy Abbey	2'02''1/2
1929	Walter Dear	The Laurel Hall	W. Cox	Volomite	2'02''3/4
1930	Hanover's Bertha	Peter Volo	T. Berry	Larkspur	2'03''
1931	Calumet Butler	Truax	R. McMahon	Keno	2'03''1/4
1932	The Marchioness	Peter Volo	W. Caton	Invader	2'01''1/4 (1)
1933	Mary Reynolds	Peter The Brewer	B. White	Brown Berry	2'03''3/4
1934	Lord Jim	Guy Axworthy	H. Parshall	Muscletone	2'01''3/4
1935	Greyhound	Guy Abbey	S. Palin	Warwell Worthy-Pedro T.	2'02''1/4
1936	Rosalind	Scotland	B. White	Brownie Hanover	2'01''3/4
1937	Shirley Hanover	Mr. Mc Elwyn	H. Thomas	De Sota-Farr	2'01''1/2
1938	McLin Hanover	Mr. Mc Elwyn	H. Thomas	Earl's Princess Martha	2'02''1/4
1939	Peter Astra	Peter Volo	H. Parshall	Gauntlet	2'04''1/4
1940	Spencer Scott	Scotland	F. Egan	Remus	2'02''
1941	Bill Gallon	Sandy Flash	L. Smith	His Excellency	2'05''
1942	The Ambassador	Scotland	B. White	Pay Ub	2'04''
1943	Volo Song*	Volomite	B. White	Worthy Boy*	2'02''1/2
1944	Yankee Maid	Volomite	H. Thomas	Emily Scott	2'04''
1945	Titan Hanover	Calumet Chuck	H. Pownall	Kimberly Hanover-Axomite	2'04''
1946	Chestertown	Volomite	T. Berry	Victor Song	2'02''1/2
1947	Hoot Mon	Scotland	S. Palin	Rodney	2'00''
1948	Demon Hanover	Dean Hanover	H. Hoyt	Rollo	2'02''
1949	Miss Tilly	Nibble Hanover	F. Egan	Volume	2'01''2/5
1950	Lusty Song	Volomite	D. Miller	Star's Pride	2'02''
1951	Mainliner	Worthy Boy	G. Cripper	Spennib	2'02''3/5
1952	Sharp Note	Phonograph	B. Shively	Hit Song	2'02''3/5
1953	Helicopter	Hoot Mon	H. Harvey	Morse Hanover*	2'01''3/5
1954	Newport Dream	Axomite	A. Cameron	Princess Rodney	2'02''4/5
1955	Scott Frost	Hoot Mon	J. O'Brien	Galophone-Leopold H.	2'00''3/5
1956	The Intruder	Scotland	N. Bower	Valiant Rodney	2'01''2/5
1957	Hickory Smoke	Titan Hanover	J. Simpson	Hoot Song	2'00''1/5
1958	Emily's Pride	Star's Pride	F. Nipe	Little Rocky	1'59''4/5
1959	Diller Hanover	Star's Pride	F. Ervin	Tie Silk	2'01''1/5
1960	Blaze Hanover	Hoot Mon	J. O'Brien	Quick Song	1'59''3/5 (2)
1961	Harlan Dean	Harlan	J. Arthur	Caleb	1'58''2/5
1962	A C's Viking	Hoot Mon	S. Russel	Isaac	1'59''3/5
1963	Speedy Scot	Speedster	R. Baldwin	Florlis*	1'57''3/5*
1964	Ayres	Star's Pride	J. Simpson	Big John	1'56''4/5
1965	Egyptian Candor	Star's Pride	A. Cameron	Armbro Flight*	2'03''4/5*
1966	Kerry Way	Star's Pride	F. Ervin	Polaris	1'58''4/5
1967	Speedy Streak	Speedster	A. Cameron	Keystone Pride	2'01''
1968	Nevele Pride	Star's Pride	S. Dancer	Keystone Spartan	1'59''2/5
1969	Lindy's Pride	Star's Pride	H. Beissinger	The Prophet	1'57''3/5
1970	Timothy T	Ayres	J. Simpson, Jr.	Formal Notice*	1'58''2/5*
1971	Speedy Crown	Speedy Scot	H. Beissinger	Savoir	1'57''2/5
1972	Super Bowl	Star's Pride	S. Dancer	Delmonica Hanover	1'56''2/5
1973	Flirth	Florican	R. Baldwin	Florinda	1'57''1/5

1974	Christopher T	Ayres	W. Haughton	Nevele Diamond	1'58''3/5
1975	Bonefish	Nevele Pride	S. Dancer	Yankee Bambino*	1'59''*
1976	Steve Lobell	Speedy Count	W. Haughton	Zoot Suit	1'56''2/5
1977	Green Speed	Speedy Rodney	W. Haughton	Texas	1'55''3/5
1978	Speedy Somolli*	Speedy Crown	H. Beissinger	Florida Pro*	1'55''
1979	Legend Hanover	Super Bowl	G. Sholty	Chiola Hanover	1'56''1/5
1980	Burgomeister*	Speedy Count	W. Haughton	Final Score*	1'56''3/5
1981	Shiaway St. Pat	Tarport Devlin	R. Remmen	Super Juan*	2'01''1/5
1982	Speed Bowl*	Super Bowl	T. Haughton	Jazz Cosmos	1'56''4/5
1983	Duenna	Green Speed	S. Dancer	Joie de Vie	1'57''2

(1) Achieved by Hollyrood Dennis.
(2) Achieved by Quick Song & Hoot Frost.
* Winner of the fastest heat.

In 1926 and 1928 run at Syracuse (NY), in 1927 and 1929 at Lexington (Ky.), from 1930 to 1942 and from 1944 to 1956 at Goshen (NY), in 1943 at the Yonkers (NY), from 1957 to 1980 at Du Quoin (Ill.) since 1981 at Meadowlands (NJ).

ROOSEVELT INTERNATIONAL TROT
(Roosevelt Raceway - Westbury)

Year	Winner	Country	Driver	Time
1959	Jamin	France	J. Riaud	3'08''2/5
1960	Hairos II	Holland	W. Geersen	2'34''
1961	Su Mac Lad	USA	St. Dancer	2'34''2/5
1962	The Silk	Canada	K. Waples	2'34''1/5
1963	Su Mac Lad	USA	St. Dancer	2'32''3/5
1964	Speedy Scot	USA	R. Baldwin	2'32''3/5
1965	Pluvier III	Sweden	G. Nordin	2'36''2/5
1966	Arbro Flight	Canada	J. O'Brien	*2'31''3/5
1967	Roquépine	France	H. Levesque	2'43''4/5
1968	Roquépine	France	J.R. Gougeon	2'38''3/5
1969	Une de Mai	France	J.R. Gougeon	2'33''2/5
1970	Fresh Yankee	Canada	J. O'Brien	2'35''1/5
1971	Une de Mai	France	J.R. Gougeon	2'34''4/5
1972	Speedy Crown	USA	H. Beissinger	2'35''1/5
1973	Delmonica Hanover	USA	J. Chapman	2'34''2/5
1974	Delmonica Hanover	USA	J. Chapman	2'34''4/5
1975	Savoir	USA	D. Insko	2'32''1/5
1976	Equiléo	France	B. Froger	2'33''3/5
1977	Delfo	Italy	S. Brighenti	2'35''2/5
1978	Cold Comfort	USA	P. Haughton	*2'31''3/5
1979	Doublemint	USA	P. Haughton	2'38''3/5
1980	Classical Way	USA	J. Simpson Jr.	2'35''2/5
1981	Idéal du Gazeau	France	E. Lefèvre	2'32''3/5
1982	Idéal du Gazeau	France	E. Lefèvre	2'36''
1983	Idéal du Gazeau	France	E. Lefèvre	2'35''2/5

Variations in the distance: in 1959 1½ miles (2,413 m); since 1960 1 mile 2 furlongs (2,011 m).
* Arbro Flight's record: 2'31''3/5 (1'15''4/km).

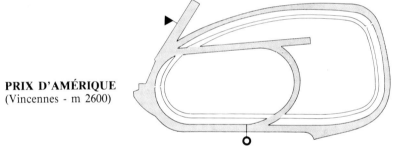

PRIX D'AMÉRIQUE
(Vincennes - m 2600)

Year	Winner	Country	Driver	Time (km)
1920	Pro Patria	France	Th. Monsieur	1'31''4/10
1921	Pro Patria	France	Th. Monsieur	1'28''
1922	Reynolds V	France	M. Gougeon	1'29''2/10
1923	Passeport	France	P. Viel	1'26''4/10
1924	Passeport	France	A. Finn	1'26''2/10
1925	Re Mac Gregor	France	Cl. Dessauze	1'26''8/10
1926	Uranie	France	V. Capovilla	1'28''2/10
1927	Uranie	France	V. Capovilla	1'28''5/10
1928	Uranie	France	V. Capovilla	1'25''2/10
1929	Templier	France	A. Butti	1'25''4/10
1930	Amazone B	France	Th. Vanlandeghem	1'26''1/10
1931	Hazleton	Italy	O. Dieffenbacher	1'27''1/10
1932	Hazleton	Italy	O. Dieffenbacher	1'27''1/10
1933	Amazone B	France	Th. Vanlandeghem	1'24''1/10
1934	Walter Dear	France	Ch. Mills	1'26''3/10
1935	Muscletone	Italy	A. Finn	1'23''8/10
1936	Javari	France	M. Perlbarg	1'24''9

CHAMPIONSHIP RECORDS

(Prix d'Amérique continued)

GRAND CIRCUIT INTERNATIONAL

1937	Muscletone	Italy	A. Finn	1'23''9/10
1938	De Sota	Italy	A. Finn	1'25''5/10
1939	De Sota	Italy	A. Finn	1'24''
1946	Ovidius Naso	France	R. Céran Maillard	1'24''3/10
1947	Mistero	Italy	R. Ossani	1'25''7/10
1948	Mighty Ned	Italy	V. Antonellini	1'24''
1949	Venutar	France	F. Réaud	1'24''6/10
1950	Scotch Fez	Sweden	S. Nordin	1'22''8/10
1951	Mighty Ned	Italy	A. Finn	1'22''7/10
1952	Cancannière	France	J. Chyriacos	1'23''1/10
1953	Permit	Germany	W. Heitmann	1'23''2/10
1954	Feu Follet X	France	M. Riaud	1'21''9/10
1955	Fortunato II	France	R. Céran Maillard	1'21''8/10
1956	Gélinotte	France	Ch. Mills	1'22''2/10
1957	Gélinotte	France	Ch. Mills	1'20''8/10
1958	Jamin	France	J. Riaud	1'20''
1959	Jamin	France	J. Riaud	1'20''5/10
1960	Hairos II	Holland	W.H. Geersen	1'21''3/10
1961	Masina	France	F. Brohier	1'20''7/10
1962	Newstar	Italy	W. Baroncini	1'20''3/10
1963	Ozo	France	R. Massue	1'20''1/10
1964	Nike Hanover	Italy	J. Frömming	1'18''9/10
1965	Ozo	France	J. Frömming	1'20''5/10
1966	Roquépine	France	J.R. Gougeon	1'18''6/10
1967	Roquépine	France	H. Levesque	1'19''7/10
1968	Roquépine	France	J.R. Gougeon	1'19''1/10
1969	Upsalin	France	L. Sauvé	1'17''6/10
1970	Toscan	France	M.M. Gougeon	1'18''3/10
1971	Tidalium Pélo	France	J. Mary	1'17''5/10
1972	Tidalium Pélo	France	J. Mary	1'17''1/10
1973	Dart Hanover	Sweden	B. Lindstedt	1'17''3/10
1974	Delmonica Hanover	USA	J. Frömming	1'18''4/10
1975	Bellino II	France	J.R. Gougeon	1'17''8/10
1976	Bellino II	France	J.R. Gougeon	1'19''1/10
1977	Bellino II	France	J.R. Gougeon	1'17''9/10
1978	Grandpré	France	P.D. Allaire	1'16''9/10
1979	High Echelon	France	J.P. Dubois	1'18''2/10
1980	Éléazar	France	L. Verroken	1'18''2/10
1981	Idéal du Gazeau	France	E. Lefèvre	1'17''4/10
1982	Hymour	France	J.P. Dubois	1'16''9/10
1983	Idéal du Gazeau	France	E. Lefèvre	1'18''7/10
1984	Lurabo	France	M.M. Gougeon	1'17''4/10

Not run in 1940 and 1941. From 1942 to 1945 it was replaced by the Grand Prix d'Hiver for 4- and 8-year olds foaled and bred in France. In 1946 and 1947 it was run at Enghien. In 1946, due to the excessive number of runners, it was held in two heats and the final run seven days later. Variations in the distance: from 1920 to 1928 1 mile 4½ furlongs (2,500 m) in 1929 1 mile 4 furlongs 150 yds (2,550 m); in 1946 and 1948 1 mile 6 furlongs (2,800 m). Since 1965 winners of previous races no longer required to concede ground.

From 1965 to 1975 the race started with the mobile barrier; since 1976 up to eight competitors started with the mobile barrier; for more than eight, the start was announced over the loudspeaker. Thirteen runners in 1976, 18 runners from 1977 to 1984.

Since 1956 Europe, like North America since the last century, has also had its Grand Circuit International sponsored by the Union Européenne du Trot. It involves a series of major heats (usually 13), selected each year by a special commission, from the most important trotting competitions held in the various countries belonging to this union. The countries involved have been France, Germany, Italy, Sweden, Denmark, Holland, Belgium, Norway and Finland. Each race operates a points system (five points for first place, three points for second, two points for third and one point for fourth) on the basis of which a final place-list is compiled establishing the best European performer, especially as regards consistency. Since the system was introduced, very few great champions have failed to have their name included in this, the cream of championship records, and some have achieved it more than once.

GRAND CIRCUIT INTERNATIONAL

Year	Winner	Breeding
1956	Gélinotte	Kairos - Rhyticière
1957	Gélinotte	Kairos - Rhyticière
1958	Jariolain	Carioca II - Poulaine
1959	Jamin	Abner - Dladys
1960	Hairos II	Kairos - Salambo II
1961	Tornese	Pharaon - Balboa
1962	Nicias Grandchamp	Fandango-Altesse de Grandchamp
1963	Ozo	Vermont - Qozo
1964	Nike Hanover	Star's Pride - Nana Hanover
1965	Elaine Rodney	Rodney - Honor Bright
1966	—	
1967	Roquépine	Atus II - Jalna IV
1968	Roquépine	Atus II - Jalna IV
1969	Une de Mai	Kerjacques - Luciole III
1970	Une de Mai	Kerjacques - Luciole III
1971	Une de Mai	Kerjacques - Luciole III
1972	Dart Hanover	Hoot Mon - Delicia Hanover
1973	Buffet II	Nonant le Pin - Paola III
1974	Timothy T	Ayres - Flicka Frost
1975	Bellino II	Boum III - Belle de Jour III
1976	Bellino II	Boum III - Belle de Jour III
1977	Éléazar	Kerjacques - Quérida
1978	Éléazar	Kerjacques - Quérida
1979	Pershing	Nevele Pride - Flying Cloud
1980	Idéal du Gazeau	Alexis III - Venise du Gazeau
1981	Idéal du Gazeau	Alexis III - Venise du Gazeau
1982	Idéal du Gazeau	Alexis III - Venise du Gazeau
1983	Ianthin	Vesuve T - Cadence II

United States

June	The Titan – 1 mile (1,609 m) – Classic 3-year-olds and over – New York (Goshen)
June	Yonkers Trot – 1 mile (1,609 m) – 3-year-old Classic – New York (Yonkers)
July	Handicap Open – 1 mile (1,609 m) – Handicap – New York (Roosevelt)
July	The Messenger Stake – 1 mile (1,609 m) – 2 heats and final 3-year-old pacers – New York (Roosevelt)
July	Dexter Cup – 1 mile (1,609 m) – 3-year-old Classic – New York (Roosevelt)
July	American Trotting Championship – 1 mile (1,609 m) – classic – New York (Roosevelt)
July	Roosevelt International Trot – 1¼ miles (2,011 m) – international – 3-year-olds and over – New York (Roosevelt)
July	Challenge Cup – 1½ miles (2,413 m) – international – New York (Roosevelt)
August	Hambletonian Stake – 1 mile (1,609 m) – win two races – 3-year-old Classic – Meadowlands
August	The Cane Pace – 1 mile (1,609 m) – 2 heats and final – 3-year-old pacers – New York (Yonkers)
September	Castleton Trot – 1 mile (1,609 m) – win two heats – 2-year-old Classic – Du Quoin
September	Colonial Trot – 1 mile (1,609 m) – 3-year-old Classic – Philadelphia (Liberty Bell)
September	The Little Brown Jug – 1 mile (1,609 m) – 3-year-old pacers – Delaware
October	Kentucky Futurity – 1 mile (1,609 m) – win two races – 3-year-old Classic – Lexington

France

January	Prix de Cornulier – 1 mile 5 furlongs (2,600 m) – mounted – Paris
January	Prix d'Amérique – 1 mile 5 furlongs (2,600 m) – international – Paris
February	Prix de France – 1 mile 2½ furlongs (2,100 m) – international – Paris
February	Critérium des Jeunes – 1 mile 3 furlongs 43 yds (2,250 m) – 3-year-old Classic – Paris
February	Prix de Paris – 1 mile 7¾ furlongs (3,150 m) – international – Paris
February	Prix de Sélection – 1 mile 3 furlongs 70 yds (2,275 m) – French 4- to 6-year-old Classic – Paris
March	Grand Critérium de Vitesse de la Côte d'Azur 1 mile (1,609 m) – international – Cagnes-sur-Mer
April	Prix de l'Atlantique – 1 mile 2 furlongs 153 yds (2,150 m) – international – Enghien
May	Critérium des Quatre Ans – 1 mile 6 furlongs (2,800 m) – classic – Paris
June	Prix René Ballière – international – Paris
August	Prix d'Europe – 1 mile 6 furlongs (2,100 m) – international – Enghien
August	Critérium Continental – 1 mile 2½ furlongs (2,100 m) – classic – Paris
September	Prix des Élites – 1 mile 3 furlongs 43 yds (2,250 m) – Paris

Italy

February	Premio Encat – 1 mile 2½ furlongs (2,100 m) – Italian horses – Milan
March	Gran Premio d'Europa – 1 mile 2½ furlongs (2,100 m) – 4-year-old European horses – Milan
March	Gran Premio Costa Azzurra – 1 mile 32 yds (1,640 m) – international – Turin
April	Gran Premio Lotteria Nazionale – 1 mile (1,600 m) – 3 heats + final – international – Naples
April	Premio R. Orlandi (formerly Premio Ghirlandina) 1 mile (1,600 m) – internationàl – Modena
April	Gran Premio della Fiera – 1 mile 2 furlongs 131 yds (2,130) – international – Milan
May	Gran Premio Regione Siciliana – 1 mile 2 furlongs 120 yds (2,120 m) – international – Palermo
May	City of Ravenna Cup – 1 mile 13 yds (1,620 m) – international – Ravenna
June	Premio della Repubblica – 1 mile 32 yds (1,640 m) – international – Bologna
June	Premio Duomo – 1 mile 57 yds (1,660 m) – 2 heats and final – international – Florence
June	Premio T. Triossi – 1 mile 2½ furlongs (2,100 m) – 4-year-old European horses – Rome
July	Gran Premio Nazionale – 1 mile 2½ furlongs (2,100 m) 3-year-old Italian horses – Milan
July	Premio Lido di Roma – 1 mile 2½ furlongs (2,100 m) – international – Rome
August	City of Montecatini Grand Prix – 1 mile 32 yds (1,640 m) – international – Montecatini
September	European Championship – 1 mile 32 yds (1,640 m) – win two races – international – Cesena
September	Premio Continentale – 1 mile 2½ furlongs 54 yds (2,060 m) – 4-year-old European horses – Bologna
October	Italian Trotting Derby – 1 mile 2½ furlongs (2,100 m) 3-year-old Italian horses – Rome
October	Premio della Vittoria – 1 mile 2½ furlongs (2,100 m) – international – Bologna
November	Premio Paola e Orsino Orsi Mangelli – 1 mile (1,600 m) 3-year-old – international – Milan
November	Gran Premio Freccia d'Europa – 1 mile (1,600 m) – international – Naples
November	Nations' Cup – 1 mile 2½ furlongs (2,100 m) – international – Milan
December	Gran Premio Allevatori – 1 mile (1,600 m) – 2-year-old – international – Rome
December	Premio Tor di Valle – G. Turilli – 1 mile 2½ furlongs (2,100 m) – international – Rome

Germany

May	Grosser Preis von Bayern – 1 mile 2½ furlongs (2,100 m) – international – Munich
July	Elite-Rennen – 1 mile 4½ furlongs (2,500 m) – international – Gelsenkirchen
September	Grosser Preis von Dinslaken – 1 mile 4½ furlongs (2,500 m) – international – Dinslaken
October	Preis der Besten – 1 mile 5 furlongs 13 yds – international – Munich

Belgium

February	Grand Prix d'Hiver – 1 mile 3½ furlongs (2,300 m) – international – Brussels
October	Grand Prix F. Talpe – 1 mile 3½ furlongs (2,300 m) – international – Courtrai

Holland

June	Grote Preis der Lage Landen – 1 mile 5 furlongs (2,600 m) – international – Duindigt
October	Prijs der Giganten – 1 mile (1,609 m) – 2 races – international – Hilversum

Sweden

May	Solvallas Internationella Elitlopp – 1 mile (1,609 m) – 2 heats and final – international – Stockholm
September	Aby Stora Pris – 1 mile 2 furlongs 142 yds (2,140 m) – international – Gothenburg

The calendar may vary from one year to the next due to planning requirements.

247

GLOSSARY

ACTION: the movement of a horse in its various gaits.

BOOKMAKER: person authorized to take bets.

BREAKING: when a trotter moves from a trot to a gallop.

BROKEN DOWN: a horse that has received a more or less serious injury to the tendons of the flexor muscles of the phalanges. This injury usually involves the front legs and its seriousness is always such as to prejudice the horse's future career.

BROKEN TROT: unnatural gait where the horse trots with the forelegs and gallops with the hindlegs.

BROOD MARE: mare used for breeding purposes.

CANTER: daily exercise run for race-horses.

COB: a small horse (14.1–15.1 hh (1.44–1.54 m)) but strong and sturdy with short legs and good bones.

CONCEDING GROUND: involves the advantage that one competitor must give to another as laid down by the conditions of the race.

CONVERSION TO THE MILE (KM): time recorded by a horse and related to the mile (km).

CRITERIUM: important flat race for two-year-olds.

DEAD-HEAT: the arrival of two or more horses at the winning post at exactly the same time, approved by the finish line judge, normally with the aid of the photo-finish camera.

DISTANCE: set route along which a race is run.

DOLICHOMORPHIC: horse with a longilineal morphology and constitution and a remarkable sprinting ability.

ENTIRE HORSE: male horse capable of reproducing.

FAR OFF: when a horse reaches the post such a long way behind the horse in front of him that the distance can no longer be calculated in lengths.

FETLOCK: joint which connects the cannon-bone to the pastern.

FIELD: number of horses taking part in a race.

FINISHING STRAIGHT: straight which includes the winning post.

FOAL: a horse of either sex up to the age of one.

FREE-LEGGED: pacer that does not require hobbles.

FULL BROTHER: son of the same sire and same dam.

FURLONG: 220 yards (approximately 200 meters).

GELDING: male horse no longer able to reproduce as a result of castration.

GIG: training cart with a platform on which to rest one's feet. It is heavier than the sulky and has thicker wheels.

HANDICAP: lead in feet (meters) conceded to a competitor in trotting races, set by racing conditions.

HANDICAPPER: official responsible for establishing a scale of the values of the runners, either by weight allotment or by fixing the distance to be run, depending on whether flat racing or trotting racing is involved.

HANDIDCAP RACE: race in which different weights are allotted to the competitors with the aim of giving all an equal chance, as far as possible, of winning. In trotting races the weight difference is replaced by conceding ground.

HEAD: distance that can separate one competitor from another at the post, corresponding to the length of a horse's head. Shorter gaps than this are the nose and the nostril.

HEAT: single competition making up part of one race.

HEAVY GOING: very difficult muddy ground.

HOCK: region between the leg and cannon-bone made up of the tarsus and the ends of the tibia and metatarsus, on the hind leg.

INBREEDING: crossing between horses which have ancestors in common in their first five removes. An inbreeding of 3 × 4 means that one of the ancestors in common is to be found in the third remove and the other in the fourth.

LENGTH: unit of measurement used to indicate the gap that separates the competitors at the post, corresponding to the length of a horse's body.

LIGHT TWO-WHEELED CART: training gig.

MAIDEN: horse that has not yet won a race.

MATCH: race limited to two competitors.

MILER: horse with a marked ability in one-mile (1,600 m) races.

NECK: distance that can separate one horse from another at the post and which corresponds to the length of a horse's neck.

NICK: successful crossing between special blood lines.

NOSE: very small gap which can separate two competitors at the post, corresponding to the measurement of this part of a horse's head.

OPPOSITE STRAIGHT: the straight facing the finishing straight.

OUTCROSS: cross between horses born of parents who do not have ancestors in common in the first five removes.

OVER TIMBER: a typically-American hurdle-race which takes place across country.

PACE: a two-time gait where the fore and hind feet on the same side strike the ground simultaneously.

PADDOCK: enclosure where horses gather to be saddled up before the race.

PAIR: two-horse team where the horses are placed side by side.

PASTURE: fenced-off meadowland where horses may enjoy relative freedom.

PERFORMANCE: the overall results obtained by a racehorse.

PERFORMER: horse that has achieved good racing performance.

PHOTO-FINISH: photograph taken of the finish of a race.

POSTS: stakes used in hurdles. They are driven into the ground to serve as a support and have the poles fixed to them.

POLES: rods usually made of chestnut wood, about 13 ft (4 m) long and used for hurdles.

POST-AND-RAIL: typical American cross-country obstacle comprising railings with planks wedged into two side supports.

REGISTRATION: the act whereby the owner, or his representative, expresses his wish to enter a horse for a race. Horses must be registered within set times and according to a set procedure.

ROARING: veterinary term used to indicate the effect and not the cause from which it originates. This concerns the paralysis of the larynx (mostly on one side only) which produces a particular condition in which the emission of air during exhalation is accompanied by a characteristic sound similar to that made by a saw or whistle. This complaint is considered hereditary but can also be of a traumatic nature or the result of poisoning or infection.

RUNNER: horse whose participation in a race has been confirmed.

SECOND DAM: maternal grandam.

SELLING RACES: low caliber races in which the winner is put up for auction.

SNAFFLES: a type of bit to which the reins are connected.

SOCK: white marking covering a lesser or greater proportion of the lower limbs.

SPACING: relegation in the order of arrival as a result of causing injury to another competitor or for some other irregularity.

SPRINTER: horse who shows his ability in races over short distances.

STALLION: male horse used for breeding.

START: moment and point at which a race begins.

STARTER: official responsible for starting the race.

STAYER: horse suited to long-distance races.

STAYING POWER: ability to run long distances or, sometimes, resistance to tiredness.

STUD BOOK: pedigree book in which the births of all horses belonging to the breed are recorded.

STUD RECORD: overall performance of a stallion at stud.

SULKY: very light two-wheeled cart mounted on rubber wheels and used in trotting races.

TIMEFORM: English weekly publication that gives an alphabetical list of all the horses in Great Britain with racing form, showing the relative assessments expressed in pounds (lbs).

TOP WEIGHT: horse running in a handicap race and carrying the highest weight.

TRAINER: person holding a license which empowers him to be in charge of training racehorses.

TRIAL: timed race in which one horse is accompanied by two others in order to create competitive conditions.

UNPLACED: horse that comes in after fourth place at the post.

WALK-OVER: race in which all the horses except one have been withdrawn, thus leaving the latter to run unrivalled.

WINNING POST: finishing post of a race.

WITHDRAWAL: pulling out of a race for which a horse has previously been entered.

WITHERS: region of the body between the neck and the back, positioned above the shoulders and covering the first eight dorsal vertebrae.

WORK-OUT: trial to test a horse's training.

YEARLING: horse of either sex, between being a foal and the age of two.

INDEX

(Numbers in bold refer to illustrations)

251

253

254

255